A BEGINNER'S GUIDE TO CRITICAL READING

An anthology of literary texts

Richard Jacobs

Routledge
Taylor & Francis Group

LONDON AND NEW YORK

First published 2001
by Routledge
2 Park Square, Milton Park, Abingdon, Oxon OX14 4RN

Simultaneously published in the USA and Canada
by Routledge
270 Madison Ave, New York, NY 10016

Transferred to Digital, Padstow, Cornwall

Routledge is an imprint of the Taylor & Francis Group, an informa business

© 2001 Compilation and editorial material Richard Jacobs

The right of Richard Jacobs to be identified as the Author of this work has
been asserted by him in accordance with the Copyright, Design and Patents
Act 1988

British Library Cataloguing in Publication Data
A catalogue record for this book is available from the British Library

Library of Congress Cataloging in Publication Data
Jacobs, Richard
A beginner's guide to critical reading : an anthology of
literary texts / Richard Jacobs.
p. cm.
Includes bibliographical references (p.).
1. English literature – History and criticism. 2. American
literature – History and criticism.
3. American literature. 4. English literature. I. Title.
PR83 .J34 2001
820.9 – dc21 00–051743

ISBN 10: 0-415-23468-9 (pbk)
ISBN 10: 0-415-23467-0 (hbk)
ISBN 13: 978-0-415-23468-9 (pbk)
ISBN 13: 978-0-415-23467-2 (hbk)

For Winnie (who doesn't read) and Rose (who does a bit)

CONTENTS

vii

CONTENTS

ACKNOWLEDGEMENTS

Warmest thanks to Talia Rodgers of Routledge for her enthusiastic commitment to the project from commissioning it onwards. Liz Brown of Routledge has been a source of calm and expert advice throughout. Almost as indispensable has been Routledge's Reader D, here unmasked as Hugh Epstein: his successive reader-reports, so full of positive and discriminating support, were of great help. Thanks also to Sarah Pearsall for her patient and skilful copy-editing, and to Kevin Eaton and his team at RefineCatch.

This book would have been unthinkable without the many years of friendship, encouragement and support of colleagues at Collyer's College, Horsham, particularly Penelope Maynard and Paul Clarke but, above all, Martin Nichols who improved many passages in the commentaries in his unfailingly generous way. Ed Tattersall's Ovid translation graces the Appendix. Thanks to all who helped at Collyer's. Many hundreds of students, at Collyer's and more recently at Brighton University, contributed so much in daily classroom discussions. A number of institutions and associations generously allowed me to try out bits of the book on groups of teachers, student-teachers and students. I'm very grateful in this regard to Viv Ellis and Carol Fox, to NATE and the English Association, and to Jane Ogborn.

Acknowledgements are offered below to publishers for granting permission to reproduce copyright material. A personal note of thanks is due to Mr S. Yorke for generously allowing the *Living* extract and to Professor Gordon Campbell for the Milton and Marvell.

ACKNOWLEDGEMENTS

Milton, excerpts from *The Complete English Poems*, edited and introduced by Gordon Campbell, © 1990, David Campbell Publishers Ltd, reprinted by permission.

Marvell, from *Everyman's Poetry* selection, © 1997, J. M. Dent, reprinted by permission.

Emily Dickinson poems 193, 926, 1004, 1456, 1611, 1747, 320, 220, 563, 588, 1607: reprinted by permission of the publishers and the Trustees of Amsherst College from *The Poems of Emily Dickinson*, ed. Ralph W. Franklin, Cambridge, Mass.: The Belknap Press of Harvard University Press, Copyright © 1998 by the President and Fellows of Harvard College. Copyright © 1951, 1955, 1979 by the President and Fellows of Harvard College.

Henry Green, excerpts from Chapters 18 and 19 of *Living* (1929). Reprinted by kind permission of Mr S. Yorke.

Jean Rhys, *Good Morning, Midnight* (pp. 12–13, 16–19, 21–6, 79–81), Penguin Books, 1969, © 1939 by Jean Rhys. Reproduced by permission of Penguin Books Ltd.

Tennessee Williams, excerpts from *A Streetcar Named Desire*, copyright © 1947 by University of the South. Reprinted by permission of New Directions Publishing Corp. and Casarotto Ramsay Ltd. Excerpts from *Cat on a Hot Tin Roof*, copyright © 1954, 1955, 1971, 1975 by University of the South. Reprinted by permission of New Directions Publishing Corp. and Casarotto Ramsay Ltd.

Geoffrey Hill, poems from *Geoffrey Hill: Collected Poems* (pp. 67, 129), 'September Song' first published in *King Log* (1968) and 'Mercian Hymn XXV Opus Anglicanum', first published in *Mercian Hymns* (1971): Penguin Books, 1985, copyright © Geoffrey Hill, 1968, 1971, 1985. Reproduced by permission of Penguin Books Ltd. 'Mercian Hymn XXV' and 'September Song' from *New and Collected Poems 1952–1992*. Copyright © 1994 by Geoffrey Hill. Reprinted by permission of Houghton Mifflin Co. All rights reserved.

ACKNOWLEDGEMENTS

Samuel Beckett, *Not 1*. Copyright © 1973 by Samuel Beckett, reprinted by permission of Grove/Atlantic Inc. and Faber & Faber.

John Berryman. Reprinted by permission of Farrar, Straus and Giroux, LLC: 'He Resigns' from *Collected Poems 1937–1971* by John Berryman. Copyright © 1989 by Kate Donahue Berryman. 'Dream Song 1' from *The Dream Songs* by John Berryman. Copyright © 1969 by John Berryman. Copyright renewed © 1997 by Kate Donahue Berryman. Reprinted by permission of Faber & Faber.

Elizabeth Bishop. Reprinted by permission of Farrar, Straus and Giroux, LLC: 'Casabianca' and 'One Art' from *The Complete Poems 1927–1979* by Elizabeth Bishop. Copyright © 1979, 1983 by Alice Helen Methfessel.

INTRODUCTION

What this book is

This book is a short collection of texts and extracts, in twenty-four chronologically arranged chapters, with critical commentaries attached to each chapter. The texts in each chapter range in length from a couple of short poems or a single Shakespeare scene to most of a long story or an entire short play. The commentaries are designed to encourage you to see texts and their contexts as inter-related, and to introduce you to a variety of different ways of approaching literary texts.

Who this book is for

This book is for anyone with an appetite for reading. It assumes that you enjoy the challenge of reading widely and reflectively and that you have an interest in seeing what different contemporary critical approaches can bring to the understanding of texts. Some chapters are more demanding than others but the texts featured and the critical commentaries are designed to be accessible in a stimulating way.

Why this book is different

First, it's a hybrid, two books in one. It can be read as a highly selective anthology of literature in English from about 1530 to about 1980, an anthology designed to reflect, even in its very brief compass, the complex map of literature as that map has been drawn and redrawn over the course of literary-critical history. Like other anthologies, this book aims to stimulate further reading, but it is also designed to be used, and I hope enjoyed, as a critical companion. The commentaries are designed to send you off with more confidence in your own literary-critical adventures.

So, as a hybrid, this is an unusual book. But another difference should be emphasised. This book is unashamedly personal, both in its selection of texts and in the style and manner of the commentaries. The choice of texts reflects what one teacher and lecturer has enjoyed working with in real classrooms and with real students. This is material that I like reading, thinking about and discussing in class. It is not meant to be a representative sampling of English and American literature over 450 years. It can't be, because of its length, and if it was it might be a rather blander collection. The large number of famous names omitted is very obvious and partly intentional, given the way readers and students tend to get presented with the same 'classic' texts. I hope the book does something to question the very notion of why certain authors tend to get taught and others don't. And I hope the book gives a little more currency to writers who perhaps have not received the attention of others. Nor is there in this book a properly weighted representation of writers according to gender, ethnicity, race or sexuality. Such treatment would be beyond the compass of this short book. But you should find that issues of pressing significance are raised in a lively way in the course of the book.

And the commentaries are designed to be personal in their voice. I didn't want to come across here as the voice of neutral academic authority because (partly through ignorance) that's the last thing I feel. The critical angles from which the commentaries emerge are as highly selective as the choice of texts. They just happen to be where this particular reader is at with that particular text at the time of writing. I hope the commentaries are engaging enough for you to want to read them, and therefore the accompanying texts, with a sense of discovery and with the confidence to debate and disagree.

How to use this book

This book can be read on your own, at your own pace, the chapters chosen in any order, following your own connections, or of course the book can be read sequentially.

Connections are made from chapter to chapter and these work cumulatively. But if, say, you find yourself meeting the poetry of Andrew Marvell it would make sense to read Chapters 5 and 6 where you'll find some of his poems and commentaries placing them in the context of the mid-seventeenth-century revolution and in connection with the writings of his contemporaries, John Milton and Gerrard Winstanley. These chapters discuss Adam and Eve's expulsion from Eden: this might lead you to the following chapter on Swift where the expulsion from Eden is pursued further. That chapter raises the issue of the slave-trade which is also dealt with in Chapter 8 where the focus is on literary London in the late 1770s. The colonial issue raised in connection with slavery could lead you to later chapters on *The Yellow Wallpaper* (16) and *Good Morning, Midnight* (20), where the contexts include post-colonialism. Or the treatment of women as exhibits in the *Good Morning, Midnight* chapter might take you to the discussion of a scene from Shakespeare's *Troilus and Cressida* (3). Or notions of desire, of madness, of social outcasts and misfits, of the politics of charity, of journeying, of the role of folk-tales in literature, might be among other ways of plotting your own routes. The last chapter explicitly pulls out one particular thread that the book is concerned with. But browsing through the extracts, picking on what you like the look of, is as good a way as any to read this book.

This book is designed also to be used as an induction text for students coming to advanced literary study for the first time. It can easily lend itself to be used in class. The texts are short enough to be read by groups in advance of a class or seminar, and the commentaries are informal and open enough to be used as a taking-off point for discussion and disagreement. The scope of the book, and the connections made between the texts, are such that essays and dissertations exploring texts comparatively could be derived from it.

Each chapter is prefaced by a headnote and concluded by an endnote. The headnote briefly introduces you to the presented text and outlines the contexts with which the commentary puts the text into play. The endnote points towards the interpretative strategies used in the chapter, which you could take forward in your own reading and critical thinking. It also provides you with a shortlist of further reading, partly to underline that the commentary is offered only as partial and selective in its ways of reading, not as an exhaustive survey providing 'answers'. You'll find an endnote to this Introduction, suggesting some books of general recommendation.

An Appendix contains a translation of Ovid's story of Echo and Narcissus, specially done for this book by Ed Tattersall.

Critical positions represented in this book

If there is one assumption that runs through the commentaries it is this: that texts and contexts are always in dynamic and volatile relations with each other and that the contexts of a text are multiple, changing over time and from reader to reader. The 'common sense' view that texts are self-sufficient and that context is the supplementary stuff in the background (biographical, historical) against which the text can be simply measured is still widely held. It's an attractive view because it encourages a simple and one-directional view of what reading does. It assumes that the meanings of texts are unchanging, universal and uncontradictory, and that the reader just has to get the meaning out like getting the nut out of the shell. The context is then there as a stable set of facts and truths for the reader to check responses against. Got the nut out? Now, does it look and taste like the history book and the biography say it should? And this model assumes that the writer is the sole controller of the meaning-process, conveying that meaning unaffected by anything outside his little garden of nut-trees.

Instead we need to think of the making of meaning as a process that happens between the text and the reader, and that such meaning is socially and culturally produced, changing and various and multiple. We need to think of the writer as a product as well as a producer, and of texts as interventions in social process. And we need to think of contexts as a network of pressures and debates in which all readers are entangled. Readers too are products, subject to contexts. Contexts are the changing conditions of possibility for the production and consumption of the text. Contexts are the process whereby the text finds and makes a place in the world, the ways in which it is enabled to speak and the ways in which it makes a difference.

There is no one school of criticism or theory dominant in this book. By definition the book is designed to be open and plural. But, as explained above, this book comes principally out of one reader's

4

critical responses, not from a committee or from an agreed consensus, so inevitably it carries signs of what has spoken most forcibly to that reader over the years.

Literary theory, during the earlier years of its ascendancy, fought as much against itself in factions as against older, traditional critical approaches. The air was thick with accusations and counter-accusations issued in the name of often terrifyingly difficult theorists whose books would be waved around like flags as much as they were read and understood. But those heady days are over and now the shops are full of guides to the dominant schools of criticism and theory. Those dominant schools seem to me to be coming together now, not pulling apart, and a model of contemporary critical practice is seeping into most areas of cultural and educational work, a model that draws on the most socially and politically informed of new literary-critical approaches. These would include so-called New Historicist or Cultural Materialist criticism (in effect two names for the same set of presuppositions), feminist studies (in all their different emph-ases), psychoanalysis, and critical studies recovering the hidden histories of people marginalised in traditional political and literary culture.

The contexts you will most often encounter in this book are historical-political, psychoanalytic, and those relating to sexuality and gender. I've tried, in every case, to show how the act of contextualising is an opening of doors on to other contexts, an opening out that returns us to the text in an adventure that never finishes. What name we give to the critical directions we're coming from or going to next, as we read and re-read, doesn't really matter. Perhaps, soon, literary theory and all its different schools will just be called good reading. Good reading is the asking of questions that generate more and better questions.

Texts, sources, and how to get help

This is not a scholarly book. The texts have been presented in a way that is designed to be helpful and clear to students and other readers, not scholars. The texts in the earlier chapters have been modernised and come from a variety of sources with no particular authority. The exceptions to this are the excerpts from Milton and Marvell (Chapters 5 and 6) where permission was kindly granted to use Gordon

Campbell's authoritatively modernised Everyman editions, and the Emily Dickinson poems (Chapter 12) where copyright and other issues have led to the adoption of the text as established by Thomas H. Johnson. Acknowledgements to holders of copyright and others are offered in a separate section.

The extracts are often abridged, for reasons of space. The headnote will indicate if that has been the case. In the course of the text, ellipses in square brackets (that is: [. . .]) indicate editorial cuts. Most of the chapters simply present the text uninterrupted, followed by the commentary. In the case of a few, notably Chapters 5, 6 and 8 where it was thought that the reader needed more guidance, the commentary is dispersed among the textual extracts.

The briefest of annotations follow immediately under the text to which they relate. Again for reasons of space, these are the bare minimum. I've had to assume that readers have access to a good dictionary and encyclopedia. More help, in the form of fuller annotations and critical discussions, is readily available in full-length editions of the texts concerned. These are often recommended in the endnotes.

A final note

In the planning stages of this book it was wondered whether it lent itself to any of the usual labels. Is it an anthology? Guidebook? Handbook? Companion? Coursebook? Workbook? Textbook? Critical reader? Saying yes and no to these (or, rather, no, pretty firmly, to 'workbook' and 'textbook') didn't really get us very far. But perhaps its disinclination to have a pre-labelled tail stuck on it works to its and to your advantage. For I hope that the book speaks personally, that the commentaries help the texts speak to you personally, and that the combination of texts and commentaries helps you engage energetically and creatively with literature and with the critical reading of literature, as you read this book and over the years to come. Perhaps 'companion-anthology' is closest. I hope you enjoy its company.

The endnotes to each chapter recommend books specific to that chapter. Here are a dozen or so books that might head up a wish-list for the reader starting advanced literary study. An excellent starting-point is Rob Pope's The

English Studies Book (London, Routledge, 1998), the most helpful and comprehensive guide to advanced literary study available in one volume. Also excellent, and in a complementary way, is Andrew Bennett and Nicholas Royle's *Introduction to Literature, Criticism and Theory* (expanded edition, Hemel Hempstead, Prentice Hall, 1999), which I read too belatedly to do more than recommend here. This offers cogent and lucid essays on a range of literary topics and includes outstanding reading-lists. Robert Eaglestone's *Doing English* (London, Routledge, 2000) is a short and straightforward guide aimed at less confident students. Jonathan Culler's *Literary Theory: A Very Short Introduction* (Oxford, Oxford University Press, 1997) is by an authority with a gift for making difficult material accessible. The new edition of Terry Eagleton's famous *Literary Theory* (2nd edn, Oxford, Blackwell, 1996) has a fine new introductory survey of developments since the book was first published. The book retains its engagingly knock-about manner. It's worth buying *The Penguin Book of Renaissance Verse* (Harmondsworth, Penguin, 1993) for David Norbrook's editorial matter alone; it's also a marvellous anthology. Marilyn Butler's *Romantics, Rebels and Reactionaries* (Oxford, Oxford University Press, 1981) is a landmark study of romantic literature in its contexts. The crucial interdependence of literature and Empire is powerfully explored in Edward Said's *Culture and Imperialism* (London, Chatto and Windus, 1993). But work such as Said's and Butler's, and cultural materialist criticism generally, would have been unthinkable without the pioneering work of Raymond Williams from the 1950s onwards. *The Country and the City* (London, Chatto and Windus, 1973) is his masterpiece. Ronald Carter and John McRae's *Routledge History of Literature in English* (London, Routledge, 1997) is wide-ranging and particularly attentive to language developments. Ross Murfin and Supryia M. Ray's *Bedford Glossary of Critical and Literary Terms* (Boston, Bedford Books, 1997) is a comprehensive handbook. Of the many collections of critical and theoretical essays, the two companion volumes edited by David Lodge, *Twentieth Century Literary Criticism* (Harlow, Longman, 1972) and *Modern Criticism and Theory* (expanded edition, Harlow, Longman, 2000), range the most widely and include the most illustrious names.

1

WYATT'S 'THEY FLEE FROM ME'
Sexual politics and metrical history

This first chapter looks at a famous love-poem, or two famous love-poems.
The contexts suggested for thinking about it are very different but happen to
be locked together in the history of this poem. They are sexual politics (the
social history of the relations between men and women) and metrics or
prosody, the patterns of rhythm and stress in English poetic metre (with its
own history). We'll see that ideas of the 'original' are less simple than they
seem.

Here's a poem. Or is it two poems? Or two versions of the same poem?
What could be the relations between them? Can they both be a, or
the, 'real' poem? They date from the early sixteenth century, more than
fifty years before Shakespeare wrote his best-known plays. It is/they
are apparently by Sir Thomas Wyatt, one of Henry VIII's courtiers and
diplomats, whom Wyatt might have seriously displeased by getting
entangled with Anne Boleyn. A man is reflecting on the fact that women,
and one in particular, seem to be 'forsaking' him, to use the word in the
poem and in the title to one of them. The spelling has been
modernised.

(A)
The lover showeth how he is forsaken of such as he sometime enjoyed

They flee from me, that sometime did me seek
With naked foot stalking within my chamber.
Once have I seen them gentle, tame, and meek,
That now are wild, and do not once remember
That sometime they have put themselves in danger,

To take bread at my hand, and now they range,
Busily seeking in continual change.

Thanked be fortune, it hath been otherwise
Twenty times better: but once especiall,
10 In thin array, after a pleasant guise,
When her loose gown did from her shoulders fall,
And she me caught in her arms long and small,
And therewithal, so sweetly did me kiss,
And softly said: 'Dear heart, how like you this?'

It was no dream: for I lay broad awaking.
But all is turned now through my gentleness,
Into a bitter fashion of forsaking:
And I have leave to go of her goodness,
And she also to use newfangleness.
20 But, since that I unkindly so am served:
How like you this, what hath she now deserved?

(B)

They flee from me, that sometime did me seek
With naked foot stalking in my chamber.
I have seen them gentle, tame, and meek
That now are wild, and do not remember
That sometime they put themself in danger
To take bread at my hand; and now they range,
Busily seeking with a continual change.

Thanked be fortune it hath been otherwise
30 Twenty times better, but once in special,
In thin array after a pleasant guise
When her loose gown from her shoulders did fall,
And she me caught in her arms long and small,
Therewithal sweetly did me kiss,
And softly said, 'Dear heart, how like you this?'

It was no dream: I lay broad waking.

But all is turned through my gentleness
Into a strange fashion of forsaking,
And I have leave to go of her goodness,
40 And she also to use newfangleness.
But since that I so kindly am served,
I would fain know what she hath deserved.

The sexiness of the second verse – the dress coming off and the 'small' (= slender) arms catching the man who thought it was his place to do the catching – may be the first thing to strike you, and reasonably enough. Bodies are often eroticised in Renaissance literature but this is particularly beguiling. Then you might wonder about the image in the first verse: what are the women, in this man's life, compared to here, and what do we make of it? Readers often think the comparison is to birds but what if 'heart' is a pun on 'hart' (= male deer), and indeed 'dear' on 'deer'? Issues of tame and wild, in the sexual politics of the poem, become even more pointed when we think of those deer kept in royal parks, somehow both aloof and vulnerable, stalked and stalking.

For who is stalking or indeed seducing whom here? The speaker may have assumed that the power was his and, in the light of his experience with one particular woman, seems to need to express a response appropriate to the changed circumstances of the new sexual politics. But isn't his response rather different in the two versions? If you read them again, perhaps aloud, and then highlight or list the differences, even the tiny and apparently trivial ones, what are you led to suspect? How might this help us reconstruct some sort of explanation for the two versions?

Readers, once they've heard the two versions a few times, nearly always prefer (A). It's smoother, more 'poem-like'. The differences, with one exception, mean that many lines are a little longer, with the resulting rhythmical smoothening effect. More to the point, the speaker has evidently been treated 'unkindly' and not 'kindly', and is likely to feel that the newfangled fashion of women choosing to seduce and then leave men is 'bitter' to him rather than 'strange'. The final gesture of repeating the seducing woman's 'how like you this?' in turning to the reader (by implication male) for confirmation of the speaker's vindictive feelings has a nice ironic force as he turns her own words against her now. The end of (B) – 'I would fain know' (= I'd like to know) – seems oddly muted in comparison.

The impresssion of a smoother rhythm in (A) is no accident. You may have noticed that (A) is in regular iambic pentameter. In contrast (B) sounds more halting and more like speech. So, taken together, the rhythmical differences and the emotional-dramatic differences point towards (A) being the 'real poem' and (B) being – what? A draft? A careless copy? A stolen or poorly remembered version? The first page of the *Penguin Book of English Verse*, a best-selling collection continuously in print since 1956 when it first appeared, authenticates this impression of (A), for there it is in unmodernised form on page 1, complete with a jaunty title, the first poem in Penguin's great march of English poetry.

But Wyatt wrote (B). A man called Tottel concocted (A) in about 1557, and what he did, or so it seems, was to think to himself that Wyatt was trying to write iambic pentameter and that he couldn't do it, poor chap. Tottel also seems to have thought that Wyatt had shirked his duty when expressing the appropriate male responses to these women throwing their weight about. So Tottel added those pretty fatuous extra words, shifted the order around a bit for more smoothing, thus reducing the swish-swish effect of the gown falling from her shoulders, beefed up the bitterness and the public-attention-getting voice of the ending, and added the flag-waving title.

Wyatt's muted irony in 'kindly' and the suggestive notes of old-world courtesy in 'through my gentleness' (where the word, as in Chaucer, evokes the codes of gentility appropriate to being a gentleman) and in 'I have leave to go of her goodness' sit rather awkwardly with the confident aggression in Tottel's last lines where the voice is coarser, overcertain, more male. The title is coming out of the same confidence. ('Enjoyed' there presumably means 'sexually had his way with', but the *Oxford English Dictionary* inexplicably only allows this meaning from the 1590s.) And as part of the same process of alteration the rhythm loses its halting, bemused diffidence. The rhythm becomes regular and predictable; the emotion loses its sense of muted, painful uncertainty. A difficult moment in the long history of male–female sexual relations meets with a difficult moment in the long history of English poetic metre. It's a twinned moment of anxiety, resolved in a doubly unfortunate way by an editor, not a poet.

11

And Tottel had his way: Wyatt's poem was published, which it wasn't in his lifetime; his manuscript versions languished in libraries; and the *Penguin Book of English Verse*, which could have chosen Wyatt's manuscript version but instead began with Tottel's influential 1557 collection called *Songes and Sonettes*, continues to perpetuate this imposition of metrical and male-sexual orthodoxy on a delicate, moving poem.

The point about the altered metre and rhythm, the imposition of the pentameter, needs a little more elaboration. What was Wyatt writing if not pentameters? Scholars and editors disagree about what they think Wyatt was trying to do. For example, is the final '-ed' at the end of verbs sounded or not? However, they seem to agree that the oppressively orthodox reign of the iambic pentameter was not yet established in the sort of power that it later exercised over poets. So it is a moment of uncertain power for this poetic form as much as for male–female power-relations. My guess, hearing (B) in my head, is that the poem shows the influence of a much more ancient form of organising the English poetic line: the Anglo-Saxon technique of lines in two halves, with each containing two stressed syllables which could come any-where in the half-line. This is known as an accentual rather than a syllabic technique. Try sounding it this way. It's more like conversation; it feels right for the halting, uncertain voice. It also feels more folky, more earthy and earthed, as if the rhythm is obscurely appealing to old authorities in the sexual dilemma, in these difficult modern times of women exercising power.

A related example of this kind of echo of Anglo-Saxon verse comes at the end of *King Lear*. Kent is going off to die, presumably of a broken heart after the death of his loved king. There are two crucially different early printings of the play and editors disagree about which is Shakespeare's 'real' version. In the first, Kent says 'I have a journey sir, shortly to go, / My master calls, and I must not say no', where the second line falls into a pentameter; in the later text he says 'I have a journey sir, shortly to go, / My master calls me, I must not say no.' The effect here is of something like a spell, an old rite, with a bare, spare simplicity, as if prehistoric, like the play. Wyatt's 'They flee from me' (B) seems to need to connect with something of this spare, earthy ordin-ariness, but charged like a spell. Whatever it is, Tottel steamrollers over it, raising the volume and playing to the gallery.

But here's a note of scepticism. What if someone, tomorrow, proves that before he died Wyatt gave Tottel his revised and 'improved' version (A) and that it's a mere accident that the earlier version (B) escaped the waste-paper basket? Or what if Wyatt gave Tottel the poem (B) and told him to do what he wanted with it, whenever he wanted, with the poet meanwhile circulating it among 'his private friends' – the phrase used later to describe those alleged to have been the first readers of at least some of Shakespeare's sonnets? The new orthodoxy about King Lear is that the two texts make quite separate claims to being authoritative, though the publishers of the second would have expected the first to end up in the waste-paper basket. The versions of Kent's last lines may represent Shakespeare or an actor improving during revision or rehearsal. But they may just be misreadings or misprintings of each other. The 'original' King Lear is a problem of definition, even a mirage. Is there, anyway, a danger of making too much of the idea of the 'original'? Aren't all texts, let alone versions of texts, equally unstable entities? Tomorrow I might find in my cellar an earlier version of 'They flee from me' which is closer to (A) than to (B). Or Wyatt's ghost might tell me in a seance that he's had a good look at all the versions around and – got a pencil? – he'd like to dictate to me his final stab at the thing before retiring for ever.

The poem, perhaps because Penguin placed it (or Tottel) on its first page, has enjoyed an enormous currency, rather more than any other pre-seventeenth-century lyric poem. Rumour has it that T.S. Eliot was the guiding influence behind the editor's choice for the Penguin anthology. Perhaps there was some logic in Eliot, a poet and critic not exactly in the vanguard of liberal attitudes towards women, preferring the Tottel.

Anyway, in whatever version it is known, this is among the world's favourite love poems, if polls of such things can be believed. And versions continue to proliferate. An English examination board recently asked its candidates to compare a parody by Gavin Ewart with a poem purporting to be the Wyatt but which turned out to be a bizarre stitching together of bits of Tottel and bits of Wyatt. It also shifted the emphasis of the last line so that it read: ' "How like you this?" – what hath she now deserved?' which changes Tottel's speaker's question to the reader into an incredulously sarcastic mocking of what the woman said to him (which this version also italicised). That turns up the volume and the aggression yet further, a strange note for the examiners to want to strike, unless the intention was to goad students into a response. So rewrite the poem. But, then, why not? All texts are randomised collections of words, most editions of *King Lear* are a stitching together of bits from the two early printings, and these days, with downloading, editing, cutting and pasting at our fingertips, why not randomise or customise further? So why not? But why?

You might valuably explore in the area of different versions of texts. It's a contentious issue in Shakespeare studies. Good modern editions of *Hamlet* and *King Lear* will have the details. Particularly illuminating is Rene Weis's parallel text edition of *King Lear* (Harlow, Longman, 1993). Drafts of poems are useful illustrations of changes made during composition, though study of drafts tends to overemphasise the achieved and final goal of the published version. We've suggested something more provisional about all versions in this chapter. There are some notorious examples of poets rewriting their poems: W.H. Auden is worth investigating in this context. The last chapter of this book offers another striking example. The problem of how to hear the rhythms of Wyatt's poetry is discussed in R.A. Rebholz's edition of Wyatt's complete poems (Harmondsworth, Penguin, 1978), though the conclusions offered there are uncertain. A polemical survey of English metrical history is offered in Anthony Easthope's *Poetry as Discourse* (London, Methuen, 1983). Penguin have just launched a *New Penguin Book of English Verse*, edited by Paul Keegan, but John Hayward's volume, discussed above, remains in print.

2

SHAKESPEARE'S *THE MERCHANT OF VENICE*
Framing the outsiders

In this and the next chapter we look at two scenes from Shakespeare plays. Here it's a short scene from *The Merchant of Venice*. We'll be looking at the purpose and function of the frame that is placed around the two stories told in the scene and we'll consider the effect of the framing on the representation of two types of outsider in the play in the context of late Elizabethan culture and society.

In this scene from *The Merchant of Venice*, often cut in productions, two interchangeably shallow young men-about-town (Salerio and Solanio, as interchangeable as their names) are chatting about recent news. Each has a juicy item of gossip.

One of them updates the news, which is hilarious to them, that Shylock the Jew's daughter, Jessica, has eloped with Lorenzo, a Christian friend of theirs, helping herself as she leaves to her father's money (his ducats), with the resulting anguish to Shylock. The other tells the story of how their elder friend Antonio, the merchant of the title, has had to say goodbye to another amorous adventurer friend of theirs, Bassanio, to whom Antonio is especially close. Those two are parting because Bassanio is setting sail for Belmont (= beautiful mountain) to woo the rich heiress Portia. The sharp hinge between these moments, conveyed exactly half-way through the scene, as indeed a hinge, is the rumour that Antonio may have lost much of his wealth in a shipwreck. This is sharp because Antonio is indebted, on Bassanio's behalf, to Shylock, and if his merchandising enterprises have, as rumoured, indeed 'miscarried' it spells bad news for him.

Both bits of plot are very dramatisable and would have made good theatre. But Shakespeare, as elsewhere in his plays, chooses instead to convey the narrative content of this scene in reportage, in minor characters describing and quoting the protagonists, and giving their own reactions to what they're reporting. The history of this technique goes back a long way, to ancient Greek theatre in which a Chorus of anonymous figures would carry a considerable amount of the play's narrative. But a chorus's role is by definition depersonalised. In Shakespeare the narrative matter is conveyed by characters with very evident feelings and opinions. Their reliability, as well as their strong opinions, is at stake. What does this do to the matter that's being discussed?

> SALERIO: Why man, I saw Bassanio under sail,
>   With him is Gratiano gone along,
>   And in their ship I am sure Lorenzo is not.
> SOLANIO: The villain Jew with outcries raised the duke,
>   Who went with him to search Bassanio's ship.
> SALERIO: He came too late, the ship was under sail.
>   But there the duke was given to understand
>   That in a gondola were seen together
>   Lorenzo and his amorous Jessica.
> 10 Besides, Antonio certified the duke
>   They were not with Bassanio in his ship.
> SOLANIO: I never heard a passion so confused,
>   So strange, outrageous, and so variable,
>   As the dog Jew did utter in the streets:
>   'My daughter! O my ducats! O my daughter!
>   Fled with a Christian! O my Christian ducats!
>   Justice! The law! My ducats, and my daughter!
>   A sealed bag, two sealed bags of ducats,
>   Of double ducats, stolen from me by my daughter,
> 20 And jewels, two stones, two rich and precious stones,
>   Stolen by my daughter. Justice! Find the girl!
>   She hath the stones upon her, and the ducats.'
> SALERIO: Why, all the boys in Venice follow him,
>   Crying, his stones, his daughter, and his ducats.
> SOLANIO: Let good Antonio look he keep his day
>   Or he shall pay for this.
> SALERIO: Marry, well remembered.

        I reasoned with a Frenchman yesterday,
        Who told me, in the narrow seas that part
        The French and English, there miscarried
30   A vessel of our country richly fraught.
        I thought upon Antonio when he told me,
        And wished in silence that it were not his.
   SOLANIO: You were best to tell Antonio what you hear,
        Yet do not suddenly, for it may grieve him.
   SALERIO: A kinder gentleman treads not the earth.
        I saw Bassanio and Antonio part,
        Bassanio told him he would make some speed
        Of his return. He answered, 'Do not so,
        Slubber not business for my sake Bassanio,
40   But stay the very riping of the time,
        And for the Jew's bond which he hath of me,
        Let it not enter in your mind of love.
        Be merry, and employ your chiefest thoughts
        To courtship and such fair ostents of love
        As shall conveniently become you there.'
        And even there, his eye being big with tears,
        Turning his face, he put his hand behind him,
        And with affection wondrous sensible
        He wrung Bassanio's hand, and so they parted.
50 SOLANIO: I think he only loves the world for him.
        I pray thee let us go and find him out
        And quicken his embraced heaviness
        With some delight or other.
   SALERIO: Do we so.

27 reasoned: talked
30 fraught: laden
39 slubber: spoil
45 ostents: displays
48 sensible: strongly felt
52 quicken: liven up

                            (Act II, scene viii)

The two bits of plot are framed, put into the frames of Salerio and
Solanio's opinionated narratives. Frames draw attention to what

they're framing. They objectify it, define its relations with the space around it, give it added status and value, attract commentary and judgement to it, stop it moving and seeping away, control or police it. These two young men are framing in the other sense as well. Like bent policemen Salerio and Solanio are framing these stories, implicating them in other narratives, those of their choice, to their own purposes and agenda.

Solerio and Solanio have a clear enough agenda. Their opinions and world-view, the view of the power-holders in the Venice of this play, could hardly be more sharply edged than they are in this double-framed picture. The diametrically opposing representations of Shylock and Antonio are framed together in these narratives, like pictures hanging together, the frames awkwardly almost touching, on a gallery wall. The high noisy comedy of the one narrative – Shylock blundering through the streets, shouting confusedly about his daughter and his money, pursued by boys mocking him in mimicry – is the ironic opposite of the grave pathos of the other – Antonio's gentle tact in hiding his tears from Bassanio after selflessly insisting (in a speech of mirroring length to Shylock's) that his friend takes as long as he likes on his mission. The contrast between the casually sadistic racism of the one narrative (Shylock is never named, is merely 'the dog Jew') and the reverential deference to Antonio ('A kinder gentleman treads not the earth') doesn't, of course, occur to Salerio and Solanio. The framing technique of the reported narrative makes sure that we, on the other hand, can't miss it and can't not be disturbed by it.

If nothing else, we can't avoid reading the scene against its grain, given the very obvious presuppositions of its narrators. Thus we might be troubled by the malicious relish over the humiliation of one older man, forced into the public spectacle of general contempt in the gutters of Venice, while another is caressingly indulged, framed at the moment of his most theatrical gesture, the turned head and the clasped hand. It is as if a private spectacle has been recorded by the onlookers it's actually intended for (as one might suspect about this as about other gestures by Antonio), but the self-sacrificing spectacle may seem a little hollow compared to Shylock's humiliated despair.

What we might also be disturbed by, and what, we can be pretty sure, hasn't entered the Venetian consciousness, is something else that the double-framing does: it makes us, if only unconsciously, see the connections between the two pictures. For this scene forces the uneasy recognition that Shylock and Antonio have much more in common than they could admit, which is perhaps why their antagonism is so sharp. They are both aliens, though the play only treats one of them as literally alien. The alienation is, for one of them, public, externalised in form, a matter of loud expressing and equally loud mocking; for the other it's private, internalised, silenced. The one is the ironic complement of the other, which is what the technique of the scene mutedly insists. They are united in loss, obviously enough: Shylock of his daughter (and his money), Antonio of Bassanio. The one's 'passion so confused, / So strange, outrageous, and so variable' is the other's 'affection wondrous sensible'. Shylock had nothing, in an antagonistic Venice, but his daughter and his money. Antonio, in Solanio's uncharacteristically observant words, 'only loves the world' for Bassanio. The publicly branded outsider is a version of what the other calls himself later: a 'tainted wether of the flock', the weakest fruit that falls earliest to the ground (IV.i.114–15). This play locks together two versions of being outsiders: the public scapegoat, the private self-exile; the Jew, the silent homosexual.

What Shakespeare's audience would have made of Shylock, what kind of preconceptions about Jews and Jewishness they would have brought with them to the theatre, and how, if at all, the play would have altered or challenged those preconceptions, are questions much discussed in the debate over this play. A comic-villainous Jew had been presented on the London stage only a few years earlier in Marlowe's *Jew of Malta*. Jews, having been expelled much earlier, were virtually unknown in Shakespeare's London. But, conversely, a Jewish doctor was the victim of a vicious and hysterical witch-hunt, accused falsely of trying to poison the Queen, a few years before this play. Since the Nazi holocaust the debate has sharpened further. Was this play received as anti-Semitic in late sixteenth-century London and can it now – in Europe, in Israel, in America – be received as other than anti-Semitic? There are cities today where it is neither performed nor studied for that reason. Or is it the opposite? Unlike Marlowe's Jew, Shylock is certainly a figure of strong, if awkward, pathos by the end. And this scene we've been looking at seems designed to challenge the stereotype, to make us feel uneasy about its casual racism. And it does this by associating Shylock, in the scene's clearly patterned construction, with his analogue Antonio.

What Shakespeare's audience would have made of Antonio is another vexed issue. Homosexual affections and behaviour were nothing new or surprising to late sixteenth- and early seventeenth-century society in England or on the continent, and Shakespeare's Achilles has his 'sweet' Patroclus as boyfriend and the Trojan princess Polyxena as girlfriend, not that he ever sees her. However, what would have been an unrecognised notion at the time was the descriptive label, homosexual as noun or adjective, as a way of defining or labelling (framing) a man. This developed, along with criminological medical ways of 'dealing' with it, only in the nineteenth century. In Antonio (as, oddly, in another Antonio, in *Twelfth Night*), Shakespeare seems to have anticipated, if in not quite bodily realised form, the much later notion, whether liberating or tyrannical, that now seems so commonplace to us – the idea that a human being's sexual direction is his or her ultimately determining characteristic. Not quite realised, and Antonio's way of describing himself (the tainted wether, the weakest fruit) seems not quite to embody it. But that sense of his own expendability seems more psychologically 'modern' than attempts to label him as an Elizabethan melancholic, like Jacques in *As You Like It*. Perhaps Antonio's not-quite-embodiedly realised psychology is only realisable as a kind of double or shadow to the all-too-embodiedly alien Shylock (it's apt that he wants a bit of Antonio's body as his due, later in the plot) and this is most telling at the level of doubled narrative and framed reportage in this apparently insubstantial, troublingly expressive little scene.

What makes the issue even more pointed is that Antonio is a very recognisable representative of what was a newly emergent and increasingly dominant class in Shakespeare's world, coexisting with older forms of an economic system that we associate with feudalism. Antonio is a merchant, a mercantile venture-capitalist as we might describe him, his fortune riding on the new hazards and opportunities of the market – and dependent on being able to secure capital from sources such as Jewish money-lenders. The Christian hatred of Shylock has a source in that monetary dependence. And if Venice and Antonio represent new capitalism, Portia's Belmont looks back to the old rituals and patriarchal obligations of feudal relations. She, unlike

Jessica, is in thrall to the will of her father. Jessica blithely cuts those old ties.

It's remarkable that Shakespeare seems to have intuited the sense of hollow alienation that later analysts would associate with capitalism, in his shadowy drawing of Antonio, emotionally alien in the most busy and volatile centre of the new merchant-capitalist world.

Framing is, as we've seen, a matter of both structure and representation. You'll be able to find other examples in Shakespeare in which events are reported in ways that both shape and colour those events. Two of the greatest of the plays, *King Lear* and *Antony and Cleopatra*, have opening scenes which are framed by characters commenting on the action before and after we see it ourselves. The problem is that the commentators' point of view may be challengingly different from ours. The challenge is to disentangle what we think from what we're told in both ends of the frame. A complex variation on this device is presented in the next chapter of this book. Issues of alienation in regard to the two protagonists of the *Merchant* can be pursued in the very extensive literature both on the play and on Shylock himself, and on representations of race and sexuality in early modern culture. Shylock is the subject of more than one book, notable among which is John Gross's *Shylock: Four Hundred Years in the Life of a Legend* (London, Chatto and Windus, 1992). The best starting-point for Shakespeare in contemporary critical contexts is Sean McEvoy's excellent *Shakespeare: The Basics* (London, Routledge, 2000) which is wide-ranging, politically engaged, and full of ideas for further reading. Alan Sinfield's 'How to Read the *Merchant of Venice* without being Heterosexist', in *Alternative Shakespeares, Vol. 2*, edited by Terence Hawkes (London, Routledge, 1996), is stylish and scholarly. Mention is made above of the older feudal world coming up against the emerging capitalist order. Shakespeare's plays generally show signs of the tensions inherent in this crucial shift. The play that makes the most profound and telling use of this is *Hamlet*, most sharply manifested in the rival father-figures and world-views of old Hamlet and Claudius.

3

SHAKESPEARE'S *TROILUS AND CRESSIDA*
Men reading and writing a woman

Here we read a painful and moving scene from *Troilus and Cressida*. We'll see that both Cressida and our own responses to her are put under intense pressure from men in the play and in history, as we show by putting Cressida's story in the context of the history of her 'character' as it emerges from earlier texts.

What happens to young lovers in Shakespeare is, across the board, pretty awful – whether they're in so-called comedies (where, after the ordeals, at least it tends to come out happily by the end) or tragedies (where it doesn't). But perhaps the sharpest story of young love hit by disaster is in a play that, unsettlingly, seems neither comedy nor tragedy but a hybrid, the black comedy or tragic farce, *Troilus and Cressida*. Let's look at its most painful scene.

The lovers of the title are Trojan and the Trojans are in the middle of their war with the Greeks. Cressida's father Calchas has defected to the Greek camp and she says she has forgotten him. Her uncle Pandarus brings the two lovers together, she more awkward and bashful than she earlier pretended, he rather worryingly cocksure and rhapsodic, and they share a first night of love. This is their only night of love because, next morning, as part of an exchange of prisoners, Cressida is transferred to her father in the Greek camp. The lovers part in despair, exchanging tokens of loyalty (his sleeve, her glove). On arrival at the Greek camp Cressida is casually passed around the military top-brass for leering approval and parcelled out to one of them, Diomedes, for (as it were) safe keeping.

In this scene, Act V, scene ii, Diomedes comes invited to her father's tent where he expects an amorous rendezvous with Cressida. Calchas delivers his daughter to her new suitor. But she is, as you'll see, very uncertain what to do. Her uncertainty is made even sharper to the audience because this painful scene is being watched, not only by us but by onstage audiences as well. Troilus has been smuggled into the area by the Greek Ulysses to witness the encounter. And they, unknowingly, are being watched too, as are Cressida and Diomedes, by the bitter commentator Thersites. (What follows is lightly abridged.)

> *Enter Diomedes*
> DIOMEDES: What, are you up here, ho? Speak.
> CALCHAS: (*within*) Who calls?
> DIOMEDES: Diomed. Calchas, I think? Where's your daughter?
> CALCHAS: (*within*) She comes to you.
> *Enter Troilus and Ulysses at a distance; after them, Thersites*
> ULYSSES: Stand where the torch may not discover us.
> *Enter Cressida*
> TROILUS: Cressid comes forth to him.
> DIOMEDES: How now, my charge?
> CRESSIDA: Now, my sweet guardian! Hark, a word with you.
> *She whispers to him*
> TROILUS: Yea, so familiar!
> 10 ULYSSES: She will sing any man at first sight.
> THERSITES: And any man may sing her, if he can take her cliff: she's noted.
> DIOMEDES: Will you remember?
> CRESSIDA: Remember? Yes.
> DIOMEDES: Nay, but do, then,
> And let your mind be coupled with your words.
> TROILUS: What should she remember?
> ULYSSES: List!
> CRESSIDA: Sweet honey Greek, tempt me no more to folly.
> 20 THERSITES: Roguery!
> DIOMEDES: Nay then –
> CRESSIDA: I'll tell you what –
> DIOMEDES: Foh, foh, come, tell a pin! You are forsworn.
> CRESSIDA: In faith I cannot; what would you have me do?

THERSITES: A juggling trick – to be secretly open.

DIOMEDES: What did you swear you would bestow on me?

CRESSIDA: I prithee, do not hold me to mine oath;
Bid me do anything but that, sweet Greek.

DIOMEDES: Good night.

30 TROILUS: Hold, patience!

ULYSSES: How now, Trojan?

CRESSIDA: Diomed –

DIOMEDES: No, no, good night; I'll be your fool no more.

TROILUS: Thy better must.

CRESSIDA: Hark, one word in your ear.

TROILUS: O plague and madness!

ULYSSES: You are moved, Prince; let us depart, I pray.you,
Lest your displeasure should enlarge itself
To wrathful terms. This place is dangerous,

40 The time right deadly; I beseech you, go.

TROILUS: Behold, I pray you.

ULYSSES: Nay, good my lord, go off.
You flow to great distraction; come, my lord.

TROILUS: I pray thee, stay.

ULYSSES: You have not patience; come.

TROILUS: I pray you, stay; by hell and all hell's torments,
I will not speak a word.

DIOMEDES: And so, good night.

CRESSIDA: Nay, but you part in anger.

TROILUS: Doth that grieve thee?
O withered truth!

ULYSSES: Why, how now, lord?

TROILUS: By Jove
I will be patient.

50 CRESSIDA: Guardian! Why, Greek?

DIOMEDES: Foh, foh, adieu; you palter.

CRESSIDA: In faith, I do not: come hither once again.

ULYSSES: You shake, my lord, at something; will you go?
You will break out.

TROILUS: She strokes his cheek!

ULYSSES: Come, come.

TROILUS: Nay, stay; by Jove, I will not speak a word.
There is between my will and all offences
A guard of patience; stay a little while.

THERSITES: How the devil luxury, with his fat rump and
potato-finger, tickles these together! Fry, lechery, fry!

60 DIOMEDES: But will you, then?

CRESSIDA: In faith I will, la; never trust me else.

DIOMEDES: Give me some token for the surety of it.

CRESSIDA: I'll fetch you one.

Exit

ULYSSES: You have sworn patience.

TROILUS: Fear me not, sweet lord;
I will not be myself, nor have cognition
Of what I feel: I am all patience.

Enter Cressida

THERSITES: Now the pledge; now, now, now!

CRESSIDA: Here, Diomed, keep this sleeve.

TROILUS: O beauty, where is thy faith?

70 ULYSSES: My lord –

TROILUS: I will be patient; outwardly I will.

CRESSIDA: You look upon that sleeve; behold it well.
He loved me – O false wench! – Give't me again.

DIOMEDES: Whose was't?

CRESSIDA: It is no matter, now I have't again.
I will not meet with you tomorrow night;
I prithee, Diomed, visit me no more.

THERSITES: Now she sharpens – well said, whetstone!

DIOMEDES: I shall have it.

80 CRESSIDA: What, this?

DIOMEDES: Ay, that.

CRESSIDA: O all you gods! O pretty, pretty pledge!
Thy master now lies thinking in his bed
Of thee and me, and sighs, and takes my glove,
And gives memorial dainty kisses to it
As I kiss thee – Nay, do not snatch it from me;
He that takes that doth take my heart withal.

DIOMEDES: I had your heart before; this follows it.

TROILUS: I did swear patience.

90 CRESSIDA: You shall not have it, Diomed, faith, you shall not;
I'll give you something else,

DIOMEDES: I will have this. Whose was it?

CRESSIDA: It is no matter.

DIOMEDES: Come, tell me whose it was.

CRESSIDA: 'Twas one's that loved me better than you will.
But now you have it, take it.

DIOMEDES: Whose was it?

CRESSIDA: By all Diana's waiting-women yond,
And by herself I will not tell you whose.

DIOMEDES: Tomorrow will I wear it on my helm;
And grieve his spirit that dares not challenge it.

100 TROILUS: Wert thou the devil, and wor'st it on thy horn,
It should be challenged.

CRESSIDA: Well, well, 'tis done, 'tis past – and yet it is not;
I will not keep my word.

DIOMEDES: Why then, farewell;
Thou never shalt mock Diomed again.

CRESSIDA: You shall not go; one cannot speak a word
But it straight starts you.

DIOMEDES: I do not like this fooling.

THERSITES: Nor I, by Pluto: but that that likes not you
Pleases me best.

DIOMEDES: What, shall I come? The hour?

CRESSIDA: Ay, come – O Jove! – do come: I shall be
plagued.

DIOMEDES: Farewell till then.

110 CRESSIDA: Good night; I prithee come.

Exit Diomedes

Troilus, farewell! One eye yet looks on thee,
But with my heart the other eye doth see.
Ah, poor our sex! This fault in us I find,
The error of our eye directs our mind;
What error leads must err – O, then conclude,
Minds swayed by eyes are full of turpitude.

Exit

THERSITES: A proof of strength she could not publish more,
Unless she say 'My mind is now turned whore.'

ULYSSES: All's done, my lord.

TROILUS: It is.

ULYSSES: Why stay we then?

120 TROILUS: To make a recordation to my soul
      Of every syllable that here was spoke.
      But if I tell how these two did co-act,
      Shall I not lie in publishing a truth?
      Sith yet there is a credence in my heart,
      An esperance so obstinately strong,
      That doth invert th'attest of eyes and ears,
      As if those organs had deceptious functions,
      Created only to calumniate.
      Was Cressid here?

ULYSSES: I cannot conjure, Trojan.

130 TROILUS: She was not, sure.

ULYSSES: Most sure she was.

TROILUS: Why, my negation hath no taste of madness.

ULYSSES: Nor mine, my lord: Cressid was here but now.

TROILUS: Let it not be believed for womanhood.
      Think, we had mothers: do not give advantage
      To stubborn critics, apt, without a theme
      For depravation, to square the general sex
      By Cressid's rule; rather think this not Cressid.

ULYSSES: What hath she done, Prince, that can soil our
140   mothers?

TROILUS: Nothing at all, unless that this were she.

THERSITES: Will he swagger himself out on's own eyes?

TROILUS: This she? No, this is Diomed's Cressida.
      If beauty have a soul, this is not she;
      If souls guide vows, if vows are sanctimony,
      If sanctimony be the gods' delight,
      If there be rule in unity itself,
      This is not she. O madness of discourse,
      That cause sets up with and against itself!

150   Bifold authority, where reason can revolt
      Without perdition, and loss assume all reason
      Without revolt. This is, and is not, Cressid!

                    [. . .]

O Cressid! O false Cressid! False, false, false!
Let all untruths stand by thy stainèd name,
And they'll seem glorious.
ULYSSES: O, contain yourself;
Your passion draws ears hither.

Enter Aeneas

AENEAS: I have been seeking you this hour, my lord.
Hector by this is arming him in Troy.
190   Ajax, your guard, stays to conduct you home.
TROILUS: Have with you, Prince. My courteous lord, adieu.
Farewell, revolted fair! – and, Diomed,
Stand fast, and wear a castle on thy head!
ULYSSES: I'll bring you to the gates.
TROILUS: Accept distracted thanks.

Exeunt Troilus, Aeneas, and Ulysses

THERSITES: Would I could meet that rogue Diomed! I would
croak like a raven; I would bode, I would bode. Patroclus will
give me anything for the intelligence of this whore; the parrot
will not do more for an almond than he for a commodious
drab. Lechery, lechery, still wars and lechery; nothing else
holds fashion! A burning devil take them!

Exit

12 cliff: musical key; vulva
51 palter: prevaricate
58 luxury: lustfulness
59 potatoes were considered aphrodisiac
126 attest: evidence
199 commodius drab: obliging prostitute

(Act V, scene ii)

Cressida's difficulty is acute. She has had one experience of love, in effect her induction into womanhood, and after it she is brutally torn from her lover and taken to enemy territory where men see her as mere commodity. It was Ulysses, now watching her, who earlier, on her arrival at the Greek camp, decided just forty lines after setting eyes on her that she was one of those 'sluttish spoils of opportunity, / And daughters of the game' (IV.v.62–3). That reading, incidentally, wasn't restricted to the Greek generals. In the middle of the liberal 1960s a male editor, in one of the most popular and widely available editions of the play, described Cressida in that scene at the Greek camp as happily parading and as a brassy and degraded slut. And now in her isolation another man is wanting her and is offering her his protection: he calls her his 'charge'; she calls him her 'guardian' – as well she might, given her father's casual handing her over with the ironically charged 'she comes to you'. Yet she can't forget Troilus, though every time she wavers because of her memories of him it is interpreted by Diomedes as her playing hard to get.

So there she is – being interpreted. By four variously partial, variously uncomprehending, uniformly hostile male witnesses (readers, critics): Diomedes expecting an easy sexual conquest; Troilus resolutely focused on his own anguish and determined not to notice hers, watching the two of them; Ulysses applying brutal man-to-man 'common sense' and his equally brutal misogyny ('She will sing any man at first sight'), watching Troilus watch them, as he is too; Thersites turning all the evidence to chortling satiric derision, watching the scene's various interconnected watchings, on the edge of the stage's visual layers, relishing it the more distressing, to everyone else, it becomes.

And here are we, positioned at the outermost rim in this series of interlocked readings (and thus, ironically, forced closest to Thersites), made to be accomplices in these multiple pressures exerted on Cressida who, vulnerably at the centre, is thus squeezed, in effect, into the male-determined role that is the only remaining function for her. Her assertion to Diomedes that Troilus 'loved me better' than he ever could carries particular pathos. It's as if the scene and its readings tighten a series of knots around the increasingly fragile sense of Cressida's freedom, choice of action, autonomous identity and selfhood. And the complexity of the layered interpretations also exerts pressure on us – to try to get through the thicket of readings to the vulnerable, frightened, confused young woman at the centre who, forced by the scene's cruel comedy, has to keep using the word 'come', forced into suggesting the sexual meaning of the word. Her total experience of men so far: one night of love.

At the end of the play she writes to that lover of one night. He reads the letter, to himself. Asked what it says, Troilus replies 'words, words, mere words, no matter from the heart'. There's literary criticism at its brutalising worst. For what does he know of her heart? For Diomedes, as we've seen, her heart is as (in)significant as her love-token sleeve. And then – 'go, wind to wind' – he tears it up (V.iii.108–10). I think this is the only letter sent and read in Shakespeare whose contents the audience never discover. It's an emblem of the way in which Cressida and her attempts at self-definition and identity are pressurised to the point of abandonment and dissolution, a page torn up and scattered.

*   *   *

Shakespeare's story of Cressida is part of a long process to which the figure of Cressida is subjected in a history of texts. A thumbnail sketch of these follows.

In Homer's ancient Greek epic the *Iliad*, written some 500 years after the events it describes, the story is told of two young women captured by the Greek hero-warrior Achilles during the Trojan War. They're called Chryseis (daughter of Chryses) and Briseis (daughter of Briseus). Achilles keeps Briseis for himself and Chryseis is allotted to the Greek commander Agamemnon. When the god Apollo intervenes to return Chryseis to her father, Agamemnon insists that Achilles hand Briseis over to him. In pique Achilles removes himself and his private army from the war-effort and the long stalemate in the war (where Shakespeare starts his play) is the result.

Rather more than a thousand years after Homer, two books, attributed to Dictys and Dares, retell the Trojan story. Dares notes that Briseis's eyebrows are joined, a mark of beauty and passion in Ancient Greece. After another 600 years, in twelfth-century France, Benoit de St Maure's *Roman de Troie* tells what appears to be a wholly new story, of how Briseida (the name is picked up from Dares) has to separate from her lover Troilus and be handed over to his rival Diomede: her father Calcas is responsible for this separation. Later in his book Benoit tells another story, derived from Dictys, of the two young women captured by Achilles – named Hippodamia (daughter of Briseus) and Astynome (daughter of Chryses). It doesn't seem to have occurred to Benoit that he's got a Briseida and a Briseus not attached to each other. But he does say that Briseida's eyebrows are joined, for him a flaw to her beauty. In another episode he tells how Achilles catches sight of and falls in love with Polyxena, a daughter of Priam, in the temple: Shakespeare picks this up and uses it casually in his play.

In fourteenth-century Italy Boccaccio writes *Il Filostrato*, telling the full-length story of Criseida and Troilo, starting at how Troilo fell in love, and for this the main source is Benoit's story of Achilles and Polyxena in the temple. Boccaccio's young woman is called Criseida and not Briseida (as in Benoit), either because he knew from the Latin poet Ovid of the Homeric story of Achilles and Briseis, or because he was misled by Ovid into supposing that Chryseis was the daughter of Calcas – as supported by Benoit who makes Calcas the father (of Briseida, if you're still with me).

Chaucer in the 1370s draws heavily but not exclusively on Boccaccio in his great poem *Troilus and Criseyde*. It's suggested that he may have based his account of Troilus falling in love with Criseyde at the temple directly on the Polyxena episode and on another story in another romance by Boccaccio called the *Filocolo*. But falling in love with a young woman at worship in a temple is something of a literary formula: it happened famously to medieval Italy's two most famous poets, Dante and Petrarch. Chaucer may have drawn, for his portrait of Criseyde, on Ovid's description of Helen of Troy.

Some 7,000 lines into his 8,000-line poem Chaucer describes Criseyde properly for the first time. She is sober, simple, wise, charitable, stately, tender-hearted and (the last in his list) 'slyding of corage' (V.118). (The 'browes joineden' (V. 117) are, as in Benoit, her single physical flaw.) Slyding of corage? What might this mean, at the end of that list of compliments? The Everyman edition suggests 'of unstable courage' (London, Dent, 1953, p. 296). The Oxford editor is of loftier mind: he says it means a deficiency in 'the loyalty that suffers and endures' (*Works*, Oxford, Oxford University Press, 1966, p. 387). The Penguin translator adds a word: '. . . but she had a sliding heart' (Harmondsworth, Penguin, 1971, p. 272). So there she is, fixed with that 'but', the heart like the eyebrows. It is true that Chaucer, a little earlier, had predicted that Troilus and Troy shall 'through-out her herte slyde' (V. 110) but in his poem this doesn't actually happen. Chaucer is quite clear in his sympathies for Criseyde's plight, once the crisis occurs, and quite explicit that she decided to stay with Diomede because 'she was alone and hadde neede/Of friendes' helpe' (V. 147). He's also reluctant to be taken to be speaking on behalf of men who feel betrayed, and anxious rather to speak 'most for women' and to warn them to be 'war' (wary) of men (V. 255). But his editors and translators, and history generally, have found it all too easy to read the poem as a demonstration of Criseyde's failure to measure up. 'She had not the strength which the code [i.e. the code of courtly love] demanded of her' (Penguin edition, p. xxii). For the Oxford edition the sliding heart was the source of her 'condemnation' (p. 387).

Not long after Chaucer, the Scots poet Henryson clearly felt the need to put the male case as strongly as possible. His continuation of the Chaucer story is explicitly designed for the instruction of 'worthie wemen' who are urged at the end to avoid 'fals deceptioun' (*The Testament of Cresseid*, 610–13). His Cresseid is punished with the disfigurements and brandings of leprosy (confused in those days with venereal disease) – because, according to Henryson's insistence, her 'feminitie' changed to 'filth' in her taking 'foull plesance' in 'fleschlie lust' (ibid. 80–3). Henryson's appeal to what his sympathetic editor calls 'selfrighteous male morality' (*The Middle Scots Poets*, London, Edward Arnold, 1970, p. 24) was widely heard and appreciated. Cressida became a byword for falsehood, punished appropriately. In Shakespeare's own *Twelfth Night*, written more or less at the same time as *Troilus and Cressida*, a clown casually remarks that 'Cressida was a beggar' (III.i.52). Thirty years later the translator Sidnam felt impelled to abandon his version of Chaucer because he felt so disgusted with what he took to be Criseyde's behaviour – acting with properly outraged male paranoia.

In Shakespeare's *Troilus* the male-aggressive readings (history's judgement) are, as we've seen, conspiring to squeeze out the voice of a vulnerable and confused young woman. The scene we've looked at dramatises that process in a particularly painful way – and implicates us in that process. The play's audience knows what history has prepared for Cressida. It knows that she will be used up by Diomedes and abandoned to leprosy (even in this scene she is made to say 'I shall be plagued'). The shreds of paper that Troilus tears up at the end of the play are a poignant reminder of what this thumbnail sketch of her literary-history suggests: Cressida's identity, which she struggles so hard to evolve and materialise in Shakespeare's play, is always being constituted and reconstituted and read and unread by men, a tissue of fragments and figments.

The history of Cressida is exemplary in the sense that it shows how women's representation and even their subjectivity are controlled and written in the terms of male language, male desire, male ownership. She's also, of course, a counter and a commodity in the economics of war. Rene Girard's *Deceit, Desire and the Novel* (Baltimore, Johns Hopkins University Press, 1965) and Eve Sedgwick's *Between Men* (New York, Columbia University Press, 1985) show that male–male relations, as here the rivalry between Troilus and Diomedes, reduce the woman to a secondary role and have a source in the anthropological exchange of women which structured the economy of male relations in earlier culture. We'll come across this notion later, particularly in the chapter on Dickens's *Our Mutual Friend*. There's a good third-series Arden edition of *Troilus* (London, Thomas Nelson, 1998), edited by David Bevington. As mentioned in the endnote to the last chapter, Sean McEvoy's *Shakespeare: The Basics* (London, Routledge, 2000) is the first place to go for contemporary thinking about the plays. *Troilus* has become one of the most popular of the plays in performance after earlier neglect. You might like to consider why, once you've had the chance to get to know the play.

4

SHAKESPEARE'S SONNETS
Courtly patronage and the homoerotic

In this chapter we look at four of Shakespeare's sonnets. The contexts for thinking about them are largely historical: the particular cultural tastes and interests of King James's court; the patronage system of the time, in which poets addressed patrons in certain ways for certain monetary gains; and early seventeenth-century and previous models of writing real or fictionalised love-poems, particularly sonnets. It is suggested that this was a volume of poems which proved very unsettling to its readers.

Shakespeare's sonnets are the most highly regarded and most appreciated love-poems in our culture – and the most controversial and most argued-over of any poems ever. These two states of extremes seem to get on happily together: readers enjoy the sonnets, quote them, learn them by heart; and critics find it difficult to agree with each other about anything to do with them, from the simplest of problems (when were they written?) to the most fundamental (are they even love-poems?).

I don't suppose anything resembling a critical consensus will ever be reached about these poems but in recent years something approaching a scholarly consensus has emerged and the following is an outline of the current position. Katherine Duncan-Jones's excellent Arden edition of the sonnets lies behind many of the findings below and I draw on her work gratefully. The propositions that follow often flatly contradict earlier received wisdom – such as the idea that the poems were first published in a collection cobbled together without Shakespeare's knowledge or consent.

- The 1609 volume containing the 154 sonnets and the longer poem *A Lover's Complaint* falls into a recognisable pattern of volumes from the period containing related but disparate poems in known generic categories, and looks carefully designed to be recognised as such. The designing is much more likely to be the poet's than his publisher's.

- The publisher, Thomas Thorpe, had a good reputation to defend. He wouldn't have risked it by publishing these poems without their author's consent and collaboration.

- Although in some cases originally drafted earlier, probably in the period 1596–8, the poems were worked on and revised for publication in the first decade of the new century, most intensively during plague years when the theatres were closed. The sonnets include reference to Queen Elizabeth's death (1603) and in their dark and often satiric tone reflect the milieu of King James's new court. Publication in 1609 was when the plague was most devastating in London. Closed theatres meant restricted income for theatre shareholders like Shakespeare.

- The order of the poems in the volume is most unlikely to correspond to the exact order of composition. Much more likely is a consciously patterned organisation, when the volume was being prepared for publication, with careful numerological significances in the ordering which early seventeenth-century readers would have responded to more easily than we can.

- The first 126 sonnets are provocatively homoerotic love-poems addressed to a publicity-conscious young aristocrat whom the poet also identifies as his patron. The homoerotic content is unusual for the period but not entirely unknown elsewhere. As such, these poems are designed to appeal to the self-consciously 'homosocial' Jacobean court. These 126 poems chart an uneven and unequal relationship of remarkable intensity, self-scrutiny and devotion.

- William Herbert, third Earl of Pembroke, a leading light of James's court, a man then in his mid-twenties and much celebrated for his physical appeal, his closeness to the King and his generous patronage of the arts, is the young man most likely to be the originating figure behind the loved youth of these poems. More materially, he would have been the volume's patron, as he was later of the first posthumous collection of Shakespeare's plays. Duncan-Jones has found a remarkable eye-witness account of

James's coronation, by an Italian diplomat, which gives a flavour of Pembroke at court. In a letter home to the Venetian senate the visitor wrote this: 'The Earl of Pembroke, a handsome youth, who is always with the King, and always joking with him, actually kissed his Majesty's face, whereupon the King laughed and gave him a little cuff' (Duncan-Jones, 1997, p. 67). As Duncan-Jones says, the bold and public intimacy there is certainly remarkable. Shakespeare's theatre company was specifically adopted by James when he became King and carried the name 'The King's Men'. It has long been recognised that Ben Jonson, at least, seems to have identified Pembroke as the dedicatee of the sonnets, his evidence suggesting that the volume was considered by Jonson and others as rather too dangerously radical.

- Sonnets 127 to 152 are bitter and wry reflections on the poet's sexual entanglement with a woman – who is, in turn, entangled with the youth at the expense of Shakespeare's relations with both of them. These poems, too, are pitched to match the sardonic, misogynistic flavour of the early Jacobean court, though some evidence suggests that these were among the first poems in the collection to be composed.

- The young Pembroke was a voracious womaniser even if he was also modishly homoerotic in his public behaviour. But in his early youth he exasperated his family by refusing to fall in with their plans to marry him off before his father's death. The first seventeen sonnets urge the youth to marry and beget children. Pembroke's mother, a very influential patroness of the arts, may have commissioned Shakespeare to write these poems on the occasion of the boy's seventeenth birthday (1597), at the time when his refusals to marry were a matter of court gossip. It's difficult to think of other reasons why the first seventeen sonnets would have been written. After Pembroke became Earl he might, with only a little incongruity, still have been referred to as 'Mr [i.e. master] W.H.', the puzzling figure to whom Thorpe's 1609 edition of the sonnets is dedicated, especially if Thorpe is drawing attention to these first seventeen poems. In the dedication he is described as the 'only begetter' of 'these insuing sonnets'. The pun, Christ as God's only begotten son, plays on the fact that all Herbert can, so far, beget is sonnets, even though he's a godlike inspirer of such poetry and thence the 'eternity' promised both by the dedication and the poems themselves.

- There's another poet who is presented in the sonnets as rivalling, successfully, for the youth's attention and patronage. As in the case of the seductive woman of Sonnets 127 to 152, it seems possible that this, however grounded in actual biography, might be a composite figure. The same, of course, might be said against the case made above for identifying Pembroke as the youth. The Arden editor comes close to this position by suggesting that Shakespeare's earlier patron, the Earl of Southampton, might have been the original addressee of some of the earlier poems. He was seven years older than Pembroke. This presumably makes him, for modern sensibilities, that much less of a source of anxieties about inappropriately young love-objects.

- Compared to the many testimonials to the success of the plays, and, more pointedly still, the success and indeed notoriety of his early 1590s narrative poems dedicated to Southampton, the 1609 edition of the sonnets seems to have attracted little notice. Perhaps the sexual radicalism, and the darkly intimated realism of the narrative drama involved, were just too disquieting, or embarrassing, or awkward for the sonnets to be the kind of success that Shakespeare, at 45 and at the peak of his fame, and his young and ambitious publisher, Thomas Thorpe, might have anticipated. These are difficult poems, prickly and raw at once, not to mention unprecedentedly dense and complex. Duncan-Jones suggests that the typical response of readers to what might have been a long-anticipated volume was stunned disappointment. There was no second edition in Shakespeare's lifetime. A textually corrupt edition of 1640 significantly got away with altering many poems to suggest that they were all written to a woman.

- My guess is that the young Thorpe helped persuade the older Shakespeare into putting together the collection. The process would have involved Shakespeare revising and knocking it into shape, mixing public and personal stuff, including, bizarrely, what looks like a courtship poem for Anne Hathaway, clearing it with Pembroke, whose career as a public investor in expeditionary journeys to the New World was by then as notable as his generous patronage of poets, and drafting or letting Thorpe draft a stylishly beguiling dedication. But the evidence is that the resulting volume didn't exactly fly out of the booksellers, even though the likelihood is that Pembroke paid generously for the dedication of this unprecedented volume of poems. Duncan-Jones suggests something between £5 and £10.

Here are four poems. In each case text is in intriguing relations with context. Together they suggest something radically unstable about the way the sonnets present the relationship between Shakespeare and the youth.

20

A woman's face with Nature's own hand painted
Hast thou, the master-mistress of my passion,
A woman's gentle heart, but not acquainted
With shifting change as is false women's fashion,
An eye more bright than theirs, less false in rolling,
Gilding the object whereupon it gazeth,
A man in hue, all hues in his controlling,
Which steals men's eyes and women's souls amazeth.
And for a woman wert thou first created,
10 Till Nature as she wrought thee fell a-doting,
And by addition me of thee defeated
By adding one thing to my purpose nothing.
    But since she prick'd thee out for women's pleasure,
    Mine be thy love, and thy love's use their treasure.

10 wrought: crafted
10 a-doting: infatuated

29

When, in disgrace with Fortune and men's eyes,
I all alone beweep my outcast state,
And trouble deaf heaven with my bootless cries,
And look upon myself and curse my fate,
Wishing me like to one more rich in hope,

Featur'd like him, like him with friends possess'd,
Desiring this man's art, and that man's scope,
With what I most enjoy contented least:
Yet in these thoughts myself almost despising,
10　Haply I think on thee, and then my state
(Like to the lark at break of day arising)
From sullen earth sings hymns at heaven's gate;
　　For thy sweet love remember'd such wealth brings
　　That then I scorn to change my state with kings.

3　bootless: pointless
10　haply: by chance

57

Being your slave what should I do but tend
Upon the hours and times of your desire?
I have no precious time at all to spend,
Nor services to do till you require.
Nor dare I chide the world-without-end hour
Whilst I (my sovereign) watch the clock for you,
Nor think the bitterness of absence sour
When you have bid your servant once adieu;
Nor dare I question with my jealous thought
10　Where you may be, or your affairs suppose,
But like a sad slave stay and think of naught
Save, where you are, how happy you make those.
　　So true a fool is love that in your Will,
　　(Though you do anything) he thinks no ill.

1　tend: wait
10　affairs: occupations
14　Will: desire; Shakespeare

62

Sin of self-love possesseth all mine eye,
And all my soul, and all my every part;
And for this sin there is no remedy,
It is so grounded inward in my heart.

Methinks no face so gracious is as mine,
No shape so true, no truth of such account,
And for myself mine own worth do define
As I all other in all worths surmount.
But when my glass shows me myself indeed,
10 Beated and chopp'd with tann'd antiquity,
Mine own self-love quite contrary I read:
Self so self-loving were iniquity.
    'Tis thee (my self) that for myself I praise,
    Painting my age with beauty of thy days.

12 iniquity: wickedness

Sonnet 20 has caused considerable consternation over the years, especially among those for whom the National Poet is part of Britain's imperial destiny or heritage industry. Closer to where I'm writing this now, some teachers in England might hesitate to teach this poem in class for fear of being prosecuted for 'promoting homosexuality'. For it's pretty obvious to most readers that the sonnet, while apparently saying that Shakespeare's interest in the youth is not a physical-bodily interest, subversively and very wittily suggests that that is exactly where his interests lie and where his love is focused. It's a wry and comic exercise in double-speak, and it is driven stylishly along through *double entendres*, sexy and sexual puns. Editors disagree about the extent of these, apart from the obvious 'pricked', but the wordplay would include 'not acquainted' (not equipped with a cunt), probably 'steals men's eyes and women's souls amazeth' (where the bawdy terms for male and female genitalia – 'eyes' and 'souls' – have been comically attached to the wrong gender and where 'steals' suggests 'steels', as in 'hardens', and 'amazeth' suggests knee-trembling sexual excitement) and, most notoriously, the idea that Nature, falling in love herself with the woman she was intending to fashion, added 'one thing to my purpose nothing', thereby making a man instead. This line brilliantly focuses the two incompatible readings. On the surface: your 'thing' (penis) is nothing to me because my love transcends sexual expression. Subversively: your thing is, for me, equivalent to a 'nothing' (a vagina – Hamlet makes the same pun to Ophelia before the performance of 'The Mousetrap' (III.ii.116)).

The poem's very line-endings are part of the joke. This is the only sonnet in the collection where every line has a so-called 'feminine ending' in the eleventh syllable. The overall effect is of a poem in drag, a camp poem. Oscar Wilde may have been fantasising when he argued that Shakespeare's youth was his star, cross-dressing boy-actor but one senses the rightness of his instinct in this poem. Sonnet 20 does have the air of naughty-but-nice titillation that the boy-actors in drag would, it seems, have elicited in both men and women in the theatre audiences, and which a play like *Twelfth Night* exploits so expressively. (Lorenzo, when he eloped with Jessica in *The Merchant of Venice*, liked the fact that she cross-dressed for the purpose, commenting with approval on her having adopted 'the lovely garnish of a boy' (II.vi.45).) But camp, crucially, depends on readers getting the joke. And so the point to make is that this poem makes most contextual sense in the light of its presumed original readership who would have appreciated the joke: the fashionable homo-erotic, misogynistic court of King James and his favourite young men, such as Pembroke. For the poem, of course, derives from the twin notions that the youth, in including female characteristics, transcends female weaknesses like falsity and 'shifting change' and that, being his 'master-mistress', the youth and being in love with him involve higher orders of intensity (including sexual expression) than heterosexuality. The poem shares the joke with its coterie male readership.

Have another look at Sonnet 29 (p. 38).

Surprisingly the new Arden editor makes no mention of an important and persuasive essay on this sonnet by John Barrell, part of the argument of which I shall draw gratefully on here. But perhaps it's not that surprisingly absent from the Arden. For what it does is radically destabilise the very idea of the love that Shakespeare is apparently exploring in these poems. Barrell does this by demonstrating, through very close attention to its language and punctuation, that the poem crucially deploys what he calls the 'discourse of patronage'. Barrell contends that readers and editors 'edit out' this context by reading the language of the poem as conventionally romantic-idealist − readings that transcend the conditions in which the poem was produced. Barrell's aim, in recovering the poem's discourse of patronage, is to 'do something to situate the poem at the historical moment of its production' and to identify 'the social position of the narrator' (Barrell, 1988, pp. 30, 21).

What was that moment? As mentioned above, the 1609 volume called *Shakespeare's Sonnets* was a commercial commodity not just in the sense that it hoped to sell itself to lots of readers but, prior to that and at a time of financial difficulty for theatre workers, it was dedicated to a patron who almost certainly rewarded the poet in cash. Barrell develops the point like this. The moment of production was when

> the commercial market for writing was not so developed as to enable a writer to be a professional writer in the sense that he could hope to be supported by his sales, and be exempt from the need for patronage; but a moment, also, when the growth of literacy and learning, and other more purely economic factors, meant that there were far more petitioners for patronage than the potential patrons were able or willing to patronise.
>
> (ibid., p. 30)

Barrell locates this poem as part of a sub-genre of literature in the period, that of complaints about the lack of patronage. That is, typical readings that represent the poem as, essentially, saying that when he's feeling a bit low and depressed Shakespeare only has to think of 'thy sweet love' to cheer himself up are editing out a range of meanings in words and phrases such as 'disgrace', 'fortune', 'outcast state', 'bootless', 'rich in hope', 'with friends possessed', 'art', 'scope', 'enjoy' and even 'love' that together and collectively produce a reading that specifically points towards issues of patronage and Shakespeare's need of it.

Barrell finds other examples from the period that suggest clearly that 'hope', in the phrase 'more rich in hope', carries the idea of 'financial rewards' – as in 'booty' which is what 'bootless' then highlights in its meaning. 'Friends', then, would suggest the rich and influential 'whose love', in Barrell's words, 'is represented by the disbursement of money' (ibid., p. 27). The discourse of patronage moves 'Fortune' from merely meaning 'fate' to meaning 'lucky prosperity', and the 'disgrace' that the poet feels is shame at his poverty. The 'art' and the 'scope' that the poet envies in other men are the social skills in securing patronage and the freedom of opportunity that such patronage would bring. And, for Barrell 'most crucial of all', when the poet is weeping his 'outcast state' he's not meaning his low spirits but, in the *Oxford English Dictionary* definition, his state 'in regard to welfare and prosperity' (ibid., p. 28).

When it comes to the end of the poem and the word 'love' we must focus on the implications of the meanings just discussed. What they suggest is that the issue of personal relations is represented here as economic relations. What 'love' does is disguise those economic relations in the suggestion that the patron's love is like the love of God in making the poet's money problems seem trivial. As Barrell points out, the 'thee' and the 'thy sweet love' in this poem, if it was read in isolation from the other sonnets, would, for most readers, be God, if only because of the 'hymns at heaven's gate'. It's part of the strategy of asking for patronage not to be too obviously holding out the hand. Mystifying the patron as godlike is good tactics. It makes asking for money sound like basking in the divine love that makes money irrelevant. Less cynically, it is a fact that in this period 'love' is the word used to describe the feelings for a hoped-for patron and the relations between patron and patronised. The love we're talking about was one that expected financial reward. In Barrell's nicely blunt paraphrase, what Sonnet 29 is saying by not-saying is this: 'when I'm pushed for money, with all the degradation that poverty involves, I sometimes remember you, and you're always good for a couple of quid' (ibid., p. 30).

Have another look at Sonnet 57 (p. 39).

By the time they've reached Sonnet 57 readers tend to have told themselves an unfolding narrative story, picking up on what may be narrative clues in the poems – a story involving Shakespeare coming to know the youth more and to idealise him rather less, especially under the impact of the triangular relationship involving the two of them and his mistress. But if it is an unfolding narrative-dramatic story of that or of any kind, it is one that readers make themselves rather more than one told them by Shakespeare. But 57, it seems, does mark a kind of pointer or landmark in the sequence, if sequence is the word.

In terms of Shakespeare's devotion to the youth this has few or no parallels. Its parallels are, perhaps, elsewhere, for the context suggested by this poem is what literary scholars call Petrarchanism. This name derives from the fourteenth-century Italian poet Petrarch, whose sonnet sequence was among the earliest and most influential; and the kind of love associated with Petrarchanism presented the beauty and cruelty of the worshipped woman and the suffering of the typically unrequited man who was doing the worshipping. The term courtly love, which we associate more with early French literature and Chaucer, involves related concerns. What many find remarkable about Shakespeare's sonnets, apart from the male gender of their addressee, is their hard realism in contrast to the rather weakened Petrarchanism of the sonnet-writers in England in the 1590s when sonnet-writing became very fashionable. But 57 seems to present the selfless suffering of the 'slave' lover for his aloof 'sovereign' in peculiarly pure form.

But the very purity and abject servility of the lover's devotion invite a contrary or subversive reading. As with 20 and 29 we seem to have two discourses in play together. These two readings might in each three cases be termed 'innocent' and 'worldly'. In this poem the innocent reading of Petrarchan servility breaks down perhaps most obviously in the notion of Shakespeare thinking only, in the youth's absence, of 'how happy' the youth is making those he's with when he's not with Shakespeare, who seems reduced to hanging around waiting for him. I'm so glad that you're making others happy? Er, a joke? The 'jealous' lover's attitude towards those others might be presumed to be rather more murderous than that.

So what we have here looks like a ferocious attack, the most bitterly sarcastic onslaught delivered on this apparently casual and indifferent youth in any of these poems. Every line, every idea needs inverting on its head in a spirit of violent anti-Petrarchanism. The prevailing voice of heavily loaded irony is saying something like – how dare you treat me so debasingly? I'm not a slave, you're not my sovereign, I have plenty of other things to do with my life, thanks very much, rather than hanging about on your whims, while you're sleeping around with others, and on the off-chance that you'll keep our appointment.

But I think there's a third way of looking at it, one which starts from the recognition that the person Shakespeare is most woundingly attacking is himself. This reading involves turning the poem back on its feet again and hearing it as a desperate statement of a literal situation. Shakespeare's devotion is such that he is reduced to an abject servility that is more than the Petrarchan literary formula. It's actual, it's happening, he loathes himself for its self-consuming hopeless-ness, but he's unable to extricate himself from it. It's as if the poem reanimates the dead clichés in Petrarchanism, rediscovers the terrible and wasting degradations that such devotion can bring. Even the apparently absurd notion of the poet thinking 'of naught / Save, where you are, how happy you make those', which we used earlier as signal-ling the ironic reading, even this now makes painful and literal sense. It's as if the poet is desperately clutching at straws: perhaps the situ-ation isn't quite as bad as all that: you are at least making someone happy . . .

As the reader shuttles among these three readings the poem, and particularly the presentation of the love and the lover and the loved youth, becomes so unstable as in effect to become unknowable. The notion of the loved youth himself, as well as whatever it is that the speaker is saying to him, seems to move out of focus in the process, leaving Shakespeare in more than an actual loneliness: leaving his love as a kind of self-love.

Have another look at Sonnet 62 (p. 39).

Sonnet 62 seems more than usually unstable, not least in its implicit instruction to the reader to read in a 'quite contrary' way. The poem certainly reads its immediate context, the story of Narcissus, in an interesting way. Shakespeare is in love with himself, like Narcissus, but in a way quite contrary to Narcissus he looks in the glass to fall out of love with himself and into the odd notion that when he loves himself he's actually loving the boy (helpfully called here 'myself'). So he is in love with himself. Or not. Right at the start of the sequence, in Sonnet 3, the boy was told to 'look in thy glass', to recognise his own narcis-sism, and to recognise that 'thou art thy mother's glass, and she in thee / Calls back the lovely April of her prime' – that is, that his mother as it were uses her son narcissistically. In Sonnet 53 the speaker, in wonder but also in some exasperation, asks the boy, 'what is your substance, whereof are you made, / That millions of strange shadows on you tend?' The notion seems to be that the loved-object can only be a series of endlessly self-generated reflections with which one narcis-sistically engages. But love is like that. (You'll find more material on Narcissus in the next chapter and in the Appendix.)

Self and other seem to float bizarrely into air in the process of Son-net 62. The more we read the two terms in a 'quite contrary' way the more the poem's logic disappears. But the possible sexual puns on 'eye', 'soul' and 'part' and the odd idea that self-love is a 'sin' suggest that Shakespeare may be occupying his lonely time engaged in something rather less metaphysical than thinking this stuff through.

The four poems under discussion seem so radically different in tone, address, manner and function as to make the idea of a poet addressing his lover seem a very peculiar one. The voices with which Shakespeare's 'love' is ventriloquised, in all four of these poems, seem so multiple and so shifting that the reader is permanently in a state of destabilised uncertainty. That is, we seem to know less and less, the more the sonnets unravel individually and accumulate collectively. It's not surprising that, in a kind of desperation, we add up the signs to make a pseudo-coherent story. The collection as it stands may be neatly organised into its large generic groupings but the experience of reading the volume is, and perhaps was intended to be, a dazzling affront to the sentimental notion that love is coherent at all. Stunned disappointment may, indeed, have been the response in 1609.

The critical literature on the sonnets is something between a mountain and a graveyard. Good minds have been turned mad by trying to solve the problems they pose, or just by reading the entirety of what's been written about them. The new Arden edition edited by Katherine Duncan-Jones (London, Thomas Nelson, 1997) is something of a radical breakthrough in its bold and convincing contextualising. Stephen Booth's edition (London, Yale University Press, 1977) is dazzlingly attentive to wordplay. Martin Seymour-Smith's edition (London, Heinemann, 1963) is very lively but has been inexplicably replaced. John Barrell's essay 'Editing Out: The Discourse of Patronage and Shakespeare's 29th sonnet' is in his *Poetry, Language and Politics* (Manchester, Manchester University Press, 1988). The chapter on Milton's sonnets is particularly recommended. There's an important essay in Eve Sedgwick's *Between Men* (New York, Columbia University Press, 1985), and two typically rich and subtle essays in Rosalie Colie's distinguished *Shakespeare's Living Art* (Princeton, Princeton University Press, 1974). A very good way of contextualising the poetry of the period is by exploring in the excellent *Penguin Book of Renaissance Verse*, edited by David Norbrook and Henry Woudhuysen (Harmondsworth, Penguin, 1993) which is wide-ranging, scholarly and contains very fine editorial contributions. Another good way is to read or see *All's Well that Ends Well* where the central relationship between Helena and the aristocratic Bertram is emotionally and socially very close to the love in the first 126 sonnets. Oscar Wilde's *The Portrait of Mr W.H.* (conveniently printed with his fairy-tales in the *Complete Shorter Fiction* (Oxford, Oxford

University Press, 1980)) is very much worth a read, especially as Duncan-Jones shows how damaging the Wilde trials were to the advance of good readings of the sonnets. We meet Wilde and his fairytales in a later chapter. Tennyson's *In Memoriam* is another Victorian text that could hardly have been written without the sonnets. The recent film *Shakespeare in Love* shows how hard it is, even now, for the cultural establishment to accept the notion of Shakespeare involved in anything but 'normal' relationships.

5

MILTON'S *PARADISE LOST*
Republican politics and the canon

This and the next chapter are to be read together. Here we have substantial extracts from a great and demanding poem, Milton's *Paradise Lost* (revised edition, 1674). The commentary runs between the extracts and is designed to contextualise the poem in the years of England's republic and commonwealth, following the civil wars of the 1640s. Focusing on the poem's presentation of the Adam and Eve story, and drawing on the work of leading historians, it is argued that the poem is an act of radical and republican politics.

There's a very funny passage in Cyril Connolly's *Enemies of Promise* (1938) where Connolly remembers the way the grand tradition of English poetry was presented to young schoolboys of his time, in the years of the First World War. He puts it in the voice of a typical private-school master, brought up on the language of the Old Testament.

> There is a natural tradition in English poetry [. . .] Chaucer begat Spenser, Spenser begat Shakespeare, Shakespeare begat Milton, Milton begat Keats, Coleridge, Shelley, Wordsworth, and they begat Tennyson who begat Longfellow, Stevenson, Kipling [. . .] There are a few bad boys we do not speak about – Donne, Dryden, Pope, Blake, Byron, Browning [. . .] and Oscar Wilde who was a criminal degenerate [. . .] A poem is good either because it is funny [. . .] or because it makes you want to cry. Some funny poems make you want to cry [. . .] that is because you are not a healthy little boy. You need more Character. The best poems have the most beautiful lines in them; these lines can be detached, they are purple patches and are Useful in Examinations [. . .] When you come to a purple

48

patch you can tell it by an alarm clock going off, you feel a cold shiver, a lump in the throat, your eyes fill with tears, and your hair stands on end [. . .] Nobody wrote so many purple patches as Tennyson, and he had character too [. . .] Kipling is the only great poet alive today. Poetry is romantic, purple – a help in time of trouble – or else it is clever and funny [. . .] – or has Character [. . .] It is also something to be ashamed of, like sex, and (except with the chaplain) religion.

(Harmondsworth, Penguin, 1961, pp. 181–3)

So what has changed in the way poetry and poets get taught today? What critics call the canon, the list of who gets taught and read and the 'bad boys' – and bad girls – who don't, is a very live issue. The idea of poets 'begetting' other poets as if they were fathers and sons in Oedipal conflict, apparently without mothers around, is an influential critical notion, associated particularly with the controversial critic Harold Bloom. But it's not just a matter of hot-headed arguments in university staffrooms. The canon and what's in it are important to those who regulate education at every level. There's a selection of books and authors that the British government lays down as a shortlist from which teachers should choose to teach students in secondary education. The assumptions behind the selection don't seem particularly different from those parodied by Connolly sixty years ago. But the most common assumption behind the shaping of the canon today, as in Connolly's day, is that politics should be kept out of poetry and its teaching. The poet this has impacted on most is Milton.

John Milton is a very great poet. The point about putting it so bluntly is that up to about 1940 the point wouldn't have needed putting at all. It was obvious. He was a compulsory author in post-16 studies in England till not that long ago, though he came off that holiest of lists before Chaucer, leaving now just Shakespeare. And his *Paradise Lost* was, with equal obviousness, recognised as one of the two or three greatest long poems in English. But then a number of things happened, more or less simultaneously, in the period from the 1930s that together had the effect of redrawing the canon and diminishing Milton.

It was largely as a result of the attempt, led by the poet T.S. Eliot and the critic F.R. Leavis, to drag English Studies into a bright new hard-edged future. Like all such projects, there was an unwritten political dimension to this and, by the time the powerful institution of so-called New Criticism had worked itself down through the universities and into the schools on both sides of the Atlantic, the result was a set of ideas about what constituted the proper study of literature, particularly poetry, that was presented as natural, timeless, and obvious.

These ideas promoted the short poem against the long (as easier to teach 'whole'), the lyric against the narrative, and criticism meant the closely focused analysis of the poem as timeless object in its complex inwardness and inner tensions. The critic's job was to tease out such tensions and to show how the dense concentrations of language work together in an organic self-sufficient whole. 'Organic' is Leavis's key-word; he purveyed the notion that England once had an organic community and that the proper reading of the 'felt life' of proper poems and properly grown-up novels could restore us to it. Texts are to be studied with more or less ruthless disregard for their social or biographical contexts, encouraging as a matter of high principle the idea that literature is self-sufficient and sealed-off from the world. So history and politics get relegated to the sidelines, reduced to supplementary background. It is only now, as I write, that the study of literature post-16 has broken with this enormously influential tradition in insisting that students show awareness of the inter-relations between texts and their contexts. Thus, of course, this book.

In addition, the favouring of the short intense lyric against the long or narrative poem decisively shifted the teaching of seventeenth-century poetry away from Milton, whose language was considered by Eliot and Leavis too elevated and unfamiliar, and towards the hitherto 'bad boy' Donne whose love lyrics and religious poems are, on the face of it, more attractively direct in expression. That Donne was, like Eliot, an orthodox Christian and a supporter of court and king was helpful to his promotion.

For Milton, emphatically, was neither. And this was why Eliot and Leavis were most concerned to dislodge him. In Connolly's day, Milton, at school, would have meant studying *Paradise Lost* with the same kind of attentiveness to language and form as applied to Greek and Roman epic poetry and to Shakespeare, who, in the post-Victorian education-world-view, propped up the Empire and begat Milton. But what was coming closer into focus in the following generations was that Milton was, first and foremost, a revolutionary republican, propagandist-in-chief for the forces that cut off the king's head, an aggressively liberal and unorthodox theological controversialist and, crucially, that his great poem is not just about Adam and Eve in the Garden of Eden but is our country's most deeply and powerfully political poem. This much was obvious to Blake in the 1790s.

So the down-grading of Milton was a political act masquerading as a poetic revaluation. (Typical of Eliot's assessments, in his 1936 'A Note on the Verse of John Milton', is that the mythology of *Paradise Lost* 'would have been better left in the Book of Genesis, upon which Milton has not improved' (Eliot, 1953, p. 130).) And his recovery is still a matter of effort and urgency. There are students today who have never heard of him or his poem, and that, on the face of it, is one big astonishing fact. It's like never having heard of Beethoven or Michelangelo or Dickens. But, then, perhaps not all students are aware of the amazing events in the middle of the seventeenth century when England had its revolution and chopped the king's head off, about 150 years before the more famous French version. Students don't tend to hear much in schools about the English revolutionary years, in which Milton was such a prominent figure. There's rather more reference these days to 1660 and 1688 when the monarchy was restored and our Constitution invented, where State works in such, er, sweet and natural harmony with Crown. This is the Constitution which Dickens's Podsnap, in *Our Mutual Friend*, assumes is so blazingly and wonderfully obvious to foreign visitors. Here he talks to a hapless Frenchman.

'Do You Find, Sir', pursued Mr Podsnap, with dignity, 'Many Evidences that Strike You, of our British Constitution in the Streets Of The World's Metropolis, London, Londres, London?'

The foreign gentleman begged to be pardoned, but did not altogether understand.

'The Constitution Britannique', Mr Podsnap explained, as if he was teaching in an infant school. 'We Say British, But You Say Britannique, You Know' (forgivingly, as if that were not his fault). 'The Constitution, Sir.'

The foreign gentleman said, 'Mais, yees; I know eem.'

'[. . .] We Englishmen are Very Proud of our Constitution, Sir. It was Bestowed Upon Us By Providence. No Other Country is so Favoured as This Country [. . .] It was the Charter of the Land. This Island was Blest, Sir, to the Direct Exclusion of such Other Countries as – as there may happen to be.'

(Book I, Ch. xi)

What actually happened in the years of England's revolution and civil war is complex and subject to historical argument. (Right-wing revisionist historians are at work denying that anything particularly radical at all happened in England's revolutionary years, just as the more notorious revisionist historians of the Second World War deny the Holocaust.) But, in a word or two, for the heady years of the 1640s and early 1650s, the unthinkable happened. England became a republic. The country got on without kings and queens. The House of Lords was closed and bishops were abolished. Communitarian socialism not only got itself invented but materialised in communes. There was an astonishing proliferation of radical political-religious sects which, taking advantage of the now uncensored press, led to an unleashing of pamphlets (2,000 in 1642 alone) in a republic of letters. (Of those sects, Quakers are the most famous survivors.) The most extreme of these sects, the Ranters, practised free love in public to prove that sin didn't exist. Women prophesied, like Eleanor Davies who had as early as 1633 predicted Charles's death sixteen years before the event, when her printed evidence became a useful political tool. (At the time of the prediction she was fined £3,000 and imprisoned.)

In all this Milton was a very formidable player, even more respected on the Continent than at home, which probably saved his neck at the Restoration. And for Milton, pamphleteering – for divorce, for the freedom of expression, for the survival of the republic itself – and the writing of epic poetry would have been far less discontinuous activities than they now seem to us.

His *Paradise Lost* is from the end of the period. It used to be thought that the poem marks Milton's retreat into political inactivity after his devastating disappointment at the failure of the revolution, with all its brave hopes. But, following the pioneering researches of Christopher Hill and David Norbrook, whose work I draw gratefully on here, it's clearer than ever that the poem is deeply imbued with republican impulses and ambitions, if in a way that would have been designed to challenge and unsettle republican as well as royalist sympathisers. It's characteristic, for instance, of the poem's challenge to the reader that

Satan often sounds and is clearly designed to sound like a staunch and very reasonable republican. And when Satan says of Hell that 'here at least / We shall be free' (I.258–9) he sounds, as Gordon Campbell nicely puts it, 'like a New England colonist escaping persecution' (Campbell, 1996, p. xvii). But as he moves towards earth his language and his tactics become more indirect, more, well, fallen.

However we read the poem, Milton's Adam, Eve and Satan play out a fraught, intensely human drama of expectation, ambition and frustration. At every turn of the unfolding drama we can hear republican impulses being tried and questioned. The poem conveys intensely realised political understanding of what can and can't be achieved by humans working with realisable aspirations.

And in the middle of the period is an equally stubborn polemical figure. Not an internationally revered poet but a proto-communist visionary and a penetrating political analyst. This is Gerrard Winstanley, a Digger or True Leveller, who founded and ran a commune at St George's Hill, near Weybridge in Surrey, now among the richest bits of real estate on the planet. And in pamphlet after pamphlet Winstanley wrote, in some of the most vivid and vigorous prose from this marvellous century, to Cromwell's generals urging them to push the revolution forward, to rescue the country from the yoke of private property which, in a typically brilliant piece of demystifying, Winstanley identified as the fall in the biblical fall of man. But the generals were too busy consolidating or defending their own interests to listen, the radicals were crushed and the communes were broken up, the revolution stalled and even went into reverse when commonwealth became Protectorate and Cromwell more or less became king, and, apart from a few months when a second go at the republic was tried, the revolutionary moment was over.

Winstanley, and others like him, are not and never have been canonical writers. Why not? The canon, as suggested above, is designed to give the impression of a timeless and 'natural selection' of great literature. Too much obvious politics doesn't go down too well with the canon-formers; nor do so-called lesser genres of literature like essays or pamphlets. But why not?

The third writer from the revolutionary years whose work is presented in the two chapters that follow is another poet, Andrew Marvell, a friend of Milton. He may well have intervened, as an MP, in Milton's defence at the Restoration. Marvell was a favourite of T.S. Eliot and Eliot propagated the view which persists today of Marvell as a writer of somehow disembodiedly poised lyric poems, classical and serene. But that's not the only way of reading them. Marvell is one of the few people in this period whose political affiliations seem to have moved from right to left, from royalist to republican. He was a canny political operator, playing his sympathies very close to his chest. And through his lyrics we can hear, in his almost obsessive fondness for notions of green-ness and gardens and falling, in his sense of loss, of uncommunicated or frustrated longing, a muted debate that connects him so expressively to the more overtly explicit Milton and Winstanley. This is the big seventeenth-century debate and it animates these three great writers in their radically different ways. It is simply put: is Paradise lost? And of what would it consist if we could find it?

* * *

What follows are two linked chapters, designed to be read together. The first presents extracts from *Paradise Lost* up to the fall, and the second presents a non-chronological sequence of poems and extracts by Marvell and Winstanley, followed by the end of *Paradise Lost*. Marvell and Winstanley investigate the fallen world in radically enquiring ways, and in ways that illuminate Milton's parallel project of investigating and reclaiming the radical potential in the story that is the most fundamental of all to western culture.

Here are some extracts from *Paradise Lost*. They're not representative; they can't be, here. They selectively focus on the human story. We start with Satan, newly arrived in Paradise on his mission to ruin God's work, in revenge for his own fall from grace having led an unsuccessful rebellion in a war in Heaven. He sees, and through him we see, for the first time, Adam and Eve. It's as if we're seeing ourselves.

285   The fiend
     Saw undelighted all delight, all kind
     Of living creatures, new to sight and strange.
     Two of far nobler shape, erect and tall,
     God-like erect, with native honour clad
290   In naked majesty, seemed lords of all,
     And worthy seemed; for in their looks divine

The image of their glorious maker shone,
Truth, wisdom, sanctitude severe and pure –
Severe, but in true filial freedom placed,
295 Whence true authority in men: though both
Not equal, as their sex not equal seemed;
For contemplation he and valour formed,
For softness she and sweet attractive grace;
He for God only, she for God in him;
300 His fair large front and eye sublime declared
Absolute rule; and hyacinthine locks
Round from his parted forelock manly hung
Clustering, but not beneath his shoulders broad:
She as a veil down to the slender waist,
305 Her unadornèd golden tresses wore
Dishevelled, but in wanton ringlets waved
As the vine curls her tendrils – which implied
Subjection, but required with gentle sway,
And by her yielded, by him best received
310 Yielded, with coy submission, modest pride,
And sweet reluctant amorous delay.
Nor those mysterious parts were then concealed;
Then was not guilty shame, dishonest shame
Of nature's works, honour dishonourable,
315 Sin-bred, how have ye troubled all mankind
With shows instead, mere shows of seeming pure,
And banished from man's life his happiest life,
Simplicity and spotless innocence.
So passed they naked on, nor shunned the sight
320 Of God or angel, for they thought no ill:
So hand in hand they passed, the loveliest pair
That ever since in love's embraces met –
Adam the goodliest man of men since born
His sons; the fairest of her daughters Eve.
325 Under a tuft of shade that on a green
Stood whispering soft, by a fresh fountain-side,
They sat them down, and after no more toil
Of their sweet gardening labour than sufficed
To recommend cool Zephyr, and made ease

330 More easy, wholesome thirst and appetite
　　More grateful, to their supper-fruits they fell –
　　Nectarine fruits, which the compliant boughs
　　Yielded them, sidelong as they sat recline
　　On the soft downy bank damasked with flowers:
335 The savoury pulp they chew, and in the rind,
　　Still as they thirsted, scoop the brimming stream;
　　Nor gentle purpose, nor endearing smiles
　　Wanted, nor youthful dalliance, as beseems
　　Fair couple linked in happy nuptial league,
　　Alone as they,

300 front: forehead
310 coy: modest

(IV.285–340)

There is so much suggestive here but we should start with a point made forcibly by Norbrook. The unadorned but also vividly eroticised nakedness of the human couple, shocking for many earlier readers, is designed as a provocatively direct republican icon. It retains its power to provoke, leading T.S. Eliot, for instance, to one of his most royalist condescensions: 'I for one can get pleasure from the verse only by the deliberate effort not to visualize Adam and Eve in their surroundings' (Eliot, 1953, p. 129). Norbrook says that Milton 'would have known how Michelangelo's David had embodied the spirit of the young Florentine republic; in their different way the newly-created Adam and Eve speak for a republican delight in returning to the beginning, in stripping away false customs' (Norbrook, 1999, p. 481). On the other hand we can't but respond to the clear statement of Eve's inequality, with Adam made 'for God only, she for God in him'. We'll return to this after the extract that follows.

　　A few lines later Eve tells the story of her creation, as she recalls it. Satan then spies on their embraces in bitter fury. His ferocious pun in 'imparadised' – 'these two, / Imparadised in one another's arms, / The happier Eden, shall enjoy their fill / Of bliss on bliss' (IV.505–8) – is perhaps the most telling in the entire poem. It identifies sharply the central place in the story of sexualised love, even suggesting that that itself is paradise, a happier Eden. (The significance of this is made even more clear at the end of the poem.) And it simultaneously identifies hell as the opposite of sexualised love, the state of pining in 'fierce desire . . . unfulfilled, with pain of longing' (IV.509–11). Here's Eve.

'That day I oft remember, when from sleep
450 I first awaked, and found myself reposed,
Under a shade on flowers, much wondering where
And what I was, whence thither brought, and how.
Not distant far from thence a murmuring sound
Of waters issued from a cave, and spread
455 Into a liquid plain, then stood unmoved,
Pure as the expanse of heaven; I thither went
With unexperienced thought, and laid me down
On the green bank, to look into the clear
Smooth lake, that to me seemed another sky.
460 As I bent down to look, just opposite
A shape within the watery gleam appeared,
Bending to look on me; I started back,
It started back, but pleased I soon returned,
Pleased it returned as soon with answering looks
465 Of sympathy and love; there I had fixed
Mine eyes till now, and pined with vain desire,
Had not a voice thus warned me: "What thou seest,
What there thou seest, fair creature, is thyself:
With thee it came and goes: but follow me,
470 And I will bring thee where no shadow stays
Thy coming, and thy soft embraces – he
Whose image thou art; him thou shalt enjoy
Inseparably thine; to him shalt bear
Multitudes like thyself, and thence be called
475 Mother of human race"; what could I do,
But follow straight, invisibly thus led?
Till I espied thee, fair indeed and tall,
Under a platan; yet methought less fair,
Less winning soft, less amiably mild,
480 Than that smooth watery image; back I turned;
Thou, following, cried'st aloud, "Return, fair Eve;
Whom fliest thou? Whom thou fliest, of him thou art,
His flesh, his bone; to give thee being I lent

Out of my side to thee, nearest my heart,
485 Substantial life, to have thee by my side
Henceforth an individual solace dear:
Part of my soul I seek thee, and thee claim
My other half"; with that thy gentle hand
Seized mine: I yielded, and from that time see
490 How beauty is excelled by manly grace
And wisdom, which alone is truly fair.'
    So spake our general mother, and with eyes
Of conjugal attraction unreproved,
And meek surrender, half-embracing leaned
495 On our first father; half her swelling breast
Naked met his under the flowing gold
Of her loose tresses hid; he in delight
Both of her beauty and submissive charms,
Smiled with superior love, as Jupiter
500 On Juno smiles when he impregns the clouds
That shed May flowers, and pressed her matron lip
With kisses pure; aside the devil turned
For envy, yet with jealous leer malign
Eyed them askance, and to himself thus plained:
505   'Sight hateful, sight tormenting! Thus these two,
Imparadised in one another's arms,
The happier Eden, shall enjoy their fill
Of bliss on bliss, while I to hell am thrust,
Where neither joy nor love, but fierce desire,
510 Among our other torments not the least,
Still unfulfilled, with pain of longing pines;
Yet let me not forget what I have gained
From their own mouths; all is not theirs, it seems:
One fatal tree there stands, of knowledge called,
515 Forbidden them to taste: knowledge forbidden?
Suspicious, reasonless: Why should their Lord
Envy them that? Can it be sin to know,
Can it be death? And do they only stand
By ignorance, is that their happy state,
520 The proof of their obedience and their faith?
O fair foundation laid whereon to build

Their ruin! Hence I will excite their minds
With more desire to know, and to reject
Envious commands, invented with design
525 To keep them low, whom knowledge might exalt
Equal with gods; aspiring to be such,
They taste and die: what likelier can ensue?
But first with narrow search I must walk round
This garden, and no corner leave unspied;
530 A chance but chance may lead where I may meet
Some wandering spirit of heaven, by fountain-side,
Or in thick shade retired, from him to draw
What further would be learned. Live while ye may,
Yet happy pair; enjoy, till I return,
535 Short pleasures; for long woes are to succeed.'

470 stays: waits for
478 platan: plane tree
486 individual: inseparable

(IV.449–535)

Later we'll hear Adam's parallel account of how he remembers his
creation. It's unsurprisingly full of upright vigour. Eve, in contrast, is
pictured lying near murmuring waters and a liquid plain. Liquidity has
been asssociated with women in a long tradition, usually in antagonism
and fear, not as here. But, for Milton's readers more obviously perhaps
than for us, she's even more directly associated with Narcissus, who
preferred his own image in the water to his unlucky suitors. (The Narcissus story is the most profoundly influential of all the stories told in
Ovid's *Metamorphoses*. It says some very far-reaching things about the
nature of desire, a subject which recurs in this book. For that reason
you'll find a new translation in the Appendix to this volume.) Eve prefers
her own watery image to Adam when she first sees him, but learns to
value his 'manly grace / And wisdom' (IV.490–1) over her own beauty.
But most telling of all is that she identifies her original Narcissus-state
as one in which she would have for ever 'pined with vain desire'
(IV.466). The words, of course, are the ones Satan uses just forty lines
later.

A detailed analysis, which we have no space for here, could show the

way in which Milton's Eve, in these first extracts, embodies contradictory suggestions of agency and passivity, independence and submission, sexual power and dutiful humility. Nor is Adam's attitude to her a
simple matter of asserted possessiveness. But there is undoubted
inequality in the representations and it must qualify what Norbrook
calls the 'polemical, and to some extent egalitarian, element in the
presentation of Adam and Eve' (Norbrook, 1999, p. 482). Norbrook
argues that Milton would have been very conscious that early feminist
writers in the period considered their cause better served in court and
Royalist circles than in traditional Puritanism which emphasised the
woman's role in the carefully separated domestic sphere. Later, Satan
tempts Eve in the distinctive language of courtly flattery. Eve's presentation is difficult partly because of these contradictory impulses and
contexts.

What might be the language of mutualised love, as opposed to
courtly flattery? One place to find it might be a seventeenth-century
love-lyric. Here it is, the most touching thing of its kind. And it's
Milton's Eve, a hundred lines after Satan's bitter curse.

> With thee conversing, I forget all time,
> 640 All seasons, and their change; all please alike.
> Sweet is the breath of morn, her rising sweet,
> With charm of earliest birds; pleasant the sun,
> When first on this delightful land he spreads
> His orient beams, on herb, tree, fruit, and flower,
> 645 Glistering with dew; fragrant the fertile earth
> After soft showers; and sweet the coming-on
> Of grateful evening mild; then silent night,
> With this her solemn bird, and this fair moon,
> And these the gems of heaven, her starry train:
> 650 But neither breath of morn, when she ascends
> With charm of earliest birds, nor rising sun
> On this delightful land, nor herb, fruit, flower,
> Glistering with dew, nor fragrance after showers,
> Nor grateful evening mild, nor silent night,
> 655 With this her solemn bird, nor walk by moon,
> Or glittering starlight, without thee is sweet.

(IV.639–656)

The couple then make love, Milton thus radically insistent that there was sex before the fall. He calls it 'wedded love, mysterious law, true source/Of human offspring, sole propriety/In Paradise of all things common else' (IV.750–2). By 'propriety' Milton insists that sexualised love is the one exclusive human ownership. Then, again in his own voice, Milton bids the couple goodnight.

> These, lulled by nightingales, embracing slept,
> And on their naked limbs the flowery roof
> Showered roses, which the morn repaired. Sleep on,
> Blest pair; and O yet happiest if ye seek
> 775 No happier state, and know to know no more.
>
> (IV.771–5)

It's the still point of the whole poem. Its disquiet is ominous, but most pointed of all is another suggestive parallel. The language Milton gives to himself uneasily evokes Satan's own farewell 240 lines earlier: 'Live while ye may, / Yet happy pair; enjoy, till I return, / Short pleasures; for long woes are to succeed.' It also, more generally, evokes the God in the poem who knows what's going to happen but chooses to or has to let it happen. The sense that Milton, too, is deeply implicated and entangled in the desires and ambitions of the poem, its power structures, is crucial to its impact.

The next extract has Eve waking from a dream that Satan has induced. She describes it to Adam.

> Now Morn, her rosy steps in the eastern clime
> Advancing, sowed the earth with orient pearl,
> When Adam waked, so customed; for his sleep
> Was airy light, from pure digestion bred,
> 5 And temperate vapours bland, which the only sound
> Of leaves and fuming rills, Aurora's fan,
> Lightly dispersed, and the shrill matin song
> Of birds on every bough; so much the more
> His wonder was to find unwakened Eve,
> 10 With tresses discomposed, and glowing cheek,
> As through unquiet rest; he on his side
> Leaning half raised, with looks of cordial love

61

Hung over her enamoured, and beheld
Beauty which, whether waking or asleep,
15 Shot forth peculiar graces; then with voice
Mild as when Zephyrus on Flora breathes,
Her hand soft touching, whispered thus: 'Awake,
My fairest, my espoused, my latest found,
Heaven's last, best gift, my ever-new delight;
20 Awake, the morning shines, and the fresh field
Calls us; we lose the prime to mark how spring
Our tended plants, how blows the citron grove,
What drops the myrrh, and what the balmy reed,
How nature paints her colours, how the bee
25 Sits on the bloom extracting liquid sweet.'
   Such whispering waked her, but with startled eye
On Adam; whom embracing, thus she spake:
   'O sole in whom my thoughts find all repose,
My glory, my perfection, glad I see
30 Thy face, and morn returned; for I this night –
Such night till this I never passed – have dreamed,
If dreamed, not as I oft am wont, of thee,
Works of day past, or morrow's next design,
But of offence and trouble, which my mind
35 Knew never till this irksome night; methought
Close at mine ear one called me forth to walk
With gentle voice; I thought it thine; it said,
"Why sleep'st thou, Eve? Now is the pleasant time,
The cool, the silent, save where silence yields
40 To the night-warbling bird, that now awake
Tunes sweetest his love-laboured song; now reigns
Full-orbed the moon, and with more pleasing light,
Shadowy sets off the face of things – in vain,
If none regard; heaven wakes with all his eyes,
45 Whom to behold but thee, nature's desire,
In whose sight all things joy, with ravishment
Attracted by thy beauty still to gaze?"
I rose as at thy call, but found thee not:
To find thee I directed then my walk;
50 And on, methought, alone I passed through ways

That brought me on a sudden to the tree
Of interdicted knowledge; fair it seemed,
Much fairer to my fancy than by day;
And as I wondering looked, beside it stood
55   One shaped and winged like one of those from heaven
By us oft seen: his dewy locks distilled
Ambrosia; on that tree he also gazed;
And, "O fair plant," said he, "with fruit surcharged,
Deigns none to ease thy load and taste thy sweet,
60   Nor God nor man? Is knowledge so despised?
Or envy, or what reserve forbids to taste?
Forbid who will, none shall from me withhold
Longer thy offered good, why else set here?"
This said, he paused not, but with venturous arm
65   He plucked, he tasted; me damp horror chilled
At such bold words vouched with a deed so bold;
But he thus, overjoyed: "O fruit divine,
Sweet of thyself, but much more sweet thus cropped,
Forbidden here, it seems, as only fit
70   For gods, yet able to make gods of men;
And why not gods of men, since good, the more
Communicated, more abundant grows,
The author not impaired, but honoured more?
Here, happy creature, fair angelic Eve,
75   Partake thou also: happy though thou art,
Happier thou may'st be, worthier canst not be;
Taste this, and be henceforth among the gods
Thyself a goddess, not to earth confined,
But sometimes in the air, as we; sometimes
80   Ascend to heaven, by merit thine, and see
What life the gods live there, and such live thou."
So saying, he drew nigh, and to me held,
Even to my mouth of that same fruit held part
Which he had plucked: the pleasant savoury smell
85   So quickened appetite that I, methought,
Could not but taste. Forthwith up to the clouds
With him I flew, and underneath beheld
The earth outstretched immense, a prospect wide

And various; wondering at my flight and change
90　To this high exaltation, suddenly
My guide was gone, and I, methought, sunk down,
And fell asleep; but O how glad I waked
To find this but a dream!'

(V.1–93)

As so often, it's the shocking eroticism in the poem that startles
here. The angel in the dream (Satan) wonders why none deigns 'to
ease thy load and taste thy sweet' (V.59) and, after eating, Eve 'Forthwith up to the clouds / With him I flew' (V.86–7) in what is easy to
read as orgasm. Now let's hear Adam describing his creation, in
conversation with the archangel Raphael.

As new-waked from soundest sleep,
Soft on the flowery herb I found me laid,
255　In balmy sweat, which with his beams the sun
Soon dried, and on the reeking moisture fed.
Straight toward heaven my wondering eyes I turned,
And gazed a while the ample sky, till, raised
By quick instinctive motion, up I sprung,
260　As thitherward endeavouring, and upright
Stood on my feet; about me round I saw
Hill, dale, and shady woods, and sunny plains,
And liquid lapse of murmuring streams; by these,
Creatures that lived and moved, and walked or flew,
265　Birds on the branches warbling; all things smiled;
With fragrance and with joy my heart o'erflowed.
Myself I then perused, and limb by limb
Surveyed, and sometimes went, and sometimes ran
With supple joints, as lively vigour led;
270　But who I was, or where, or from what cause,
Knew not; to speak I tried, and forthwith spake;
My tongue obeyed, and readily could name
What'er I saw. 'Thou sun,' said I, 'fair light,
And thou enlightened earth, so fresh and gay,
275　Ye hills and dales, ye rivers, woods, and plains,
And ye that live and move, fair creatures, tell,

Tell, if ye saw, how came I thus, how here.
Not of myself; by some great maker then,
In goodness and in power pre-eminent;
280 Tell me, how may I know him, how adore,
From whom I have that thus I move and live,
And feel that I am happier than I know.'
While thus I called, and strayed I knew not whither,
From where I first drew air, and first beheld
285 This happy light, when answer none returned,
On a green shady bank, profuse of flowers,
Pensive I sat me down; there gentle sleep
First found me, and with soft oppression seized
My drowsed sense, untroubled, though I thought
290 I then was passing to my former state
Insensible, and forthwith to dissolve:
When suddenly stood at my head a dream,
Whose inward apparition gently moved
My fancy to believe I yet had being,
295 And lived; one came, methought, of shape divine,
And said, 'Thy mansion wants thee, Adam; rise,
First man, of men innumerable ordained
First father; called by thee, I come thy guide
To the garden of bliss, thy seat prepared.'
300 So saying, by the hand he took me, raised,
And over fields and waters, as in air
Smooth sliding without step, last led me up
A woody mountain, whose high top was plain,
A circuit wide, enclosed, with goodliest trees
305 Planted, with walks and bowers, that what I saw
Of earth before scarce pleasant seemed. Each tree
Loaden with fairest fruit, that hung to the eye
Tempting, stirred in me sudden appetite
To pluck and eat; whereat I waked, and found
310 Before mine eyes all real, as the dream
Had lively shadowed; here had new begun
My wandering, had not he who was my guide
Up hither from among the trees appeared,
Presence divine. Rejoicing, but with awe,

315 In adoration at his feet I fell
Submiss; he reared me, and, 'Whom thou sought'st I am,'
Said mildly, 'author of all this thou seest
Above, or round about thee, or beneath.
This Paradise I give thee; count it thine
320 To till and keep, and of the fruit to eat;
Of every tree that in the garden grows
Eat freely with glad heart; fear here no dearth;
But of the tree whose operation brings
Knowledge of good and ill, which I have set
325 The pledge of thy obedience and thy faith,
Amid the garden by the tree of life –
Remember what I warn thee – shun to taste,
And shun the bitter consequence: for know,
The day thou eat'st thereof, my sole command
330 Transgressed, inevitably thou shalt die,
From that day mortal, and this happy state
Shalt loose, expelled from hence into a world
Of woe and sorrow.'

263 lapse: flow

(VIII.253–333)

This is many thousands of lines, and three entire books, later than the last extract, but you'll see some more parallels that seem designed to make us uneasy. Adam's account of how, in his dream, God took him by the hand, 'raised,/ And over fields and waters, as in air/ Smooth sliding without step' (VIII.300–2) gives a strange retrospective justification to Eve's flight. If he then why not she? And Adam's view of trees 'Loaden with fairest fruit, that hung to the eye/ Tempting, stirred in me sudden appetite/ To pluck and eat' (VIII.307–9) seems intended to evoke Satan, in Eve's dream, addressing the tree 'with fruit surcharged' with its 'load' of sweetness, as well as his subsequent holding to her mouth the fruit 'which he had plucked' and her 'quickened appetite' which ensured she 'could not but taste' (V.58–86). The effect is designed to unsettle and undermine the poem's own telling of the orthodox story. That is, despite the clear boundaries between them and their motives, these parallels draw Satan, Adam and Eve together into a web of personal ambition and personal weakness in which all three are entangled. It's in this respect that this epic poem may also be called a tragedy.

Not many lines later, Adam notes, reasonably enough, that the animals come in pairs. So God makes Eve. You'll see that Adam's version leaves out Eve's unwillingness to stay with him and the subsequent plea he made to Eve, as in her telling of the story earlier.

460 Mine eyes he closed, but open left the cell
      Of fancy, my internal sight, by which,
      Abstract as in a trance, methought I saw,
      Though sleeping, where I lay, and saw the shape
      Still glorious before whom awake I stood;
465 Who, stooping, opened my left side, and took
      From thence a rib, with cordial spirits warm,
      And life-blood streaming fresh; wide was the wound,
      But suddenly with flesh filled up and healed;
      The rib he formed and fashioned with his hands;
470 Under his forming hands a creature grew,
      Man-like, but different sex, so lovely fair
      That what seemed fair in all the world seemed now
      Mean, or in her summed up, in her contained
      And in her looks, which from that time infused
475 Sweetness into my heart unfelt before
      And into all things from her air inspired
      The spirit of love and amorous delight.
      She disappeared, and left me dark; I waked
      To find her, or for ever to deplore
480 Her loss, and other pleasures all abjure:
      When, out of hope, behold her not far off,
      Such as I saw her in my dream, adorned
      With what all earth and heaven could bestow
      To make her amiable; on she came,
485 Led by her heavenly maker, though unseen
      And guided by his voice, nor uninformed
      Of nuptial sanctity and marriage rites;
      Grace was in all her steps, heaven in her eye,
      In every gesture dignity and love.
490 I, overjoyed, could not forbear aloud:

'This turn hath made amends; thou hast fulfilled
Thy words, creator bounteous and benign,
Giver of all things fair – but fairest this
Of all thy gifts – nor enviest. I now see
495 Bone of my bone, flesh of my flesh, my self
Before me; woman is her name, of man
Extracted; for this cause he shall forgo
Father and mother, and to his wife adhere,
And they shall be one flesh, one heart, one soul.'
500   She heard me thus, and, though divinely brought,
Yet innocence and virgin modesty,
Her virtue and the conscience of her worth,
That would be wooed, and not unsought be won,
Not obvious, not obtrusive, but retired,
505 The more desirable – or, to say all,
Nature herself, though pure of sinful thought –
Wrought in her so, that seeing me, she turned;
I followed her; she what was honour knew,
And with obsequious majesty approved
510 My pleaded reason. To the nuptial bower
I led her blushing like the morn; all heaven,
And happy constellations, on that hour
Shed their selectest influence; the earth
Gave sign of gratulation, and each hill;
515 Joyous the birds; fresh gales and gentle airs
Whispered it to the woods, and from their wings
Flung rose, flung odours from the spicy shrub,
Disporting, till the amorous bird of night
Sung spousal, and bid haste the evening star
520 On his hill-top to light the bridal lamp.

462 Abstract: withdrawn
509 obsequious: obedient

(VIII.460–520)

The most radical aspect of this great humanitarian poem is its emphatic stress on eroticised human love in the wedded relationship. Milton, in the passage referred to above where he celebrates 'wedded love', pointedly opposes such love to what he calls 'court amours'

(IV.750, 767) – the court-inspired sex-entanglements that, as Milton might have dreaded, indeed became the dominant mode of literary love in Restoration comedy later. When Adam first sees Eve, in his half-dream, he falls in love.

Falling in love is rarer than one might have thought in Renaissance literature and this is it. 'What seemed fair in all the world seemed now/Mean, or in her summed up' and her beauty 'infused/Sweetness into my heart unfelt before' (VIII.472–5). In one of the most moving moments in all poetry, 'She disappeared, and left me dark; I waked/To find her, or for ever to deplore/Her loss' (VIII.478–80). Adam's first waking experience of love is loss. (The Narcissus story is again relevant here.) It's the possibility of losing each other that most crucially informs the radical one-ness of Adam and Eve's relationship. A little later the archangel Raphael warns Adam about overvaluing outside appearances and the sexual act. Adam, in a marvellous moment of republican questioning of authority, answers that it's not just the sex but 'those graceful acts,/Those thousand decencies, that daily flow/From all her words and actions' (VIII.600–2). (That idea of the little decencies so momentously accumulating has crucial force at the poem's ending.) And he compounds the undermining of angelic authority by asking Raphael whether, anyway, angels make love or not. Raphael has the decency to blush.

* * *

We're approaching the fall itself. Satan, in the form of the serpent, finds Eve alone and, in another marvellous moment, falls momentarily in love with her. It makes him 'stupidly good' (IX.465) (in a stupor). But his malice returns and he seductively approaches.

> He bolder now, uncalled before her stood,
> But as in gaze admiring; oft he bowed
> 525 His turret crest and sleek enamelled neck,
> Fawning, and licked the ground whereon she trod.
> His gentle dumb expression turned at length
> The eye of Eve to mark his play; he, glad
> Of her attention gained, with serpent tongue
> 530 Organic, or impulse of vocal air,
> His fraudulent temptation thus began:

'Wonder not, sovereign mistress – if perhaps
Thou canst who are sole wonder – much less arm
Thy looks, the heaven of mildness, with disdain,
535 Displeased that I approach thee thus, and gaze
Insatiate, I thus single, nor have feared
Thy awful brow, more awful thus retired.
Fairest resemblance of thy maker fair,
Thee all things living gaze on, all things thine
540 By gift, and thy celestial beauty adore,
With ravishment beheld – there best beheld
Where universally admired; but here
In this enclosure wild, these beasts among,
Beholders rude, and shallow to discern
545 Half what in thee is fair, one man except,
Who sees thee (and what is one?) who shouldst be seen
A goddess among gods, adored and served
By angels numberless, thy daily train?'
So glozed the tempter, and his proem tuned.
550 Into the heart of Eve his words made way,
Though at the voice much marvelling; at length,
Not unamazed, she thus in answer spake:
'What may this mean? Language of man pronounced
By tongue of brute, and human sense expressed?
555 The first at least of these I thought denied
To beasts, whom God on their creation-day
Created mute to all articulate sound;
The latter I demur, for in their looks
Much reason, and in their actions, oft appears.
560 Thee, serpent, subtlest beast of all the field
I knew, but not with human voice endued;
Redouble then this miracle, and say,
How cam'st thou speakable of mute, and how
To me so friendly grown above the rest
565 Of brutal kind that daily are in sight:
Say, for such wonder claims attention due.'
To whom the guileful tempter thus replied.
'Empress of this fair world, resplendent Eve,
Easy to me it is to tell thee all

70

570 What thou command'st, and right thou shouldst be obeyed;
    I was at first as other beasts that graze
    The trodden herb, of abject thoughts and low,
    As was my food, nor aught but food discerned
    Or sex, and apprehended nothing high:
575 Till on a day, roving the field, I chanced
    A goodly tree far distant to behold,
    Loaden with fruit of fairest colours mixed,
    Ruddy and gold; I nearer drew to gaze,
    When from the boughs a savoury odour blown,
580 Grateful to appetite, more pleased my sense
    Than smell of sweetest fennel, or the teats
    Of ewe or goat dropping with milk at even,
    Unsucked of lamb or kid, that tend their play.
    To satisfy the sharp desire I had
585 Of tasting those fair apples, I resolved
    Not to defer; hunger and thirst at once,
    Powerful persuaders, quickened at the scent
    Of that alluring fruit, urged me so keen.
    About the mossy trunk I wound me soon,
590 For, high from ground, the branches would require
    Thy utmost reach, or Adam's: round the tree
    All other beasts that saw, with like desire
    Longing and envying stood, but could not reach.
    Amid the tree now got, where plenty hung
595 Tempting so nigh, to pluck and eat my fill
    I spared not, for such pleasure till that hour
    At feed or fountain never had I found.
    Sated at length, ere long I might perceive
    Strange alteration in me, to degree
600 Of reason in my inward powers, and speech
    Wanted not long, though to this shape retained.
    Thenceforth to speculations high or deep
    I turned my thoughts, and with capacious mind
    Considered all things visible in heaven,
605 Or earth, or middle, all things fair and good;
    But all that fair and good in thy divine
    Semblance and in thy beauty's heavenly ray,

United I beheld – no fair to thine
Equivalent or second; which compelled
610 Me thus, though importune perhaps, to come
And gaze, and worship thee of right declared
Sovereign of creatures, universal dame.'

530 Organic: like an organ
549 proem: prelude

(IX.524–612)

They reach the tree and Satan successfully argues the good sense of eating the fruit. Flattering Eve with royalist extravagance (calling her 'queen of this universe'), his arguments seem reasonable, particularly when he calls the prohibition a 'petty trespass' which it would be courageous to ignore in the pursuit of knowledge, and when he suggests that God's motives are 'to keep ye low and ignorant' (IX.684, 693, 704). This is a familiar political argument against oppression and, in this period, would also evoke the Puritan attacks on the mystifying authorities of the priesthood, designed to perpetuate ignorance for the priests' own gain. That is, Milton is deploying, in a way that again seems designed to unsettle, arguments which he and others like him (including Winstanley) regularly used in their fight for freedom. But Satan's purposes are the opposite of those of a freedom-fighter. The last four lines of Eve's subsequent reflections lead to the poem's dramatic climax.

'Here grows the cure of all, this fruit divine,
Fair to the eye, inviting to the taste,
Of virtue to make wise; what hinders, then,
To reach, and feed at once both body and mind?'
780 So saying, her rash hand in evil hour
Forth reaching to the fruit, she plucked, she ate;
Earth felt the wound, and nature from her seat,
Sighing through all her works, gave signs of woe
That all was lost. Back to the thicket slunk
785 The guilty serpent, and well might, for Eve,
Intent now only on her taste, naught else
Regarded; such delight till then, as seemed,
In fruit she never tasted, whether true,

Or fancied so through expectation high
790 Of knowledge; nor was godhead from her thought.
Greedily she engorged without restraint,
And knew not eating death; satiate at length,
And heightened as with wine, jocund and boon,
Thus to herself she pleasingly began:
795 'O sovereign, virtuous, precious of all trees
In Paradise, of operation blest
To sapience, hitherto obscured, infamed,
And thy fair fruit let hang, as to no end
Created; but henceforth my early care,
800 Not without song, each morning, and due praise,
Shall tend thee, and the fertile burden ease
Of thy full branches, offered free to all;
Till dieted by thee I grow mature
In knowledge, as the gods who all things know;
805 Though others envy what they cannot give –
For had the gift been theirs, it had not here
Thus grown. Experience, next to thee I owe,
Best guide: not following thee, I had remained
In ignorance; thou open'st wisdom's way,
810 And giv'st access, though secret she retire.
And I perhaps am secret: heaven is high –
High, and remote to see from thence distinct
Each thing on earth; and other care perhaps
May have diverted from continual watch
815 Our great forbidder, safe with all his spies
About him. But to Adam in what sort
Shall I appear? Shall I to him make known
As yet my change, and give him to partake
Full happiness with me, or rather not,
820 But keep the odds of knowledge in my power
Without copartner? So to add what wants
In female sex, the more to draw his love,
And render me more equal, and perhaps –
A thing not undesirable – sometime
825 Superior; for, inferior, who is free?
This may be well; but what if God have seen,

73

And death ensue? Then I shall be no more;
And Adam, wedded to another Eve,
Shall live with her enjoying, I extinct;
830 A death to think. Confirmed, then, I resolve
Adam shall share with me in bliss or woe;
So dear I love him that with him all deaths
I could endure, without him live no life.'

(IX.776–833)

Adam is on his way to meet her, with a garland of flowers. Eve hastily tells her story and urges him to 'also taste, that equal lot/May join us, equal joy, as equal love' (IX.881–2). There follows the first death in paradise (the roses), and the poem's most radically anti-authoritarian moment, its emotional heart. Adam chooses love for Eve over obedience to, and love for, God. In the words Milton used himself in his summary of this Book of the poem: Adam 'resolves through vehemence of love'. He eats as an act of 'extenuating the trespass' (Campbell, 1990, p. 334). The word 'extenuate' means to lessen or thin out. That's Adam's purpose, to lessen the fall, as if to wrest its authority away. And the word 'vehemence' means what you think it means and what Milton makes it mean elsewhere: force, violence, fervour of personal feeling (*Oxford English Dictionary*, meanings 2 and 3). But the editor of the standard scholarly, if Christianising edition intervenes at this point, telling the reader to remember that the root meaning of the Latin word 'vehementia' is mindlessness (Harlow, Longman, 1971, p. 433). That is to rewrite Milton's great and radical insistence on Adam's love. He knows what he's doing. There's nothing mindless about it.

On the other side, Adam, soon as he heard
The fatal trespass done by Eve, amazed,
890 Astonied stood and blank, while horror chill
Ran through his veins, and all his joints relaxed.
From his slack hand the garland wreathed for Eve
Down dropped, and all the faded roses shed;
Speechless he stood and pale, till thus at length
895 First to himself he inward silence broke:
    'O fairest of creation, last and best

74

Of all God's works, creature in whom excelled
Whatever can to sight or thought be formed,
Holy, divine, good, amiable, or sweet!
900 How art thou lost, how on a sudden lost,
Defaced, deflowered, and now to death devote?
Rather, how hast thou yielded to transgress
The strict forbiddance, how to violate
The sacred fruit forbidden? Some cursed fraud
905 Of enemy hath beguiled thee, yet unknown,
And me with thee hath ruined; for with thee
Certain my resolution is to die;
How can I live without thee, how forgo
Thy sweet converse, and love so dearly joined,
910 To live again in these wild woods forlorn?
Should God create another Eve, and I
Another rib afford, yet loss of thee
Would never from my heart; no, no, I feel
The link of nature draw me: flesh of flesh,
915 Bone of my bone thou art, and from thy state
Mine never shall be parted, bliss or woe.'

901 devote: doomed

(IX.888–916)

Those words are spoken to himself. To Eve he speaks equivalently and
'in calm mood', insisting that 'if death / Consort with thee, death is to
me as life' because 'our state cannot be severed; we are one, / One
flesh; to lose thee were to lose myself' (IX.920, 953–9). Eve urges him
that the outcome ('event') is life, not death, and urges him to taste.
They then make fallen love, though love doesn't seem to be the right
word. Their 'guilty shame' after sleep – 'confounded', 'stricken mute',
'abashed' (IX.1058–65) – is all too expressive.

'I feel
Far otherwise the event – not death, but life
985 Augmented, opened eyes, new hopes, new joys,
Taste so divine that what of sweet before
Hath touched my sense flat seems to this and harsh.
On my experience, Adam, freely taste,

75

And fear of death deliver to the winds.'
990   So saying, she embraced him, and for joy
Tenderly wept, much won that he his love
Had so ennobled, as of choice to incur
Divine displeasure for her sake, or death.
In recompense (for such compliance bad
995 Such recompense best merits), from the bough
She gave him of that fair enticing fruit
With liberal hand; he scrupled not to eat,
Against his better knowledge, not deceived,
But fondly overcome with female charm.
1000 Earth trembled from her entrails, as again
In pangs, and nature gave a second groan;
Sky loured, and muttering thunder, some sad drops
Wept at completing of the mortal sin
Original; while Adam took no thought,
1005 Eating his fill, nor Eve to iterate
Her former trespass feared, the more to soothe
Him with her loved society; that now,
As with new wine intoxicated both,
They swim in mirth, and fancy that they feel
1010 Divinity within them breeding wings
Wherewith to scorn the earth; but that false fruit
Far other operation first displayed,
Carnal desire inflaming; he on Eve
Began to cast lascivious eyes, she him
1015 As wantonly repaid; in lust they burn,
Till Adam thus 'gan Eve to dalliance move:
    'Eve, now I see thou art exact of taste
And elegant – of sapience no small part;
Since to each meaning savour we apply,
1020 And palate call judicious; I the praise
Yield thee, so well this day thou hast purveyed.
Much pleasure we have lost, while we abstained
From this delightful fruit, nor known till now
True relish, tasting; if such pleasure be
1025 In things to us forbidden, it might be wished
For this one tree had been forbidden ten.

But come; so well refreshed, now let us play,
As meet is, after such delicious fare;
For never did thy beauty since the day
1030 I saw thee first and wedded thee, adorned
With all perfections, so inflame my sense
With ardour to enjoy thee, fairer now
Than ever – bounty of this virtuous tree.'
    So said he, and forbore not glance or toy
1035 Of amorous intent, well understood
Of Eve, whose eye darted contagious fire.
Her hand he seized, and to a shady bank
Thick overhead with verdant roof embowered
He led her, nothing loath; flowers were the couch,
1040 Pansies, and violets, and asphodel,
And hyacinth – earth's freshest, softest lap.
There they their fill of love and love's disport
Took largely, of their mutual guilt the seal,
The solace of their sin, till dewy sleep
1045 Oppressed them, wearied with their amorous play.
    Soon as the force of that fallacious fruit,
That with exhilarating vapour bland
About their spirits had played, and inmost powers
Made err, was now exhaled, and grosser sleep,
1050 Bred of unkindly fumes, with conscious dreams
Encumbered, now had left them, up they rose
As from unrest, and each the other viewing,
Soon found their eyes how opened, and their minds
How darkened; innocence, that as a veil
1055 Had shadowed them from knowing ill, was gone;
Just confidence, and native righteousness
And honour, from about them, naked left
To guilty shame: he covered, but his robe
Uncovered more.

1034 toy: caressing

(IX.983–1059)

That Adam chooses Eve over God, love over obedience, is a moment of
extraordinary force, not least because it is clearly designed to seem

right, despite the poem's explicit purpose, stated at the outset, of justifying 'the ways of God to men' (I.26). This act of conscious choice, knowing what it entails, also has the force of equivalent moments in Shakespearean tragedy. That is, it's a moment of radical humanism, of enlarged human consciousness. Historians have helped contextualise the force of this, apart from its radical theology, by seeing the moment as part of the momentous shift in the seventeenth century, driven by libertarians such as Milton, from thinking about marital relations as grounded in obedience to parental and other duties towards relations grounded in individualised mutual affection.

Another way of contextualising this moment is to look at what sex is like after the fall. You'll recall that sex before the fall is explicitly contrasted to 'court amours'. Now Adam and Eve are 'wantonly' inflamed with 'lascivious' and 'carnal desire' (IX.1013–15), words which directly evoke the sexual licence Milton earlier linked to court culture. And when Adam 'seized' Eve's hand here (IX.1037) we're looking at aggressive assertiveness, not mutuality. For poets like Milton language is always politicised. This is clear from his Preface to the second edition of the poem where he defends his use of blank verse as opposed to rhyme. Milton describes his act of poetic intervention as 'an example set . . . of ancient liberty recovered to heroic poem from the troublesome and modern bondage of rhyming' (Campbell, 1990, p. 148). Rhyme is the bondage of royalty. Language isn't decorative. It's where action is materialised and formalised.

Adam and Eve have, as it were, fallen into post-republicanism.

This chapter began with reflections on the politics of the canon and its making. The early chapters on the rise of English in Terry Eagleton's famous *Literary Theory* (2nd edition, Oxford, Blackwell, 1996) are incisive and entertaining on the issue. Frank Kermode's *Forms of Attention* (Chicago, University of Chicago Press, 1985) and *History and Value* (Oxford, Clarendon Press, 1988) are authoritative and subtle in their discussions of the canon. Reading seventeenth-century poetry, Milton especially, historically and politically is an important counter-balance to the tendency which prevailed roughly from the 1930s to the 1970s, which was to read the period principally for its clever 'metaphysical' lyric poems and to read Milton as a rather antiquated 'baroque' or 'sublime' oddity. T.S. Eliot, as we saw above, was crucial in devaluing Milton. His 1936 Milton essay gained wide currency from his *Selected Prose* (Harmondsworth, Penguin, 1953). Christopher Hill's *Milton and the English Revolution* (London, Faber, 1977) was the crucial turning-point in reclaiming Milton as a radical poet. Hill's work made possible the formid-able scholarship of David Norbrook whose *Writing the English Republic* (Cam-bridge, Cambridge University Press, 1999) I draw on above. The collection of essays on Milton edited by Annabel Patterson in the Longman Critical Readers series (Harlow, Longman, 1992) has many distinguished and theor-etically advanced contributions and Patterson's introduction is a fine survey. At a simpler level, Peter Weston's *Paradise Lost* (Harmondsworth, Penguin, 1987) is a very clear guide to the poem; Margarita Stocker's volume in The Critics Debate series is lively (London, Macmillan, 1998); and *John Milton: Introductions*, edited by John Broadbent (Cambridge, Cambridge University Press, 1973), has a wealth of supporting material. The same critic's *Paradise Lost: An Introduction* (Cambridge, Cambridge University Press, 1972) is equally useful. Broadbent's two-volume paperback anthology of seventeenth-century poetry (New York, Signet, 1974), long out of print but worth ransacking bookshops for, is the most inspirational thing of its kind I know. The edition of *Paradise Lost* used in this and the next chapter is Gordon Campbell's excellent Everyman edition, *Milton: The Complete English Poems* (London, David Campbell Publishers, 1990). Professor Campbell's Everyman's Poetry paperback selection of Milton (London, J.M. Dent, 1996) includes the first two books of *Paradise Lost*. Philip Pullman's recently completed trilogy, *His Dark Materials* (ostensibly for young adults), is a work of profound imaginative reach that engages vividly with *Paradise Lost*.

6

MARVELL, WINSTANLEY, MILTON

Gardens, communes, and losing Paradise

This chapter is designed to be read with the preceding chapter in which the contents of this chapter were briefly indicated and its writers introduced. Here we read a selection of poems by Andrew Marvell (probably from the 1650s), extracts from pamphlets by the radical activist Gerrard Winstanley, and finally the end of Milton's *Paradise Lost*. As in the last chapter, our concern is with versions of the fall of man in the contexts of England's revolutionary years.

And what was the fall anyway?

Here are some texts that unsettle the very notion of falling or the fall. For Marvell, Eden is not so much the erotic one-ness of the heterosexual couple as something closer to auto-eroticism.

Here is 'The Garden'. It opens by wondering why men seek military, political or artistic fame when the repose of a garden is so superior. With similar playfulness, stanza 3 wittily plays on the romantic notion of love-sick boys carving their girlfriends' names on trees. These trees, says Marvell's speaker, will have their own names on them instead. Stanza 4 turns some famous myths upside down: the joke here is that the gods Apollo and Pan, chasing their unwilling humans, actually wanted them to turn into trees. The idea is that trees are sexier.

Marvell's fruit is certainly sexy and the fall that his speaker undergoes in this poem, 'ensnared with flowers' rather than by Satan, is full of almost infantile pleasure. His mind equivalently turns inwards and, again as in a child's fantasy, creates and annihilates at will. (Marvell, here as elsewhere, suggests that acts of creation need prior acts of annihilation.) What his soul then does is somehow both a transcendent flight and a hair-combing. But, then, the garden itself seems at once an Eden and a highly manicured and constructed gentleman's retreat and an image of a state. The multiple vision places us oddly nowhere. Or everywhere. But wherever the speaker is, his ecstasy and his journey are solitary ones. Milton's Satan recognised that Adam and Eve's 'happier' Eden is being 'imparadised in one another's arms' (IV.506–7); for Marvell's speaker 'two paradises 'twere in one/To live in paradise alone'. Marvell's way of destabilising the fall is different from Milton's but comes out of the same sceptical temper.

The Garden

1

How vainly men themselves amaze
To win the palm, the oak, or bays,
And their uncessant labours see
Crowned from some single herb or tree,
Whose short and narrow vergèd shade
Does prudently their toils upbraid,
While all flow'rs and all trees do close
To weave the garlands of repose.

2

Fair Quiet, have I found thee here,
10 And Innocence, thy sister dear!
Mistaken long, I sought you then
In busy companies of men.
Your sacred plants, if here below,
Only among the plants will grow.
Society is all but rude,
To this delicious solitude.

3

No white nor red was ever seen
So am'rous as this lovely green.
Fond lovers, cruel as their flame,
20 Cut in these trees their mistress' name.
Little, alas, they know, or heed,
How far these beauties hers exceed!

81

Fair trees! wheres'e'er your barks I wound,
No name shall but your own be found.

4

When we have run our passion's heat,
Love hither makes his best retreat.
The gods, that mortal beauty chase,
Still in a tree did end their race.
Apollo hunted Daphne so,
30 Only that she might laurel grow.
And Pan did after Syrinx speed,
Not as a nymph, but for a reed.

5

What wondrous life is this I lead!
Ripe apples drop about my head;
The luscious clusters of the vine
Upon my mouth do crush their wine;
The nectarine, and curious peach,
Into my hands themselves do reach;
Stumbling on melons, as I pass,
40 Ensnared with flowers, I fall on grass.

6

Meanwhile the mind, from pleasures less,
Withdraws into its happiness:
The mind, that ocean where each kind
Does straight its own resemblance find,
Yet it creates, transcending these,
Far other worlds, and other seas,
Annihilating all that's made
To a green thought in a green shade.

7

Here at the fountain's sliding foot,
50 Or at some fruit-tree's mossy root,
Casting the body's vest aside,
My soul into the boughs does glide:

There like a bird it sits, and sings,
Then whets, and combs its silver wings;
And, till prepared for longer flight,
Waves in its plumes the various light.

8

Such was that happy garden-state,
While man there walked without a mate:
After a place so pure, and sweet,
60 What other help could yet be meet!
But 'twas beyond a mortal's share
To wander solitary there:
Two paradises 'twere in one
To live in paradise alone.

9

How well the skilful gardener drew
Of flowers and herbs this dial new,
Where from above the milder sun
Does through a fragrant zodiac run;
And, as it works, the industrious bee
70 Computes its time as well as we.
How could such sweet and wholesome hours
Be reckoned but with herbs and flowers!

5 vergèd shade: deflected shadow
37 curious: desirable
54 whets: preens

There's another pseudo-Eden, again presented in an air somewhere between irony and ecstasy, in Marvell's 'Bermudas'. This has a precise socio-religious context. Marvell knew and lived for a time in the house of John Oxenbridge who, with many others, faced with the intolerant and persecuting bishops of the pre-war years, fled to the New World where their non-conformist religion could be practised. Thus the poem's reference to the 'prelate's rage'. There's more eroticised fruit here and, again, we're somehow both in an enchanting Eden and an enamelled world, even on a 'stage' (if the word is a pun). The little boat is apparently going nowhere and, in a nice inversion, the 'falling' oars are being used to keep the singing in time, as opposed to the expected opposite. Again this is a moment of strange stillness, in an Eden, the Bermudas, nowhere, a 'falling' in stillness.

Bermudas

Where the remote Bermudas ride
In th' ocean's bosom unespied,
From a small boat, that rowed along,
The listening winds received this song.
   'What should we do but sing his praise
That led us through the watery maze,
Unto an isle so long unknown,
And yet far kinder than our own?
Where he the huge sea-monsters wracks,
10 That lift the deep upon their backs,
He lands us on a grassy stage,
Safe from the storms, and prelate's rage.
He gave us this eternal spring,
Which here enamels everything,
And sends the fowl to us in care,
On daily visits through the air.
He hangs in shades the orange bright,
Like golden lamps in a green night,
And does in the pom'granates close
20 Jewels more rich than Ormus shows.
He makes the figs our mouths to meet,
And throws the melons at our feet,
But apples plants of such a price,
No tree could ever bear them twice.
With cedars, chosen by his hand,
From Lebanon, he stores the land,
And makes the hollow seas, that roar,
Proclaim the ambergris on shore.
He cast (of which we rather boast)
30 The gospel's pearl upon our coast,
And in these rocks for us did frame
A temple, where to sound his name.

Oh let our voice his praise exalt,
Till it arrive at heaven's vault:
Which thence (perhaps) rebounding, may
Echo beyond the Mexique Bay.'
 Thus sung they, in the English boat,
An holy and a cheerful note,
And all the way, to guide their chime,
With falling oars they kept the time.

23 apples: pineapples
28 ambergris: secretion from sperm-whales

And here are eleven stanzas from Marvell's great long poem 'Upon Appleton House'. Here too the speaker (it seems more than usually important, in Marvell, to avoid identifying the poet with the speaker) is in an erotically solitary Eden and undergoes a pseudo-fall or anti-fall, reverting or falling into auto-erotic bliss and what sounds like masochistic bondage. There's barbed comedy in stanza 74, when the speaker compares himself to a 'great prelate' with an 'antic cope': this would evoke the religious persecutions of the 1630s again, as in 'Bermudas'. And the evoking of the river as a serpent or snake, both 'wanton' and 'harmless', as well as the sun pining 'Narcissus-like', might lead Marvell's readers, highly attuned to such allusiveness of language, to sceptical reflection on the biblical fall. But to speak of Marvell's readers is a problem. His lyrics remained unpublished at his death.

Upon Appleton House

71

Thus I, easy philosopher,
Among the birds and trees confer.
And little now to make me wants
Or of the fowls, or of the plants:
Give me but wings as they, and I
Straight floating on the air shall fly:
Or turn me but, and you shall see
I was but an inverted tree.

72

Already I begin to call
570 In their most learn'd original:
And where I language want, my signs
The bird upon the bough divines;
And more attentive there doth sit
Than if she were with lime-twigs knit.
No leaf does tremble in the wind.
Which I, returning, cannot find.

73

Out of these scattered sibyl's leaves
Strange prophecies my fancy weaves:
And in one history consumes,
580 Like Mexique paintings, all the plumes.
What Rome, Greece, Palestine, ere said
I in this light mosaic read.
Thrice happy he who, not mistook,
Hath read in Nature's mystic book.

74

And see how chance's better wit
Could with a mask my studies hit!
The oak leaves me embroider all,
Between which caterpillars crawl:
And ivy, with familiar trails,
590 Me licks, and clasps, and curls, and hales.
Under this antic cope I move
Like some great prelate of the grove.

75

Then, languishing with ease, I toss
On pallets swoll'n of velvet moss,
While the wind, cooling through the boughs,
Flatters with air my panting brows.
Thanks for my rest, ye mossy banks;
And unto you, cool zephyrs, thanks,
Who, as my hair, my thoughts too shed,
600 And winnow from the chaff my head.

76

How safe, methinks, and strong, behind
These trees have I encamped my mind:
Where beauty, aiming at the heart,
Bends in some tree its useless dart;
And where the world no certain shot
Can make, or me it toucheth not,
But I on it securely play,
And gall its horsemen all the day.

77

Bind me, ye woodbines, in your twines,
610 Curl me about, ye gadding vines,
And, oh, so close your circles lace,
That I may never leave this place:
But lest your fetters prove too weak,
Ere I your silken bondage break,
Do you, O brambles, chain me too,
And, courteous briars, nail me through.

78

Here in the morning tie my chain,
Where the two woods have made a lane,
While, like a guard on either side,
620 The trees before their Lord divide;
This, like a long and equal thread,
Betwixt two labyrinths does lead.
But where the floods did lately drown,
There at the evening stake me down.

79

For now the waves are fall'n and dried,
And now the meadows fresher dyed,
Whose grass, with moister colour dashed,
Seems as green silks but newly washed.
No serpent new nor crocodile
630 Remains behind our little Nile,
Unless itself you will mistake,

Among these meads the only snake.

80

See in what wanton harmless folds
It everywhere the meadow holds;
And its yet muddy back doth lick,
Till as a crystal mirror slick,
Where all things gaze themselves, and doubt
If they be in it or without.
And for his shade which therein shines,
640 Narcissus-like, the sun too pines.

81

O what a pleasure 'tis to hedge
My temples here with heavy sedge,
Abandoning my lazy side,
Stretched as a bank unto the tide,
Or to suspend my sliding foot
On th' osier's underminèd root,
And in its branches tough to hang,
While at my lines the fishes twang!

We left *Paradise Lost* at Adam and Eve's post-fall guilt. Marvell's lyrics, probably from the 1650s, presumably pre-date Milton's writing of Book IX but it's very tempting to think that one great poet was consciously responding to another, Marvell to Milton, when we compare Marvell's stanzas 76 and 77 ('Bind me, ye woodbines' etc.) with this, Adam's lament: 'O might I here/In solitude live savage, in some glade/Obscured ... Cover me, ye pines;/Ye cedars, with innumerable boughs/Hide me ... ' (IX.1084–90). It's not necessary, though, to presume that Marvell had seen bits of Milton before the epic was published. It's enough to see that Marvell's temperament led him to rewrite the fall as a comic-ecstatic self-flagellation.

As in 'The Garden', we seem to be, in 'Appleton House', everywhere and nowhere, an Eden, an England in the aftermath of civil war, a country garden in an estate owned by someone. In this case, the someone was Lord Fairfax, once Cromwell's most senior general, who had withdrawn from his position in protest at Cromwell's policy towards the

Scots. Marvell was for a time tutor to his daughter Maria. The penultimate stanza of 'Appleton House' has an almost jaunty statement of the modern world being a 'rude heap' and addresses Maria Fairfax as an emblem of a world in 'more decent order'. If Paradise exists or ever existed it's in the lap, not of the gods, but of this young girl.

96

'Tis not, what once it was, the world,
But a rude heap together hurled,
All negligently overthrown,
Gulfs, deserts, precipices, stone.
Your lesser world contains the same,
But in more decent order tame;
You, heaven's centre, Nature's lap,
And paradise's only map.

And Fairfax, oddly enough, would have known Gerrard Winstanley too, though it's unlikely that Marvell did. Fairfax met Winstanley a year or so before employing Marvell.

In early 1649, amid considerable disappointment and anger at Cromwell and his army among the Levellers and other radical supporters of the Commonwealth, whose hopes for a genuinely reformed democratic society the republic was failing to deliver, and in the unrest and mutinous mood at a 'terrifying time for the men of property' (in the words of Christopher Hill whose editon of Winstanley's writings I draw gratefully on here (Hill, 1973, p. 26)), a remarkable thing happened. A group of poor men began digging and planting on the waste land on St George's Hill, near Weybridge, Surrey. This was a time of particularly sharp hardship and starvation for the poor. So they took action into their own hands. The number of Diggers or True Levellers (the other Levellers they considered insufficiently radical in their politics) grew to the point of seriously alarming local landowners and military assistance was called for. Fairfax interviewed Winstanley and later visited the Digger colony. He seems to have found them eccentric but harmless. Winstanley, in a nice turn of phrase, explained to Fairfax that landowners' claims to common land had been 'cut off with the King's head'. A Digger manifesto was then published declaiming that 'the old world' is 'running up like parchment in the fire' (ibid., p. 27).

Fairfax was less concerned than the local property-owners who made sure the colony was repeatedly raided and the Diggers arrested, fined and their property seized. By the autumn of 1649 the colony was forced to move on to Cobham, but there too they were arrested, fined and the commune eventually forcibly broken up. But other Digger colonies were springing up across the country and, though they all, like Winstanley, disappeared into the margins of history, the moment of peacefully and actually achieved communist organisation was real.

Here's Gerrard Winstanley rewriting the fall in typical demystifying fashion, exposing the myth to what modern critics would call a materialist reading. Modern political historians have wistfully suggested that private property is a consequence of the fall. Winstanley, three hundred years earlier, put it the other way round. The fall was, and is in everyday terms, 'that power that hedges some into the earth and hedges others out', the enclosing, buying, selling of and systematic exclusion of others from property. Property was indeed a crucial point of argument between republicans, the left-wing radical Levellers arguing for the vote to be extended much further than just to men who owned property. This was, typically, too much for Cromwell and the less radical of his generals.

What the blessing is that restores him again

'But how came man's fall in at the first?' I answer, the outward objects of riches, honours, being set before the living soul, imaginary covetousness, which is the absence of the true light, moves the man to close with those objects, and to seek content without him; and through this dark night power, wars, divisions and discontent arises in mankind, to tear and devour itself; and so it is said to mankind, that his destruction is of himself. And the misery of mankind came in by these degrees:

First, when whole mankind walked in singleness and simplicity each to other, some bodies were more strong than others, as the elder brother was stronger than the younger, and the stronger did work for the weaker, and the whole earth was common to all without exception. But this singleness and simplicity was subject to corruption and change; and the change came in thus:

The stronger or elder brother, seeing the outward objects before him, thereupon imagines and saith, 'Why should I that do all the work be such a servant to these that do least work, and be equal with them? It is fit I should have some larger part of the earth than they, and be in some more esteem than others; and that they should acknowledge me in some degree above them.'

This imagination is the serpent that deceives the man; and as lust is thus conceived within, and the heart or the living soul consenting to these imaginary inventions, presently death is brought forth, and mankind falls from single simplicity to be full of divisions; and one member of mankind is separated from another, which before were all one, and looked upon each other as all one.

This is the first step of the fall, consent within being moved by outward objects of pleasure, riches and honour for one to be above another; whereas it was the honour of the elder to help the younger, and not to tread him down.

Secondly, it breaks forth into outward action: for this imaginary invention in the elder brother moves him to set about to enclose parcels of the earth into several divisions, and calls those enclosures proper or peculiar to himself, and that the younger or weaker brother should lay no claim to it, and the younger brother lets it go so; and presently their nakedness appears, that is, the imaginary covetousness of the heart is uncovered and laid open to the view hereby.

[. . .]

Then next to this, mankind began to buy and sell these enclosures of land, one of another, which the creating spirit of righteousness gave them no command to do. For by reason of this bargaining, the younger or weaker brother is more forcibly shut out of the earth; and so here is a foundation laid to steal the earth by craft, and to murder one another by the sword.

'For now,' saith the buyer, 'this parcel of land is mine; I have paid the fruit of my labours for it, to be properly my own'. But the younger brother comes in and saith, 'The land is our portion by creation as well as yours, and we give no consent to be shut out; therefore what authority had you to buy, or the other to sell? By thus doing you cheat us and cast us out of the earth'. And from hence now divisions and wars begins to arise between the brothers.

[. . .]

The stronger brother goes further in his imaginary ambitious invention, and makes war against the younger or weaker brother, and takes their enclosures by force from them; and either kills them or turns them out of the land which they had bestowed labour upon; and so did break Moses's law, which said, thou shall not kill, thou shalt not steal.

And now divisions and enmity is risen to the height, and the power of the sword is the very strength of the curse, and is the murderer; for this takes not away property from others by labour or by buying and selling; but by cruel violence and force, casting down one, setting up another by force; and now mankind is in the extremity of division.

And they that enjoy the land, they or their fathers got it by the sword, and they keep possession by the sword, and no man regards the law of righteous creation, or of Moses's law of equity; for every man seeks himself, and thinks it equity for others to regard him, and is offended at those that do not regard him; and the whole earth is filled with this devouring self-righteousness.

[. . .]

This power of the sword doth not only kill and rob; but by his laws, made and upheld by his power, he hedges the weak out of the earth, and either starves them or else forces them through poverty to take from others, and then hangs them for so doing.

They that have the greatest power of the sword in their hands do kill and take away the labours of others, and say it is righteous; but if a weaker hand doth but take from others to supply necessaries, the other calls this unrighteous, and hangs them for it. Surely the King of righteousness is not so partial a God as to call one and the same action good in his hand that is the stronger, and bad in his hand that is the weaker brother.

No, no; this is the righteousness of the Man of Sin: this is the righteousness of the scribes, Pharisees and Judas, that counts every thing righteous that pleases them, and every thing unrighteous that displeases them. This is the extremity of the curse; and yet this is the law that everyone nowadays dotes upon; when the plain truth is the law of property is the shameful nakedness of mankind, and as far from the law of Christ as light from darkness.

And yet soldiers and lawyers and all that cry up this power of property, which is both brought in and upheld by the murdering sword, would be called saints and members of Christ.

Truly you are all deceived, you are members and actors of the curse, which is the destruction and bondage of the creation; you are that power that hedges some into the earth and hedges others out; and takes to yourselves, by the power of the killing sword, a liberty to rule over the labours and persons of your fellow-creatures, who are flesh of your flesh and bone of your bone. And you do the very same things, in a higher degree and nature, for which you hang other men for, punishing others for such actions as you call sin; and yet you live in the daily action yourselves, taking the earth from the weaker brother, and so killing him by poverty or prison all day long.

[. . .]

Look upon a child that is new born, or till he grows up to some few years: he is innocent, harmless, humble, patient, gentle, easy to be entreated, not envious; and this is Adam, or mankind in his innocence; and this continues till outward objects entice him to pleasure or seek content without him. And when he consents, or suffers the imaginary covetousness within to close with the objects, then he falls and is taken captive, and falls lower and lower.

First into the slavery of that power of lusts within, leading him forth to act all manner of selfishness, with greediness to the destruction of others;

And then falls from this delight into trouble of mind and touch of conscience and inward torment, and so falls deeper and deeper into hell, till the seed or blessing rise up in him to work deliverance and then carry him back again, and lead him into the ways of truth.

And thus we see how mankind came to fall from his

93

innocence; and that was by closing to outward objects for content with inward imaginary covetousness, to find life in those objects without him.

And man's recovery will he to reject outward objects, and to close with the spirit of truth, life and peace within, preferring this kingdom within before the outward kingdom.

(*Fire in the Bush* in Hill, 1973, pp. 263–9)

Christopher Hill has provocatively linked Winstanley with Thomas Traherne, a writer of mystical and devotional texts from the 1670s. Traherne, in his poem 'Wonder', calls private property 'cursed ill-devised proprieties' and says that they are among the 'fiends that spoil even Paradise', which does suggest that he might have read Winstanley as well as Milton. Traherne also laments the 'hedges, ditches, limits, narrow bounds', the boundaries imposed on the landscape. Here he not only connects with Winstanley but also with later nineteenth-century writers like John Clare, whose anger was directed at the enclosure movement in which previously common land was forcibly taken to further the interests of large landowners and the new intensive agriculture. We associate the enclosure movement with later developments but historians have shown that three-quarters of English enclosure had taken place by 1700.

Winstanley's suggestion that Adam is no more than every child in infancy is remarkable in its modernity. And it too seems to have been taken up directly by Traherne. His version, in a prose meditation, is this. 'Certainly Adam in Paradise had not more sweet and curious apprehensions of the world, than I when I was a child.' Winstanley's notion that when we 'close with' what he calls 'outward objects' we fall and are 'taken captive' and fall 'lower and lower' is a proposition little different from that offered by contemporary anti-corporative eco-warriors. And the following idea that recovering Paradise is to prefer the 'kingdom within before the outward kingdom' echoes, as we'll see, with the end of *Paradise Lost*.

* * *

A challenging guide to the fallen world is Marvell. His poetry is Milton's opposite. Milton's is declamatory, rhetorical, tense with the authorial voice, sentences strung powerfully across large structures in which

94

meaning is at last gratifyingly made clear. It makes a kind of bold and dramatic bet with the reader: stick with its confidence and it will make sense. Marvell's is ventriloquised, as if personal voice has fallen away into echoes (suggesting the Narcissus myth again), the verse's movement an ebbing and flowing, the rhymes never quite completing a pattern, the rhythm so poignantly shadowed by disaster. It's difficult to describe. It's unforgettable. It's a poetry fallen but in suspension, in every sense, neither quite liquid nor solid, never reaching either fulfilment or free fall.

The speakers of Marvell's lyrics are usually solitary and they speak of loss, desire getting nowhere, souls and bodies dislocated and condemned to speak in, as it were, different theatres. But the lyric impulse keeps alive and what it keeps alive reads like a series of displaced and distanced responses to the political-historical moment, dramatised as voices speaking in their strangely charged sorrows and isolations. Annabel Patterson, in a very suggestive recent book, has it that Marvell saw that 'religion, sex and politics are names for the different (and sometimes crossing) paths of desire towards its unknown object' (Patterson, 1994, p. 64). The most poignant of these lyrics is 'The Nymph Complaining For the Death of her Fawn', an extraordinary piece of ventriloquising in which a young girl laments the random killing of her fawn, itself a gift from her unfaithful boyfriend.

The Nymph Complaining for the Death of her Fawn

> The wanton troopers riding by
> Have shot my fawn, and it will die.
> Ungentle men! They cannot thrive
> To kill thee! Thou ne'er didst alive
> Them any harm: alas, nor could
> Thy death yet do them any good.
> I'm sure I never wished them ill;
> Nor do I for all this; nor will:
> But if my simple prayers may yet
> 10 Prevail with heaven to forget
> Thy murder, I will join my tears
> Rather than fail. But, O my fears!
> It cannot die so. Heaven's King

Keeps register of everything:
And nothing may we use in vain.
E'en beasts must be with justice slain,
Else men are made their deodands.
Though they should wash their guilty hands
In this warm life-blood, which doth part
20 From thine, and wound me to the heart,
Yet could they not be clean: their stain
Is dyed in such a purple grain,
There is not such another in
The world, to offer for their sin.

Unconstant Sylvio, when yet
I had not found him counterfeit,
One morning (I remember well),
Tied in this silver chain and bell
Gave it to me: nay, and I know
30 What he said then; I'm sure I do.
Said he, 'Look how your huntsman here
Hath taught a fawn to hunt his dear.'
But Sylvio soon had me beguiled.
This waxèd tame, while he grew wild,
And quite regardless of my smart,
Left me his fawn, but took his heart.

Thenceforth I set myself to play
My solitary time away
With this: and very well content,
40 Could so mine idle life have spent.
For it was full of sport; and light
Of foot, and heart; and did invite
Me to its game; it seemed to bless
Itself in me. How could I less
Than love it? O I cannot be
Unkind, t'a beast that loveth me.

Had it lived long, I do not know
Whether it too might have done so
As Sylvio did: his gifts might be
50 Perhaps as false or more than he.
But I am sure, for ought that I

Could in so short a time espy,
Thy love was far more better than
The love of false and cruel men.
   With sweetest milk, and sugar, first
I it at mine own fingers nursed.
And as it grew, so every day
It waxed more white and sweet than they.
It had so sweet a breath! And oft
60 I blushed to see its foot more soft,
And white (shall I say than my hand?)
Nay, any lady's of the land.
   It is a wondrous thing, how fleet
'Twas on those little silver feet.
With what a pretty skipping grace,
It oft would challenge me the race:
And when 't had left me far away,
'Twould stay, and run again, and stay.
For it was nimbler much than hinds;
70 And trod, as on the four winds.
   I have a garden of my own
But so with roses overgrown,
And lilies, that you would it guess
To be a little wilderness.
And all the springtime of the year
It only lovèd to be there.
Among the beds of lilies, I
Have sought it oft, where it should lie;
Yet could not, till itself would rise,
80 Find it, although before mine eyes.
For, in the flaxen lilies' shade,
It like a bank of lilies laid.
Upon the roses it would feed,
Until its lips e'en seemed to bleed:
And then to me 'twould boldly trip,
And print those roses on my lip.
But all its chief delight was still
On roses thus itself to fill:
And its pure virgin limbs to fold

97

90 In whitest sheets of lilies cold.
     Had it lived long, it would have been
     Lilies without, roses within.
        O help! O help! I see it faint:
     And die as calmly as a saint.
     See how it weeps. The tears do come
     Sad, slowly dropping like a gum.
     So weeps the wounded balsam: so
     The holy frankincense doth flow.
     The brotherless Heliades
100 Melt in such amber tears as these.
       I in a golden vial will
     Keep these two crystal tears; and fill
     It till it do o'erflow with mine;
     Then place it in Diana's shrine.
       Now my sweet fawn is vanished to
     Whither the swans and turtles go:
     In fair Elysium to endure,
     With milk-white lambs, and ermines pure.
     O do not run too fast: for I
110 Will but bespeak thy grave, and die.
       First my unhappy statue shall
     Be cut in marble; and withal,
     Let it be weeping too; but there
     The engraver sure his art may spare,
     For I so truly thee bemoan,
     That I shall weep though I be stone:
     Until my tears (still dropping) wear
     My breast, themselves engraving there.
     Then at my feet shalt thou be laid,
120 Of purest alabaster made:
     For I would have thine image be
     White as I can, though not as thee.

 17 deodands: forfeited objects that have caused death
106 turtles: turtledoves

The fawn was killed by a 'trooper' randomly riding by, a concentrated reminder of the war years in one casual word. Troopers were members of an invading Scottish army in 1640, an invasion against Charles's absolutism that was one trigger for the civil wars that followed. The word itself dates from 1640. Its use here is clearly strategic. But what Marvell's nymph is up to in this poem is far from clear and seems designed to resist clarity. As in 'The Garden' and 'Appleton House' we seem to need to read on multiple levels simultaneously. For a start, whether by accident or not, the notion that Sylvio's fawn became 'tame, while he grew wild', with the puns on dear/deer and heart/hart, seems like a gender-inverted rewrite of Wyatt's 'They flee from me'. Beyond Wyatt the poem is gesturing back to classical antecedents in which girls lament the death of a pet.

But Marvell's poem has a longer reach than the merely literary. That the fawn, Sylvio's gift before he left her, is a love-substitute or sex-substitute is clear enough. The word fawn connects, at its roots, with the word foetus which is very suggestive. When its blood is pictured as in 'purple grain' and its killers are pictured washing 'their guilty hands' in sin, readers would presumably picture Christ and/or Charles at his execution. Marvell's own 'Horatian Ode', which was published in his lifetime and which is vigorously pro-Cromwell, says that at the scaffold 'the armed bands/ Did clap their bloody hands'.

But the fawn, as argued in a challenging essay by Jonathan Goldberg, is perhaps best seen as a representation of desire's illusionary goals, a substitute in a chain of merely repetitive substitutes, an 'it' (Goldberg counts 26 references to the fawn as an 'it' in 38 lines (Goldberg, 1986, p. 26)), an impossibility, a dream object, like the weeping marble statue the nymph turns herself into at the end, with the fawn turned into even more precious 'purest alabaster' at her feet. Patterson calls this 'an almost pure expression of desire in its essence' (Patterson, 1994, p. 64). The story of Narcissus and Echo, to which Patterson's words might also be applied, and the story of Pygmalion, who fell in love with his own statue, are certainly important in the poem, but in a typically elusive way. In effect the poem, and the fawn and the nymph (and Sylvio), seem determined to avoid definition and capture. And what Marvell, as opposed to the nymph, is 'saying' in the poem is definitively elusive. He says nothing. The entire poem belongs to its speaker. But then nymphs don't exist anyway and meaning is always escaping in the fallen world.

Let's go to three of Marvell's love-poems in classical-pastoral mode, the love-sick shepherd Damon here modified into a mower with scythe, a more ominous if also more comic figure, typically threatening that 'flow'rs, and grass, and I and all,/ Will in one common ruin fall' or claiming that glow-worms predict 'the grass's fall'. Damon tries to give Juliana tokens of his love, notably including a snake 'harmless' and 'disarmed'; then, while 'depopulating all the ground', in a strangely worded act of annihilation, he cuts into his own ankle and falls, mowing himself down in yet another anti-fall. 'The Mower mown' is Marvell at his most funny and worrying, at the same time. We need to remember that the pastoral genre is always a form of political writing in classical and Renaissance literature. Virgil's pastoral *Eclogues*, on which Marvell draws provocatively, open with shepherds complaining about their land being confiscated for war veterans.

Damon the Mower

1

Hark how the Mower Damon sung,
With love of Juliana stung!
While everything did seem to paint
The scene more fit for his complaint.
Like her fair eyes the day was fair,
But scorching like his am'rous care.
Sharp like his scythe his sorrow was,
And withered like his hopes the grass.

2

'Oh what unusual heats are here,
10 Which thus our sunburned meadows sear!
The grasshopper its pipe gives o'er;
And hamstringed frogs can dance no more.
But in the brook the green frog wades;
And grasshoppers seek out the shades.
Only the snake, that kept within,
Now glitters in its second skin.

3

'This heat the sun could never raise,

Nor Dog Star so inflame the days.
It from an higher beauty grow'th,
20 Which burns the fields and mower both:
Which mads the dog, and makes the sun
Hotter than his own Phaëton.
Not July causeth these extremes,
But Juliana's scorching beams.

4

'Tell me where I may pass the fires
Of the hot day, or hot desires.
To what cool cave shall I descend,
Or to what gelid fountain bend?
Alas! I look for ease in vain,
30 When remedies themselves complain.
No moisture but my tears do rest,
Nor cold but in her icy breast.

5

'How long wilt thou, fair shepherdess,
Esteem me, and my presents less?
To thee the harmless snake I bring,
Disarmèd of its teeth and sting;
To thee chameleons, changing hue,
And oak leaves tipped with honey dew.
Yet thou, ungrateful, hast not sought
40 Nor what they are, nor who them brought.

6

'I am the Mower Damon, known
Through all the meadows I have mown.
On me the morn her dew distils
Before her darling daffodils.
And, if at noon my toil me heat,
The sun himself licks off my sweat,
While, going home, the evening sweet
In cowslip-water bathes my feet.

7

'What, though the piping shepherd stock
50 The plains with an unnumbered flock,
This scythe of mine discovers wide
More ground than all his sheep do hide.
With this the golden fleece I shear
Of all these closes every year.
And though in wool more poor than they,
Yet am I richer far in hay.

8

'Nor am I so deformed to sight,
If in my scythe I lookèd right;
In which I see my picture done,
60 As in a crescent moon the sun.
The deathless fairies take me oft
To lead them in their dances soft:
And, when I tune myself to sing,
About me they contract their ring.

9

'How happy might I still have mowed,
Had not Love here his thistles sowed!
But now I all the day complain,
Joining my labour to my pain:
And with my scythe cut down the grass,
70 Yet still my grief is where it was:
But, when the iron blunter grows,
Sighing, I whet my scythe and woes.'

10

While thus he threw his elbow round,
Depopulating all the ground,
And, with his whistling scythe, does cut
Each stroke between the earth and root,
The edgèd steel by careless chance
Did into his own ankle glance;
And there among the grass fell down,
80 By his own scythe, the Mower mown.

11

'Alas!' said he, 'these hurts are slight
To those that die by love's despite.
With shepherd's-purse, and clown's-all-heal,
The blood I staunch, and wound I seal.
Only for him no cure is found,
Whom Juliana's eyes do wound.
'Tis death alone that this must do:
For Death thou art a Mower too.'

28 gelid: frozen
33 remedies for bleeding

The Mower to the Glowworms

1

Ye living lamps, by whose dear light
The nightingale does sit so late,
And studying all the summer night,
Her matchless songs does meditate;

2

Ye country comets, that portend
No war, nor prince's funeral,
Shining unto no higher end
Than to presage the grass's fall;

3

Ye glowworms, whose officious flame
10 To wandering mowers shows the way,
That in the night have lost their aim,
And after foolish fires do stray;

4

Your courteous lights in vain you waste,
Since Juliana here is come,
For she my mind hath so displaced
That I shall never find my home.

9 officious: attentive

The Mower's Song

1

My mind was once the true survey
Of all these meadows fresh and gay,
And in the greenness of the grass
Did see its hopes as in a glass;
When Juliana came, and she
What I do to the grass, does to my thoughts and me.

2

But these, while I with sorrow pine,
Grew more luxuriant still and fine,
That not one blade of grass you spied,
10   But had a flower on either side;
When Juliana came, and she
What I do to the grass, does to my thoughts and me.

3

Unthankful meadows, could you so
A fellowship so true forgo,
And in your gaudy May-games meet,
While I lay trodden under feet?
When Juliana came, and she
What I do to the grass, does to my thoughts and me.

4

But what you in compassion ought,
20   Shall now by my revenge be wrought:
And flow'rs, and grass, and I and all,
Will in one common ruin fall.
For Juliana comes, and she
What I do to the grass, does to my thoughts and me.

5

And thus, ye meadows, which have been
Companions of my thoughts more green,

Shall now the heraldry become
With which I will adorn my tomb;
For Juliana comes, and she
30 What I do to the grass, does to my thoughts and me.

And we end this selection from Marvell with the terrifying, because so bizarrely voiced, 'Definition of Love' and 'Dialogue between the Soul and Body'. The notion, in the first of these, that human love is the result of the coupling of two parents called Despair and Impossibility, and that the resulting lovers in such parallel unity 'can never meet', is an astonishing insight into the elemental loneliness of human longing with which contemporary theory and psychoanalysis are so concerned. And the brilliantly paradoxical 'Dialogue' gives us soul and body talking in parallel and separately lonely universes, as if they were characters in a text by a twentieth-century modernist writer like Samuel Beckett, the two entities complementarily compelled to speak of their dizzyingly unendurable entrapments. This poem contains Marvell's one and only nightmarish fall, the body's sense of the soul 'stretched upright' impaling it so that 'mine own precipice I go', the nightmare of an endless fall going nowhere, never reaching bottom.

The Definition of Love

1

My love is of a birth as rare
As 'tis for object strange and high:
It was begotten by Despair
Upon Impossibility.

2

Magnanimous Despair alone
Could show me so divine a thing,
Where feeble Hope could ne'er have flown
But vainly flapped its tinsel wing.

3

And yet I quickly might arrive
10 Where my extended soul is fixed,

105

But Fate does Iron wedges drive,
And always crowds itself betwixt.

4

For Fate with jealous eye does see
Two perfect loves, nor lets them close:
Their union would her ruin be,
And her tyrannic power depose.

5

And therefore her decrees of steel
Us as the distant poles have placed,
(Though Love's whole world on us doth wheel)
20 Not by themselves to be embraced,

6

Unless the giddy heaven fall,
And earth some new convulsion tear;
And, us to join, the world should all
Be cramped into a planisphere.

7

As lines (so loves) oblique may well
Themselves in every angle greet:
But ours so truly parallel,
Though infinite, can never meet.

8

Therefore the love which us doth bind,
30 But Fate so enviously debars,
Is the conjunction of the mind,
And opposition of the stars.

A Dialogue between the Soul and Body

SOUL

O, who shall from this dungeon raise
A soul, enslaved so many ways,
With bolts of bones, that fettered stands
In feet, and manacled in hands;
Here blinded with an eye; and there
Deaf with the drumming of an ear,
A soul hung up, as 'twere, in chains
Of nerves, and arteries, and veins,
Tortured, besides each other part,
10 In a vain head, and double heart?

BODY

O, who shall me deliver whole,
From bonds of this tyrannic soul,
Which, stretched upright, impales me so,
That mine own precipice I go;
And warms and moves this needless frame
(A fever could but do the same),
And, wanting where its spite to try,
Has made me live to let me die,
A body that could never rest,
20 Since this ill spirit it possessed?

SOUL

What magic could me thus confine
Within another's grief to pine,
Where, whatsoever it complain,
I feel, that cannot feel, the pain,
And all my care itself employs,
That to preserve, which me destroys:
Constrained not only to endure
Diseases, but, what's worse, the cure:
And ready oft the port to gain,
30 Am shipwrecked into health again?

BODY

But physic yet could never reach
The maladies thou me dost teach:
Whom first the cramp of hope does tear,
And then the palsy shakes of fear;
The pestilence of love does heat,
Or hatred's hidden ulcer eat;
Joy's cheerful madness does perplex,
Or sorrow's other madness vex;
Which knowledge forces me to know,
40 And memory will not forgo
What but a soul could have the wit
To build me up for sin so fit?
So architects do square and hew,
Green trees that in the forest grew.

* * *

We left Marvell's speaker in both of his dungeons. He's pointing back to Hamlet's 'Denmark's a prison' (II.ii.242) and forward to Blake's 'mind-forged manacles' ('London') 150 years later. But he's more frightening than either. Winstanley is characteristically more robust and demystifying. 'England', he says in his New year's Gift sent to the Parliament and Army, 'is a prison; the variety of subtleties in the laws preserved by the sword are bolts, bars and doors of the prison; the lawyers are jailors, and poor men are the prisoners'.

Here are extracts from this pamphlet. It tells of Winstanley's own experiences as a persecuted Digger. It urges the generals to push the revolution much further, in the name of the 'head Leveller' Christ and in the certainty that the claim, 'The poor shall inherit the earth, is really and materially to be fulfilled. For the earth is to be restored from the bondage of sword property, and it is to become a common treasury [. . .] every one shall delight to let each other enjoy the pleasures of the earth, and shall hold each other no more in bondage.' That would be to cancel the fall into property bondage, the fall itself. And Cromwell's reaction to the Digger argument that a social revolution is needed to complete the Digger he himself had started? 'I was by birth a gentleman. You must cut these people in pieces or they will cut you in pieces' (quoted in Morton, 1965, p. 257).

A
New year's Gift
SENT TO THE
PARLIAMENT
AND
ARMY

Gentlemen of the Parliament and Army: you and the common
people have assisted each other to cast out the head of oppression which was kingly power seated in one man's hand, and
that work is now done; and till that work was done you called
upon the people to assist you to deliver this distressed bleeding
dying nation out of bondage; and the people came and failed
you not, counting neither purse nor blood too dear to part with
to effect this work.

The Parliament after this have made an act to cast out kingly
power, and to make England a free commonwealth. These acts
the people are much rejoiced with, as being words forerunning
their freedom, and they wait for their accomplishment that
their joy may be full; for as words without action are a cheat
and kills the comfort of a righteous spirit, so words performed
in action does comfort and nourish the life thereof.

Now Sirs, wheresoever we spy out kingly power, no man I
hope shall be troubled to declare it, nor afraid to cast it out,
having both act of Parliament, the soldiers' oath and the common people's consent on his side; for kingly power is like a
great spread tree, if you lop the head or top bough, and let the
other branches and root stand, it will grow again and recover
fresher strength.

[. . .]

While this kingly power reigned in one man called Charles,
all sorts of people complained of oppression, both gentry and
common people, because their lands, enclosures and copyholds
were entangled, and because their trades were destroyed by
monopolizing patentees, and your troubles were that you could
not live free from oppression in the earth. Thereupon you that
were the gentry, when you were assembled in Parliament, you
called upon the poor common people to come and help you,

and cast out oppression; and you that complained are helped and freed, and that top bough is lopped off the tree of tyranny, and kingly power in that one particular is cast out. But alas, oppression is a great tree still, and keeps off the sun of freedom from the poor commons still; he hath many branches and great roots which must be grubbed up, before everyone can sing Sion's songs in peace.

As we spy out kingly power we must declare it and cast it out, or else we shall deny the Parliament of England and their acts, and so prove traitors to the land by denying obedience thereunto. Now there are three branches more of kingly power, greater than the former, that oppresses this land wonderfully; and these are the power of the tithing priests over the tenths of our labours; and the power of lords of manors, holding the free use of the commons and waste land from the poor; and the intolerable oppression either of bad laws, or of bad judges corrupting good laws. These are branches of the Norman conquest and kingly power still, and wants a reformation.

For as for the first, William the Conqueror promised that if the clergy would preach him up, so that the people might be bewitched so as to receive him to be God's anointed over them, he would give them the tenths of the land's increase yearly; and they did it, and he made good his promise. And do we not yet see that if the clergy can get tithes or money, they will turn as the ruling power turns, any way: to popery, to protestantism; for a king, against a king; for monarchy, for state-government; they cry 'Who bids most wages?' They will be on the strongest side, for an earthly maintenance; yea, and when they are lifted up, they would rule too, because they are called spiritual men. It is true indeed, they are spiritual; but it is of the spiritual power of covetousness and pride; for the spiritual power of love and righteousness they know not; for if they knew it, they would not persecute and rail against him as they do.

The clergy will serve on any side, like our ancient laws that will serve any master. They will serve the papists, they will serve the protestants, they will serve the king, they will serve the states; they are one and the same tools for lawyers to work with under any government. O you Parliament-men of

110

England, cast those whorish laws out of doors, that are so common, that pretend love to every one and is faithful to none: for truly, he that goes to law (as the proverb is) shall die a beggar: so that old whores and old laws picks men's pockets, and undoes them. If the fault lie in the laws (and much does), burn all your old law-books in Cheapside, and set up a government upon your own foundation. Do not put new wine into old bottles; but as your government must be new, so let the laws be new, or else you will run farther into the mud where you stick already, as though you were fast in an Irish bog; for you are so far sunk that he must have good eyes that can see where you are: but yet all are not blind, there are eyes that sees you. But if the fault lies in the judges of the law, surely such men deserve no power in a reforming commonwealth, that burdens all sorts of people.

And truly I'll tell you plain, your two acts of Parliament are excellent and righteous: the one to cast out kingly power, the other to make England a free commonwealth. Build upon these two, it is a firm foundation, and your house will be the glory of the world; and I am confident, the righteous spirit will love you. Do not stick in the bog of covetousness: let not self-love so bemuddy your brain that you should lose yourselves in the thicket of bramble-bush words, and set never a strong oak of some stable action for the freedom of the poor oppressed that helped you when you complained of oppression. Let not pride blind your eyes, that you should forget you are the nation's servants, and so prove Solomon's words good in yourselves, that servants ride on horseback and coaches, whenas princes, such as chose you and set you there, go on foot: and many of them, through their love to the nation, have so wasted themselves that now they can hardly get bread, but with great difficulty. I tell you this is a sore evil, and this is truth; therefore think upon it, it is a poor man's advice, and you shall find weight in it, if you do as well as say.

Then secondly for lords of manors, they were William the Conqueror's colonels and favourites, and he gave a large circuit of land to every one, called a lordship, that they might have a watchful eye that if any of the conquered English should begin to plant themselves upon any common or waste land, to live out of sight or out of slavery, that then some lord of manor or other might see and know of it, and drive them off, as these lords of manors nowadays endeavours to drive off the diggers from digging upon the commons. But we expect the rulers of the land will grant unto us their friends the benefit of their own acts against kingly power, and not suffer that Norman power to crush the poor oppressed who helped them in their straits, nor suffer that Norman power to bud fresher out, and so in time may come to over-top our dear-bought freedom more than ever.

Search all your laws, and I'll adventure my life (for I have little else to lose) that all lords of manors hold title to the commons by no stronger hold than the king's will, whose head is cut off; and the king held title as he was a conqueror. Now if you cast off the king who was the head of that power, surely the power of lords of manors is the same; therefore perform your own act of Parliament, and cast out that part of the kingly power likewise, that the people may see you understand what you say and do, and that you are faithful.

For truly the kingly power reigns strongly in the lords of manors over the poor. For my own particular, I have in other writings as well as in this declared my reasons that the common land is the poor people's property; and I have digged upon the commons, and I hope in time to obtain the freedom to get food and raiment therefrom by righteous labour, which is all I desire; and for so doing, the supposed lord of that manor hath arrested me twice; first, in an action of £20 trespass for plough-ing upon the commons, which I never did; and because they would not suffer me to plead my own cause, they made shift to pass a sentence of execution against some cows I kept, suppos-ing they had been mine, and took them away; but the right owner reprieved them, and fetched the cows back. So greedy are these thieves and murderers after my life for speaking the truth, and for maintaining the life and marrow of the Parliament's cause in my actions.

And now they have arrested me again in an action of £4 trespass for digging upon the commons, which I did, and own the work to be righteous and no trespass to any. This was the attorney of Kingston's advice, either to get money on both sides, for they love money as dearly as a poor man's dog do his breakfast in a cold morning (but regard not justice), or else that I should not remove it to a higher court, but that the cause might be tried there; and then they know how to please the lords of manors, that have resolved to spend hundreds of pounds but they will hinder the poor from enjoying the commons. For they will not suffer me to plead my own cause, but I must fee an enemy, or else be condemned and executed without mercy or justice as I was before, and so to put me in prison till I pay their unrighteous sentence; for truly attorneys are such neat workmen that they can turn a cause which way those that have the biggest purse will have them: and the country knows very well that Kingston court is so full of the kingly power that some will rather lose their rights than have their causes tried there. One of the officers of that court told a friend of mine that if the digger's cause was good, he would pick out such a jury as should overthrow him. And upon my former arrest they picked out such a jury as sentenced me to pay £10 damages for ploughing upon the commons, which I did not do, neither did any witness prove it before them. So that from Kingston juries, lords of manors and kingly power, good Lord deliver us.

Do these men obey the Parliament's acts, to throw down kingly power? O no: the same unrighteous doing that was complained of in King Charles's days, the same doings is among them still. Monies will buy and sell justice still: and is our 8 years' wars come round about to lay us down again in the kennel of injustice as much or more than before? Are we no farther learned yet? O ye rulers of England, when must we turn over a new leaf? Will you always hold us in one lesson? Surely you will make dunces of us: then all the boys in other lands will laugh at us. Come, I pray, let us take forth and go forward in our learning.

You blame us who are the common people as though we would have no government; truly gentlemen, we desire a righteous government with all our hearts, but the government we have gives freedom and livelihood to the gentry to have abundance, and to lock up treasures of the earth from the poor, so that rich men may have chests full of gold and silver, and houses full of corn and goods to look upon; and the poor that works to get it can hardly live, and if they cannot work like slaves, then they must starve. And thus the law gives all the land to some part of mankind whose predecessors got it by conquest, and denies it to others who by the righteous law of creation may claim an equal portion; and yet you say this is a righteous government. But surely it is no other but selfishness, which is the great red dragon, the murderer.

England is a prison; the variety of subtleties in the laws preserved by the sword are bolts, bars and doors of the prison; the lawyers are jailors, and poor men are the prisoners; for let a man fall into the hands of any from the bailiff to the judge, and he is either undone or weary of his life.

[. . .]

Yea that kingly power in the laws appointed the conquered poor to work for them that possess the land, for three pence and four pence a day; and if any refused, they were to be imprisoned; and if any walked a-begging and had no dwelling, he was to be whipped; and all was to force the slaves to work for them that had taken their property of their labours from them by the sword, as the laws of England are yet extant. And truly most laws are but to enslave the poor to the rich, and so they uphold the conquest and are laws of the great red dragon.

And at this very day poor people are forced to work in some places for 4, 5 and 6 pence a day; in other places for 8, 10 and 12 pence a day, for such small prizes now (corn being dear) that their earnings cannot find them bread for their family. And yet if they steal for maintenance, the murdering law will hang them; whenas lawyers, judges and court officers can take bribes by wholesale to remove one man's property by that law into another man's hands: and is not this worse thievery than the poor man's that steals for want? Well, this shews that if this be law, it is not the law of righteousness; it is a murderer, it is the law of covetousness and self-love; and this law that frights people and forces people to obey it by prisons, whips and gallows is the very kingdom of the devil and darkness which the creation groans under at this day.

And if any poor enslaved man that dares not steal begins to mourn under that bondage and saith, 'We that work most have least comfort in the earth, and they that work not at all, enjoy all'; contrary to the Scripture which saith, *The poor and the meek shall inherit the earth*:

Presently the tithing priest stops his mouth with a slam and tells him that is meant of the inward satisfaction of mind which the poor shall have, though they enjoy nothing at all; and so poor creatures, it is true, they have some ease thereby, and [are] made to wait with patience, while the kingly power swims in fulness and laughs at the other's misery: as a poor Cavalier gentlewoman presented a paper to the General in my sight, who looked upon the woman with a tender countenance; but a brisk little man and two or three more colonels pulled back the paper, not suffering the General to receive it, and laughed at the woman, who answered them again: 'I thought,' said she, 'you had not sat in the seat of the scornful'. This was done in Whitehall upon the 12 of December, 1649.

[. . .]

For I tell you and your preachers, that Scripture which saith *The poor shall inherit the earth*, is really and materially to be fulfilled. For the earth is to be restored from the bondage of sword property, and it is to become a common treasury in reality to whole mankind; for this is the work of the true saviour to do, who is the true and faithful Leveller, even the spirit and power of universal love, that is now rising to spread himself in the whole creation, who is the blessing, and will spread as far as the curse had spread, to take it off and cast him out, and who will set the creation in peace.

This powerful saviour will not set up his kingdom nor rule his creation with sword and fighting, as some think and fear; for he hath declared to you long since that they that take the sword to save themselves shall perish with the sword.

But this shall be the way of his conquest: even as in the days of the Beast, the whole world wondered after him, set him up and was subject to him, and did persecute universal love and made war against him and his saints, and overcame them for a time:

Even so the spirit of love and blessing shall arise and spread in mankind like the sun from east to west, and by his inward power of love, light and righteousness shall let mankind see the abomination of the swordly kingly power, and shall loathe themselves in dust and ashes, in that they have owned and upheld him so long; and shall fall off from him, loathe him and leave him.

And this shall be your misery, O you covetous oppressing tyrants of the earth, not only you great self-seeking powers of England but you powers of all the world. The people shall all fall off from you, and you shall fall on a sudden like a great tree that is undermined at the root. And you powers of England, you cannot say: 'another day'; but you had warning, this falling off is begun already, divisions shall tear and torture you till you submit to community. O come in, come in to righteousness that you may find peace.

You or some of you hate the name Leveller, and the chiefest of you are afraid and ashamed to own a Leveller, and you laugh and jeer at them. Well, laugh out, poor blind souls; the people and common soldiers both lets you alone, but they laugh in their hearts at you, and yet desire that you did know the things that concern your peace.

The time is very near that the people generally shall loathe and be ashamed of your kingly power, in your preaching, in your laws, in your counsels, as now you are ashamed of the Levellers. I tell you Jesus Christ who is that powerful spirit of love is the head Leveller; and *as he is lifted up, he will draw all men after him*, and leave you naked and bare, and make you ashamed in yourselves. His appearance will be with power; therefore kiss the son, O ye rulers of the earth, lest his anger fall upon you. The wounds of conscience within you from him shall be sharper than the wounds made by your sword, he shook heaven and earth when Moses's law was cast out, but he will shake heaven and earth now to purpose much more, and nothing shall stand but what is lovely. Be wise, scorn not the counsel of the poor, lest you be whipped with your own rod.

This great Leveller, Christ our King of righteousness in us, shall cause men to beat their swords into ploughshares and spears into pruning hooks, and nations shall learn war no more; and every one shall delight to let each other enjoy the pleasures of the earth, and shall hold each other no more in bondage: then what will become of your power? Truly he must be cast out for a murderer; and I pity you for the torment your spirit must go through, if you be not fore-armed, as you are abundantly fore-warned from all places. But I look upon you as part of the creation who must be restored, and the spirit may give you wisdom to foresee a danger, as he hath admonished divers of your rank already to leave those high places, and to lie quiet and wait for the breakings forth of the powerful day of the Lord. Farewell, once more. *Let Israel go free.*

(A New year's Gift in Hill, 1973, pp. 161–204)

*   *   *

Here, at last, is the end of *Paradise Lost*. After Adam and Eve's repentance God has delivered the penalty and archangel Michael has given Adam a prophetic look into the future, including the promise that Eve's seed will eventually yield the birth of Christ and human redemption.

    He ended; and thus Adam last replied:
    'How soon hath thy prediction, seer blest,
    Measured this transient world, the race of time,
555 Till time stand fixed; beyond is all abyss –
    Eternity, whose end no eye can reach.
    Greatly instructed I shall hence depart,
    Greatly in peace of thought, and have my fill
    Of knowledge, what this vessel can contain;
560 Beyond which was my folly to aspire.
    Henceforth I learn that to obey is best,
    And love with fear the only God, to walk
    As in his presence, ever to observe
    His providence, and on him sole depend,
565 Merciful over all his works, with good
    Still overcoming evil, and by small
    Accomplishing great things – by things deemed weak

117

Subverting worldly-strong, and wordly-wise
By simply meek; that suffering for truth's sake
570 Is fortitude to highest victory,
And to the faithful death the gate of life –
Taught this by his example whom I now
Acknowledge my Redeemer ever blest.'
    To whom thus also the angel last replied:
575 'This having learned, thou hast attained the sum
Of wisdom; hope no higher, though all the stars
Thou knew'st by name, and all the ethereal powers,
All secrets of the deep, all nature's works,
Or works of God in heaven, air, earth, or sea;
580 And all the riches of this world enjoy'dst,
And all the rule, one empire; only add
Deeds to thy knowledge answerable, add faith,
Add virtue, patience, temperance, add love,
By name to come called Charity, the soul
585 Of all the rest: then wilt thou not be loath
To leave this Paradise, but shalt possess
A paradise within thee, happier far.
Let us descend now, therefore, from this top
Of speculation; for the hour precise
590 Exacts our parting hence; and see, the guards,
By me encamped on yonder hill, expect
Their motion, at whose front a flaming sword,
In signal of remove, waves fiercely round;
We may no longer stay; go, waken Eve;
595 Her also I with gentle dreams have calmed,
Portending good, and all her spirits composed
To meek submission: thou at season fit
Let her with thee partake what thou hast heard –
Chiefly what may concern her faith to know,
600 The great deliverance by her seed to come
(For by the woman's seed) on all mankind –
That ye may live, which will be many days,
Both in one faith unanimous; though sad
With cause for evils past, yet much more cheered
605 With meditation on the happy end.'

He ended, and they both descend the hill;
Descended, Adam to the bower where Eve
Lay sleeping ran before, but found her waked;
And thus with words not sad she him received:
610   'Whence thou return'st and whither went'st I know;
For God is also in sleep, and dreams advise,
Which he hath sent propitious, some great good
Presaging, since, with sorrow and heart's distress
Wearied, I fell asleep; but now lead on;
615   In me is no delay; with thee to go
Is to stay here; without thee here to stay
Is to go hence unwilling; thou to me
Art all things under heaven, all places thou,
Who for my wilful crime art banished hence.
620   This further consolation yet secure
I carry hence: though all by me is lost,
Such favour I unworthy am vouchsafed,
By me the promised seed shall all restore.'
       So spake our mother Eve, and Adam heard
625   Well pleased, but answered not; for now too nigh
The archangel stood, and from the other hill
To their fixed station, all in bright array,
The cherubim descended, on the ground
Gliding meteorous, as evening mist
630   Risen from a river o'er the marish glides,
And gathers ground fast at the labourer's heel
Homeward returning. High in front advanced,
The brandished sword of God before them blazed,
Fierce as a comet; which with torrid heat,
635   And vapour as the Libyan air adust,
Began to parch that temperate clime; whereat
In either hand the hastening angel caught
Our lingering parents, and to the eastern gate
Led them direct, and down the cliff as fast
640   To the subjected plain – then disappeared.
They looking back, all the eastern side beheld
Of Paradise, so late their happy seat,
Waved over by that flaming brand; the gate

With dreadful faces thronged and fiery arms;
645 Some natural tears they dropped, but wiped them soon,
The world was all before them, where to choose
Their place of rest, and providence their guide;
They hand in hand with wandering steps and slow,
Through Eden took their solitary way.

630 marish: marsh
640 subjected: situated at a lower level

(XII.552–649)

For many readers this is the most moving passage in western poetry. Particularly moving is that last extended image, so sharply different from the poem's usual recourse to classical and epic imagery, where the descent of the cherubim is compared to mist 'at the labourer's heel / Homeward returning' (XII.631–2). Adam's punishment is to labour at the earth but it's the quiet stress on an ordinary working figure, at the close of the poem, and his returning home, that carries such poignancy in this context.

Adam's understanding that man is capable of 'by small / Accomplishing great things – by things deemed weak / Subverting worldly-strong, and worldly-wise / By simply meek' (XII.566–9) carries crucial political weight. Far from being a post-Restoration statement of despair, it's a recognition of creative political practicalities, a recognition of how progress is achieved. This passage also poignantly looks back to where Adam, defying Raphael, celebrated Eve's 'thousand decencies that daily flow / From all her words and actions' (VIII.601–2). The notion in both cases is that seemingly small graces and small acts accumulate momentously and have irresistible force. The connection between the passages has the effect of underlining yet again the poem's radical insistence on human love.

Even more telling is Michael's following advice: 'only add / Deeds to thy knowledge answerable ... add love, / By name to come called Charity, the soul / Of all the rest: then wilt thou not be loath / To leave this Paradise, but shalt possess / A paradise within thee, happier far' (XII.581–7). Love is called charity in biblical texts. But this poem would rather call it love, for that is what it is for Milton, human 'wedded love', the humanitarian 'soul of all the rest'. And, in great daring, this passage returns us to Satan's bitter spying on Adam and Eve's embraces, seeing in that erotic self-expression 'the happier Eden' (IV.507). Satan was right. It's as if the fall has never happened. Or as if, even if it has, it's now a relative rather than an absolute matter, now that the happier paradise is within. This is where we rejoin Milton the radical pamphleteer. He argued that a proper education system would 'repair the ruins of our first parents' (quoted in Hill, 1975, p. 395), an idea whose radical force looks rather amazing now. One way of assessing the distance between the 1640s and the 1980s may just be to mention a British Conservative Chancellor's assessment that the education system should be geared to preparing large sectors of the population for jobs with no skills, no prospects, or for no jobs at all. Milton, never at a loss for angry words, might still have been speechless with rage at that.

In the poem's final anti-authoritarian gesture, the last spoken word is given to Eve; and the word is 'restore' (XII.623). (None of Shakespeare's thirty-seven plays ends with a woman speaking; only one so begins.) For Milton, as for Winstanley, 'restore' means nothing to do with monarchy; it means the restoration of liberties and the political struggle to secure them.

The poem's penultimate word is 'solitary', the word so crucial in Marvell. But Adam and Eve are also 'hand in hand'.

Christopher Hill's edition of Winstanley's writings is *The Law of Freedom and Other Writings* (Harmondsworth, Penguin, 1973). Hill's *The World Turned Upside Down* (Harmondsworth, Penguin, 1975) is a wonderful guide to radical ideas in the English revolution and it ends with the material on Traherne referred to above. The collection *1642: Literature and Power in the 17th Century* (Colchester, University of Essex Press, 1981), edited by Francis Barker et al., contains essays on Traherne and Winstanley, on the Levellers, and a suggestive piece by Fredric Jameson on *Paradise Lost*. Christopher Hill also wrote significantly on Marvell. His essay 'Society and Andrew Marvell' (1946) is in the Penguin Critical Anthology on Marvell (Harmondsworth, Penguin, 1969): this contains many good essays, notably by both William Empson and Frank Kermode on 'The Garden'. There are some excellent pages on 'Upon Appleton House' in Raymond Williams's classic *The Country and the City* (London, Chatto and Windus, 1973). Annabel Patterson's *Andrew Marvell* (London, Northcote House, 1994) and Jonathan Goldberg's essay on the 'Nymph Complaining' in his *Voice Terminal Echo* (London, Methuen, 1986) are commended above. Gordon Campbell's succinct Marvell selection for Everyman's Poetry (London, Dent, 1997) is this chapter's copy-text. The best way of capturing the revolutionary moment of this period is by seeing Caryl

Churchill's brilliant play *Light Shining in Buckinghamshire* (London, Hern, 1989): the name was originally the title of a Digger pamphlet. Reference is made above to the enclosure movement and the early nineteenth-century poet John Clare. Another modern play, Edward Bond's *The Fool* (London, Eyre Methuen, 1976), is a strong and moving account of Clare's life. A.L. Morton's *A People's History of England* (1938, revised edition, London, Lawrence and Wishart, 1965) is still the best thing of its kind. If you visit Florence try to see Masaccio's fresco painting of Adam and Eve expelled from Eden (about 1425) in the newly restored Brancacci chapel in Santa Maria del Carmine. Take *Paradise Lost* with you to see how radically forward-looking Milton's ending is in comparison.

7

SWIFT'S
GULLIVER'S TRAVELS
Colonialism and Eden lost again

In this chapter we'll be looking at the end of Swift's *Gulliver's Travels* (1726). As in many later chapters problems of endings are considered, here in the light of a recent televised version of the travels. We'll see that Gulliver's departure from Houyhnhnm-land can be read as a loss of Eden, which connects this chapter with the last two, and that Houyhnhnm myths of the Yahoo origins make interesting sense in the context of eighteenth-century colonialism and the slavery-trade.

Here is the end, or most of it, of *Gulliver's Travels*. This is from the fourth and last book, 'A Voyage to the Country of the Houyhnhnms', an island where a race of fabulously rational horses, with the unpronounceable name, live a blameless and guilt-free and apparently Utopian existence, bothered only by the other race on the island, which they have subjugated, the gross and savage but humanoid Yahoos. When Lemuel Gulliver ('first a surgeon, and then a captain of several ships') arrives, after being dumped on the island by his mutinous ship's crew, the horses are presented with the puzzle of what this creature is. He is, they decide, a kind of freak Yahoo, docile and teachable. Gulliver's violent response to this identification, and desire instead to imitate and live for ever in happy contemplation of the Houyhnhnms, despising what he takes to be the Yahoos of our Europe to which he has no wish to return, leads to the uneasy position here, at the beginning of Chapter IX. It's uneasy partly because the Yahoos, who started by shitting on him, have recently been noticed fancying him.

Gulliver has been on the island now for three years. He starts by telling us about one of the grand assemblies held by the Houyhnhnms every four years. Our extract continues uninterrupted to the end of the

123

book's penultimate chapter, which is the end of this voyage. A rather less remarkable, more bookishly eighteenth-century last chapter surveys all four of the travels. But endings are problematic in these travels. The end of Chapter XI is, as you'll see, distinctly disturbing. This ending proved a major stumbling block when a 1996 British film-version was being put together. Its American co-funders, NBC television, insisted on a rewrite of the scriptwriter's original ending, demanding that Gulliver and Mrs Gulliver were shown reconciled in a happily and lovingly re-united ending. The scriptwriter effectively had no choice, as financial success in the USA was considered too important a consideration. You may well consider the end of Chapter XI unmarketable in today's film industry.

Chapter IX

A grand debate at the general assembly of the Houyhnhnms, *and how it was determined. The learning of the* Houyhnhnms. *Their buildings. Their manner of burials. The defectiveness of their language.*

One of these grand assemblies was held in my time, about three months before my departure, whither my master went as the representative of our district. In this council was resumed their old debate, and indeed, the only debate which ever happened in that country; whereof my master after his return gave me a very particular account.

The question to be debated, was, whether the *Yahoos* should be exterminated from the face of the earth. One of the members for the affirmative offered several arguments of great strength and weight, alleging, that as the *Yahoos* were the most filthy, noisome, and deformed animal which nature ever produced, so they were the most restive and indocible, mischievous and malicious: they would privately suck the teats of the *Houyhnhnms'* cows, kill and devour their cats, trample down their oats and grass, if they were not continually watched, and commit a thousand other extravagancies. He took notice of a general tradition, that *Yahoos* had not been always in that country; but, that many ages ago, two of these brutes appeared together upon a mountain; whether produced by the heat of the sun upon corrupted mud and slime, or from the ooze and froth of the sea, was never known. That these *Yahoos* engendered, and their brood in a short time grew so numerous as to over-run and infest the whole nation. That the *Houyhnhnms* to get rid of this evil, made a general hunting, and at last enclosed the whole herd; and destroying the elder, every *Houyhnhnm* kept two young ones in a kennel, and brought them to such a degree of tameness, as an animal so savage by nature can be capable of acquiring; using them for draught and carriage. That there seemed to be much truth in this tradition, and that those creatures could not be *Ylnhniamshy* (or *aborigines* of the land), because of the violent hatred the *Houyhnhnms*, as well as all other animals, bore them; which although their evil disposition sufficiently deserved, could never have arrived at so high a degree, if they had been aborigines, or else they would have long since been rooted out. That the inhabitants taking a fancy to use the service of the *Yahoos*, had very imprudently neglected to cultivate the breed of asses, which were a comely animal, easily kept, more tame and orderly, without any offensive smell, strong enough for labour, although they yield to the other in agility of body; and if their braying be no agreeable sound, it is far preferable to the horrible howlings of the *Yahoos*.

Several others declared their sentiments to the same purpose, when my master proposed an expedient to the assembly, whereof he had indeed borrowed the hint from me. He approved of the tradition mentioned by the honourable member, who spoke before, and affirmed, that the two *Yahoos* said to be first seen among them, had been driven thither over the sea; that coming to land, and being forsaken by their companions, they retired to the mountains, and degenerating by degrees, became in process of time, much more savage than those of their own species in the country from whence these two originals came. The reason of his assertion was, that he had now in his possession a certain wonderful *Yahoo* (meaning myself) which most of them had heard of, and many of them had seen. He then related to them, how he first found me: that my body was all covered with an artificial composure of the skins and hairs of other animals: that I spoke in a language of my own, and had thoroughly learned theirs: that I had related to him the accidents which brought me thither: that when he saw me without my covering, I was an exact *Yahoo* in every part, only of a whiter colour, less hairy, and with shorter claws. He added, how I had endeavoured to persuade him, that in my own and other countries the *Yahoos* acted as the governing, rational animal, and held the *Houyhnhnms* in servitude: that he observed in me all the qualities of a *Yahoo*, only a little more civilized by some tincture of reason, which however was in a degree as far inferior to the *Houyhnhnm* race, as the *Yahoos* of their country were to me: that, among other things, I mentioned a custom we had of castrating *Houyhnhnms* when they were young, in order to render them tame; that the operation was easy and safe; that it was no shame to learn wisdom from brutes, as industry is taught by the ant, and building by the swallow. (For so I translate the word *lyhannh*, although it be a much larger fowl.) That this invention might be practised upon the younger *Yahoos* here, which, besides rendering them tractable and fitter for use, would in an age put an end to the whole species without destroying life. That in the mean time the *Houyhnhnms* should be exhorted to cultivate the breed of asses, which, as they are in all respects more valuable brutes, so they have this advantage, to be fit for service at five years old, which the others are not till twelve.

This was all my master thought fit to tell me at that time, of what passed in the grand council. But he was pleased to conceal one particular, which related personally to myself, whereof I soon felt the unhappy effect, as the reader will know in its proper place, and from whence I date all the succeeding misfortunes of my life.

The *Houyhnhnms* have no letters, and consequently their knowledge is all traditional. But there happening few events of any moment among a people so well united, naturally disposed to every virtue, wholly governed by reason, and cut off from all commerce with other nations, the historical part is easily preserved without burthening their memories. I have already observed, that they are subject to no diseases and therefore can

have no need of physicians. However, they have excellent medicines composed of herbs, to cure accidental bruises and cuts in
the pastern or frog of the foot by sharp stones, as well as other
maims and hurts in the several parts of the body.

They calculate the year by the revolution of the sun and
moon, but use no subdivision into weeks. They are well enough
acquainted with the motions of those two luminaries,
and understand the nature of eclipses; and this is the utmost
progress of their astronomy.

In poetry they must be allowed to excel all other mortals;
wherein the justness of their similes, and the minuteness, as
well as exactness of their descriptions, are indeed inimitable.
Their verses abound very much in both of these, and usually
contain either some exalted notions of friendship and benevolence, or the praises of those who were victors in races, and
other bodily exercises. Their buildings, although very rude and
simple, are not inconvenient, but well contrived to defend
them from all injuries of cold and heat. They have a kind of
tree, which at forty years old loosens in the root, and falls with
the first storm: it grows very straight, and being pointed like
stakes with a sharp stone (for the *Houyhnhnms* know not the use
of iron), they stick them erect in the ground about ten inches
asunder, and then weave in oat-straw, or sometimes wattles
betwixt them. The roof is made after the same manner, and so
are the doors.

The *Houyhnhnms* use the hollow part between the pastern
and the hoof of their fore-feet, as we do our hands, and this
with greater dexterity, than I could at first imagine. I have seen
a white mare of our family thread a needle (which I lent her on
purpose) with the joint. They milk their cows, reap their oats,
and do all the work which requires hands, in the same manner.
They have a kind of hard flints, which by grinding against
other stones, they form into instruments, that serve instead of
wedges, axes, and hammers. With tools made of these flints,
they likewise cut their hay, and reap their oats, which there
groweth naturally in several fields: the *Yahoos* draw home the
sheaves in carriages, and the servants tread them in certain
covered huts, to get out the grain, which is kept in stores. They

make a rude kind of earthen and wooden vessels, and bake the former in the sun.

If they can avoid casualties, they die only of old age, and are buried in the obscurest places that can be found, their friends and relations expressing neither joy nor grief at their departure; nor does the dying person discover the least regret that he is leaving the world, any more than if he were upon returning home from a visit to one of his neighbours. I remember my master having once made an appointment with a friend and his family to come to his house upon some affair of importance, on the day fixed, the mistress and her two children came very late; she made two excuses, first for her husband, who, as she said, happened that very morning to *lhnuwnh*. The word is strongly expressive in their language, but not easily rendered into English; it signifies, *to retire to his first mother*. Her excuse for not coming sooner, was, that her husband dying late in the morning, she was a good while consulting her servants about a convenient place where his body should be laid; and I observed she behaved herself at our house as cheerfully as the rest. She died about three months after.

They live generally to seventy or seventy-five years, very seldom to fourscore: some weeks before their death they feel a gradual decay, but without pain. During this time they are much visited by their friends, because they cannot go abroad with their usual ease and satisfaction. However, about ten days before their death, which they seldom fail in computing, they return the visits that have been made them by those who are nearest in the neighbourhood, being carried in a convenient sledge drawn by *Yahoos;* which vehicle they use, not only upon this occasion, but when they grow old, upon long journeys, or when they are lamed by any accident. And therefore when the dying *Houyhnhnms* return those visits, they take a solemn leave of their friends, as if they were going to some remote part of the country, where they designed to pass the rest of their lives.

I know not whether it may be worth observing, that the *Houyhnhnms* have no word in their language to express any thing that is evil, except what they borrow from the deformities or ill qualities of the *Yahoos*. Thus they denote the folly of a servant, an omission of a child, a stone that cuts their feet, a continuance of foul or unspeakable weather, and the like, by adding to each the epithet of *Yahoo*. For instance, *Hhnm Yahoo, Whnaholm Yahoo, Ynlhmnawihlma Yahoo*, and an ill-contrived house *Ynholmhnmrohlnw Yahoo*.

I could with great pleasure enlarge further upon the manners and virtues of this excellent people; but intending in a short time to publish a volume by itself expressly upon that subject, I refer the reader thither. And in the mean time, proceed to relate my own sad catastrophe.

Chapter X

The Author's economy, and happy life among the Houyhnhnms. *His great improvement in virtue, by conversing with them. Their conversations. The Author has notice given him by his master that he must depart from the country. He falls into a swoon for grief, but submits. He contrives and finishes a canoe, by the help of a fellow-servant, and puts to sea at a venture.*

I had settled my little economy to my own heart's content. My master had ordered a room to be made for me after their manner, about six yards from the house; the sides and floors of which I plastered with clay, and covered with rush-mats of my own contriving; I had beaten hemp, which there grows wild, and made of it a sort of ticking: this I filled with the feathers of several birds I had taken with springes made of *Yahoos'* hairs, and were excellent food. I had worked two chairs with my knife, the sorrel nag helping me in the grosser and more laborious part. When my clothes were worn to rags, I made myself others with the skins of rabbits, and of a certain beautiful animal about the same size, called *nnuhnoh*, the skin of which is covered with a fine down. Of these I likewise made very tolerable stockings. I soled my shoes with wood which I cut from a tree, and fitted to the upper leather, and when this was worn out, I supplied it with the skins of *Yahoos* dried in the sun. I often got honey out of hollow trees, which I mingled with water, or ate it with my bread. No man could more verify the truth of these two maxims, *That nature is very easily satisfied;* and

That necessity is the mother of invention. I enjoyed perfect health of body, and tranquillity of mind; I did not feel the treachery or inconstancy of a friend, nor the injuries of a secret or open enemy. I had no occasion of bribing, flattering or pimping, to procure the favour of any great man or of his minion. I wanted no fence against fraud or oppression; here was neither physician to destroy my body, nor lawyer to ruin my fortune; no informer to watch my words and actions, or forge accusations against me for hire: here were no gibers, censurers, backbiters, pick-pockets, highwaymen, housebreakers, attorneys, bawds, buf-foons, gamesters, politicians, wits, splenetics, tedious talkers, controvertists, ravishers, murderers, robbers, virtuosos; no leaders or followers of party and faction; no encouragers to vice, by seducement or examples; no dungeon, axes, gibbets, whipping-posts, or pillories; no cheating shopkeepers or mech-anics; no pride, vanity, or affection; no fops, bullies, drunkards, strolling whores, or poxes; no ranting, lewd, expensive wives; no stupid, proud pedants; no importunate, overbearing, quarrelsome, noisy, roaring, empty, conceited, swearing companions; no scoundrels, raised from the dust for the sake of their vices, or nobility thrown into it on account of their virtues; no lords, fiddlers, judges, or dancing-masters.

I had the favour of being admitted to several *Houyhnhnms*, who came to visit or dine with my master; where his Honour graciously suffered me to wait in the room, and listen to their discourse. Both he and his company would often descend to ask me questions, and receive my answers. I had also sometimes the honour of attending my master in his visits to others. I never presumed to speak, except in answer to a question; and then I did it with inward regret, because it was a loss of so much time for improving myself: but I was infinitely delighted with the station of an humble auditor in such conversations, where nothing passed but what was useful, expressed in the fewest and most significant words; where (as I have already said) the greatest decency was observed, without the least degree of ceremony; where no person spoke without being pleased him-self, and pleasing his companions; where there was no interrup-tion, tediousness, heat, or difference of sentiments. They have a notion, that when people are met together, a short silence doth much improve conversation: this I found to be true; for during those little intermissions of talk, new ideas would arise in their thoughts, which very much enlivened the discourse. Their subjects are generally on friendship and benevolence, or order and economy; sometimes upon the visible operations of nature, or ancient traditions; upon the bounds and limits of virtue; upon the unerring rules of reason, or upon some determinations to be taken at the next great assembly; and often upon the various excellencies of poetry. I may add, without vanity, that my presence often gave them sufficient matter for discourse, because it afforded my master an occasion of letting his friends into the history of me and my country, upon which they were all pleased to descant in a manner not very advantageous to human kind; and for that reason I shall not repeat what they said: only I may be allowed to observe, that his Honour, to my great admiration, appeared to understand the nature of *Yahoos* much better than myself. He went through all our vices and follies, and discovered many which I had never mentioned to him, by only supposing what qualities a *Yahoo* of their country, with a small proportion of reason, might be capable of exerting; and concluded, with too much probability, how vile as well as miserable such a creature must be.

I freely confess, that all the little knowledge I have of any value, was acquired by the lectures I received from my master, and from hearing the discourses of him and his friends; to which I should be prouder to listen, than to dictate to the greatest and wisest assembly in Europe. I admired the strength, comeliness, and speed of the inhabitants; and such a constellation of virtues in such amiable persons produced in me the highest veneration. At first, indeed, I did not feel that natural awe which the *Yahoos* and all other animals bear towards them; but it grew upon me by degrees, much sooner than I imagined, and was mingled with a respectful love and gratitude, that they would condescend to distinguish me from the rest of my species.

When I thought of my family, my friends, my countrymen, or human race in general, I considered them as they really were,

Yahoos in shape and disposition; perhaps a little more civilized, and qualified with the gift of speech, but making no other use of reason, than to improve and multiply those vices, whereof their brethren in this country had only the share that nature allotted them. When I happened to behold the reflection of my own form in a lake or fountain, I turned away my face in horror and detestation of myself, and could better endure the sight of a common *Yahoo*, than of my own person. By conversing with the *Houyhnhnms*, and looking upon them with delight, I fell to imitate their gait and gesture, which is now grown into a habit, and my friends often tell me in a blunt way, that *I trot like a horse;* which, however, I take for a great compliment. Neither shall I disown, that in speaking I am apt to fall into the voice and manner of the *Houyhnhnms*, and hear myself ridiculed on that account without the least mortification.

In the midst of all this happiness, and when I looked upon myself to be fully settled for life, my master sent for me one morning a little earlier than his usual hour. I observed by his countenance that he was in some perplexity, and at a loss how to begin what he had to speak. After a short silence, he told me, he did not know how I would take what he was going to say; that in the last general assembly, when the affair of the *Yahoos* was entered upon, the representatives had taken offence at his keeping a *Yahoo* (meaning myself) in his family more like a *Houyhnhnm* than a brute animal. That he was known frequently to converse with me, as if he could receive some advantage or pleasure in my company; that such a practice was not agreeable to reason or nature, or a thing ever heard of before among them. The assembly did therefore exhort him, either to employ me like the rest of my species, or command me to swim back to the place from whence I came. That the first of these expedients was utterly rejected by all the *Houyhnhnms* who had ever seen me at his house or their own: for they alleged, that because I had some rudiments of reason, added to the natural pravity of those animals, it was to be feared, I might be able to seduce them into the woody and mountainous parts of the country, and bring them in troops by night to destroy the *Houyhnhnms'* cattle, as being naturally of the ravenous kind, and averse from labour.

My master added, that he was daily pressed by the *Houyhn-hnms* of the neighbourhood to have the assembly's exhortation executed, which he could not put off much longer. He doubted it would be impossible for me to swim to another country, and therefore wished I would contrive some sort of vehicle resembling those I had described to him, that might carry me on the sea; in which work I should have the assistance of his own servants, as well as those of his neighbours. He concluded, that for his own part, he could have been content to keep me in his service as long as I lived; because he found I had cured myself of some bad habits and dispositions, by endeavouring, as far as my inferior nature was capable, to imitate the *Houyhnhnms*.

I should here observe to the reader, that a decree of the general assembly in this country is expressed by the word *hnh-loayn*, which signifies an exhortation, as near as I can render it; for they have no conception how a rational creature can be compelled, but only advised, or exhorted; because no person can disobey reason, without giving up his claim to be a rational creature.

I was struck with the utmost grief and despair at my master's discourse; and being unable to support the agonies I was under, I fell into a swoon at his feet; when I came to myself, he told me, that he concluded I had been dead (for these people are subject to no such imbecilities of nature). I answered, in a faint voice, that death would have been too great an happiness; that although I could not blame the assembly's exhortation, or the urgency of his friends; yet, in my weak and corrupt judgment, I thought it might consist with reason to have been less rigorous. That I could not swim a league, and probably the nearest land to theirs might be distant above an hundred: that many materials, necessary for making a small vessel to carry me off, were wholly wanting in this country, which, however, I would attempt in obedience and gratitude to his Honour, although I concluded the thing to be impossible, and therefore looked on myself as already devoted to destruction. That the certain prospect of an unnatural death was the least of my evils: for, supposing I should escape with life by some strange adventure, how could I think with temper, of passing my days among *Yahoos*, and relapsing into my old corruptions, for want of examples to lead and keep me within the paths of virtue? That I knew too well upon what solid reasons all the determinations of the wise *Houyhnhnms* were founded, not to be shaken by arguments of mine, a miserable *Yahoo*; and therefore, after presenting him with my humble thanks for the offer of his servants' assistance in making a vessel, and desiring a reasonable time for so difficult a work, I told him I would endeavour to preserve a wretched being; and, if ever returned to England, was not without hopes of being useful to my own species, by celebrating the praises of the renowned *Houyhnhnms*, and proposing their virtues to the imitation of mankind.

My master in a few words made me a very gracious reply, allowed me the space of two months to finish my boat; and ordered the sorrel nag, my fellow-servant (for so at this distance I may presume to call him) to follow my instructions, because I told my master, that his help would be sufficient, and I knew he had a tenderness for me.

In his company my first business was to go to that part of the coast where my rebellious crew had ordered me to be set on shore. I got upon a height, and looking on every side into the sea, fancied I saw a small island, towards the north-east: I took out my pocket-glass, and could then clearly distinguish it about five leagues off, as I computed; but it appeared to the sorrel nag to be only a blue cloud: for, as he had no conception of any country beside his own, so he could not be as expert in distinguishing remote objects at sea, as we who so much converse in that element.

After I had discovered this island, I considered no farther; but resolved it should, if possible, be the first place of my banishment, leaving the consequence to fortune.

I returned home, and consulting with the sorrel nag, we went into a copse at some distance, where I with my knife, and he with a sharp flint fastened very artificially, after their manner, to a wooden handle, cut down several oak wattles about the thickness of a walking-staff, and some larger pieces. But I shall not trouble the reader with a particular description of my own mechanics; let it suffice to say, that in six weeks time, with the help of the sorrel nag, who performed the parts that required most labour, I finished a sort of Indian canoe, but much larger, covering it with the skins of *Yahoos* well stitched together, with hempen threads of my own making. My sail was likewise composed of the skins of the same animal; but I made use of the youngest I could get, the older being too tough and thick; and I likewise provided myself with four paddles. I laid in a stock of boiled flesh, of rabbits and fowls, and took with me two vessels, one filled with milk, and the other with water.

I tried my canoe in a large pond near my master's house, and then corrected in it what was amiss; stopping all the chinks with *Yahoos'* tallow, till I found it staunch, and able to bear me, and my freight. And when it was as complete as I could possibly make it, I had it drawn on a carriage very gently by *Yahoos* to the sea-side, under the conduct of the sorrel nag, and another servant.

When all was ready, and the day came for my departure, I took leave of my master and lady, and the whole family, my eyes flowing with tears, and my heart quite sunk with grief. But his Honour, out of curiosity, and, perhaps (if I may speak it without vanity) partly out of kindness, was determined to see me in my canoe, and got several of his neighbouring friends to accompany him. I was forced to wait above an hour for the tide, and then observing the wind very fortunately bearing towards the island, to which I intended to steer my course, I took a second leave of my master: but as I was going to prostrate myself to kiss his hoof, he did me the honour to raise it gently to my mouth. I am not ignorant how much I have been censured for mentioning this last particular. For my detractors are pleased to think it improbable, that so illustrious a person should descend to give so great a mark of distinction to a creature so inferior as I. Neither have I forgot, how apt some travellers are to boast of extraordinary favours they have received. But if these censurers were better acquainted with the noble and courteous disposition of the *Houyhnhnms*, they would soon change their opinion.

I paid my respects to the rest of the *Houyhnhnms* in his Honour's company; then getting into my canoe, I pushed off from shore.

Chapter XI

The Author's dangerous voyage. He arrives at New Holland, *hoping to settle there. Is wounded with an arrow by one of the natives. Is seized and carried by force into a* Portuguese *ship. The great civilities of the Captain. The Author arrives at* England.

I began this desperate voyage on February 15, 1714–15, at 9 o'clock in the morning. The wind was very favourable; however, I made use at first only of my paddles; but considering I should soon be weary, and that the wind might chop about, I ventured to set up my little sail; and thus, with the help of the tide, I went at the rate of a league and a half an hour, as near as I could guess. My master and his friends continued on the shore, till I was almost out of sight; and I often heard the sorrel nag (who always loved me) crying out, *Hnuy illa nyha majah Yahoo*, Take care of thyself, gentle *Yahoo*.

My design was, if possible, to discover some small island uninhabited, yet sufficient by my labour to furnish me with the necessaries of life, which I would have thought a greater happiness than to be first minister in the politest court of Europe; so horrible was the idea I conceived of returning to live in the society and under the government of *Yahoos*. For in such a solitude as I desired, I could at least enjoy my own thoughts, and reflect with delight on the virtues of those inimitable *Houyhnhnms*, without any opportunity of degenerating into the vices and corruptions of my own species.

The reader may remember what I related when my crew conspired against me, and confined me to my cabin. How I continued there several weeks, without knowing what course we took; and when I was put ashore in the long-boat, how the sailors told me with oaths, whether true or false, that they knew not in what part of the world we were. However, I did then believe us to be about ten degrees southward of the Cape of Good Hope, or about 45 degrees southern latitude, as I gathered from some general words I overheard among them, being I supposed to the southeast in their intended voyage to Madagascar. And although this were little better than conjecture, yet I resolved to steer my course eastward, hoping to reach the south-west coast of New Holland, and perhaps some such island as I desired, lying westward of it. The wind was full west, and by six in the evening I computed I had gone eastward at least eighteen leagues, when I spied a very small island about half a league off, which I soon reached. It was nothing but a rock with one creek, naturally arched by the force of tempests. Here I put in my canoe, and climbing up a part of the rock, I could plainly discover land to the east, extending from south to north. I lay all night in my canoe; and repeating my voyage early in the morning, I arrived in seven hours to the south-east point of New Holland. This confirmed me in the opinion I have long entertained, that the maps and charts place this country at least three degrees more to the east than it really is; which thought I communicated many years ago to my worthy friend Mr. Herman Moll, and gave him my reasons for it, although he hath rather chosen to follow other authors.

I saw no inhabitants in the place where I landed, and being unarmed, I was afraid of venturing far into the country. I found some shellfish on the shore, and ate them raw, not daring to kindle a fire, for fear of being discovered by the natives. I continued three days feeding on oysters and limpets, to save my own provisions; and I fortunately found a brook of excellent water, which gave me great relief.

On the fourth day, venturing out early a little too far, I saw twenty or thirty natives upon a height, not above five hundred yards from me. They were stark naked, men, women, and children round a fire, as I could discover by the smoke. One of them spied me, and gave notice to the rest; five of them advanced towards me, leaving the women and children at the fire. I made what haste I could to the shore, and getting into my canoe, shoved off: the savages observing me retreat, ran after me; and before I could get far enough into the sea, discharged an arrow, which wounded me deeply on the inside of my left knee (I shall carry the mark to my grave). I apprehended the arrow might be poisoned, and paddling out of the reach of their darts (being a calm day), I made a shift to suck the wound, and dress it as well as I could.

I was at a loss what to do, for I durst not return to the same landing-place, but stood to the north, and was forced to paddle; for the wind, though very gentle, was against me, blowing north-west. As I was looking about for a secure landing-place, I saw a sail to the north-north-east, which appearing every minute more visible, I was in some doubt whether I should wait for them or no; but at last my detestation of the *Yahoo* race prevailed, and turning my canoe, I sailed and paddled together to the south, and got into the same creek from whence I set out in the morning, choosing rather to trust myself among these barbarians, than live with European *Yahoos*. I drew up my canoe as close as I could to the shore, and hid myself behind a stone by the little brook, which, as I have already said, was excellent water.

The ship came within half a league of this creek, and sent her long-boat with vessels to take in fresh water (for the place it seems was very well known), but I did not observe it till the boat was almost on shore, and it was too late to seek another hiding-place. The seamen at their landing observed my canoe, and rummaging it all over, easily conjectured that the owner could not be far off. Four of them well armed searched every cranny and lurking-hole, till at last they found me flat on my face behind the stone. They gazed awhile in admiration at my strange uncouth dress; my coat made of skins, my wooden-soled shoes, and my furred stockings; from whence, however, they concluded I was not a native of the place, who all go naked. One of the seamen in Portuguese bid me rise, and asked who I was. I understood that language very well, and getting upon my feet, said, I was a poor *Yahoo*, banished from the *Houyhnhnms*, and desired they would please to let me depart. They admired to hear me answer them in their own tongue, and saw by my complexion I must be an European; but were at a loss to know what I meant by *Yahoos* and *Houyhnhnms*, and at the same time fell a laughing at my strange tone in speaking, which resembled the neighing of a horse. I trembled all the while betwixt fear and hatred: I again desired leave to depart, and was gently moving to my canoe; but they laid hold of me, desiring to know, what country I was of? whence I came? with many other questions. I told them, I was born in England, from whence I came about five years ago, and then their country and ours were at peace. I therefore hoped they would not treat me as an enemy, since I meant them no harm, but was a poor *Yahoo*, seeking some desolate place where to pass the remainder of his unfortunate life.

When they began to talk, I thought I never heard or saw any thing so unnatural; for it appeared to me as monstrous as if a dog or a cow should speak in England, or a *Yahoo* in *Houyhnhnm-land*. The honest Portuguese were equally amazed at my strange dress, and the odd manner of delivering my words, which however they understood very well. They spoke to me with great humanity, and said they were sure their Captain would carry me *gratis* to Lisbon, from whence I might return to my own country; that two of the seamen would go back to the ship, inform the Captain of what they had seen, and receive his orders; in the mean time, unless I would give my solemn oath not to fly, they would secure me by force. I thought it best to comply with their proposal. They were very curious to know my story, but I gave them very little satisfaction; and they all conjectured, that my misfortunes had impaired my reason. In two hours the boat, which went loaden with vessels of water, returned with the Captain's command to fetch me on board. I fell on my knees to preserve my liberty; but all was in vain, and the men having tied me with cords, heaved me into the boat, from whence I was taken into the ship, and from thence into the Captain's cabin.

His name was Pedro de Mendez; he was a very courteous and generous person; he entreated me to give some account of myself, and desired to know what I would eat or drink; said, I should be used as well as himself, and spoke so many obliging things, that I wondered to find such civilities from a *Yahoo*. However, I remained silent and sullen; I was ready to faint at the very smell of him and his men. At last I desired something to eat out of my own canoe; but he ordered me a chicken and some excellent wine, and then directed that I should be put to bed in a very clean cabin. I would not undress myself, but lay on the bed-clothes, and in half an hour stole out, when I thought the crew was at dinner, and getting to the side of the ship was going to leap into the sea, and swim for my life, rather than continue among *Yahoos*. But one of the seamen prevented me, and having informed the Captain, I was chained to my cabin.

After dinner Don Pedro came to me, and desired to know my reason for so desperate an attempt; assured me he only meant to do me all the service he was able; and spoke so very movingly, that at last I descended to treat him like an animal which had some little portion of reason. I gave him a very short relation of my voyage; of the conspiracy against me by my own men; of the country where they set me on shore, and of my three years residence there. All which he looked upon as if it were a dream or a vision; whereat I took great offence; for I had quite forgot the faculty of lying, so peculiar to *Yahoos* in all countries where they preside, and, consequently the disposition of suspecting truth in others of their own species. I asked him, whether it were the custom in his country to *say the thing that was not?* I assured him I had almost forgot what he meant by falsehood, and if I had lived a thousand years in *Houyhnhnm-land*, I should never have heard a lie from the meanest servant; that I was altogether indifferent whether he believed me or no; but however, in return for his favours, I would give so much allowance to the corruption of his nature, as to answer any objection he would please to make, and then he might easily discover the truth.

The Captain, a wise man, after many endeavours to catch me tripping in some part of my story, at last began to have a better opinion of my veracity. But he added, that since I professed so inviolable an attachment to truth, I must give him my word of honour to bear him company in this voyage, without attempting any thing against my life, or else he would continue me a prisoner till we arrived at Lisbon. I gave him the promise he required; but at the same time protested that I would suffer the greatest hardships rather than return to live among *Yahoos.*

Our voyage passed without any considerable accident. In gratitude to the Captain I sometimes sat with him at his earnest request, and strove to conceal my antipathy to human kind, although it often broke out, which he suffered to pass without observation. But the greatest part of the day, I confined myself to my cabin, to avoid seeing any of the crew. The Captain had often entreated me to strip myself of my savage dress, and offered to lend me the best suit of clothes he had. This I would not be prevailed on to accept, abhorring to cover myself with any thing that had been on the back of a *Yahoo.* I only desired he would lend me two clean shirts, which having been washed since he wore them, I believed would not so much defile me. These I changed every second day, and washed them myself.

We arrived at Lisbon, Nov. 5, 1715. At our landing the Captain forced me to cover myself with his cloak, to prevent the rabble from crowding about me. I was conveyed to his own house, and at my earnest request, he led me up to the highest room backwards. I conjured him to conceal from all persons what I had told him of the *Houyhnhnms,* because the least hint of such a story would not only draw numbers of people to see me, but probably put me in danger of being imprisoned, or burnt by the Inquisition. The Captain persuaded me to accept a suit of clothes newly made; but I would not suffer the tailor to take my measure; however, Don Pedro being almost of my size, they fitted me well enough. He accoutred me with other necessaries all new, which I aired for twenty-four hours before I would use them.

The Captain had no wife, nor above three servants, none of which were suffered to attend at meals, and his whole deportment was so obliging, added to very good *human* understanding, that I really began to tolerate his company. He gained so far upon me, that I ventured to look out of the back window. By degrees I was brought into another room, from whence I peeped into the street, but drew my head back in a fright. In a week's time he seduced me down to the door. I found my terror gradually lessened, but my hatred and contempt seemed to increase. I was at last bold enough to walk the street in his company, but kept my nose well stopped with rue, or sometimes with tobacco.

In ten days, Don Pedro, to whom I had given some account of my domestic affairs, put it upon me as a matter of honour and conscience, that I ought to return to my native country, and live at home with my wife and children. He told me, there was an English ship in the port just ready to sail, and he would furnish me with all things necessary. It would be tedious to repeat his arguments, and my contradictions. He said it was altogether impossible to find such a solitary island as I desired to live in; but I might command in my own house, and pass my time in a manner as recluse as I pleased.

I complied at last, finding I could not do better. I left Lisbon the 24th day of November, in an English merchant-man, but who was the master I never inquired. Don Pedro accompanied me to the ship, and lent me twenty pounds. He took kind leave of me, and embraced me at parting, which I bore as well as I could. During this last voyage I had no commerce with the master or any of his men; but pretending I was sick, kept close in my cabin. On the fifth of December, 1715, we cast anchor in the Downs about nine in the morning, and at three in the afternoon I got safe to my house at Rotherhith.

My wife and family received me with great surprise and joy, because they concluded me certainly dead; but I must freely confess the sight of them filled me only with hatred, disgust, and contempt, and the more by reflecting on the near alliance I had to them. For, although since my unfortunate exile from the *Houyhnhnm* country, I had compelled myself to tolerate the sight of *Yahoos*, and to converse with Don Pedro de Mendez; yet my memory and imagination were perpetually filled with the virtues and ideas of those exalted *Houyhnhnms*. And when I began to consider, that by copulating with one of the *Yahoo* species I had become a parent of more, it struck me with the utmost shame, confusion, and horror.

As soon as I entered the house, my wife took me in her arms, and kissed me; at which, having not been used to the touch of that odious animal for so many years, I fell in a swoon for almost an hour. At the time I am writing it is five years since my last return to England: during the first year, I could not endure my wife or children in my presence, the very smell of them was intolerable; much less could I suffer them to eat in the same room. To this hour they dare not presume to touch my bread, or drink out of the same cup, neither was I ever able to let one of them take me by the hand. The first money I laid out was to buy two young stone-horses, which I keep in a good stable, and next to them the groom is my greatest favourite; for I feel my spirits revived by the smell he contracts in the stable. My horses understand me tolerably well; I converse with them at least four hours every day. They are strangers to bridle or saddle; they live in great amity with me, and friendship to each other.

It's often said that Gulliver has gone mad, and that must be true, in a sense. But is the voice we've just heard the voice of a madman? The eerie simplicity of it, the calmness and control of the simple language in which the sheer awfulness of isolation and loneliness is conveyed, seems too aware of its bleakness to be mad. It's as if Gulliver knows the absurdity of his situation but has moved beyond absurdity to this strange state of blank and unelaborated statement of the facts as they stand, such as his calm awareness of the fact that Pedro de Mendez was 'very courteous and generous'. The last two sentences of the book are, in content, 'mad' but in their calm colourlessness, as if voice has been drained of all movement and energy, 'mad' doesn't seem the word at all. 'My horses understand me tolerably well; I converse with them at least four hours every day. They are strangers to bridle or saddle; they live in great amity with me, and friendship to each other.' Something in that, but I'm not sure what (those gravely placed semi-colons?), sounds sane.

One of the many hotly debated problems about Book Four is how to disentangle the points of view of Gulliver and Swift. (Who speaks the amazing paragraph listing all the categories of people Gulliver is pleased to miss in Houyhnhnm-land?) What I find most eerie in Chapter XI is the way the problem of Swift's presentation of Gulliver seems to disappear, the way Gulliver's 'character' here seems to have mutated into something much more unsettling. He seems to have become a figure of suddenly awkward pathos. This seems quite different from the roles he inhabited earlier, from the sensible if limited observer and reporter to the comically self-satisfied and self-ignorant figure whom we've heard earlier – and hear again in the following and final chapter, where, as I say, something seems rather irritatingly ordinary after the end of Chapter XI. The 'character' of Gulliver in Chapter XI is, if I can put it this way, something which the text itself in the sheer grip of Swift's visionary logic or illogic has, as if in overdrive, developed. Gulliver becomes here, in a radical sense, genuinely representative man, a kind of anti-socialised essential Man. He is man lost in his isolation. For that's what Gulliver is, a man of essential loss. His paradise is lost. He had it. It was 'my little economy to my own heart's content'. By 'economy' he means the complete management of his life.

This way of reading the ending of *Gulliver's Travels* has received less attention than others but the experience Gulliver undergoes when he leaves Houyhnhnm-land, and the subsequent trauma, is a loss of Eden, an expulsion from the garden, however we read the garden itself, as Utopia-Paradise or as totalitarian, even proto-fascist state. Or, as I think I do, as both. (Earlier we hear that in marriage the horses 'are exactly careful to choose such colours as will not make any disagree-able mixture in the breed' and we've noticed them casually debating wholesale extermination.) For Gulliver, the experience feels like an expulsion. I think it may be the purest thing of its kind, outside Milton. You may also be reminded, as I often am when reading of Gulliver's expulsion, of the sharp loss that a child feels when first expelled from his mother's bed or, in some other way, first sent away from the nest. Gulliver, after all, is treated like an indulged child and seems happy to be so. Perhaps the power of Book Four is something to do with regression to childhood – and the subsequent expulsion from it.

To think of Gulliver as an Adam expelled from Eden seems even more appropriate in the light of what we hear at the beginning of our extract, where Gulliver reports two Houyhnhnm versions of the origin of the Yahoos. The first version is that 'two of these brutes' appeared sud-denly, 'whether produced by the heat of the sun upon corrupted mud and slime, or from the ooze and froth of the sea'. The second, for which Gulliver's history unwittingly supplies evidence, is that the first couple came from overseas and 'degenerating by degrees' became savage. In both cases these are myths of origin that deny aboriginal status to the

Yahoo couple. That is, they lend logic to the Houyhnhnms' arguments for expelling Gulliver. It's as if he has to be either an Adam as biological mistake or an Adam as foreigner in the wrong garden.

But in neither case need the Houynhnms be right. Both versions may be no more than convenient fictions. These horses can't apparently 'say the thing that is not', but they do appeal to 'general tradition'. General tradition is often convenient fiction. Indeed, the reader can even go down the dizzying route of seeing the whole edifice of Houyhnhnm theory and practice as self-serving fiction. At two points in our extract I think this more or less happens. In the first, we learn that Houyhnhnm friends and relations express 'neither joy nor grief' when one of their number dies. This sounds fine, in a Utopian sort of way, and the notion that death is the return to the 'first mother' is touchingly Edenic. We then hear about a horse bereaved that day behaving 'as cheerfully as the rest' on an evening visit. At this point Gulliver, presumably unaware of what he's suggesting, adds: 'she died about three months after'. And what, as we know, does one partner so soon die of, after the death of the other? Of grief. Er, right.

And the other is this. In preparation for Gulliver's departure we hear that he uses Yahoo skins and tallow in the making of his canoe. It's specified that the sail is made from the skins of 'the youngest I could get'. Gulliver is typically unaware of the suggestion of infanticide but readers might well be reminded of Swift's notorious *Modest Proposal*, three years later (1729), in which a mad proposer proposes the eating of Irish babies to ease the crisis in that country. (Both texts were anonymously published.) But the sharpest sting here is to follow, just half a dozen lines later. Yahoos draw the completed canoe, made with the bodies of their youngest, on a carriage to the seaside. And they draw it 'very gently'. Oh right, so they are, or at least can be, gentle, after all. This amounts to the book pretty comprehensively deconstructing itself, to use an overused term. And in case we missed that crucial word, within moments, at the beginning of the next chapter, Gulliver tells how the sorrel nag, a servant (not the pure breed, therefore capable of love), calls after him as he disappears to the seas 'take care of thyself, gentle Yahoo'.

Let's return to the two Houyhnhnm versions of the origin of Yahoos. In both stories we can hear the arguments of the European colonial invaders justifying their policy of violence and land-seizure from aboriginal inhabitants, labelled inherently corrupt or gradually degenerated, whichever fits more with political usefulness. The argument that Yahoos can't be aboriginal because of the 'violent hatred' the horses feel for them looks particularly dubious. Violent hatred may easily be political antagonism naturalised. Perhaps Swift was remembering Caliban in *The Tempest*. But that Swift was intervening in a debate about colonialism and slavery seems even more likely when we move sideways again to something else in this extract, in yet another pattern of difference and sameness with yet further dizzying effect.

This is the brief passage about yet another inhabited land. Gulliver escapes to it and is eventually forcibly removed, again, from it. It's inhabited by humans, 'stark naked, men, women, and children round a fire, as I could discover by the smoke'. So, in miniature, here's another tale of adventure and here we are again, seeing ourselves, this time another version of ourselves at the start of civilisation, as represented by the fire. They're not Yahoos. And, significantly, they're not colonised. The Portuguese use the place, which they know 'very well', for water but leave the inhabitants alone, naked and unprovoked. This must provoke parallels with Houyhnhnm-land. On the other hand, in yet another move calculated to cut the ground from beneath the reader's feet, these naked and simple people attack Gulliver when they see him. So it's another rejection and expulsion. But perhaps they thought Gulliver had come to colonise them.

Swift is notoriously difficult to categorise and place. But Edward Said is surely right to insist that Swift was principally a re-active intellectual, oppositional in temperament and in politics. Efforts to turn him into what Said nicely describes as a 'pipesmoking armchair philosopher' (Said, 1983, p. 77) damagingly misrepresent his characteristic stance as 'perhaps the most worldly' of writers, with each and every work a work of intervention, a performative act of '*writing* in a world of power' (ibid., pp. 87–8).

And Said is right to identify Swift's most persistent target as 'human aggression' and 'organised human violence'. Swift was robust in his horror of war, of 'colonial oppression, religious factionalism' and 'the victimisation of the poor' (ibid., p. 84). Swift's furious anger on behalf of the Irish poor was driven by direct experience of colonial oppression in that country. In a finely bitter reflection on warfare, and international law, earlier in this journey Swift makes Gulliver claim that 'if a prince send forces into a nation where the people are poor and ignorant, he may lawfully put half of them to death, and make slaves of the rest, in order to civilize and reduce them from their barbarous way of living'. We might remember that the wars that were fought prior to the composition of these travels were colonial wars to the extent that they were about protecting or extending colonial control. As one result, Britain from 1710 onwards secured the monopoly of supplying the Spanish colonies with African slaves. In the period between 1690 and 1807 the British transported some 2.8 million slaves, an average of some 25,000 slaves every year, with appalling numbers, typically 20 per cent, dying during the voyage. The savages' response to Gulliver is understandable enough.

But turn to that last little bit of the text yet again and something else rich and strange emerges. The savages wound Gulliver with an arrow which 'wounded me deeply on the inside of my left knee (I shall carry the mark to my grave)'. For readers, like Swift's, attuned to classical mythology this bizarrely turns Gulliver into Chiron, the wisest of centaurs, half-man and half-horse, accidentally wounded in his knee, from which wound he pleaded with the gods for early death. Readers attuned to the classics have often seen in Houyhnhnm society and culture echoes of the lives idealised in Homer and in Spartan civilisation. Like Lemuel Gulliver, Chiron the centaur was a healer. And Gulliver, a man who would rather be a horse, in effect wants out of it all at the end, as we've seen.

This seems to have got us to a position in which I feel I don't know where we are. I have a feeling that that's exactly where Swift wanted us to be.

Using the contexts of Eden-loss and colonialism, and the connections between them, can only be a very partial response to Swift's habit of 'vexing' the reader, cutting the ground from beneath our feet. But Eden-loss, as seen in the last two chapters, is a crucial narrative in western culture, one which helped structure our sense of ourselves. It is suggestive that Swift's friend, the poet Alexander Pope, turned to another crucial narrative-myth, the end of the world apocalypse, at the end of his satire *The Dunciad* (1743), which is worth exploring in relation to *Gulliver*. Brian Tippett's guide to *Gulliver's Travels* (London, Macmillan, 1989) is one of the best in the 'Critics Debate' series. Two volumes were put together for the 1996 film: *Gulliver and Beyond*, edited by Paul Barker (London, Channel 4 Television, 1996), brings together contemporary reflections on the social targets of Swift's satire; and a shortened and annotated edition of the travels, made for school work (London, English and Media Centre, 1997), has an account of the changes imposed on the ending of the televised film. Edward Said's essays on Swift are in his ground-breaking *The World, the Text and the Critic* (Cambridge, Mass., Harvard University Press, 1983). The slave-trade was, in Swift's day, beginning to attract organised opposition, key early figures being Pope and the philosopher John Locke. Duncan Clarke's *Slaves and Slavery* (London, Grange Books, 1998) is a clear survey. Robin Blackburn's *The Making of New World Slavery* (London, Verso, 1997) is authoritative. John Updike's *The Centaur* (London, Andre Deutsch, 1963) is a fine novel, exploring the story of Chiron in a contemporary American setting.

8

JOHNSON AND OTHERS
Toryism, the slave-trade, poverty, being and reading a character

Here the text is a series of short extracts from the third and last quarter of the eighteenth century, dispersed through a more discursive commentary which invites you to consider London at the time, with its prevailing attitudes towards poverty and the slave-trade, with its colourful literary 'characters' and its evolving interest in characterisation itself.

This chapter starts by inviting you to meet the inhabitants of 8, Bolt Court, just off Fleet Street in London, in about 1777. But the chances of getting them all together and sitting quietly enough to be met properly would have been slim as they were usually quarrelling. The historian Macaulay called them a 'menagerie'.

Anyway, we'll have a go. Anna Williams, hostess and general provider to the household, elderly and blind but still adept at pouring tea without spillage. Robert Levet or Levett, unqualified doctor servicing the London poor, who would walk miles, even in his seventies as now, to help the sick with rudimentary skills picked up from doctors he'd served as a waiter and mixed with in Paris. He would often walk home drunk because the poor would gratefully press gin on him and he was too delicate to refuse them. The widowed Mrs Desmoulins, a recent arrival in her sixties, and put in charge of the kitchen, an arrangement that Levet resented. Her daughter, a woman of about 30. Poll Carmichael, a prostitute who had been brought to the house sick and exhausted from the streets. She had somehow been deprived of a legacy from her father. Mrs Desmoulins, and presumably her daughter, resented having to share their room with Poll. Frank Barber, about 30, nominally a valet and food-provisioner to the household and occasionally a waiter at table, but actually of higher status than that. He was respected by the others, apart from Mrs Williams who resented the money spent on his education (some £300). Frank married at about this time and, on Mrs Williams's death, moved his wife and two infant daughters into the household. Two servants, whose duties were more nominal than real: Mrs Williams's Scottish maid and a Mrs White, an elderly and rather pitiful woman, ostensibly the housekeeper. Then there were others who came and went. And a cat called Hodge which, when old and sick, would only eat oysters.

Oh, and Samuel Johnson, writer. He had taken all these into his household, at various times, and provided for them. He'd found Poll Carmichael lying in the street and had carried her home on his back. The general appearance of 8, Bolt Court, says the biographer W. Jackson Bate (on whose great work this chapter draws gratefully), was of 'an informal home for the destitute and infirm' (Bate, 1977, p. 501). And the quarrelling among what Bate calls the 'inmates' (ibid.) was such that Johnson was often afraid of going home at night to be met with their complaints against each other. He explained to Mrs Thrale: 'Williams hates everybody. Levet hates Desmoulins, and does not love Williams. Desmoulins hates them both; Poll loves none of them.' And, elsewhere to the Thrales, 'a general anarchy prevails in my kitchen' (Boswell, Penguin edition, 1979, pp. 351, 349). But Johnson told another of his friends, John Hawkins, that 'if I do not assist them, no one else would, and they would be lost in want' (Bate, 1977, p. 503).

In 1937 a then unknown playwright embarked on a play he never finished, about Johnson and Mrs Thrale, which pictures Mrs Desmoulins (knitting), Mrs Williams (meditating) and Miss Carmichael (reading), sitting together. Hodge is on stage (sleeping). You might like to guess the playwright. The answer will be apparent from a later chapter in this book.

MRS D: He is late.
　　　Silence
MRS D: God grant all is well.
　　　Silence
MRS D: Puss puss puss puss puss.
MRS W: What are you reading, young woman?
MISS C: A book, Madam.

MRS W: Ha!
Silence.

I've left out one fact about Frank Barber. He was black, a liberated orphan slave from Jamaica, and he had been handed over to Johnson aged about 10 by a friend of Johnson who couldn't manage his upkeep and whose father had originally brought Frank with him when he had left Jamaica. Johnson paid for his schooling, and his position in the household was something close to a son. When Hodge was ill it was Johnson himself, not Frank, who went out to buy oysters: Johnson couldn't risk offending Frank's dignity by sending him out to buy food for a cat. Frank became the principal beneficiary in Johnson's will.

The period between, say, Swift's *Gulliver's Travels* (1726) and, say, Wordsworth and Coleridge's *Lyrical Ballads* (1798) is a period in English literary history that students tend to have little to do with. Anthologies often pass over it in silence. The result is that Johnson, whose writing career falls exactly into this period, tends to get missed out too. This would have much amazed those many who recognised in him, in his later years and for long after, the larger-than-life figure of literary legend. But that was part of the problem. Turned into a legendary figure, even in his own lifetime and most forcibly later in James Boswell's famous biography, Johnson became like a figure in a museum, taking the mid-eighteenth century with him. He became a 'character', more respectfully acknowledged than energetically engaged with, apart from by specialists in the period and the many small groups of amateur Johnson-devotees around the world who would gather together to share anecdotes. And they seemed happy to keep Johnson – as opposed to Boswell's Johnson – to themselves, devoted to him in an intensely personal way, as Johnson scholars and Johnson amateurs tend to be.

And to consider the sheer bulk and sheer range of Johnson's work is enough to induce a kind of sea-sickness. His output is the opposite of the manageably small and easily anthologisable work that readers and students feel safer and more comfortable with, like the poetry of Donne or Blake. The problem is that Johnson isn't a poet, novelist, playwright, essayist, critic, historian, biographer, parliamentary reporter, moralist, sermon-maker, translator, ghost-writer of other people's public addresses, editor or dictionary-maker. Because he is all of those and, as the production-line writer just getting on with the job, he also happened to redefine the parameters in most of these fields while being tied to the production of the millions of words which meant day-to-day survival. To even contemplate reading his complete works – which incidentally included writings in Greek, Latin and French – is like squaring up to a hurricane. And this is to say nothing of the fact that everything he wrote in English is written in a language, usual to the period but taken to a new degree of polish and intensity in Johnson, that puts unusual demands on modern readers. The sentences are long and complex, the vocabulary abstract and classical. It takes some practice to be able to tune into its rich pleasures.

For these reasons and others, Johnson is always in danger of disappearing into his own, or rather Boswell's, legend. And we 'know' legends so we don't need to read them. And what we perhaps 'know' about Johnson is that he was a comfortably-off man of letters, dispensing well-turned put-downs and majestic judgements from the power-bases of literary London, in its salons and at its dinner-tables, a lover of church and crown, of authority and tradition, an enemy of anything new and radical, a sage who knew everything and who lived happily and at peace with the world, rather amused by it all, unbothered by such minor anxieties as love or sex: above all, a Tory. That is, someone more or less entirely out of step with students today.

But this is Boswell's spin on Johnson (I've exaggerated it crudely), a figure that the young Boswell needed as a romantically reactionary father-figure, for very personal reasons. The Johnson that knew himself all too well and too painfully, the Johnson as recovered by scholars like Bate, could hardly have been more different. He was permanently fighting depression and illness, his eyesight and hearing were woefully impaired after the traumas of a childhood scrofula, he suffered from humiliatingly dreadful and obsessional convulsions which made him unemployable as the schoolmaster he planned to be, he was in constant battle with frustrated fantasies, and was forced to live from hand to mouth till late in his career, in his fifties (when Boswell got to know him).

He regularly feared the onset of madness. Once, in his thirties, working as a hack-writer for the publisher and editor Edward Cave, he insisted on hiding himself behind a screen while ostensibly having dinner with Cave, embarrassed that the other dinner-guest might see his scruffily clothed figure. At this period he was writing 'parliamentary debates' for Cave's magazine, records of political speeches purporting to be those actually delivered in Parliament, and widely regarded to be such, but actually Johnson's inventions, half a million words rushed out at about two thousand words an hour, anonymous hackwork that came to be anthologised as great works of oratory by the major political figures of the day. The little money he managed to save from work of this kind went to his much older and alcoholic wife Tetty, from whom he later separated – and to the poor unfortunates who, as we've seen, he collected in his household, and to the begging poor in the streets.

He was a Tory. And it's here that Donald Greene, Jackson Bate and others have done vital and illuminating work. For to be a Tory in Johnson's day, as opposed to a Whig, was to be something almost the opposite of what it means to be a Tory today or in the twentieth century. The reasonable enough assumption that Tories are Tories whenever they are has helped perpetuate the quite misguided and misleading picture of Johnson that we inherit today.

We associate Toryism today with *laissez-faire* economics and the free power of the market. But *laissez-faire* economics was, in Bate's words, 'the essence of Whiggism in Johnson's day' (1977, p. 191). It was the Whigs who represented the interests of what we now call conservatism. They were the party of property and commercial interest, the powerful merchants, the money-men and the biggest landowners. They were driving the country in its new mercantile and financial world-power, its colonial conquests. That power was generated by something that historians have put at the centre of Britain's domination of trade and money, making it all possible. That something is the slave-trade.

The Tories of Johnson's day were the unfashionable underdogs. They were the party of the lesser landowners, the country clergymen, and they were a minority party in Parliament for most of Johnson's lifetime. Johnson knew many Whigs and mixed with them socially. But his instincts, throughout his life, were intensely humanitarian, driven by a raw fellow-feeling with the suffering and outcast, the poor and the exploited, and for Johnson the *laissez-faire* economics of Whiggism was the crude and cruel logic of dog-eat-dog. Boswell records an exchange between Johnson and a Lady MacLeod. She asked him whether man was not 'naturally good'. Johnson replied, 'No, madam, no more than a wolf'. The startled Lady Macleod said in a low voice, 'This is worse than Swift' (Bate, 1977, p. 196).

And that's why Johnson, in Mrs Thrale's words, 'loved the poor as I never yet saw any one else do'. In Whig society, not many felt they needed to. Johnson knew poverty for years after arriving in London. He had to leave Oxford without finishing his degree-course because of poverty. This humiliation prompted the first of his protracted and near-suicidal depressions. In London, even when still poor himself, he would press money into the hands of children sleeping rough in the streets. To the common middle-class claim that money given to beggars is only wasted on gin (we'll be meeting this issue in relation to Oscar Wilde's *The Happy Prince*), Johnson would answer, 'And why should they be denied such sweeteners of their existence?' What Johnson would have thought of today's so-called zero-tolerance towards beggars in the streets of London and New York can be assessed when we look at the passage from Mrs Thrale at greater length.

> Severity towards the poor was, in Dr. Johnson's opinion (as is visible in his Life of Addison particularly), an undoubted and constant attendant or consequence upon whiggism; and he was not contented with giving them relief, he wished to add also indulgence. He loved the poor as I never yet saw any one else do, with an earnest desire to make them happy. – What signifies, says some one, giving halfpence to common beggars? they only lay it out in gin or tobacco. 'And why should they be denied such sweeteners of their existence (says Johnson)? it is surely very savage to refuse them every possible avenue to pleasure, reckoned too coarse for our own acceptance. Life is a pill which none of us can bear to swallow without gilding; yet for the poor we delight in stripping it still barer, and are not ashamed to show even visible displeasure, if ever the bitter taste is taken from their mouths.' In consequence of these principles he nursed whole nests of people in his house, where the lame, the blind, the sick, and the sorrowful found a sure retreat from all the evils whence his little income could secure them.
>
> (quoted in *Eighteenth-Century Prose*, Harmondsworth, Pelican, 1956, pp. 58–9)

For Johnson the logic of Whiggism is that 'we delight in stripping [the life of the poor] still barer, and are not ashamed to show even visible displeasure, if ever the bitter taste is taken from their mouths'. When challenged by a lady as to why he persisted in giving money to beggars he replied, 'Madam, to enable them to beg *on*' (Bate, 1977, p. 196). Two years before his death, much troubled by sickness, he went out of his way to write to Boswell about the 'calamity' of being poor.

This year has afflicted me with a very irksome and severe disorder. My respiration has been much impeded, and much blood has been taken away. I am now harrassed by a catarrhous cough, from which my purpose is to seek relief by change of air; and I am, therefore, preparing to go to Oxford.

Whether I did right in dissuading you from coming to London this spring, I will not determine. You have not lost much by missing my company; I have scarcely been well for a single week. I might have received comfort from your kindness; but you would have seen me afflicted, and, perhaps, found me peevish. Whatever might have been your pleasure or mine, I know not how I could have honestly advised you to come hither with borrowed money. Do not accustom yourself to consider debt only as an inconvenience; you will find it a calamity. Poverty takes away so many means of doing good, and produces so much inability to resist evil, both natural and moral, that it is by all virtuous means to be avoided. Consider a man whose fortune is very narrow; whatever be his rank by birth, or whatever his reputation by intellectual excellence, what good can he do? or what evil can he prevent? That he cannot help the needy is evident, he has nothing to spare. But, perhaps, his advice or admonition may be useful. His poverty will destroy his influence: many more can find that he is poor, than that he is wise; and few will reference the understanding that is of so little advantage to its owner. I say nothing of the personal wretchedness of a debtor, which, however, has passed into a proverb. Of riches, it is not necessary to write the praise. Let it, however, be remembered, that he who has money to spare, has it always in his power to benefit others; and of such power a good man must always be desirous.

(Chapman, 1962, pp. 430–1)

And so he took people like Robert Levet and Poll Carmichael into his household. Typically, he was too delicate to Poll's dignity to tell even close friends like Mrs Thrale the truth of Poll's history. He told the Thrales that he didn't 'rightly remember' how she came to be in his house. It is to be hoped that he kept Boswell, an inveterate and obsessional consumer of the services of street-prostitutes (his secret, unknown to Johnson), in the dark about Poll.

For Boswell, who felt distinctly proprietorial towards anything to do with Johnson, was never easy about the claims made on his hero's time and affections by the 'inmates' of the household, especially when, like Levet, their acquaintance with Johnson far preceded his own. Describing Levet as 'grotesque' in appearance he also rather tartly commented on Johnson's 'predilection for him, and fanciful estimation of his moderate abilities' (Boswell, 1979, p. 72). In apparent indifference, he varies his surname from Levet to Levett. One of the sharpest moments in Boswell's entire life of Johnson is this, from 1776. 'Being irritated by hearing a gentleman ask Mr Levet a variety of questions concerning him, when he was sitting by, he broke out, "Sir, you have but two topics, yourself and me. I am sick of both"' (ibid., p. 216). The 'him', 'he' and 'he' there are all Johnson (for Boswell was only interested in Levet as a source of information) and the gentleman was Boswell. It was Levet's privacy Johnson was protecting there as well as his own.

Levet died in 1782, two years before Johnson. The two men would meet for long and silent breakfasts throughout their thirty-six-year acquaintance. Levet, in fact, was a more or less completely silent figure in the household. Johnson seems to have valued that. Boswell has this:

> In one of the memorandum-books in my possession, is the following entry:– 'January 20, Sunday. Robert Levet was buried in the churchyard of Bridewell, between one and two in the afternoon. He died on January 17, about seven in the morning, by an instantaneous death. He was an old and faithful friend; I have known him from about '46. May GOD have mercy on him. May he have mercy on me.'
>
> (ibid., p. 283)

This is the most poignant of Johnson's poems. 'Officious' means eager to serve; Christ's parable of the talents is referred to in the poem.

On the Death of Dr. Robert Levet

Condemned to hope's delusive mine,
    As on we toil from day to day,
By sudden blasts, or slow decline,
    Our social comforts drop away.

Well tried through many a varying year,
    See Levet to the grave descend;
Officious, innocent, sincere,
    Of ev'ry friendless name the friend.

Yet still he fills affection's eye,
10   Obscurely wise, and coarsely kind;
Nor, lettered arrogance, deny
    Thy praise to merit unrefined.

When fainting nature called for aid,
    And hov'ring death prepared the blow,
His vig'rous remedy displayed
    The power of art without the show.

In misery's darkest caverns known,
    His useful care was ever nigh,
Where hopeless anguish poured his groan,
20   And lonely want retired to die.

No summons mocked by chill delay,
    No petty gain disdained by pride,
The modest wants of ev'ry day
    The toil of ev'ry day supplied.

His virtues walked their narrow round,
    Nor made a pause, nor left a void;

And sure th' Eternal Master found
  The single talent well employed.

  The busy day, the peaceful night,
30   Unfelt, uncounted, glided by;
  His frame was firm, his powers were bright,
    Though now his eightieth year was nigh.

  Then with no throbbing fiery pain,
    No cold gradations of decay,
  Death broke at once the vital chain,
    And freed his soul the nearest way.

Next year, on another visit when Johnson was very ill, Boswell records
that

> he repeated to me his verses on Mr Levet, with an emotion
> which gave them full effect; and then he was pleased to say,
> 'You must be as much with me as you can. You have done me
> good. You cannot think how much better I am since you came
> in'.
>
> (ibid., p. 285)

*   *   *

The presence of Frank Barber at Bolt Court was more than habitual
charity or kindness to an old friend. Johnson, much to Boswell's patronising amusement, had an intense horror of slavery. He saw it, according to Bate, 'as the inevitable extension of the uncontrolled pursuit
of wealth' (Bate, 1977, 192–3). Boswell has Johnson startling some
'very grave men at Oxford' with the toast 'here's to the next in-
surrection of the negroes in the West Indies' (ibid., p. 194). Boswell's
attitude was the routine mercantile self-interested one, dressed up as
liberal kindness. The slave-trade for Boswell is a 'very important and
necessary branch of commercial interest', and it saves 'the African
savage . . . from massacre, or intolerable bondage in their own country,
and introduces [them] into a much happier state of life' (ibid.). To that,
one is inclined to reply with Swift's fine bitterness, quoted in the last
chapter: 'if a prince send forces into a nation where the people are

158

poor and ignorant, he may lawfully put half of them to death, and make slaves of the rest, in order to civilize and reduce them from their barbarous way of living'. The statistics again: by the 1730s the British were the dominant slaving nation, shipping some 2.8 million African slaves between 1690 and 1807, packing these goods or commodities into slaving ships, typically 600 at a time, stacked 'like books on a shelf', as one contemporary witness put it. The British dominance made for all those country-houses, of which Jane Austen's Mansfield Park was typical. Edward Said points to a very expressive 'dead silence' in the novel (1814) when Fanny Price asks Sir Thomas 'about the slave trade', the trade on which the wealth of his house and family depends (Said, 1993, p. 115).

From about 1765 the first moves towards an abolition movement in Britain began. (Here I draw directly on Duncan Clarke's *Slaves and Slavery*.) It started with the work of a civil servant called Granville Sharp who took up the cases of three fugitive slaves in London whose original colonial owners claimed they had legal hold over them. After legal wranglings it was ruled in 1772 that one slave-master's ownership-rights, claimed under Virginian law, could not override British common-law protecting individual liberty. There were some 15,000 slaves in Britain in the 1770s, working as domestic servants in the country estates and town-houses of wealthy absentee landlords of West Indian sugar plantations. They were a considerable status symbol and can be glimpsed in the paintings of the period. And there were many fewer poor but free or fugitive slaves in London and cities like Liverpool. The ruling of 1772 didn't liberate the slaves in Britain but it stopped them being forcibly returned to slave-owners in the colonies. It took nearly another forty years for abolition to become law, in 1808. A key incident, which Granville Sharp publicised, was the case of the slave ship Zong in 1783. The captain, spuriously alleging shortage of water on the vessel, had 132 sick slaves tossed overboard in order to claim the consequent property loss, at £30 each, from his insurers. Understandably enough, Colonel Bathurst, the father of Johnson's friend, who had brought the orphaned Frank Barber from Virginia in 1750, had made a point of asserting in his will six years later that he had given Frank his freedom.

If the slave-trade, for Johnson, was the inevitable result of the uncontrolled pursuit of wealth, he saw war, which he loathed as 'the extremity of evil', as of immediate benefit only to the 'paymasters and agents, contractors and commissaries' who 'laugh from their desks' while 'hoping for a new contract from a new armament'. That is, Johnson saw with prophetic clarity that war is principally in the interest of what we now call the arms-trade, that grim manifestation of military-industrial capitalism, blithely selling arms to all sides in all international conflicts. Swift's loathing of war is powerfully, sickeningly conveyed in furious passages of *Gulliver's Travels*. Johnson is more measured.

The Horrors of War

As war is the last of remedies [. . .] all lawful expedients must be used to avoid it. As war is the extremity of evil, it is surely the duty of those whose station intrusts them with the care of nations, to avert it from their charge. There are diseases of animal nature which nothing but amputation can remove; so there may, by the depravation of human passions, be sometimes a gangrene in collective life for which fire and the sword are the necessary remedies; but in what can skill or caution be better shown than preventing such dreadful operations, while there is yet room for gentler methods?

It is wonderful with what coolness and indifference the greater part of mankind see war commenced. Those that hear of it at a distance or read of it in books, but have never presented its evils to their minds, consider it as little more than a splendid game, a proclamation, an army, a battle, and a triumph. Some indeed must perish in the most successful field, but they die upon the bed of honour, *resign their lives amidst the joys of conquest, and filled with England's glory, smile in death.*

The life of a modern soldier is ill represented by heroic fiction. War has means of destruction more formidable than the cannon and the sword. Of the thousands and ten thousands that perished in our late contests with France and Spain, a very small part ever felt the stroke of an enemy; the rest languished in tents and ships, amidst damps and putrefaction; pale, torpid, spiritless, and helpless; gasping and groaning unpitied, among men made obdurate by long continuance of hopeless misery;

and were at last whelmed in pits, or heaved into the ocean, without notice and without remembrance. By incommodious encampments and unwholesome stations, where courage is useless, and enterprise impracticable, fleets are silently dispeopled, and armies sluggishly melted away.

Thus is a people gradually exhausted, for the most part, with little effect. The wars of civilized nations make very slow changes in the system of empire. The public perceives scarcely any alteration but an increase of debt; and the few individuals who are benefited, are not supposed to have the clearest right to their advantages. If he that shared the danger enjoyed the profit, and after bleeding in the battle grew rich by the victory, he might show his gains without envy. But at the conclusion of a ten years war, how are we recompensed for the death of multitudes and the expense of millions, but by contemplating the sudden glories of paymasters and agents, contractors and commissaries, whose equipages shine like meteors, and whose palaces rise like exhalations?

These are the men who, without virtue, labour, or hazard, are growing rich as their country is impoverished; they rejoice when obstinacy or ambition adds another year to slaughter and devastation; and laugh from their desks at bravery and science, while they are adding figure to figure, and cipher to cipher, hoping for a new contract from a new armament, and computing the profits of a siege or tempest.

(Chapman, 1962, pp. 288–9)

Nor was Johnson very inclined to romanticise the lives of soldiers and sailors. 'No man will be a sailor who has contrivance enough to get himself into a jail; for being in a ship is being in a jail, with the chance of being drowned ... A man in a jail has more room, better food, and commonly better company' (Boswell, 1979, p. 86). Johnson, in a typically charitable gesture, managed through intermediaries in the Admiralty to secure the discharge of a young man who had run away to sea before settling finally with the man who treated him as his father. This was Frank Barber.

* * *

We started with the problem of Johnson having become a 'character', a victim of his own legend. We're at the beginning of the period when 'character', in the modern sense, takes on new force. The late eighteenth- and early nineteenth-century novel was the genre where explorations of new forms of socially constructed subjectivity and the newly emergent middle-class consumers of such writings came conveniently together. The poets of the early Romantic period, particularly Coleridge and Keats, were speaking to a new sense of free but also lonely individualism which they found so influentially in Shakespeare, in *Hamlet* above all. Biography, according to the modern psychologically informed model, was invented in the Romantic period.

But it was Johnson who invented it, as if accidentally, in his wonderful biography of Richard Savage. Savage was a compulsive fantasist and rake, a talented minor-poet and accomplished raconteur and sponger, given to nursing grudges and violent squabbles. Preposterously, or perhaps not given the nature of the job, he applied for the post of poet-laureate. He was condemned to death for killing a gentleman in a pub brawl, but pardoned. He died in a debtors' prison. He may or may not have been the illegitimate and abandoned son of an aristocrat. His case was taken up by as many people as he could interest in it. Johnson was one such. The two of them, in Johnson's early days in London, would wander the streets at night, too poor for lodgings, sleeping rough, laying elaborate plans to reform the world.

Or that's the legend. The legend is brilliantly examined and the story told in a wonderful short book about these two unlikely friends, Richard Holmes's *Dr Johnson and Mr Savage*. This is literary criticism, social history, thriller and biography in one, and what it insists on is the radical newness of Johnson's life of Savage, the first biography of its kind and Johnson's first substantial publication. In effect, the notion of the poet as outcast, which we associate with later Romantic developments, starts here in Johnson's story of Savage and Savage's stories of injustice. It's Savage's contradictory and fascinatingly self-dramatising and self-inventing character or multiplicity of characterisations that Johnson explores and, in so doing, he provides a shadowy sense of his own richly entangled psychological investment in the processes of Savage's inventiveness. Johnson's 'character', his needs and his vulnerabilities, are more revealingly at issue in his early friendship with Savage than in his much later friendship with Boswell who, understandably, found the entire episode inexplicable and rather embarrassing.

Here's a typical passage in Johnson's life. It deals with Savage as a problematic 'inmate' in the houses of those who kindly or misguidedly 'received him into their families'. With this passage we can return to where we began: Johnson's uncomplainingly making his home available to those who, like Savage, found life such a problem. The young Johnson, unknown and without employment, given to disappointment, depression and frustrated ambition, could have become a version of the extraordinary and charismatic figure with whom he suffered the pains of city poverty.

Whoever was acquainted with him was certain to be solicited for small sums, which the frequency of the request made in time considerable, and he was therefore quickly shunned by those who were become familiar enough to be trusted with his necessities; but his rambling manner of life, and constant appearance at houses of public resort, always procured him a new succession of friends, whose kindness had not been exhausted by repeated requests; so that he was seldom absolutely without resources, but had in his utmost exigences this comfort, that he always imagined himself sure of speedy relief.

It was observed that he always asked favours of this kind without the least submission or apparent consciousness of dependence, and that he did not seem to look upon a compliance with his request as an obligation that deserved any extraordinary acknowledgements; but a refusal was resented by him as an affront, or complained of as an injury: nor did he readily reconcile himself to those who either denied to lend, or gave him afterwards any intimation that they expected to be repaid.

He was sometimes so far compassionated by those who knew both his merit and distresses that they received him into their families, but they soon discovered him to be a very incommodious inmate; for, being always accustomed to an irregular manner of life, he could not confine himself to any stated hours, or pay any regard to the rules of a family, but would prolong his conversation till midnight, without considering that business might require his friend's application in the morning; and, when he had persuaded himself to retire to bed, was not, without equal difficulty, called up to dinner: it was therefore impossible to pay him any distinction without the entire sub-version of all economy, a kind of establishment which, wher-ever he went, he always appeared ambitious to overthrow.

It must therefore be acknowledged, in justification of man-kind, that it was not always by the negligence or coldness of his friends that Savage was distressed, but because it was in reality very difficult to preserve him long in a state of ease. To supply him with money was a hopeless attempt, for no sooner did he see himself master of a sum sufficient to set him free from care for a day, than he became profuse and luxurious. When once he had entered a tavern, or engaged in a scheme of pleasure, he never retired till want of money obliged him to some new expedient. If he was entertained in a family nothing was any longer to be regarded there but amusements and jollity: wher-ever Savage entered he immediately expected that order and business should fly before him, that all should thenceforward be left to hazard, and that no dull principle of domestic man-agement should be opposed to his inclination, or intrude upon his gaiety.

(Chapman, 1962, pp. 23–5)

*   *   *

We started in 1777 and we end in 1777. We've been thinking about Johnson's pioneering, pre-Romantic interest in Savage's 'character' as something mobile and provisional, not instantly available to scrutiny, inconsistent and contradictory, a model of characterisation as un-certain product and difficult process. Johnson's own persistence of self-doubt and early history of social uncertainty meant that he knew this model from the inside. And his interest in this modern notion of character is implicitly evidenced in Johnson's tolerant openness to those ignored and rejected by his society. Robert Levet and Poll Carmichael may have been characters in a menagerie to others; to Johnson they were complex individuals. We've placed this in the context of the later post-Boswell tendency to fix Johnson himself in the simple and immobile character of legend.

In 1777 the conventions of understanding character were also in the process of being rewritten somewhere else, in a way that again prefigures the work of much more celebrated critics in the early Romantic period, names like Coleridge and Hazlitt. Again this seems to have happened as if accidentally. Across the city from Fleet Street, in some government office (as I like to imagine it), a government official with particular knowledge of matters American was relaxing from his duties by writing a book. It was a book about Shakespeare, ostensibly about Falstaff, and the government official was Maurice Morgann. His book, written a few years earlier, was published in 1777. It's a leisurely, observant and detailed study of Shakespeare's Falstaff, but something very extraordinary suddenly happens when Morgann finds himself remarking that 'something should be said of the nature of Shakespeare's dramatic characters, by what arts they were formed, and wherein they differ from those of other writers'. Between the word 'characters' and the words 'by what arts' Morgann inserts a footnote. This, perhaps the most telling footnote in literary criticism, is it.

¹ The reader must be sensible of something in the composition of *Shakespeare*'s characters, which renders them essentially different from those drawn by other writers. The characters of every Drama must indeed be grouped; but in the groups of other poets the parts which are not seen, do not in fact exist. But there is a certain roundness and integrity in the forms of *Shakespeare*, which give them an independence as well as a relation, insomuch that we often meet with passages, which though perfectly felt, cannot be sufficiently explained in words, without unfolding the whole character of the speaker.
[. . .] Something which may be thought too heavy for the *text*, I shall add *here*, as a conjecture concerning the composition of *Shakespeare*'s characters: Not that they were the effect, I believe, so much of a minute and laborious attention, as of a certain comprehensive energy of mind, involving within itself all the effects of system and of labour.
    Bodies of all kinds, whether of metals, plants, or animals, are supposed to possess certain first principles of *being*, and to have an existence independent of the accidents, which form their magnitude or growth: Those accidents are supposed to be

drawn in from the surrounding elements, but not indiscriminately; each plant and each animal, imbibes those things only, which are proper to its own distinct nature, and which have besides such a secret relation to each other as to be capable of forming a perfect union and coalescence: But so variously are the surrounding elements mingled and disposed, that each particular body, even of those under the same species, has yet some *peculiar* of its own. *Shakespeare* appears to have considered the being and growth of the human mind as analogous to this system: There are certain qualities and capacities, which he seems to have considered as first principles; the chief of which are certain energies of courage and activity, according to their degrees; together with different degrees and sorts of sensibilities, and a capacity, varying likewise in the *degree*, of discernment and intelligence. The rest of the composition is drawn in from an atmosphere of surrounding things; that is, from the various influences of the different laws, religions and governments in the world; and from those of the different ranks and inequalities in society; and from the different professions of men, encouraging or repressing passions of particular sorts, and inducing different modes of thinking and habits of life; and he seems to have known intuitively what those influences in particular were which this or that original constitution would most freely imbibe, and which would most easily associate and coalesce. But all these things being, in different situations, very differently disposed, and those differences exactly discerned by him, he found no difficulty in marking every individual, even among characters of the same sort, with something peculiar and distinct.

[. . .] The reader will not now be surprised if I affirm that those characters in *Shakespeare*, which are seen only in part, are yet capable of being unfolded and understood in the whole; every part being in fact relative, and inferring all the rest. It is true that the point of action or sentiment, which we are most concerned in, is always held out for our special notice. But who does not perceive that there is a peculiarity about it, which conveys a relish of the whole? And very frequently, when no particular point presses, he boldly makes a character act and speak from those parts of the composition, which are *inferred* only, and not distinctly shown. This produces a wonderful effect: it seems to carry us beyond the poet to nature itself, and gives an integrity and truth to facts and character, which they could not otherwise obtain: And this is in reality that art in *Shakespeare*, which being withdrawn from our notice, we more emphatically call *nature*. A felt propriety and truth from causes unseen, I take to be the highest point of Poetic composition. If the characters of *Shakespeare* are thus *whole*, and as it were original, while those of almost all other writers are mere imitation, it may be fit to consider them rather as Historic than Dramatic beings; and, when occasion requires, to account for their conduct from the *whole* of character, from general principles, from latent motives, and from policies not avowed.

(Nichol Smith, 1946, pp. 170–2)

Shakespeare character-criticism has had a rough ride since the 1930s when its excesses were first violently assaulted in the name of formalist or new-critical symbolist approaches. It's still a little embarrassing in certain circles to write about Shakespearean characterisation. But the issue is paramount to what we all respond to in Shakespeare, and with Morgann we're at a critical breakthrough. His intuited insight was to notice that the apparent realness of the characters was a brilliant illusion, a technical effect whereby Shakespeare makes 'a character act and speak from those parts of the composition, which are inferred only, and not distinctly shown'. Morgann called this 'a felt propriety and truth from causes unseen'. It's the audience, in effect, that supplies what is only inferred or unseen. The ground, the theatrical space, seems to open out beneath the dialogue when this illusion works, as it so frequently does in Shakespeare. Shakespeare character-criticism takes off in vigorous style from about 1817 with Hazlitt and Coleridge. Neither of them show any acknowledgement of having read Morgann.

Johnson's interest in Shakespeare led, in the preface to his edition and the accompanying notes, to some of the most judicious remarks made by one great mind about another. We end with a note from Johnson's Shakespeare, and with a look at some of Johnson's journal entries, from the time of his Shakespeare edition and up till ten years later.

In *Measure for Measure* the Duke says this (at III.i.32). Johnson's note follows.

Measure for Measure (III.i.32)

> *Thou hast nor youth, nor age:*
> *But as it were an after dinner's sleep,*
> *Dreaming on both.*

This is exquisitely imagined. When we are young we busy ourselves in forming schemes for succeeding time, and miss the gratifications that are before us; when we are old we amuse the languour of age with the recollection of youthful pleasures or performances; so that our life, of which no part is filled with the business of the present time, resembles our dreams after dinner, when the events of the morning are mingled with the designs of the evening.

(Chapman, 1962, pp. 265–6)

A 'life, of which no part is filled with the business of the present time'? The most astonishing of all the astonishing things about Samuel Johnson was that he so regularly savaged himself, in his private journals, for not employing himself 'properly and vigorously enough' while his life steals 'unprofitably away'. A typical self-accusation is of not following his own resolutions: 'I have resolved, I hope not presumptuously, till I am afraid to resolve again.' In April 1764, just before the Shakespeare edition was published, the charge is of 'indolence' and 'sluggishness'.

> My indolence, since my last reception of the Sacrament, has sunk into grosser sluggishness, and my dissipation spread into wilder negligence. My thoughts have been clouded with sensuality and except that from the beginning of this year I have in some measure forborn excess of strong drink my appetites have predominated over my reason. A kind of strange oblivion has overspread me, so that I know not what has become of the last year, and perceive that incidents and intelligence pass over me without leaving any impression.
> This is not the life to which Heaven is promised.

168

In September of the same year, 1764, Johnson reflects on his birthday.

This is my fifty-sixth birthday, the day on which I have concluded fifty-five years.

I have outlived many friends. I have felt many sorrows. I have made few improvements. Since my resolution formed last Easter I have made no advancement in knowledge or in goodness; nor do I recollect that I have endeavoured it. I am dejected but not hopeless.

O God for Jesus Christ's Christ's sake have mercy on me.

And this is from September 1768.

I have now begun the sixtieth year of my life. How the last year has past I am unwilling to terrify myself with thinking. This day has been past in great perturbation, I was distracted at church in an uncommon degree, and my distress has had very little intermission. I have found myself somewhat relieved by reading, which I therefore intend to practise when I am able.

This day it came into my mind to write the history of my melancholy. On this I purpose to deliberate. I know not whether it may not too much disturb me.

And, finally, here is his journal entry for the 'awful' (awe-inspiring) day, Good Friday, 1775. The entry is in two parts. Boswell is with him all day. When Boswell goes, Johnson's last action is to talk with Frank Barber about Holy Communion. The entry closes. And, then, it begins again.

Apr. 14, GOOD FRIDAY.

Boswell came in before I was up. We breakfasted, I only drank tea without milk or bread. We went to church, saw Dr. Wetherel in the pew, and by his desire took him home with us. He did not go very soon, and Boswell stayed. Dilly and Millar called. Boswell and I went to church, but came very late. We then took tea, by Boswell's desire, and I ate one bun, I think, that I might not seem to fast ostentatiously. Boswell sat with me till night; we had some serious talk. When he went I gave

Francis some directions for preparation to communicate. Thus
has passed hitherto this awful day.   10°30′ p.m.

When I look back upon resolutions of improvement and
amendments, which have year after year been made and
broken, either by negligence, forgetfulness, vicious idleness,
casual interruption, or morbid infirmity, when I find that so
much of my life has stolen unprofitably away, and that I can
descry by retrospection scarcely a few single days properly and
vigorously employed, why do I yet try to resolve again? I try
because Reformation is necessary and despair is criminal. I try
in humble hope of the help of God.

As my life has from my earliest years been wasted in a morning bed my purpose is from Easter day to rise early, not later
than eight.   11°15′ p.m. D. j.

(Chapman, 1962, p. 347)

This chapter has been concerned to reposition Johnson and Johnson's poli-
tics and in so doing has perhaps been unfair to Boswell and his biography.
There's a handily abridged edition with a good introduction, edited by
Christopher Hibbert (Harmondsworth, Penguin, 1979), from which I quote
above. Other Johnson quotations are from R.W. Chapman's *Selections from
Samuel Johnson* (Oxford, Oxford University Press, 1962) and from Jackson
Bate's great biography (London, Harcourt Brace, 1977). This received some
flak from the more traditional in the Johnson industry, resistant to its psych-
ologising. A good modern selection of Johnson is edited by Donald Greene
(Oxford, Oxford University Press, 1984): this has a decent selection from
the prayers and meditations. Richard Holmes's *Dr Johnson and Mr Savage*
(London, Hodder and Stoughton, 1993) is the most accessible and com-
pulsively readable book on the period. You might like to investigate Johnson's
critical responses to Milton and Swift in his *Lives of the Poets*, the two writers
about whom he had uncharacteristically blind spots. Maurice Morgann's
essay on Falstaff is excerpted in a very useful collection of Shakespeare
criticism, 1623–1840, edited by D. Nichol Smith (Oxford, Oxford University
Press, 1946), which also has a generous selection from Johnson's edition.
Edward Said's exemplary reading of *Mansfield Park* is in his *Culture and
Imperialism* (London, Chatto and Windus, 1993).

9

WORDSWORTH'S POEMS OF BOYHOOD
Myths of initiation in revolutionary times

This chapter explores two poems by William Wordsworth (1798) by looking at them in a number of connected ways. We'll read them in terms of their psycho-sexual suggestiveness, their resemblance to myths, their debt to earlier poetry and the political-historical moment of their publication and reception.

Here are two Wordsworth poems, or rather one poem and one extract. They were both going to be in his long autobiographical poem *The Prelude*, but 'Nutting' was detached and published in *Lyrical Ballads* (1800 edition). They were written in 1798. The subtitle of *The Prelude* is 'The Growth of a Poet's Mind'.

From *The Prelude* (1850) Book I

One summer evening (led by her) I found
A little boat tied to a willow tree
Within a rocky cave, its usual home.
360 Straight I unloosed her chain, and stepping in
Pushed from the shore. It was an act of stealth
And troubled pleasure, nor without the voice
Of mountain-echoes did my boat move on;
Leaving behind her still, on either side,
365 Small circles glittering idly in the moon,
Until they melted all into one track
Of sparkling light. But now, like one who rows,
Proud of his skill, to reach a chosen point
With an unswerving line, I fixed my view

171

370 Upon the summit of a craggy ridge,
    The horizon's utmost boundary; far above
    Was nothing but the stars and the grey sky.
    She was an elfin pinnace; lustily
    I dipped my oars into the silent lake,
375 And, as I rose upon the stroke, my boat
    Went heaving through the water like a swan;
    When, from behind that craggy steep till then
    The horizon's bound, a huge peak, black and huge,
    As if with voluntary power instinct
380 Upreared its head. I struck and struck again,
    And growing still in stature the grim shape
    Towered up between me and the stars, and still,
    For so it seemed, with purpose of its own
    And measured motion like a living thing,
385 Strode after me. With trembling oars I turned,
    And through the silent water stole my way
    Back to the covert of the willow tree;
    There in her mooring-place I left my bark, –
    And through the meadows homeward went, in grave
390 And serious mood; but after I had seen
    That spectacle, for many days, my brain
    Worked with a dim and undetermined sense
    Of unknown modes of being; o'er my thoughts
    There hung a darkness, call it solitude
395 Or blank desertion. No familiar shapes
    Remained, no pleasant images of trees,
    Of sea or sky, no colours of green fields;
    But huge and mighty forms, that do not live
    Like living men, moved slowly through the mind
400 By day, and were a trouble to my dreams.

Nutting

    ——————It seems a day
    (I speak of one from many singled out)
    One of those heavenly days that cannot die;
    When, in the eagerness of boyish hope,

5   I left our cottage-threshold, sallying forth
     With a huge wallet o'er my shoulders slung,
     A nutting-crook in hand; and turned my steps
     Tow'rd some far-distant wood, a Figure quaint,
     Tricked out in proud disguise of cast-off weeds
10 Which for that service had been husbanded,
     By exhortation of my frugal Dame –
     Motley accoutrement, of power to smile
     At thorns, and brakes, and brambles, – and, in truth,
     More ragged than need was! O'er path-less rocks,
15 Through beds of matted fern, and tangled thickets,
     Forcing my way, I came to one dear nook
     Unvisited, where not a broken bough
     Drooped with its withered leaves, ungracious sign
     Of devastation; but the hazels rose
20 Tall and erect, with tempting clusters hung,
     A virgin scene! – A little while I stood,
     Breathing with such suppression of the heart
     As joy delights in; and, with wise restraint
     Voluptuous, fearless of a rival, eyed
25 The banquet; – or beneath the trees I sate
     Among the flowers, and with the flowers I played;
     A temper known to those who, after long
     And weary expectation, have been blest
     With sudden happiness beyond all hope.
30 Perhaps it was a bower beneath whose leaves
     The violets of five seasons re-appear
     And fade, unseen by any human eye;
     Where fairy water-breaks do murmur on
     For ever; and I saw the sparkling foam,
35 And – with my cheek on one of those green stones
     That, fleeced with moss, under the shady trees,
     Lay round me, scattered like a flock of sheep –
     I heard the murmur and the murmuring sound,
     In that sweet mood when pleasure loves to pay
40 Tribute to ease; and, of its joy secure,
     The heart luxuriates with indifferent things,
     Wasting its kindliness on stocks and stones,

And on the vacant air. Then up I rose,
And dragged to earth both branch and bough, with crash
45 And merciless ravage: and the shady nook
Of hazels, and the green and mossy bower,
Deformed and sullied, patiently gave up
Their quiet being: and, unless I now
Confound my present feelings with the past,
50 Ere from the mutilated bower I turned
Exulting, rich beyond the wealth of kings,
I felt a sense of pain when I beheld
The silent trees, and saw the intruding sky. –
Then, dearest Maiden, move along these shades
55 In gentleness of heart; with gentle hand
Touch – for there is a spirit in the woods.

You may be wondering whether Wordsworth was conscious of how easily these poems lend themselves to psycho-sexual interpretation. They're both clearly journeys of initiation, rites of passage, moments of crucial transition between childhood and adolescence – or perhaps they're not quite successful journeys, perhaps only partial or incompleted passages. They resemble myths or fairy-tales, which, as it happens, often had their origins in initiation or other similar rituals.

These two texts are, indeed, mythologised moments. Perhaps all our versions of autobiography, particularly the recounting or revisiting of moments we consider most crucial or most formative, are acts of mythologising. Do we ever really know our past, our histories as anything but myths, always heavy with retrospective interpretation? If your family is like mine there may be 'family legends' that get told about your childhood which, in many cases, are fictions or at least elaborations of the ordinary into the extraordinary. They get told and retold as ways of signifying 'you' despite their shaky authenticity.

And if these two poems seem to be versions of sexual initiation then that too would make mythological sense. Knowledge of sex is a mythological moment of more anxiety and significance than any other. But whether knowledge 'happens' in any discrete or highly localised way, in what Freud called 'the primal scene', as opposed to in a more general and diffuse way, is rather unlikely. And because it's unlikely we have a psychic need to compensate by elaborating stories of charged significance, telling myths, as Wordsworth may unconsciously be doing here. The story of the fall of Adam and Eve would make little sense if that need didn't exist. 'Nutting', indeed, is a version of the fall itself. But let's look first at 'One summer evening', if only because the boy in the narrative seems, if anything, at a somewhat earlier mythological moment in his story of 'the growth of the poet's mind'.

'Her' in the first line is Nature. It's intriguing that this story of 'stealth / And troubled pleasure' is initiated by a female presence. The same is true of 'Nutting'. And it's also true of many folk-tales or more modern children's stories, from 'Little Red Riding Hood' and 'Jack and the Beanstalk' to 'Peter Rabbit' where the mother's warning, not to go into the McGregors' garden, is, in effect, an order to do exactly that. (A version of the fall can be read in the modern sci-fi thriller film *Alien*. The on-board computer that has been pro-grammed to bring the alien to earth is named Mother.) It's the mother-figure, here Mother-Nature, who launches the boy on his journey.

Fixing his eyes on what he thinks is the 'utmost boundary', the boy rows in language that suggests an act of sex – 'lustily / I dipped . . . as I rose' – only to find that the boundary has something terrifyingly behind it, 'a huge peak, black and huge', that now 'As if with voluntary power instinct / Upreared its head'. One doesn't have to be a Manhattan psychoanalyst to see here a representation of the father's phallus threatening the boy's efforts at sexual independence, nor to see in the boy's subsequent efforts of self-assertion in 'I struck and struck again' the Oedipal wish to supplant and replace the father. (That's what Peter Rabbit tries to do too, to succeed against Mr McGregor where his father had failed, and it's what Jack has to do against the giant's phallus.) 'Struck' is after all a very odd word for what was 'dipped' earlier. But the Oedipal effort is useless against the 'living thing' that 'strode after me', reducing the rower who was at first 'proud' and 'unswerving' to a state in which his oars are 'trembling' and in which he 'stole' his way home.

But it's knowledge of a kind that the boy gains here for his mind has been darkened, in effect for ever. Over his thoughts 'There hung a darkness, call it solitude / Or blank desertion'. He's lost and alone. So this too is a fall, even though as sexual initiation or Oedipal journey it's an incompletion or failure.

* * *

'Nutting' has many parallels though the central event is very different. There's no father's phallus here. But we'll see that there's a different kind of father in this poem.

As before, it's the mother-figure who delivers the boy on to his ritualistic journey. The 'dame' was actually a woman called Anne Tyson with whom Wordsworth stayed while at school. The day sounds Edenic ('One of those heavenly days that cannot die') on which the boy, wearing second-hand and unnecessarily 'ragged' clothes, 'husbanded' by his dame, goes hazelnut gathering, like Jack when the cow runs out of milk. He's in 'proud disguise', in clothing as ritualised as Red Riding Hood's, and, if the pun can be allowed, he's pretending to be a husband, not a boy, like Jack. He forces his way through 'matted' and 'tangled' vegetation and the language suggests a sexually violent entrance on to a scene itself described as 'virgin'. It's a 'dear nook / Unvisited' where 'the hazels rose / Tall and erect, with tempting clusters hung'. Once there he gets what can only be described as intense erotic pleasure from the expectation before him as he 'eyed / The banquet'. It's a kind of auto-erotic foreplay.

The violence of what follows is conveyed through the suddenness of its telling. It's a kind of rape, as the word 'ravage' suggests. The bower is 'deformed', 'sullied' and 'mutilated'. It's also shocking because the violence seems so aimless, a mere act of destruction rather than a means to an end, picking hazels. And the result, as in 'One summer evening', is a new sense of alone-ness in a world where the sky is always 'intruding'.

It's a rape and a fall. When the boy 'rose' he brought the garden down, felling it and himself in the process, its virgin beauty lost and himself, though 'rich beyond the wealth of kings', now alone in a vacant world. It's a story of intense sexual anticipation turning to equally intense sexual destructiveness. It's like a private and auto-eroticised version of the Adam and Eve story. It's a boy getting his nuts. It's Jack chopping down his father.

And the father? The father is Milton. For what distinguishes this poem from 'One summer evening' is the way the language, as well as

176

being sexually suggestive, evokes *Paradise Lost*. We met this idea at the opening of Chapter 5, the idea that poems can have anxious relations with predecessor-texts. We saw Connolly's nice comic turn in which 'Milton begat Keats, Shelley, Coleridge, Wordsworth'. A brief look at some verbal echoes might be enough to suggest the truth in that joke. (Keats famously struggled with Milton – and indeed with Wordsworth, old enough to be a kind of near-father figure.)

The verbal connections are (all but one) available by looking again at Chapter 5 (see pp. 54–77). In the Wordsworth, 'the hazels rose / Tall and erect', inescapably evoking our first sight of Adam and Eve 'erect and tall', and they 'hung' in 'clusters' just as Adam's hair 'hung / Clustering'. The hazels 'tempting . . . hung' as in Satan's account to Eve of the fruit which 'hung / Tempting'. The boy's 'dear nook' is a 'bower' which is Milton's word for Adam and Eve's place for lovemaking ('the nuptial bower'). The boy, before the sudden violence, lies where he 'heard the murmur and the murmuring sound' of 'waterbreaks', just as Eve, before she met Adam, 'laid me down' where she heard 'a murmuring sound / Of waters'. The mutilated bower is described as 'sullied', which means soiled; Adam laments (in a passage not in Chapter 5) that, after the fall, their 'wonted ornaments' are 'soiled'.

At the level of story it's perhaps not surprising that 'Nutting' reminds us of Milton's story, because both of them are so crucially sexualised, but the close echoes in language suggest something more worried about the relations between the poems. It suggests an anxiety of considerable intensity. For there's nothing in 'Nutting' that suggests Wordsworth expected the Miltonic echoes to be acknowledged. Milton is, of course, the pre-eminent poet of the pre-eighteenth-century generation, ominously behind the poets with whom Wordsworth could more easily contend ambitiously, like Swift's friend Alexander Pope whose polished and cultured satires Wordsworth was keen to advance beyond. But the real threat goes further back, is unacknowledged, and is Milton: an ominous 'peak' beyond the 'horizon's bound', to use the language of our other poem.

What is suggested is that Wordsworth had to make Milton's fall his own, to appropriate, answer and displace the father, to annihilate in the act of creation and the acquisition of power. What is striking is that the end of 'Nutting' itself is thematically about annihilating (the bower) in the act of acquisition (the nuts), as well as about the boy annihilating his own previous untroubled comforts in days that cannot die, annihilating that Eden in the 'pain' of maturity and the world's emptinesses intruding.

And there's another sense in which issues of power and creative violence are crucial to the publication of these poems. And that's a matter of historical timing whereby Wordsworth was as much a misrepresented victim as a creative agent.

It was Wordsworth and Coleridge who together compiled the volume that appeared as *Lyrical Ballads* in 1798. The second edition of 1800 contained new material, including 'Nutting' and a Preface by Wordsworth. The popular view about *Lyrical Ballads*, which Wordsworth and his supporters encouraged, is that it marked a decisive break from earlier eighteenth-century conventions into what became known as Romanticism. But recent critics, notably Marilyn Butler, have shown that the sharpest of the critical reactions were more a result of ill-timing and the crisis in the political situation than to do with the quality or nature of the poetry or the philosophy and theory in the Preface. In particular, Wordsworth's ballad-style poems in the volume, exploring the lives of simple folk in simple rhythmic forms, would have seemed unsurprising to the point of being, in Butler's words, 'ominously late' (Butler, 1981, p. 58). Ominous because anything aimed at a large audience and extolling the language and experience of ordinary people would, in 1798, have been to seem to flirt treasonably with by-then discredited revolutionary ideas from the beginning of the decade.

Butler shows that enthusiasm for and sympathy with the revolutionaries in France were at first 'marked at all levels of the population' (ibid., p. 42). Blake, with his roots traceable to the radical sects of the 1640s, is in his revolutionary poetry the most vivid and far-reaching guide to the fervour of the time, particularly in his *The Marriage of Heaven and Hell* (1790–2), which deploys Milton in a quite different way, championing his Satan's revolutionary angels in their energetic challenge to the self-satisfied establishment. Wordsworth was in France in 1792, fired by at least some of the same enthusiasm. But when from February 1793 England entered the war against France and the authorities began to whip-up and orchestrate violent loyalist reactions against radicals at home, imposing 'Gagging Acts' on public meetings, Wordsworth was not alone in moderating his earlier enthusiasm. By 1796–7 mass support for radicalism had melted away.

So for Wordsworth to publish poetry and a Preface arguing for the language of ordinary people was, in effect, to invite the kind of response it got from Francis Jeffrey, the leading critic of the age, who specifically linked Wordsworth to the most radical of all political publications from the revolutionary years, Paine's *Rights of Man* of 1791. The irony is that Wordsworth was by 1800 already on the way to adopting what Butler calls 'the public mantle of the poet of counter-revolution, celebrating . . . personal humility and service, domesticity, hearth and home'. When the French 'egalitarian revolution . . . turned into a dictatorship', says Butler, it 'made private or religious men of so many artists and intellectuals all over Europe about 1800' (1981, pp. 65–7).

Both these poems, from the crisis years of the 1790s, carry some unresolved and unconscious anxiety about power and ambition and the ambivalence in their creative destructiveness. The use of Milton in 'Nutting' is part of the anxiety. Milton in 1790–2 was a revolutionary hero to Blake. Wordsworth's investment in Milton may well have been more complex and his political position more shifting and imprecise.

We started with the idea of these poems as mythological fictions, equivalent to folk-tales. We end with the bizarre last three lines of 'Nutting', for most readers such an absurdly inadequate note on which to conclude such a poem. Perhaps that's the point. The energetically personalised, not altogether conscious anxieties suggested above might well have needed a taming, a toning down, a return to the kind of cheerful-uncle voice adopted in the last three lines, addressing a 'dearest Maiden' as if the poem is hardly about personal experience at all. As a matter of fact, after writing the main material, Wordsworth added framing lines at each end which place the incident in retrospect, warning his 'beloved friend' Lucy to 'look with feelings of fraternal love' on Nature, because the woods shrink 'from such rude intercourse' as he inflicted in his boyhood. The phrase 'fraternal love' can hardly but evoke the French republic's rallying cry; 'intercourse' is hardly less suggestive. (The *Oxford English Dictionary* dates the sexual meaning of the word from 1798. Wordsworth typically used it elsewhere with at least a suggestion of sexuality.) But Wordsworth cut all the framing material, leaving only the now rather stranded last three lines.

But another way of looking at those lines is this. It's a folk-tale ending, a prim and thin little moral as attached to the retellings of folk-tales
by the late seventeenth-century collector and reteller Charles Perrault
(and, later, partly through him, the Grimm brothers). These were massively popular in England. The definitive authority on such tales, Jack
Zipes, has shown how primitive tales conveying crucial messages
about initiation or separation-anxiety became socialised and man-
nerised for the education of higher-class children in the policing of
correctly regulated behaviour. Wordsworth's last three lines are at once
a miniature version of an equivalent domestication, a feebly childish
'romanticism', and a clear sign of failure to achieve just that, to contain
and control the energies of his own text.

We've located these poems in relation to myths and folk-tales, to Milton, to
the French revolution. Jack Zipes's many books on folk-tales are scholarly
and very readable. His *The Trials and Tribulations of Little Red Riding Hood*
(2nd edition, London, Routledge, 1993) is a model piece of research. Harold
Bloom's *The Anxiety of Influence* (2nd edition, Oxford, Oxford University Press,
1997) is his controversial statement of texts' anxious relations with
predecessor-texts. Keats's relations with Milton can be traced in his
two failed attempts at epic poems, in 'Hyperion' and 'The Fall of Hyperion'.
Marilyn Butler's *Romantics, Rebels and Reactionaries* (Oxford, Oxford
University Press, 1981) is an excellent and accessible guide to the period
1760–1830, demonstrating clearly how the study of canonical writers like
Jane Austen, Blake and Wordsworth is enriched by close attention to their
relations with immediate socio-political contexts. Roger Sales's *English
Literature in History: 1780–1830* (London, Hutchinson, 1983) has an enter-
tainingly aggressive reading of Wordsworth. *Romanticism: A Critical Reader*,
edited by Duncan Wu (Oxford, Blackwell, 1995) is a good modern collection.

10

BRONTË'S
WUTHERING HEIGHTS
Three-volume novels, centres and loss

Here we do something rather different. We'll look at the middle of *Wuthering Heights* (1847), or rather we' ll try to show that this novel has three 'centres', though its publication history has suggested otherwise. We look at that history in the light of so-called triple-decker novels and try to show that the three 'centres' at once correspond to three ways of reading and convey the vacancy and loss in the novel.

The chunk of *Wuthering Heights* that follows is the middle of the novel. It takes us from Heathcliff forcing Ellen Dean to let him have access to the sick Catherine, through her death and the birth of the younger Cathy, up to the twelve-year gap in Ellen's narrative and the young Cathy's being apparently 'perfectly contented' as a recluse in the confines of Thrushcross Grange. For reasons of space, Isabella's account of how she escaped from the violence at the Heights, and the subsequent news of Hindley's death and funeral, which Ellen insists on being 'respectable', are cut. We start at the end of Chapter 14 which is the end of Volume One.

Well, Mr Lockwood, I argued and complained, and flatly refused him fifty times; but in the long run he forced me to an agreement – I engaged to carry a letter from him to my mistress; and, should she consent, I promised to let him have intelligence of Linton's next absence from home, when he might come, and get in as he was able – I wouldn't be there, and my fellow servants should be equally out of the way.

Was it right or wrong? I fear it was wrong, though expedient. I thought I prevented another explosion by my

181

compliance; and I thought, too, it might create a favourable crisis in Catherine's mental illness: and then I remembered Mr Edgar's stern rebuke of my carrying tales; and I tried to smooth away all disquietude on my subject, by affirming, with frequent iteration, that that betrayal of trust, if it merited so harsh an appellation, should be the last.

Notwithstanding, my journey homeward was sadder than my journey thither; and many misgivings I had, ere I could prevail on myself to put the missive into Mrs Linton's hand.

But here is Kenneth – I'll go down, and tell him how much better you are. My history is *dree*, as we say, and will serve to wile away another morning.

Dree, and dreary! I reflected as the good woman descended to receive the doctor; and not exactly of a kind which I should have chosen to amuse me; but never mind! I'll extract wholesome medicines from Mrs Dean's bitter herbs; and firstly, let me beware of the fascination that lurks in Catherine Heathcliff's brilliant eyes. I should be in a curious taking if I surrendered my heart to that young person, and the daughter turned out a second edition of the mother!

[End of Volume 1]

Chapter 15 [Volume 2, Chapter 1]

Another week over – and I am so many days nearer health, and spring! I have now heard all my neighbour's history, at different sittings, as the housekeeper could spare time from more important occupations. I'll continue it in her own words, only a little condensed. She is, on the whole, a very fair narrator, and I don't think I could improve her style.

In the evening, she said, the evening of my visit to the Heights, I knew, as well as if I saw him, that Mr Heathcliff was about the place; and I shunned going out, because I still carried his letter in my pocket, and didn't want to be threatened, or teased any more.

I had made up my mind not to give it till my master went somewhere; as I could not guess how its receipt would affect Catherine. The consequence was, that it did not reach her before the lapse of three days. The fourth was Sunday, and I brought it into her room, after the family were gone to church.

There was a man servant left to keep the house with me, and we generally made a practice of locking the doors during the hours of service; but on that occasion, the weather was so warm and pleasant that I set them wide open; and to fulfil my engagement, as I knew who would be coming, I told my companion that the mistress wished very much for some oranges, and he must run over to the village and get a few, to be paid for on the morrow. He departed, and I went upstairs.

Mrs Linton sat in a loose, white dress, with a light shawl over her shoulders, in the recess of the open window, as usual. Her thick, long hair had been partly removed at the beginning of her illness; and now she wore it simply combed in its natural tresses over her temples and neck. Her appearance was altered, as I had told Heathcliff, but when she was calm, there seemed unearthly beauty in the change.

The flash of her eyes had been succeeded by a dreamy and melancholy softness: they no longer gave the impression of looking at the objects around here; they appeared always to gaze beyond, and far beyond – you would have said out of this world. Then, the paleness of her face – its haggard aspect having vanished as she recovered flesh – and the peculiar expression arising from her mental state, though painfully suggestive of their causes, added to the touching interest which she awakened; and – invariably to me, I know, and to any person who saw her, I should think – refuted more tangible proofs of convalescence and stamped her as one doomed to decay.

A book lay spread on the sill before her, and the scarcely perceptible wind fluttered its leaves at intervals. I believe Linton had laid it there, for she never endeavoured to divert herself with reading, or occupation of any kind; and he would spend many an hour in trying to entice her attention to some subject which had formerly been her amusement.

She was conscious of his aim, and in her better moods,

endured his efforts placidly, only showing their uselessness by now and then suppressing a wearied sigh, and checking him at last, with the saddest of smiles and kisses. At other times, she would turn petulantly away, and hide her face in her hands, or even push him off angrily; and then he took care to let her alone, for he was certain of doing no good.

Gimmerton chapel bells were still ringing; and the full, mellow flow of the beck in the valley came soothingly on the ear. It was a sweet substitute for the yet absent murmur of the summer foliage, which drowned that music about the Grange, when the trees were in leaf. At Wuthering Heights it always sounded on quiet days, following a great thaw or a season of steady rain – and, of Wuthering Heights, Catherine was thinking as she listened; that is, if she thought, or listened, at all; but she had the vague, distant look I mentioned before, which expressed no recognition of material things either by ear or eye.

'There's a letter for you, Mrs Linton,' I said, gently inserting it in one hand that rested on her knee. 'You must read it immediately, because it wants an answer. Shall I break the seal?'

'Yes,' she answered, without altering the direction of her eyes.

I opened it – it was very short.

'Now,' I continued, 'read it.'

She drew away her hand, and let it fall. I replaced it in her lap, and stood waiting till it should please her to glance down; but that movement was so long delayed that at last I resumed – 'Must I read it, ma'am? It is from Mr Heathcliff.' There was a start, and a troubled gleam of recollection, and a struggle to arrange her ideas. She lifted the letter, and seemed to peruse it; and when she came to the signature she sighed; yet still I found she had not gathered its import, for upon my desiring to hear her reply, she merely pointed to the name, and gazed at me with mournful and questioning eagerness.

'Well, he wishes to see you,' said I, guessing her need of an interpreter. 'He's in the garden by this time, and impatient to know what answer I shall bring.'

As I spoke, I observed a large dog, lying on the sunny grass beneath, raise its ears, as if about to bark, and then smoothing them back, announce, by a wag of the tail that some one approached whom it did not consider a stranger.

Mrs Linton bent forward, and listened breathlessly. The minute after a step traversed the hall; the open house was too tempting for Heathcliff to resist walking in: most likely he supposed that I was inclined to shirk my promise, and so resolved to trust to his own audacity.

With straining eagerness Catherine gazed towards the entrance of her chamber. He did not hit the right room directly; she motioned me to admit him; but he found it out, ere I could reach the door, and in a stride or two was at her side, and had her grasped in his arms.

He neither spoke, nor loosed his hold for some five minutes, during which period he bestowed more kisses than ever he gave in his life before, I dare say; but then my mistress had kissed him first, and I plainly saw that he could hardly bear, for downright agony, to look into her face! The same conviction had stricken him as me, from the instant he beheld her, that there was no prospect of ultimate recovery there – she was fated, sure to die.

'O, Cathy! Oh, my life! how can I bear it?' was the first sentence he uttered, in a tone that did not seek to disguise his despair.

And now he stared at her so earnestly that I thought the very intensity of his gaze would bring tears into his eyes; but they burned with anguish, they did not melt.

'What now?' said Catherine, leaning back, and returning his look with a suddenly clouded brow – her humour was a mere vane for constantly varying caprices. 'You and Edgar have broken my heart, Heathcliff! And you both come to bewail the deed to me, as if you were the people to be pitied! I shall not pity you, not I. You have killed me – and thriven on it, I think. How strong you are! How many years do you mean to live after I am gone?'

Heathcliff had knelt on one knee to embrace her; he attempted to rise, but she seized his hair, and kept him down.

'I wish I could hold you,' she continued, bitterly, 'till we

were both dead! I shouldn't care what you suffered. I care nothing for your sufferings. Why shouldn't you suffer? I do! Will
you forget me – will you be happy when I am in the earth?
Will you say twenty years hence, "That's the grave of Catherine
Earnshaw. I loved her long ago, and was wretched to lose her;
but it is past. I've loved many others since – my children are
dearer to me than she was, and, at death, I shall not rejoice that
I am going to her, I shall be sorry that I must leave them!" Will
you say so, Heathcliff?'

'Don't torture me till I'm as mad as yourself,' cried he,
wrenching his head free, and grinding his teeth.

The two, to a cool spectator, made a strange and fearful
picture. Well might Catherine deem that heaven would be a
land of exile to her, unless, with her mortal body, she cast away
her mortal character also. Her present countenance had a wild
vindictiveness in its white cheek, and a bloodless lip, and scin-
tillating eye; and she retained, in her closed fingers, a portion of
the locks she had been grasping. As to her companion, while
raising himself with one hand, he had taken her arm with the
other; and so inadequate was his stock of gentleness to the
requirements of her condition, that on his letting go, I saw four
distinct impressions left blue in the colourless skin.

'Are you possessed with a devil', he pursued, savagely, 'to
talk in that manner to me, when you are dying? Do you reflect
that all those words will be branded in my memory, and eating
deeper eternally after you have left me? You know you lie to say
I have killed you; and, Catherine, you know that I could as soon
forget you, as my existence! Is it not sufficient for your infernal
selfishness, that while you are at peace I shall writhe in the
torments of hell?'

'I shall not be at peace,' moaned Catherine, recalled to a
sense of physical weakness by the violent, unequal throbbing of
her heart, which beat visibly, and audibly, under this excess of
agitation.

She said nothing further till the paroxysm was over; then she
continued, more kindly –

'I'm not wishing you greater torment than I have, Heathcliff. I only wish us never to be parted – and should a word of

mine distress you hereafter, think I feel the same distress underground, and for my own sake, forgive me! Come here and kneel down again! You never harmed me in your life. Nay, if you nurse anger, that will be worse to remember than my harsh words! Won't you come here again? Do!'

Heathcliff went to the back of her chair, and leant over, but not so far as to let her see his face, which was livid with emotion. She bent round to look at him; he would not permit it; turning abruptly, he walked to the fireplace, where he stood, silent, with his back towards us.

Mrs. Linton's glance followed him suspiciously: every movement woke a new sentiment in her. After a pause, and a prolonged gaze, she resumed, addressing me in accents of indignant disappointment.

'Oh, you see, Nelly! he would not relent a moment to keep me out of the grave! *That* is how I'm loved! Well, never mind ! That is not *my* Heathcliff. I shall love mine yet; and take him with me – he's in my soul. And,' added she, musingly, 'the thing that irks me most is this shattered prison, after all. I'm tired, tired of being enclosed here. I'm wearying to escape into that glorious world, and to be always there; not seeing it dimly through tears, and yearning for it through the walls of an aching heart; but really with it, and in it. Nelly, you think you are better and more fortunate than I; in full health and strength – you are sorry for me – very soon that will be altered. I shall be sorry for *you*. I shall be incomparably beyond and above you all. I *wonder* he won't be near me!' She went on to herself. 'I thought he wished it. Heathcliff, dear! you should not be sullen now. Do come to me, Heathcliff.'

In her eagerness she rose, and supported herself on the arm of the chair. At that earnest appeal, he turned to her, looking absolutely desperate. His eyes wide, and wet, at last, flashed fiercely on her; his breast heaved convulsively. An instant they held asunder; and then how they met I hardly saw, but Catherine made a spring, and he caught her, and they were locked in an embrace from which I thought my mistress would never be released alive. In fact, to my eyes, she seemed directly insensible. He flung himself into the nearest seat, and on my approaching hurriedly to ascertain if she had fainted, he gnashed at me, and foamed like a mad dog, and gathered her to him with greedy jealousy. I did not feel as if I were in the company of a creature of my own species; it appeared that he would not understand, though I spoke to him; so, I stood off, and held my tongue, in great perplexity.

A movement of Catherine's relieved me a little presently: she put up her hand to clasp his neck, and bring her cheek to his, as he held her: while he, in return, covering her with frantic caresses, said wildly – 'You teach me now how cruel you've been – cruel and false. *Why* did you despise me? *Why* did you betray your own heart, Cathy? I have not one word of comfort – you deserve this. You have killed yourself. Yes, you may kiss me, and cry; and wring out my kisses and tears. They'll blight you – they'll damn you. You loved me – then what *right* had you to leave me? What right – answer me – for the poor fancy you felt for Linton? Because misery, and degradation, and death, and nothing that God or Satan could inflict would have parted us, *you*, of your own will, did it. I have not broken your heart – *you* have broken it – and in breaking it, you have broken mine. So much the worse for me, that I am strong. Do I want to live? What kind of living will it be when you – oh, God! would *you* like to live with your soul in the grave?'

'Let me alone. Let me alone,' sobbed Catherine. 'If I've done wrong, I'm dying for it. It is enough! You left me too; but I won't upbraid you! I forgive you. Forgive me!'

'It is hard to forgive, and to look at those eyes, and feel those wasted hands,' he answered. 'Kiss me again; and don't let me see your eyes! I forgive what you have done to me. I love *my* murderer – but *yours* ! How can I?'

They were silent – their faces hid against each other, and washed by each other's tears. At least, I suppose the weeping was on both sides; as it seemed Heathcliff *could* weep on a great occasion like this.

I grew very uncomfortable, meanwhile; for the afternoon wore fast away, the man whom I had sent off returned from his errand, and I could distinguish, by the shine of the westering sun up the valley, a concourse thickening outside Gimmerton chapel porch.

'Service is over,' I announced. 'My master will be here in half an hour.'

Heathcliff groaned a curse, and strained Catherine closer – she never moved.

Ere long I perceived a group of the servants passing up the road towards the kitchen wing. Mr Linton was not far behind; he opened the gate himself, and sauntered slowly up, probably enjoying the lovely afternoon that breathed as soft as summer.

'Now he is here,' I exclaimed. 'For Heaven's sake, hurry down! You'll not meet any one on the front stairs. Do be quick; and stay among the trees till he is fairly in.'

'I must go, Cathy,' said Heathcliff, seeking to extricate himself from his companion's arms. 'But, if I live, I'll see you again before you are asleep. I won't stay five yards from your window,'

'You must not go!' she answered, holding him as firmly as her strength allowed. 'You shall not, I tell you.'

'For one hour,' he pleaded earnestly.

'Not for one minute,' she replied.

'I *must* – Linton will be up immediately,' persisted the alarmed intruder.

He would have risen, and unfixed her fingers by the act – she clung fast, gasping; there was mad resolution in her face.

'No! she shrieked. 'Oh, don't, don't go. It is the last time! Edgar will not hurt us. Heathcliff, I shall die! I shall die!'

'Damn the fool! There he is,' cried Heathcliff, sinking back into his seat. 'Hush, my darling! Hush, hush, Catherine! I'll stay. If he shot me so, I'd expire with a blessing on my lips.'

And there they were fast again. I heard my master mounting the stairs – the cold sweat ran from my forehead; I was horrified.

'Are you going to listen to her ravings?' I said, passionately. 'She does not know what she says. Will you ruin her, because she has not wit to help herself? Get up! You could be free instantly. That is the most diabolical deed that ever you did. We are all done for – master, mistress, and servant.'

I wrung my hands, and cried out; and Mr Linton hastened

his step at the noise. In the midst of my agitation, I was sincerely glad to observe that Catherine's arms had fallen relaxed, and her head hung down.

'She's fainted or dead,' I thought; 'so much the better. Far better that she should be dead, than lingering a burden and a misery-maker to all about her.'

Edgar sprang to his unbidden guest, blanched with astonishment and rage. What he meant to do, I cannot tell; however, the other stopped all demonstrations, at once, by placing the lifeless-looking form in his arms.

'Look here!' he said. 'Unless you be a fiend, help her first — then you shall speak to me!'

He walked into the parlour, and sat down. Mr Linton summoned me, and with great difficulty, and after resorting to many means, we managed to restore her to sensation; but she was all bewildered; she sighed, and moaned, and knew nobody. Edgar, in his anxiety for her, forgot her hated friend. I did not. I went, at the earliest opportunity, and besought him to depart, affirming that Catherine was better, and he should hear from me in the morning, how she passed the night.

'I shall not refuse to go out of doors,' he answered; 'but I shall stay in the garden; and, Nelly, mind you keep your word tomorrow. I shall be under those larch trees, mind! or I pay another visit, whether Linton be in or not.'

He sent a rapid glance through the half-open door of the chamber, and, ascertaining that what I stated was apparently true, delivered the house of his luckless presence.

Chapter 16 [Volume 2, Chapter 2]

About twelve o'clock, that night, was born the Catherine you saw at Wuthering Heights, a puny, seven months' child; and two hours after, the mother died, having never recovered sufficient consciousness to miss Heathcliff, or know Edgar.

The latter's distraction at his bereavement is a subject too painful to be dwelt on; its after effects showed how deep the sorrow sunk.

A great addition, in my eyes, was his being left without an

heir. I bemoaned that, as I gazed on the feeble orphan; and I mentally abused old Linton for, what was only natural partiality, the securing his estate to his own daughter, instead of *his* son's.

An unwelcomed infant it was, poor thing! It might have wailed out of life, and nobody cared a morsel, during those first hours of existence. We redeemed the neglect afterwards; but its beginning was as friendless as its end is likely to be.

Next morning – bright and cheerful out of doors – stole softened in through the blinds of the silent room, and suffused the couch and its occupant with a mellow, tender glow.

Edgar Linton had his head laid on the pillow, and his eyes shut. His young and fair features were almost as deathlike as those of the form beside him, and almost as fixed; but *his* was the hush of exhausted anguish, and *hers* of perfect peace. Her brow smooth, her lids closed, her lips wearing the expression of a smile. No angel in heaven could be more beautiful than she appeared; and I partook of the infinite calm in which she lay. My mind was never in a holier frame, than while I gazed on that untroubled image of Divine rest. I instinctively echoed the words she had uttered a few hours before. 'Incomparably beyond, and above us all! Whether still on earth or now in heaven, her spirit is at home with God!'

I don't know if it be a peculiarity in me, but I am seldom otherwise than happy while watching in the chamber of death, should no frenzied or despairing mourner share the duty with me. I see a repose that neither earth nor hell can break; and I feel an assurance of the endless and shadowless hereafter – the Eternity they have entered – where life is boundless in its duration, and love in its sympathy, and joy in its fulness. I noticed on that occasion how much selfishness there is even in a love like Mr Linton's, when he so regretted Catherine's blessed release!

To be sure, one might have doubted, after the wayward and impatient existence she had led, whether she merited a haven of peace at last. One might doubt in seasons of cold reflection, but not then, in the presence of her corpse. It asserted its own tranquillity, which seemed a pledge of equal quiet to its former inhabitant.

Do you believe such people *are* happy in the other world, sir? I'd give a great deal to know.

I declined answering Mrs Dean's question, which struck me as something heterodox. She proceeded:

Retracing the course of Catherine Linton, I fear we have no right to think she is: but we'll leave her with her Maker.

The master looked asleep, and I ventured soon after sunrise to quit the room and steal out to the pure, refreshing air. The servants thought me gone to shake off the drowsiness of my protracted watch; in reality, my chief motive was seeing Mr Heathcliff. If he had remained among the larches all night he would have heard nothing of the stir at the Grange, unless, perhaps, he might catch the gallop of the messenger going to Gimmerton. If he had come nearer, he would probably be aware, from the lights flitting to and fro, and the opening and shutting of the outer doors, that all was not right within.

I wished yet feared to find him. I felt the terrible news must be told, and I longed to get it over, but *how* to do it, I did not know.

He was there – at least a few yards further in the park; leant against an old ash tree, his hat off, and his hair soaked with the dew that had gathered on the budded branches, and fell pattering round him. He had been standing a long time in that position, for I saw a pair of ousels passing and repassing, scarcely three feet from him, busy in building their nest, and regarding his proximity no more than that of a piece of timber. They flew off at my approach, and he raised his eyes and spoke:

'She's dead!' he said; 'I've not waited for you to learn that. Put your handkerchief away – don't snivel before me. Damn you all! she wants none of *your* tears!'

I was weeping as much for him as her: we do sometimes pity creatures that have none of the feeling either for themselves or others; and when I first looked into his face, I perceived that he had got intelligence of the catastrophe; and a foolish notion struck me that his heart was quelled, and he prayed, because his lips moved, and his gaze was bent on the ground.

'Yes, she's dead!' I answered, checking my sobs, and drying my cheeks. 'Gone to heaven, I hope, where we may, every one, join her, if we take due warning, and leave our evil ways to follow good!'

'Did *she* take due warning, then?' asked Heathcliff, attempting a sneer. 'Did she die like a saint? Come, give me a true history of the event. How did –'

He endeavoured to pronounce the name, but could not manage it; and compressing his mouth, he held a silent combat with his inward agony, defying, meanwhile, my sympathy with an unflinching, ferocious stare.

'How did she die?' he resumed, at last – fain, notwithstanding his hardihood, to have a support behind him, for, after the struggle, he trembled, in spite of himself, to his very finger-ends.

'Poor wretch!' I thought; 'you have a heart and nerves the same as your brother men! Why should you be anxious to conceal them? your pride cannot blind God! You tempt him to wring them, till he forces a cry of humiliation!'

'Quietly as a lamb!' I answered, aloud. 'She drew a sigh, and stretched herself, like a child reviving, and sinking again to sleep; and five minutes after I felt one little pulse at her heart, and nothing more!'

'And – did she ever mention me?' he asked, hesitating, as if he dreaded the answer to his question would introduce details that he could not bear to hear.

'Her senses never returned – she recognised nobody from the time you left her,' I said. 'She lies with a sweet smile on her face; and her latest ideas wandered back to pleasant early days. Her life closed in a gentle dream – may she wake as kindly in the other world!'

'May she wake in torment!' he cried, with frightful vehemence, stamping his foot, and groaning in a sudden paroxysm of ungovernable passion. 'Why, she's a liar to the end! Where is she? Not *there* – not in heaven – not perished – where? Oh! you said you cared nothing for my sufferings! And I pray one prayer – I repeat it till my tongue stiffens – Catherine Earnshaw, may you not rest, as long as I am living! You said I killed you – haunt me then! The murdered *do* haunt their murderers. I believe – I know that ghosts *have* wandered on earth. Be with me always – take any form – drive me mad! only *do* not leave me in this abyss, where I cannot find you! Oh God! it is unutterable! I *cannot* live without my life! I *cannot* live without my soul!'

He dashed his head against the knotted trunk; and, lifting up his eyes, howled, not like a man, but like a savage beast getting goaded to death with knives and spears.

I observed several splashes of blood about the bark of the tree, and his hands and forehead were both stained; probably the scene I witnessed was a repetition of others acted during the night. It hardly moved my compassion – it appalled me; still I felt reluctant to quit him so. But the moment he recollected himself enough to notice me watching, he thundered a command for me to go, and I obeyed. He was beyond my skill to quiet or console!

Mrs Linton's funeral was appointed to take place on the Friday following her decease; and till then her coffin remained uncovered, and strewn with flowers and scented leaves, in the great drawing-room. Linton spent his days and nights there, a sleepless guardian; and – a circumstance concealed from all but me – Heathcliff spent his nights, at least, outside, equally a stranger to repose.

I held no communication with him; still I was conscious of his design to enter, if he could; and on the Tuesday, a little after dark, when my master, from sheer fatigue, had been compelled to retire a couple of hours, I went and opened one of the windows, moved by his perseverance to give him a chance of bestowing on the fading image of his idol one final adieu.

He did not omit to avail himself of the opportunity, cautiously and briefly; too cautiously to betray his presence by the slightest noise; indeed, I shouldn't have discovered that he had been there, except for the disarrangement of the drapery about the corpse's face, and for observing on the floor a curl of light hair, fastened with a silver thread, which, on examination, I ascertained to have been taken from a locket hung round Catherine's neck. Heathcliff had opened the trinket and cast out its contents, replacing them by a black lock of his own. I twisted the two, and enclosed them together.

Mr Earnshaw was, of course, invited to attend the remains of his sister to the grave; and he sent no excuse, but he never came; so that besides her husband, the mourners were wholly composed of tenants and servants. Isabella was not asked.

The place of Catherine's interment, to the surprise of the villagers, was neither in the chapel, under the carved monument of the Lintons, nor yet by the tombs of her own relations, outside. It was dug on a green slope, in a corner of the kirkyard, where the wall is so low that heath and bilberry plants have climbed over it from the moor; and peat mould almost buries it. Her husband lies in the same spot, now; and they have each a simple headstone above, and a plain grey block at their feet, to mark the graves.

Chapter 17 [Volume 2, Chapter 3]

That Friday made the last of our fine days, for a month. In the evening, the weather broke; the wind shifted from south to north-east, and brought rain first, and then sleet, and snow.

On the morrow one could hardly imagine that there had been three weeks of summer: the primroses and crocuses were hidden under wintry drifts: the larks were silent, the young leaves of the early trees smitten and blackened – and dreary, and chill, and dismal that morrow did creep over! My master kept his room – I took possession of the lonely parlour, converting it into a nursery; and there I was sitting, with the moaning doll of a child laid on my knee; rocking it to and fro, and watching, meanwhile, the still driving flakes build up the uncurtained window, when the door opened, and some person entered, out of breath, and laughing!

My anger was greater than my astonishment for a minute; I supposed it one of the maids, and I cried,

'Have done! How dare you show your giddiness, here? What would Mr Linton say if he heard you?'

'Excuse me!' answered a familiar voice; 'but I know Edgar is in bed, and I cannot stop myself.'

With that, the speaker came forward to the fire, panting and holding her hand to her side.

'I have run the whole way from Wuthering Heights!' she continued, after a pause. 'Except where I've flown – I couldn't count the number of falls I've had – Oh, I'm aching all over! Don't be alarmed – There shall be an explanation as soon as I can give it – only just have the goodness to step out and order the carriage to take me on to Gimmerton, and tell a servant to seek up a few clothes in my wardrobe.'

The intruder was Mrs Heathcliff – She certainly seemed in no laughing predicament: her hair streaming on her shoulders, dripping with snow and water; she was dressed in the girlish dress she commonly wore, befitting her age more than her position; a low frock, with short sleeves, and nothing on either head or neck. The frock was of light silk, and clung to her with wet; and her feet were protected merely by thin slippers; add to this a deep cut under one ear, which only the cold prevented from bleeding profusely, a white face scratched and bruised, and a frame hardly able to support itself through fatigue, and you may fancy my first fright was not much allayed when I had leisure to examine her.

'My dear young lady,' I exclaimed, 'I'll stir nowhere, and hear nothing, till you have removed every article of your clothes, and put on dry things; and certainly you shall not go to Gimmerton tonight, so it is needless to order the carriage.'

'Certainly, I shall,' she said; 'walking or riding – yet I've no objection to dress myself decently; and – ah, see how it flows down my neck now ! The fire does make it smart.'

She insisted on my fulfilling her directions, before she would let me touch her; and not till after the coachman had been instructed to get ready, and a maid set to pack up some necessary attire, did I obtain her consent for binding the wound, and helping to change her garments.

'Now, Ellen,' she said, when my task was finished, and she was seated in an easy chair on the hearth, with a cup of tea before her, 'you sit down opposite me, and put poor Catherine's baby away – I don't like to see it! You mustn't think I care little for Catherine, because I behaved so foolishly on entering – I've cried too, bitterly – yes, more than any one else has reason to cry – we parted unreconciled, you remember, and I shan't forgive myself. But, for all that, I was not going to sympathise with him – the brute beast! Oh, give me the poker! This is the last thing of his I have about me.' She slipped the gold ring from her third finger, and threw it on the floor. 'I'll smash it!' she continued, striking it with childish spite. 'And then I'll burn it!' and she took and dropped the misused article among the coals. 'There! he shall buy another, if he gets me back again. He'd be capable of coming to seek me, to tease Edgar – I dare not stay, lest that notion should possess his wicked head! And besides, Edgar has not been kind, has he? And I won't come suing for his assistance; nor will I bring him into more trouble – Necessity compelled me to seek shelter here; though if I had not learnt he was out of the way, I'd have halted at the kitchen, washed my face, warmed myself, got you to bring what I wanted, and departed again to anywhere out of the reach of my accursed – of that incarnate goblin! Ah, he was in such a fury – if he had caught me! It's a pity, Earnshaw is not his match in strength – I wouldn't have run, till I'd seen him all but demolished, had Hindley been able to do it!'

'Well, don't talk so fast, Miss!' I interrupted, 'you'll disorder the handkerchief I have tied round your face, and make the cut bleed again – Drink your tea, and take breath, and give over laughing – Laughter is sadly out of place under this roof, and in your condition!'

'An undeniable truth,' she replied. 'Listen to that child! It maintains a constant wail – send it out of my hearing, for an hour; I shan't stay any longer.'

I rang the bell, and committed it to a servant's care; and then I inquired what had urged her to escape from Wuthering Heights in such an unlikely plight – and where she meant to go, as she refused remaining with us.

[. . .]

I insisted on the funeral being respectable – Mr Heathcliff said I might have my own way there, too; only, he desired me to remember, that the money for the whole affair came out of his pocket.

He maintained a hard, careless deportment, indicative of neither joy nor sorrow; if anything, it expressed a flinty gratification at a piece of difficult work, successfully executed. I observed once, indeed, something like exultation in his aspect. It was just when the people were bearing the coffin from the house; he had the hypocrisy to represent a mourner; and previous to following with Hareton, he lifted the unfortunate child on to the table, and muttered, with peculiar gusto,

'Now, my bonny lad, you are *mine*! And we'll see if one tree won't grow as crooked as another, with the same wind to twist it!'

The unsuspecting thing was pleased at this speech; he played with Heathcliff's whiskers, and stroked his cheek, but I divined its meaning, and observed tartly,

'That boy must go back with me to Thrushcross Grange, sir. There is nothing in the world less yours than he is!'

'Does Linton say so?' he demanded.

'Of course – he has ordered me to take him,' I replied.

'Well,' said the scoundrel, 'we'll not argue the subject now; but I have a fancy to try my hand at rearing a young one, so intimate to your master, that I must supply the place of this with my own, if he attempt to remove it. I don't engage to let Hareton go, undisputed; but I'll be pretty sure to make the other come! Remember to tell him.'

This hint was enough to bind our hands. I repeated its substance on my return, and Edgar Linton, little interested at the commencement, spoke no more of interfering. I'm not aware that he could have done it to any purpose, had he been ever so willing.

The guest was now the master of Wuthering Heights: he held firm possession, and proved it to the attorney, who, in his turn, proved it to Mr Linton, that Earnshaw had mortgaged every yard of land he owned for cash to supply his mania for gaming; and he, Heathcliff, was the mortgagee.

In that manner, Hareton, who should now be the first gentleman in the neighbourhood was reduced to a state of complete dependence on his father's inveterate enemy; and lives in his own house as a servant deprived of the advantage of wages, and quite unable to right himself, because of his friendlessness, and his ignorance that he has been wronged.

Chapter 18 [Volume 2, Chapter 4]

The twelve years, continued Mrs Dean, following that dismal period, were the happiest of my life: my greatest troubles, in their passage, rose from our little lady's trifling illnesses, which she had to experience in common with all children, rich and poor.

For the rest, after the first six months, she grew like a larch; and could walk and talk, too, in her own way, before the heath bloomed a second time over Mrs Linton's dust.

She was the most winning thing that ever brought sunshine into a desolate house – a real beauty in face – with the Earnshaws' handsome dark eyes, but the Lintons' fair skin and small features, and yellow curling hair. Her spirit was high, though not rough, and qualified by a heart, sensitive and lively to excess in its affections. That capacity for intense attachments reminded me of her mother; still she did not resemble her; for she could be soft and mild as a dove, and she had a gentle voice, and pensive expression: her anger was never furious, her love never fierce; it was deep and tender.

However, it must be acknowledged, she had faults to foil her gifts. A propensity to be saucy was one; and a perverse will that indulged children invariably acquire, whether they be good tempered or cross. If a servant chanced to vex her, it was always: 'I shall tell papa!' And if he reproved her, even by a look, you would have thought it a heartbreaking business: I don't believe he ever did speak a harsh word to her.

He took her education entirely on himself, and made it an amusement: fortunately, curiosity and a quick intellect urged her into an apt scholar; she learnt rapidly and eagerly, and did honour to his teaching.

Till she reached the age of thirteen, she had not once been beyond the range of the park by herself. Mr Linton would take her with him, a mile or so outside, on rare occasions, but he trusted her to no one else. Gimmerton was an unsubstantial name in her ears; the chapel, the only building she had approached or entered, except her own home. Wuthering Heights and Mr Heathcliff did not exist for her; she was a perfect recluse; and apparently perfectly contented.

Let's explore the novel's structure in the context of its publication history. It was brought out originally by a rather shifty publisher called Newby as the first two volumes of a three-volume book, with Anne Brontë's *Agnes Grey* as the third volume. Three-volume novels were financially attractive to publishers and also to the new lending libraries because it meant that novels could be read by three readers simultaneously. There is no surviving manuscript. Newby did a pretty rough job of it and subjected Brontë to a very rough financial deal (she had to pay money up front and he never repaid her, despite promising to). It seems very questionable whether Brontë had a hand in deciding on the double-volume format or where the first volume ended. Be that as it may, there would appear to be three 'centres' to the design and they work strangely together.

I'll call them centres A, B and C.

Centre A: Volume One as printed by Newby ends at the close of Chapter 14. Heathcliff forces Ellen to take a letter to the sick Cathy. In terms of plot this is an awkward place for a gap, as well as structurally marking an unequal first half. There are 34 chapters; we're 41 per cent through the chapters and 45.5 per cent through the total pages. But it is nonetheless an appropriate choice for a gap. Of the three centres under review it most clearly signals a reason to continue reading (the cliffhanger) and it does so with a nice literary (even publisher's) joke about a new 'edition'. The ending has Ellen noticing Dr Kenneth's arrival and the narrative returning to the novel's first narrator, Lockwood, and so to the outer frame around the text. In so doing we are returned to the sad-comic presentation of Lockwood's delusionary vanity, his persistent belief in his attractiveness to Cathy (and to other young women). He says this: 'let me beware of the fascination that lurks in Catherine Heathcliff's brilliant eyes. I should be in a curious taking if . . . the daughter turned out a second edition of the mother!' Lockwood likes jokes like that 'edition' and it's a good joke (his, Brontë's, Newby's?) if the volume ends there. Volume Two resumes with Lockwood talking, a week later, and returning the narrative to Ellen.

Centre B: The centre in terms of totality of pages is the end of Chapter 16 (Volume Two, Chapter 2): that is, it's the mathematical centre of the novel. This follows the only occasion in the entire novel, described in the explosive Chapter 15, when Heathcliff and Catherine are 'locked' together – a moment shadowed by the fact that she's dying (and seven months pregnant). Chapter 16 gives us Catherine's death and Heathcliff's distraught response. His plea – 'Catherine Earnshaw, may you not rest . . . haunt me' (note the 'Earnshaw') – returns the reader to Chapter 3, where Lockwood muses over the Catherine Earnshaw-Heathcliff-Linton riddle, undergoes the haunting (it that's what it is) of the child at the window, and hears Heathcliff's desperate pleading ('do come . . . once more') to the now vanished apparition.

Two crucial narrative developments now occur. First, Ellen tells how she discovers that Heathcliff has substituted Edgar's lock of hair in the locket round Catherine's neck with one of his own. Ellen twists the light with the black and 'enclosed them together'. Secondly, the chapter ends with the narrative tracking forward, in a way it does nowhere else, to anticipate Edgar's own death and burial next to Catherine. The language in this remarkable couple of sentences is somehow over and above Ellen's usual utilitarian, functional-sentimental discourse.

> It [Catherine's grave] was dug on a green slope, in a corner of the kirkyard, where the wall is so low that heath and bilberry plants have climbed over it from the moor; and peat mould almost buries it. Her husband lies in the same spot, now; and they have each a simple headstone above, and a plain grey block at their feet, to mark the graves.

This has a charged, poem-like eloquence. (And, unlike the other two centres, this could be an ending, as, in effect, it is in the famous black-and-white Olivier film.) What is intriguing is that it is recognisably the same idiom as used in the passage which it clearly anticipates, the novel's very last paragraphs, where, in just the same way, the language seems too fraught and charged for its notional speaker, in this case Lockwood.

> I sought, and soon discovered, the three headstones on the slope next the moor – the middle one, grey, and half buried in

heath – Edgar Linton's only harmonized by the turf and moss, creeping up its foot – Heathcliff's still bare.

The premonition of the novel's end (the three graves) at its centre (the two graves) is focused in the image of the locket, where the three bits of body lie together, but not quite together, for the only time, as two threads intertwined, lying on but not twined with or inside the body of the third. The sexual suggestiveness is obvious, as is the expressive image, here as elsewhere, of locks and openings (which is the novel's allowed language for the disallowed representation of sexual penetration). In that respect the locket secretly opened by Heathcliff in this passage returns us to the sexual violence of the triangular confrontation earlier where Catherine throws her key into the fire and Heathcliff smashes the lock with a poker. But it's the language that combines the centre with the end that is most expressive of all. One might say that these two textual moments, one at the exact centre, one at the end, are the novel's only recourse to a narrator beyond the doubly framing Lockwood and Ellen. It is as if they're spoken by a narrator somehow beyond the narrative. We could do worse than call this narrator Emily Brontë.

Centre C: The centre in terms of number of chapters is at the close of Chapter 17 (Volume Two Chapter 3). Why, incidentally, 34 chapters? My guess is that this is a representation of 2 times 17, the two Cathys at 17, the age at which both their fates and their statuses become so crucially altered. They both marry aged 17. Hindley dies, Heathcliff takes over at the Heights, and Nelly's narrative connects with one of the opening mysteries of the book, Hareton's status at the Heights, by explaining how Hareton came to be reduced to a state of servitude. This, in terms of Heathcliff's designs, is a hinge moment, an appropriate place for a gap. But much more obviously appropriate is the fact that between Chapters 17 and 18 is the gap of twelve years, easily the biggest gap in the narrative. (This centre is thus equivalent to the years passing at the centre of Shakespeare's *The Winter's Tale* and George Eliot's *Silas Marner*. In all three cases one is reminded of fairy-tale.) So this is a very appropriate centre in terms of the novel's chronology and in terms of Heathcliff's larger design, to take over both houses.

The three centres (a) foreground Lockwood and the sad-comic frame in which he holds the entire book; (b) foreground the novel's most formative event, Catherine's death, and encompass its dramatic-emotional reach: back to the original apparition and forward to the graves which may or may not be at peace at the end – and delivered to the reader in a voice that strangely disembodies the notional narrator(s); and (c) foreground Heathcliff's designs and the equally carefully planned design of the novel's chronology.

These may be said to correspond to three contextualising ways of reading the novel: (a) the formalist reading, which would focus on the framings, the narrators, the highly literary constructedness of the novel; (b) the sexual-politics reading, the one connecting the dead Catherine, the unfulfilled love, and the woman writing/speaking in silence (at the novel's centre, but also on the margins of the text's production and distribution, as suggested at the novel's outset in the image of the young Catherine compelled to self-expression in the margins of men's books); and (c) the reading as discovery, the unfolding of dramatic plot in a dimensionalised real-time chronology, and the primitive pleasures the reader takes from that unfolding within that illusion of real time, the pleasure equivalent to that taken by Heathcliff in the unfolding of his vengeful-sadistic design.

The fact that we, as it were, have three differently functioning centres seems to serve two larger ideas. First, the effect is of a repeatedly aching gap in the novel, one equivalent to the absent centre at the heart of the whole story – the fact that the Catherine–Heathcliff story is not really a love-story at all but a series of wounding separations and losses. There is no centre where there should be the sexualised centring of consummation. Second, the three centres seem to be arranged, in terms of hierarchy, as the one centre (where the woman writer finally speaks and what she speaks is death) secreted within the other two (where the unwinding of plot and the structuring frame are foregrounded). But in terms of casual reading this, the second centre, is the least noticeable. The others are more clearly signposted, the first with its alteration of the main narrative frame (and, of course, the end of a Volume), and the third with its twelve-year gap.

This notion lends itself to both psycho-sexual and biographical readings. Women's sexuality is, in the nineteenth-century novel, unnoticeable; Emily stayed at home and wasn't noticed by the world like Charlotte. Whatever, what we've been noticing is that these three moments in the text are wounds, gaps and centres, all at once. They figure the one obviously unavailable fact in the novel – Cathy and Heathcliff's sexualities, to each other.

In terms of the publication and marketing of the novel, whatever might have been Brontë's conscious or unconscious design in providing these three centres is obscured by what was Newby's take-it-or-leave-it deal, forcing the book into serving as the first two volumes of a three-volume commodity. And Newby himself was, perhaps, constrained to follow that convention of economic-cultural practice, the triple-decker novel with its own strange history. Charlotte's one-volume novel *The Professor* ran through the series of publishers' rejections that *Wuthering Heights* and *Agnes Grey* originally received – though one more kindly publisher, in rejecting it, 'added that a work in three volumes would meet with careful attention' (Charlotte Brontë's 'Biographical Notice', 1850). And modern editions that observe the two-volume format continue in that process of obscuring the larger design.

It may be worth adding that a number of Shakespeare plays have exact mathematical centres that are of remarkable emotional-dramatic interest: Lear's prayer to the 'poor naked wretches' and the dumb-show in *Hamlet*, for instance (two moments of strangely muted eloquence). Such centres, designed or otherwise, are equally obscured by conventions of act and scene divisions and the convention (driven by social and commercial imperatives as much as artistic ones) of plays having intervals. Shakespeare's plays were originally performed, at much greater pace than we're used to, without intervals.

The notion that texts might have dispersed centres that correspond to their awareness that centres of fulfilment or truth can never be found may repay investigation. *Hamlet*, in which everyone is chasing centres and truths and which has a long series of seemingly central moments (with the silent dumb-show blankly in the exact middle), may be a case in point. Polonius, absurdly, claims that he can always find truth 'though it were hid indeed / Within the centre' (II.ii.157–8). The temptation to think that Cathy and Heathcliff's relationship is more centred and fulfilled than it is may be partly due to the many film versions which sentimentalise it. There are two especially good editions of *Wuthering Heights*. Heather Glen's (London, Routledge, 1988) has fine and subtle essays at front and back, the first of which identifies three crucial contexts for the novel's languages. Linda H. Peterson's (Boston, Bedford Books, 1992) is one of the best in the variable Case Studies in Contemporary Criticism series. It collects important critical work from various schools of criticism, and all the essays are notable, particularly J. Hillis Miller's deconstructionist reading. The Open University's volume *The Realist Novel*, edited by Dennis Walder (London, Routledge, 1995), is a wide-ranging and important collection on the genre in its social contexts (including readership and publication issues) and it reprints key material from leading critics such as Raymond Williams and Edward Said.

11

MELVILLE'S *BARTLEBY*
The crisis of interpretation

In this chapter we'll be reading Herman Melville's *Bartleby* (1853). And the focus for the commentary that follows is the nature and the problem of interpretation. How and why do we have the need to interpret? And how does this story, particularly in its ending, challenge and unsettle us in that need? The focus is on Bartleby as a character: but what is a 'character' in a text?

Here, nearly complete, is *Bartleby,* one of the most sheerly odd of all novellas or long short stories. Readers tend to find that it helps to read it aloud or to hear it read aloud. The narrator is a Wall Street lawyer and at the start of his narrative he's rather elaborately concerned with telling us about his office-workers. These are the nicely named Turkey, Nippers and Ginger Nut. I've abridged this elaborate introduction. The situation is this: because of extra demands on his office he's obliged to hire an extra copyist (scrivener). So Bartleby appears.

Now my original business – that of a conveyancer and title hunter, and drawer-up of recondite documents of all sorts — was considerably increased by receiving the Master's office. There was now great work for scriveners. Not only must I push the clerks already with me, but I must have additional help.

In answer to my advertisement, a motionless young man one morning stood upon my office threshold, the door being open, for it was summer. I can see that figure now – pallidly neat, pitiably respectable, incurably forlorn! It was Bartleby.

After a few words touching his qualifications, I engaged him, glad to have among my corps of copyists a man of so singularly sedate an aspect, which I thought might operate

206

beneficially upon the flighty temper of Turkey and the fiery one of Nippers.

I should have stated before that ground-glass folding doors divided my premises into two parts, one of which was occupied by my scriveners, the other by myself. According to my humor, I threw open these doors or closed them. I resolved to assign Bartleby a corner by the folding doors, but on my side of them, so as to have this quiet man within easy call, in case any trifling thing was to be done. I placed his desk close up to a small side window in that part of the room, a window which originally had afforded a lateral view of certain grimy back yards and bricks, but which, owing to subsequent erections, commanded at present no view at all, though it gave some light. Within three feet of the panes was a wall, and the light came down from far above, between two lofty buildings, as from a very small opening in a dome. Still further to a satisfactory arrangement, I procured a high green folding screen, which might entirely isolate Bartleby from my sight, though not remove him from my voice. And thus, in a manner, privacy and society were conjoined.

At first, Bartleby did an extraordinary quantity of writing. As if long famishing for something to copy, he seemed to gorge himself on my documents. There was no pause for digestion. He ran a day and night line, copying by sunlight and by candlelight. I should have been quite delighted with his application, had he been cheerfully industrious. But he wrote on silently, palely, mechanically.

It is, of course, an indispensable part of a scrivener's business to verify the accuracy of his copy, word by word. Where there are two or more scriveners in an office, they assist each other in this examination, one reading from the copy, the other holding the original. It is a very dull, wearisome, and lethargic affair. I can readily imagine that, to some sanguine temperaments, it would be altogether intolerable. For example, I cannot credit that the mettlesome poet, Byron, would have contentedly sat down with Bartleby to examine a law document of, say five hundred pages, closely written in a crimpy hand.

Now and then, in the haste of business, it had been my habit to assist in comparing some brief document myself, calling Turkey or Nippers for this purpose. One object I had in placing Bartleby so handy to me behind the screen was to avail myself of his services on such trivial occasions. It was on the third day, I think, of his being with me, and before any necessity had arisen for having his own writing examined, that, being much hurried to complete a small affair I had in hand, I abruptly called to Bartleby. In my haste and natural expectancy of instant compliance, I sat with my head bent over the original on my desk, and my right hand sideways, and somewhat nervously extended with the copy, so that, immediately upon emerging from his retreat, Bartleby might snatch it and proceed to business without the least delay.

In this very attitude did I sit when I called to him, rapidly stating what it was I wanted him to do – namely, to examine a small paper with me. Imagine my surprise, nay, my consternation, when, without moving from his privacy, Bartleby, in a singularly mild, firm voice, replied, 'I would prefer not to.'

I sat awhile in perfect silence, rallying my stunned faculties. Immediately it occurred to me that my ears had deceived me, or Bartleby had entirely misunderstood my meaning. I repeated my request in the clearest tone I could assume; but in quite as clear a one came the previous reply, 'I would prefer not to.'

'Prefer not to,' echoed I, rising in high excitement, and crossing the room with a stride. 'What do you mean? Are you moon-struck? I want you to help me compare this sheet here – take it,' and I thrust it towards him.

'I would prefer not to,' said he.

I looked at him steadfastly. His face was leanly composed; his gray eyes dimly calm. Not a wrinkle of agitation rippled him. Had there been the least uneasiness, anger, impatience or impertinence in his manner; in other words, had there been anything ordinarily human about him, doubtless I should have violently dismissed him from the premises. But as it was I should have as soon thought of turning my pale plaster-of-Paris bust of Cicero out of doors. I stood gazing at him awhile, as he went on with his own writing, and then reseated myself at my desk. This is very strange, thought I. What had one best do? But my business hurried me. I concluded to forget the matter for the present, reserving it for my future leisure. So calling Nippers from the other room, the paper was speedily examined.

A few days after this, Bartleby concluded four lengthy documents, being quadruplicates of a week's testimony taken before me in my High Court of Chancery. It became necessary to examine them. It was an important suit, and great accuracy was imperative. Having all things arranged, I called Turkey, Nippers, and Ginger Nut from the next room, meaning to place the four copies in the hands of my four clerks, while I should read from the original. Accordingly, Turkey, Nippers, and Ginger Nut had taken their seats in a row, each with his document in his hand, when I called to Bartleby to join this interesting group.

'Bartleby! quick, I am waiting.'

I heard a slow scrape of his chair legs on the uncarpeted floor, and soon he appeared standing at the entrance of his hermitage.

'What is wanted?' said he, mildly.

'The copies, the copies,' said I, hurriedly. 'We are going to examine them. There' – and I held towards him the fourth quadruplicate.

'I would prefer not to,' he said, and gently disappeared behind the screen.

For a few moments I was turned into a pillar of salt, standing at the head of my seated column of clerks. Recovering myself, I advanced towards the screen and demanded the reason for such extraordinary conduct.

'*Why* do you refuse?'

'I would prefer not to.'

With any other man I should have flown outright into a dreadful passion, scorned all further words, and thrust him ignominiously from my presence. But there was something about Bartleby that not only strangely disarmed me, but, in a wonderful manner, touched and disconcerted me. 1 began to reason with him.

'These are your own copies we are about to examine. It is

labor saving to you, because one examination will answer for your four papers. It is common usage. Every copyist is bound to help examine his copy. Is it not so? Will you not speak? Answer!'

'I prefer not to,' he replied in a flutelike tone. It seemed to me that, while I had been addressing him, he carefully revolved every statement that I made; fully comprehended the meaning; could not gainsay the irresistible conclusion; but, at the same time, some paramount consideration prevailed with him to reply as he did.

'You are decided, then, not to comply with my request — a request made according to common usage and common sense?'

He briefly gave me to understand that on that point my judgment was sound. Yes: his decision was irreversible.

It is not seldom the case that, when a man is browbeaten in some unprecedented and violently unreasonable way, he begins to stagger in his own plainest faith. He begins, as it were, vaguely to surmise that, wonderful as it may be, all the justice and all the reason is on the other side. Accordingly, if any disinterested persons are present, he turns to them for some reinforcement for his own faltering mind.

'Turkey,' said I, 'what do you think of this? Am I not right?'

'With submission, sir,' said Turkey, in his blandest tone, 'I think that you are.'

'Nippers,' said I, 'what do *you* think of it?'

'I think I should kick him out of the office.'

(The reader of nice perceptions will here perceive that, it being morning, Turkey's answer is couched in polite and tranquil terms, but Nippers replies in ill-tempered ones. Or, to repeat a previous sentence, Nippers's ugly mood was on duty, and Turkey's off.)

'Ginger Nut,' said I, willing to enlist the smallest suffrage in my behalf, 'what do *you* think of it?'

'I think, sir, he's a little *luny*,' replied Ginger Nut, with a grin.

'You hear what they say,' said I, turning towards the screen, 'come forth and do your duty.'

But he vouchsafed no reply. I pondered a moment in sore

perplexity. But once more business hurried me. I determined again to postpone the consideration of this dilemma to my future leisure. With a little trouble we made out to examine the papers without Bartleby, though at every page or two Turkey deferentially dropped his opinion that this proceeding was quite out of the common; while Nippers, twitching in his chair with a dyspeptic nervousness, ground out between his set teeth occasional hissing maledictions against the stubborn oaf behind the screen. And for his (Nippers's) part, this was the first and the last time he would do another man's business without pay.

Meanwhile Bartleby sat in his hermitage, oblivious to everything but his own peculiar business there.

Some days passed, the scrivener being employed upon another lengthy work. His late remarkable conduct led me to regard his ways narrowly. I observed that he never went to dinner; indeed, that he never went anywhere. As yet I had never, of my personal knowledge, known him to be outside of my office. He was a perpetual sentry in the corner. At about eleven o'clock, though, in the morning, I noticed that Ginger Nut would advance towards the opening in Bartleby's screen, as if silently beckoned thither by a gesture invisible to me where I sat. The boy would then leave the office jingling a few pence, and reappear with a handful of gingernuts, which he delivered in the hermitage, receiving two of the cakes for his trouble.

He lives, then, on gingernuts, thought I; never eats a dinner, properly speaking; he must be a vegetarian, then; but no, he never eats even vegetables, he eats nothing but gingernuts. My mind then ran on in reveries concerning the probable effects upon the human constitution of living entirely on gingernuts. Gingernuts are so called because they contain ginger as one of their peculiar constituents, and the final flavoring one. Now, what was ginger? A hot, spicy thing. Was Bartleby hot and spicy? Not at all. Ginger, then, had no effect upon Bartleby. Probably he preferred it should have none.

Nothing so aggravates an earnest person as a passive resistance. If the individual so resisted be of a not inhumane temper, and the resisting one perfectly harmless in his passivity, then, in the better moods of the former, he will endeavor charitably to construe to his imagination what proves impossible to be solved by his judgment. Even so, for the most part, I regarded Bartleby and his ways. Poor fellow! thought I, he means no mischief; it is plain he intends no insolence; his aspect sufficiently evinces that his eccentricities are involuntary. He is useful to me. I can get along with him. If I turn him away, the chances are he will fall in with some less indulgent employer, and then he will be rudely treated, and perhaps driven forth miserably to starve. Yes. Here I can cheaply purchase a delicious self-approval. To befriend Bartleby, to humor him in his strange willfulness, will cost me little or nothing, while I lay up in my soul what will eventually prove a sweet morsel for my conscience. But this mood was not invariable with me. The passiveness of Bartleby sometimes irritated me. I felt strangely goaded on to encounter him in new opposition – to elicit some angry spark from him answerable to my own. But, indeed, I might as well have essayed to strike fire with my knuckles against a bit of Windsor soap. But one afternoon the evil impulse in me mastered me, and the following little scene ensued:

'Bartleby,' said I, 'when those papers are all copied, I will compare them with you.'

'I would prefer not to.'

'How? Surely you do not mean to persist in that mulish vagary?'

No answer.

I threw open the folding doors near by, and, turning upon Turkey and Nippers, exclaimed:

'Bartleby a second time says he won't examine his papers. What do you think of it, Turkey?'

It was afternoon, be it remembered. Turkey sat glowing like a brass boiler, his bald head steaming, his hands reeling among his blotted papers.

'Think of it?' roared Turkey. 'I think I'll just step behind his screen and black his eyes for him!'

So saying, Turkey rose to his feet and threw his arms into a pugilistic position. He was hurrying away to make good his promise when I detained him, alarmed at the effect of incautiously rousing Turkey's combativeness after dinner.

'Sit down, Turkey,' said I, 'and hear what Nippers has to say. What do you think of it, Nippers? Would I not be justified in immediately dismissing Bartleby?'

'Excuse me, that is for you to decide, sir. I think his conduct quite unusual, and indeed, unjust, as regards Turkey and myself. But it may only be a passing whim.'

'Ah,' exclaimed I, 'you have strangely changed your mind, then – you speak very gently of him now.'

'All beer,' cried Turkey; 'gentleness is effects of beer – Nippers and I dined together today. You see how gentle *I* am, sir. Shall I go and black his eyes?'

'You refer to Bartleby, I suppose. No, not today, Turkey,' I replied; 'pray, put up your fists.'

I closed the doors and again advanced towards Bartleby. I felt additional incentives tempting me to my fate. I burned to be rebelled against again. I remembered that Bartleby never left the office.

'Bartleby,' said I, 'Ginger Nut is away; just step around to the Post Office, won't you? (it was but a three minutes' walk), and see if there is anything for me'

'I would prefer not to.'

'You *will* not?'

'I *prefer* not.'

I staggered to my desk and sat there in a deep study. My blind inveteracy returned. Was there any other thing in which I could procure myself to be ignominiously repulsed by this lean, penniless wight? – my hired clerk? What added thing is there, perfectly reasonable, that he will be sure to refuse to do?

'Bartleby!'

No answer.

'Bartleby,' in a louder voice.

No answer.

'Bartleby,' I roared.

Like a very ghost, agreeably to the laws of magical invocation, at the third summons he appeared at the entrance of his hermitage.

'Go to the next room, and tell Nippers to come to me.'

'I prefer not to,' he respectfully and slowly said, and mildly disappeared.

'Very good, Bartleby,' said I, in a quiet sort of serenely severe self-possessed tone, intimating the unalterable purpose of some terrible retribution very close at hand. At the moment I half intended something of the kind. But upon the whole, as it was drawing towards my dinner hour, I thought it best to put on my hat and walk home for the day, suffering much from perplexity and distress of mind.

Shall I acknowledge it? The conclusion of this whole business was that it soon became a fixed fact of my chambers, that a pale young scrivener by the name of Bartleby had a desk there; that he copied for me at the usual rate of four cents a folio (one hundred words); but he was permanently exempt from examining the work done by him, that duty being transferred to Turkey and Nippers, out of compliment, doubtless, to their superior acuteness; moreover, said Bartleby was never, on any account, to be dispatched on the most trivial errand of any sort; and that even if entreated to take upon him such a matter, it was generally understood that he would 'prefer not to' – in other words, that he would refuse point-blank.

As days passed on, I became considerably reconciled to Bartleby. His steadiness, his freedom from all dissipation, his incessant industry (except when he chose to throw himself into a standing reverie behind his screen), his great stillness, his unalterableness of demeanor under all circumstances, made him a valuable acquisition. One prime thing was this – *he was always there* – first in the morning, continually through the day, and the last at night. I had a singular confidence in his honesty. I felt my most precious papers perfectly safe in his hands. Sometimes, to be sure, I could not, for the very soul of me, avoid falling into sudden spasmodic passions with him. For it was exceeding difficult to bear in mind all the time those strange peculiarities, privileges, and unheard-of exemptions, forming the tacit stipulations on Bartleby's part under which he remained in my office. Now and then, in the eagerness of dispatching pressing business, I would inadvertently summon Bartleby, in a short, rapid tone, to put his finger, say, on the incipient tie of a bit of red tape with which I was about compressing some papers. Of course, from behind the screen the usual answer, 'I prefer not to,' was sure to come; and then, how could a human creature, with the common infirmities of our nature, refrain from bitterly exclaiming upon such perverseness – such unreasonableness? However, every added repulse of this sort which I received only tended to lessen the probability of my repeating the inadvertence.

Here it must be said that, according to the custom of most legal gentlemen occupying chambers in densely populated law buildings, there were several keys to my door. One was kept by a woman residing in the attic, which person weekly scrubbed and daily swept and dusted my apartments. Another was kept by Turkey for convenience sake. The third I sometimes carried in my own pocket. The fourth I knew not who had.

Now, one Sunday morning I happened to go to Trinity Church, to hear a celebrated preacher, and finding myself rather early on the ground I thought I would walk round to my chambers for a while. Luckily I had my key with me, but upon applying it to the lock, I found it resisted by something inserted from the inside. Quite surprised, I called out, when to my consternation a key was turned from within, and, thrusting his lean visage at me, and holding the door ajar, the apparition of Bartleby appeared, in his shirt sleeves, and otherwise in a strangely tattered deshabille, saying quietly that he was sorry, but he was deeply engaged just then, and – preferred not admitting me at present. In a brief word or two, he moreover added, that perhaps I had better walk around the block two or three times, and by that time he would probably have concluded his affairs.

Now, the utterly unsurmised appearance of Bartleby, tenanting my law chambers of a Sunday morning, with his cadaverously gentlemanly *nonchalance*, yet withal firm and self-possessed, had such a strange effect upon me that incontinently I slunk away from my own door and did as desired. But not without sundry twinges of impotent rebellion against the mild effrontery of this unaccountable scrivener. Indeed, it was his wonderful mildness, chiefly, which not only disarmed me but unmanned me, as it were. For I consider that one, for the time, is sort of unmanned when he tranquilly permits his hired clerk to dictate to him and order him away from his own premises. Furthermore, I was full of uneasiness as to what Bartleby could possibly be doing in my office in his shirt sleeves, and in an otherwise dismantled condition, of a Sunday morning. Was anything amiss going on? Nay, that was out of the question. It was not to be thought of for a moment that Bartleby was an immoral person. But what could he be doing there? – copying? Nay again, whatever might be his eccentricities, Bartleby was an eminently decorous person. He would be the last man to sit down to his desk in any state approaching to nudity. Besides, it was Sunday; and there was something about Bartleby that forbade the supposition that he would by any secular occupation violate the proprieties of the day.

Nevertheless, my mind was not pacified, and, full of a restless curiosity, at last I returned to the door. Without hindrance I inserted my key, opened it, and entered. Bartleby was not to be seen. I looked round anxiously, peeped behind his screen, but it was very plain that he was gone. Upon more closely examining the place, I surmised that for an indefinite period Bartleby must have ate, dressed, and slept in my office, and that, too, without plate, mirror, or bed. The cushioned seat of a rickety old sofa in one corner bore that faint impress of a lean, reclining form. Rolled away under his desk I found a blanket; under the empty grate, a blacking box and brush; on a chair, a tin basin, with soap and a ragged towel; in a newspaper a few crumbs of gingernuts and a morsel of cheese. Yes, thought I, it is evident enough that Bartleby has been making his home here, keeping bachelor's hall all by himself. Immediately then the thought came sweeping across me, what miserable friendlessness and loneliness are here revealed. His poverty is great, but his solitude, how horrible! Think of it. Of a Sunday, Wall Street is deserted as Petra, and every night of every day it is an emptiness. This building, too, which of weekdays hums with industry and life, at nightfall echoes with sheer vacancy, and all through Sunday is forlorn. And here Bartleby makes his home, sole spectator of a solitude which he has seen all populous – a sort of innocent and transformed Marius brooding among the ruins of Carthage!

For the first time in my life a feeling of overpowering stinging melancholy seized me. Before, I had never experienced aught but a not unpleasing sadness. The bond of a common humanity now drew me irresistibly to gloom. A fraternal melancholy! For both I and Bartleby were sons of Adam. I remembered the bright silks and sparkling faces I had seen that day, in gala trim, swanlike sailing down the Mississippi of Broadway; and I contrasted them with the pallid copyist, and thought to myself, Ah, happiness courts the light, so we deem the world is gay, but misery hides aloof, so we deem that misery there is none. These sad fancyings – chimeras, doubtless, of a sick and silly brain – led on to other and more special thoughts, concerning the eccentricities of Bartleby. Presentiments of strange discoveries hovered round me. The scrivener's pale form appeared to me laid out, among uncaring strangers in its shivering winding sheet.

Suddenly I was attracted by Bartleby's closed desk, the key in open sight left in the lock.

I mean no mischief, seek the gratification of no heartless curiosity, thought I; besides, the desk is mine, and its contents, too, so I will make bold to look within. Everything was methodically arranged, the papers smoothly placed. The pigeonholes were deep, and, removing the files of documents, I groped into their recesses. Presently I felt something there, and dragged it out. It was an old bandanna handkerchief, heavy and knotted. I opened it, and saw it was a savings bank.

I now recalled all the quiet mysteries which I had noted in the man. I remembered that he never spoke but to answer; that, though at intervals he had considerable time to himself, yet I had never seen him reading – no, not even a newspaper; that for long periods he would stand looking out, at his pale window behind the screen, upon the dead brick wall; I was quite sure he never visited any refectory or eating house, while his pale face

clearly indicated that he never drank beer like Turkey, or tea
and coffee even, like other men; that he never went anywhere in
particular that I could learn; never went out for a walk, unless,
indeed, that was the case at present; that he had declined telling who he was, or whence he came, or whether he had any
relatives in the world; that though so thin and pale, he never
complained of ill health. And more than all I remembered a
certain unconscious air of pallid – how shall I call it? – of pallid
haughtiness, say, or rather an austere reserve about him, which
had positively awed me into my tame compliance with his
eccentricities, when I had feared to ask him to do the slightest
incidental thing for me, even though I might know, from his
long-continued motionlessness, that behind his screen he must
be standing in one of those dead-wall reveries of his.

[. . .]

I did not accomplish the purpose of going to Trinity Church
that morning. Somehow, the things I had seen disqualified me
for the time from churchgoing. I walked homeward, thinking
what I would do with Bartleby. Finally, I resolved upon this – I
would put certain calm questions to him the next morning,
touching his history, etc., and if he declined to answer them
openly and unreservedly (and I supposed he would prefer not),
then to give him a twenty-dollar bill over and above whatever I
might owe him, and tell him his services were no longer
required; but that if in any other way I could assist him, I
would be happy to do so, especially if he desired to return to his
native place, wherever that might be, I would willingly help to
defray the expenses. Moreover, if, after reaching home, he
found himself at any time in want of aid, a letter from him
would be sure of a reply.

The next morning came.

'Bartleby,' said I, gently calling to him behind his screen.

No reply.

'Bartleby,' said I, in a still gentler tone, 'come here; I am not
going to ask you to do anything you would prefer not to do – I
simply wish to speak to you.'

Upon this he noiselessly slid into view.

'Will you tell me, Bartleby, where you were born?'

'I would prefer not to.'

'Will you tell me *anything* about yourself?'

'I would prefer not to.'

'But what reasonable objection can you have to speak to me? I feel friendly towards you.'

He did not look at me while I spoke, but kept his glance fixed upon my bust of Cicero, which, as I then sat, was directly behind me, some six inches above my head.

'What is your answer, Bartleby?' said I, after waiting a considerable time for a reply, during which his countenance remained immovable, only there was the faintest conceivable tremor of the white attenuated mouth.

'At present I prefer to give no answer,' he said, and retired into his hermitage.

It was rather weak in me I confess, but his manner, on this occasion, nettled me. Not only did there seem to lurk in it a certain calm disdain, but his perverseness seemed ungrateful, considering the undeniable good usage and indulgence he had received from me.

Again I sat ruminating what I should do. Mortified as I was at his behavior, and resolved as I had been to dismiss him when I entered my office, nevertheless I strangely felt something superstitious knocking at my heart, and forbidding me to carry out my purpose, and denouncing me for a villain if I dared to breath the one bitter word against this forlornest of mankind. At last, familiarly drawing my chair behind his screen, I sat down and said: 'Bartleby, never mind, then, about revealing your history; but let me entreat you, as a friend, to comply as far as may be with the usages of this office. Say now, you will help to examine papers tomorrow or next day: in short, say now, that in a day or two you will begin to be a little reasonable: – say so, Bartleby.'

'At present I would prefer not to be a little reasonable,' was his mildly cadaverous reply.

Just then the folding doors opened and Nippers approached. He seemed suffering from an unusually bad night's rest, induced by severer indigestion than common. He overheard those final words of Bartleby.

'*Prefer not*, eh?' gritted Nippers – 'I'd *prefer* him, if I were you, sir,' addressing me – 'I'd *prefer* him; I'd give him preferences, the stubborn mule! What is it, sir, pray, that he *prefers* not to do now?'

Bartleby moved not a limb.

'Mr. Nippers,' said I, 'I'd prefer that you would withdraw for the present.'

Somehow, of late, I had got into the way of involuntarily using this word 'prefer' upon all sorts of not exactly suitable occasions. And I trembled to think that my contact with the scrivener had already and seriously affected me in a mental way. And what further and deeper aberration might it not yet produce? This apprehension had not been without efficacy in determining me to summary measures.

As Nippers, looking very sour and sulky, was departing, Turkey blandly and deferentially approached.

'With submission, sir,' said he, 'yesterday I was thinking about Bartleby here, and I think that if he would but prefer to take a quart of good ale every day, it would do much towards mending him, and enabling him to assist in examining his papers.'

'So you have got the word, too,' said I, slightly excited.

'With submission, what word, sir?' asked Turkey, respectfully crowding himself into the contracted space behind the screen, and by so doing making me jostle the scrivener. 'What word, sir?'

'I would prefer to be left alone here,' said Bartleby, as if offended at being mobbed in his privacy.

'*That's* the word, Turkey,' said I – '*that's* it.'

'Oh, *prefer*? oh yes – queer word. I never use it myself. But, sir, as I was saying, if he would but prefer——'

'Turkey,' interrupted I, 'you will please withdraw.'

'Oh certainly, sir, if you prefer that I should.'

As he opened the folding door to retire, Nippers at his desk caught a glimpse of me, and asked whether I would prefer to have a certain paper copied on blue paper or white. He did not in the least roguishly accent the word prefer. It was plain that it involuntarily rolled from his tongue. I thought to myself, surely I must get rid of a demented man, who already has in some degree turned the tongues, if not the heads, of myself and my clerks. But I thought it prudent not to break the dismission at once.

The next day I noticed that Bartleby did nothing but stand at his window in his dead-wall reverie. Upon asking him why he did not write, he said that he had decided upon doing no more writing.

'Why, how now? what next?' exclaimed I, 'do no more writing?'

'No more.'

'And what is the reason?'

'Do you not see the reason for yourself?' he indifferently replied.

I looked steadfastly at him, and perceived that his eyes looked dull and glazed. Instantly it occurred to me that his unexampled diligence in copying by his dim window for the first few weeks of his stay with me might have temporarily impaired his vision.

I was touched. I said something in condolence with him. I hinted that of course he did wisely in abstaining from writing for a while; and urged him to embrace that opportunity of taking wholesome exercise in the open air. This, however, he did not do. A few days after this, my other clerks being absent, and being in a great hurry to dispatch certain letters by the mail, I thought that, having nothing else earthly to do, Bartleby would surely be less inflexible than usual, and carry these letters to the Post Office. But he blankly declined. So, much to my inconvenience, I went myself.

Still added days went by. Whether Bartleby's eyes improved or not, I could not say. To all appearance, I thought they did. But when I asked him if they did, he vouchsafed no answer. At all events, he would do no copying. At last, in reply to my urgings, he informed me that he had permanently given up copying.

'What!' exclaimed I; 'suppose your eyes should get entirely well – better than ever before – would you not copy then?'

'I have given up copying,' he answered, and slid aside.

He remained as ever, a fixture in my chamber. Nay – if that were possible – he became still more of a fixture than before. What was to be done? He would do nothing in the office; why should he stay there? In plain fact, he had now become a millstone to me, not only useless as a necklace, but afflictive to bear. Yet I was sorry for him. I speak less than truth when I say that, on his own account, he occasioned me uneasiness. If he would but have named a single relative or friend, I would instantly have written and urged their taking the poor fellow away to some convenient retreat. But he seemed alone, absolutely alone in the universe. A bit of wreck in the mid-Atlantic. At length, necessities connected with my business tyrannized over all other considerations. Decently as I could, I told Bartleby that in six days' time he must unconditionally leave the office. I warned him to take measures, in the interval, for procuring some other abode. I offered to assist him in this endeavor, if he himself would but take the first step towards a removal. 'And when you finally quit me, Bartleby,' added I, 'I shall see that you go not away entirely unprovided. Six days from this hour, remember.'

At the expiration of that period, I peeped behind the screen, and lo! Bartleby was there.

I buttoned up my coat, balanced myself, advanced slowly towards him, touched his shoulder, and said, 'The time has come; you must quit this place; I am sorry for you; here is money; but you must go.'

'I would prefer not,' he replied, with his back still towards me.

'You *must*.'

He remained silent.

Now I had an unbounded confidence in this man's common honesty. He had frequently restored to me sixpences and shillings carelessly dropped upon the floor, for I am apt to be very reckless in such shirt-button affairs. The proceeding, then, which followed will not be deemed extraordinary.

'Bartleby,' said I, 'I owe you twelve dollars on account; here are thirty-two; the odd twenty are yours – Will you take it?' and I handed the bills towards him.

But he made no motion.

'I will leave them here, then,' putting them under a weight on the table. Then taking my hat and cane and going to the door, I tranquilly turned and added – 'After you have removed your things from these offices, Bartleby, you will of course lock the door – since everyone is now gone for the day but you – and if you please, slip your key underneath the mat, so that I may have it in the morning. I shall not see you again; so good-bye to you. If, hereafter, in your new place of abode, I can be of any service to you, do not fail to advise me by letter. Good-bye, Bartleby, and fare you well.'

But he answered not a word; like the last column of some ruined temple, he remained standing mute and solitary in the middle of the otherwise deserted room.

As I walked home in a pensive mood, my vanity got the better of my pity. I could not but highly plume myself on my masterly management in getting rid of Bartleby. Masterly I call it, and such it must appear to any dispassionate thinker. The beauty of my procedure seemed to consist in its perfect quietness. There was no vulgar bullying, no bravado of any sort, no choleric hectoring and striding to and fro across the apartment, jerking out vehement commands for Bartleby to bundle himself off with his beggarly traps. Nothing of the kind. Without loudly bidding Bartleby depart – as an inferior genius might have done – I *assumed* the ground that depart he must, and upon that assumption built all I had to say. The more I thought over my procedure, the more I was charmed with it. Nevertheless, next morning, upon awakening, I had my doubts – I had somehow slept off the fumes of vanity. One of the coolest and wisest hours a man has is just after he awakes in the morning. My procedure seemed as sagacious as ever – but only in theory. How it would prove in practice – there was the rub. It was truly a beautiful thought to have assumed Bartleby's departure; but, after all, that assumption was simply my own, and none of Bartleby's. The great point was, not whether I had assumed that he would quit me, but whether he would prefer so to do. He was more a man of preferences than assumptions.

[. . .]

As I had intended, I was earlier than usual at my office door. I stood listening for a moment. All was still. He must be gone. I tried the knob. The door was locked. Yes, my procedure had worked to a charm; he indeed must be vanished. Yet a certain melancholy mixed with this: I was almost sorry for my brilliant success. I was fumbling under the door mat for the key, which Bartleby was to have left there for me, when accidentally my knee knocked against a panel, producing a summoning sound, and in response a voice came to me from within – 'Not yet; I am occupied.'

It was Bartleby.

I was thunderstruck. For an instant I stood like the man who, pipe in mouth, was killed one cloudless afternoon long ago in Virginia by summer lightning; at his own warm open window he was killed, and remained leaning out there upon the dreamy afternoon, till someone touched him, when he fell.

'Not gone!' I murmured at last. But again obeying that wondrous ascendancy which the inscrutable scrivener had over me, and from which ascendancy, for all my chafing, I could not completely escape, I slowly went downstairs and out into the street, and while walking round the block considered what I should next do in this unheard-of perplexity. Turn the man out by an actual thrusting I could not; to drive him away by calling him hard names would not do; calling in the police was an unpleasant idea; and yet, permit him to enjoy his cadaverous triumph over me – this, too, I could not think of. What was to be done? or, if nothing could be done, was there anything further that I could *assume* in the matter? Yes, as before I had prospectively assumed that Bartleby would depart, so now I might retrospectively assume that departed he was. In the legitimate carrying out of this assumption I might enter my office in a great hurry, and, pretending not to see Bartleby at all, walk straight against him as if he were air. Such a proceeding would in a singular degree have the appearance of a home thrust. It was hardly possible that Bartleby could withstand such an application of the doctrine of assumptions. But upon second thoughts the success of the plan seemed rather dubious. I resolved to argue the matter over with him again.

'Bartleby,' said I, entering the office, with a quietly severe expression, 'I am seriously displeased. I am pained, Bartleby. I had thought better of you. I had imagined you of such a gentlemanly organization that in any delicate dilemma a slight hint would suffice – in short, an assumption. But it appears I am deceived. Why,' I added, unaffectedly starting, 'you have not even touched that money yet,' pointing to it, just where I had left it the evening previous.

He answered nothing.

'Will you, or will you not, quit me?' I now demanded in a sudden passion, advancing close to him.

'I would prefer *not* to quit you,' he replied, gently emphasizing the *not*.

'What earthly right have you to stay here? Do you pay any rent? Do you pay my taxes? Or is this property yours?'

He answered nothing.

'Are you ready to go on and write now? Are your eyes recovered? Could you copy a small paper for me this morning? or help examine a few lines? or step round to the Post Office? In a word, will you do anything at all to give a coloring to your refusal to depart the premises?'

He silently retired into his hermitage.

[. . .]

Gradually I slid into the persuasion that these troubles of mine touching the scrivener had been all predestinated from eternity, and Bartleby was billeted upon me for some mysterious purpose of an all-wise Providence, which it was not for a mere mortal like me to fathom. Yes, Bartleby, stay there behind your screen, thought I; I shall persecute you no more; you are harmless and noiseless as any of these old chairs; in short, I never feel so private as when I know you are here. At last I see it, I feel it; I penetrate to the predestinated purpose of my life. I am content. Others may have loftier parts to enact, but my mission in this world, Bartleby, is to furnish you with office room for such period as you may see fit to remain.

I believe that this wise and blessed frame of mind would have continued with me had it not been for the unsolicited and uncharitable remarks obtruded upon me by my professional friends who visited the rooms. But thus it often is that the constant friction of illiberal minds wears out at last the best resolves of the more generous. Though, to be sure, when I reflected upon it it was not strange that people entering my office should be struck by the peculiar aspect of the unaccountable Bartleby, and so be tempted to throw out some sinister observations concerning him. Sometimes an attorney having business with me, and calling at my office, and finding no one but the scrivener there, would undertake to obtain some sort of precise information from him touching my whereabouts; but without heeding his idle talk, Bartleby would remain standing immovable in the middle of the room. So, after contemplating him in that position for a time, the attorney would depart no wiser than he came.

Also, when a reference was going on, and the room full of lawyers and witnesses, and business driving fast, some deeply-occupied legal gentleman present, seeing Bartleby wholly unemployed, would request him to run round to his (the legal gentleman's) office and fetch some papers for him. Thereupon Bartleby would tranquilly decline, and yet remain idle as before. Then the lawyer would give a great stare, and turn to me. And what could I say? At last I was made aware that all through the circle of my professional acquaintance a whisper of wonder was running round, having reference to the strange creature I kept at my office. This worried me very much. And as the idea came upon me of his possibly turning out a longlived man, and keep occupying my chambers, and denying my authority; and perplexing my visitors; and scandalizing my professional reputation; and casting a general gloom over the premises; keeping soul and body together to the last upon his savings (for doubtless he spent but half a dime a day), and in the end perhaps outlive me, and claim possession of my office by right of his perpetual occupancy – as all these dark anticipations crowded upon me more and more, and my friends continually intruded their relentless remarks upon the apparition in my room, a great change was wrought in me. I resolved to gather all my faculties together and forever rid me of this intolerable incubus.

Ere revolving any complicated project, however, adapted to this end, I first simply suggested to Bartleby the propriety of his permanent departure. In a calm and serious tone, I commended the idea to his careful and mature consideration. But, having taken three days to meditate upon it, he apprised me that his original determination remained the same; in short, that he still preferred to abide with me.

What shall I do? I now said to myself, buttoning up my coat to the last button. What shall I do? what ought I to do? what does conscience say I *should* do with this man, or, rather, ghost. Rid myself of him, I must; go, he shall. But how? You will not thrust him, the poor, pale, passive mortal – you will not thrust such a helpless creature out of your door? you will not dishonor yourself by such cruelty? No, I will not, I cannot do that. Rather would I let him live and die here, and then mason up his remains in the wall. What, then, will you do? For all your coaxing, he will not budge. Bribes he leaves under your own paperweight on your table; in short, it is quite plain that he prefers to cling to you.

Then something severe, something unusual, must be done. What! surely you will not have him collared by a constable, and commit his innocent pallor to the common jail? And upon what ground could you procure such a thing to be done? – a vagrant, is he? What! he a vagrant, a wanderer, who refuses to budge? It is because he will *not* be a vagrant, then, that you seek to count him *as* a vagrant. That is too absurd. No visible means of support: there I have him. Wrong again: for indubitably he *does* support himself, and that is the only unanswerable proof that any man can show of his possessing the means so to do. No more, then. Since he will not quit me, I must quit him. I will change my offices; I will move elsewhere, and give him fair notice that if I find him on my new premises I will then proceed against him as a common trespasser.

Acting accordingly, next day I thus addressed him: 'I find these chambers too far from the City Hall; the air is unwholesome. In a word, I propose to remove my offices next week, and shall no longer require your services. I tell you this now, in order that you may seek another place.'

He made no reply, and nothing more was said.

On the appointed day I engaged carts and men, proceeded to my chambers, and, having but little furniture, everything was removed in a few hours. Throughout, the scrivener remained standing behind the screen, which I directed to be removed the last thing. It was withdrawn; and, being folded up like a huge folio, left him the motionless occupant of a naked room. I stood in the entry watching him a moment, while something from within me upbraided me.

I re-entered, with my hand in my pocket – and – and my heart in my mouth.

'Good-bye, Bartleby; I am going – good-bye; and God some way bless you; and take that,' slipping something in his hand. But it dropped upon the floor, and then – strange to say – I tore myself from him whom I had so longed to be rid of.

Established in my new quarters, for a day or two I kept the door locked, and started at every footfall in the passages. When I returned to my rooms after any little absence, I would pause at the threshold for an instant and attentively listen ere applying my key. But these fears were needless. Bartleby never came nigh me.

I thought all was going well, when a perturbed-looking stranger visited me, inquiring whether I was the person who had recently occupied rooms at No. – Wall Street.

Full of forebodings, I replied that I was.

'Then, sir,' said the stranger, who proved a lawyer, 'you are responsible for the man you left there. He refuses to do any copying; he refuses to do anything; he says he prefers not to; and he refuses to quit the premises.'

'I am very sorry, sir,' said I, with assumed tranquillity, but an inward tremor, 'but, really, the man you allude to is nothing to me – he is no relation or apprentice of mine, that you should hold me responsible for him.'

'In mercy's name, who is he?'

'I certainly cannot inform you. I know nothing about him. Formerly I employed him as a copyist; but he has done nothing for me now for some time past.'

'I shall settle him, then – good morning, sir.'

Several days passed, and I heard nothing more; and, though I often felt a charitable prompting to call at the place and see poor Bartleby, yet a certain squeamishness, of I know not what, withheld me. All is over with him, by this time, thought I at last, when, through another week, no further intelligence reached me. But, coming to my room the day after, I found several persons waiting at my door in a high state of nervous excitement.

'That's the man – here he comes,' cried the foremost one, whom I recognized as the lawyer who had previously called upon me alone.

'You must take him away, sir, at once,' cried a portly person among them, advancing upon me, and whom I knew to be the landlord of No. – Wall Street. 'These gentlemen, my tenants, cannot stand it any longer; Mr. B———,' pointing to the lawyer, 'has turned him out of his room, and he now persists in haunting the building generally, sitting upon the banisters of the stairs by day, and sleeping in the entry by night. Everybody is concerned; clients are leaving the offices; some fears are entertained of a mob; something you must do, and that without delay.'

Aghast at this torrent, I fell back before it, and would fain have locked myself in my new quarters. In vain I persisted that Bartleby was nothing to me – no more than to anyone else. In vain – I was the last person known to have anything to do with him, and they held me to the terrible account. Fearful, then, of being exposed in the papers (as one person present obscurely threatened), I considered the matter, and at length said that if the lawyer would give me a confidential interview with the scrivener, in his (the lawyer's) own room, I would, that afternoon, strive my best to rid them of the nuisance they complained of.

Going upstairs to my old haunt, there was Bartleby silently sitting upon the banister at the landing.

'What are you doing here, Bartleby?' said I.

'Sitting upon the banister,' he mildly replied.

I motioned him into the lawyer's room, who then left us.

'Bartleby,' said I, 'are you aware that you are the cause of great tribulation to me, by persisting in occupying the entry after being dismissed from the office?'

No answer.

'Now one of two things must take place. Either you must do something, or something must be done to you. Now what sort of business would you like to engage in? Would you like to re-engage in copying for someone?'

'No; I would prefer not to make any change.'

'Would you like a clerkship in a dry-goods store?'

'There is too much confinement about that. No, I would not like a clerkship; but I am not particular.'

'Too much confinement,' I cried; 'why you keep yourself confined all the time!'

'I would prefer not to take a clerkship,' he rejoined, as if to settle that little item at once.

'How would a bartender's business suit you? There is no trying of the eyesight in that.'

'I would not like it at all; though, as I said before, I am not particular.'

His unwonted wordiness inspirited me. I returned to the charge.

'Well, then, would you like to travel through the country collecting bills for the merchants? That would improve your health.'

'No, I would prefer to be doing something else.'

'How, then, would going as a companion to Europe, to entertain some young gentleman with your conversation – how would that suit you?'

'Not at all. It does not strike me that there is anything definite about that. I like to be stationary. But I am not particular.'

'Stationary you shall be, then,' I cried, now losing all patience, and, for the first time in all my exasperating connection with him, fairly flying into a passion. 'If you do not go away from these premises before night, I shall feel bound – indeed, I *am* bound – to – to – to quit the premises myself!' I rather absurdly concluded, knowing not with what possible threat to try to frighten his immobility into compliance. Despairing of all further efforts, I was precipitately leaving him, when a final thought occurred to me – one which had not been wholly unindulged before.

'Bartleby,' said I, in the kindest tone I could assume under such exciting circumstances, 'will you go home with me now – not to my office, but my dwelling – and remain there till we can conclude upon some convenient arrangement for you at our leisure? Come, let us start now, right away.'

'No; at present I would prefer not to make any change at all.'

I answered nothing, but, effectually dodging everyone by the suddenness and rapidity of my flight, rushed from the building, ran up Wall Street towards Broadway, and, jumping into the first omnibus, was soon removed from pursuit. As soon as tranquillity returned, I distinctly perceived that I had now done all that I possibly could, both in respect to the demands of the landlord and his tenants, and with regard to my own desire and sense of duty, to benefit Bartleby, and shield him from rude persecution. I now strove to be entirely carefree and quiescent, and my conscience justified me in the attempt, though, indeed, it was not so successful as I could have wished. So fearful was I of being again hunted out by the incensed landlord and his exasperated tenants that, surrendering my business to Nippers for a few days, I drove about the upper part of the town and through the suburbs in my rockaway; crossed over to Jersey City and Hoboken, and paid fugitive visits to Manhattanville and Astoria. In fact, I almost lived in my rockaway for the time.

When again I entered my office, lo, a note from the landlord lay upon the desk. I opened it with trembling hands. It informed me that the writer had sent to the police, and had Bartleby removed to the Tombs as a vagrant. Moreover, since I knew more about him than anyone else, he wished me to appear at that place and make a suitable statement of the facts. These tidings had a conflicting effect upon me. At first I was indignant, but at last almost approved. The landlord's energetic, summary disposition had led him to adopt a procedure which I do not think I would have decided upon myself; and yet, as a last resort, under such peculiar circumstances, it seemed the only plan.

As I afterwards learned, the poor scrivener, when told that he must be conducted to the Tombs, offered not the slightest obstacle, but, in his pale, unmoving way, silently acquiesced.

Some of the compassionate and curious bystanders joined the party, and, headed by one of the constables arm in arm with Bartleby, the silent procession filed its way through all the noise, and heat, and joy of the roaring thoroughfares at noon.

The same day I received the note, I went to the Tombs, or, to speak more properly, the Halls of Justice. Seeking the right officer, I stated the purpose of my call, and was informed that the individual I described was indeed within. I then assured the functionary that Bartleby was a perfectly honest man, and greatly to be compassionated, however unaccountably eccentric. I narrated all I knew, and closed by suggesting the idea of letting him remain in as indulgent confinement as possible till something less harsh might be done – though, indeed, I hardly knew what. At all events, if nothing else could be decided upon, the almshouse must receive him. I then begged to have an interview.

Being under no disgraceful charge, and quite serene and harmless in all his ways, they had permitted him freely to wander about the prison, and, especially, in the inclosed grass-platted yards thereof. And so I found him there, standing all alone in the quietest of the yards, his face towards a high wall, while all around, from the narrow slits of the jail windows, I thought I saw peering out upon him the eyes of murderers and thieves.

'Bartleby!'

'I know you,' he said, without looking round – 'and I want nothing to say to you.'

'It was not I that brought you here, Bartleby,' said I, keenly pained at his implied suspicion. 'And, to you, this should not be so vile a place. Nothing reproachful attaches to you by being here. And see, it is not so sad a place as one might think. Look, there is the sky, and here is the grass.'

'I know where I am,' he replied, but would say nothing more, and so I left him.

As I entered the corridor again, a broad meatlike man in an

apron accosted me, and, jerking his thumb over his shoulder,
said – 'Is that your friend?'

'Yes.'

'Does he want to starve? If he does, let him live on the prison
fare, that's all.'

'Who are you?' asked I, not knowing what to make of such
an unofficially speaking person in such a place.

'I am the grubman. Such gentlemen as have friends here hire
me to provide them with something good to eat.'

'Is this so?' said I, turning to the turnkey.

He said it was.

'Well, then,' said I, slipping some silver into the grubman's
hands (for so they called him), 'I want you to give particular
attention to my friend there; let him have the best dinner you
can get. And you must be as polite to him as possible.'

'Introduce me, will you?' said the grubman, looking at me
with an expression which seemed to say he was all impatience
for an opportunity to give a specimen of his breeding.

Thinking it would prove of benefit to the scrivener, I acquiesced, and, asking the grubman his name, went up with him to
Bartleby.

'Bartleby, this is a friend; you will find him very useful to
you.'

'Your sarvant, sir, your sarvant,' said the grubman, making a
low salutation behind his apron. 'Hope you find it pleasant
here, sir; nice grounds – cool apartments – hope you'll stay
with us some time – try to make it agreeable. What will you
have for dinner today?'

'I prefer not to dine today,' said Bartleby, turning away. 'It
would disagree with me; I am unused to dinners.' So saying, he
slowly moved to the other side of the inclosure and took up a
position fronting the dead-wall.

'How's this?' said the grubman, addressing me with a stare
of astonishment. 'He's odd, ain't he?'

'I think he is a little deranged,' said I, sadly.

'Deranged? deranged is it? Well, now, upon my word, I
thought that friend of yourn was a gentleman forger; they
are always pale and genteel-like, them forgers. I can't help pity

'em – can't help it, sir. Did you know Monroe Edwards?' he added, touchingly, and paused. Then, laying his hand piteously on my shoulder, sighed, 'He died of consumption at Sing-Sing. So you weren't acquainted with Monroe?'

'No, I was never socially acquainted with any forgers. But I cannot stop longer. Look to my friend yonder. You will not lose by it. I will see you again.'

Some few days after this, I again obtained admission to the Tombs, and went through the corridors in quest of Bartleby; but without finding him.

'I saw him coming from his cell not long ago,' said a turn-key, 'maybe he's gone to loiter in the yards.' So I went in that direction.

'Are you looking for the silent man?' said another turnkey, passing me. 'Yonder he lies – sleeping in the yard there. 'Tis not twenty minutes since I saw him lie down.'

The yard was entirely quiet. It was not accessible to the common prisoners. The surrounding walls, of amazing thickness, kept off all sounds behind them. The Egyptian character of the masonry weighed upon me with its gloom. But a soft imprisoned turf grew underfoot. The heart of the eternal pyramids, it seemed, wherein, by some strange magic, through the clefts, grass-seed, dropped by birds, had sprung.

Strangely huddled at the base of the wall, his knees drawn up and lying on his side, his head touching the cold stones, I saw the wasted Bartleby. But nothing stirred. I paused, then went close up to him, stooped over, and saw that his dim eyes were open; otherwise he seemed profoundly sleeping. Something prompted me to touch him. I felt his hand, when a tingling shiver ran up my arm and down my spine to my feet.

The round face of the grubman peered upon me now. 'His dinner is ready. Won't he dine today, either? Or does he live without dining?'

'Lives without dining,' said I, and closed the eyes.

'Eh! – He's asleep, ain't he?'

'With kings and counselors,' murmured I.

* * *

234

There would seem little need for proceding further in this history. Imagination will readily supply the meager recital of poor Bartleby's interment. But, ere parting with the reader, let me say that if this little narrative has sufficiently interested him to awaken curiosity as to who Bartleby was, and what manner of life he led prior to the present narrator's making his acquaintance, I can only reply that in such curiosity I fully share, but am wholly unable to gratify it. Yet here I hardly know whether I should divulge one little item of rumor which came to my ear a few months after the scrivener's decease. Upon what basis it rested, I could never ascertain, and hence how true it is I cannot now tell. But, inasmuch as this vague report has not been without a certain suggestive interest to me, however sad, it may prove the same with some others, and so I will briefly mention it. The report was this: that Bartleby had been a subordinate clerk in the Dead Letter Office at Washington, from which he had been suddenly removed by a change in the administration. When I think over this rumor, hardly can I express the emotions which seize me. Dead letters! does it not sound like dead men? Conceive a man by nature and mis-fortune prone to a pallid hopelessness, can any business seem more fitted to heighten it than that of continually handling these dead letters, and assorting them for the flames? For by the cartload they are annually burned. Sometimes from out the folded paper the pale clerk takes a ring – the finger it was meant for, perhaps, molders in the grave; a bank note sent in swiftest charity – he whom it would relieve nor eats nor hun-gers any more; pardon for those who died despairing; hope for those who died unhoping; good tidings for those who died stifled by unrelieved calamities. On errands of life, these letters speed to death.

Ah, Bartleby! Ah, humanity!

A very fundamental human need is the urge to interpret, to explain. From the child's 'why' to the most rarefied reaches of philosophical enquiry (often the same thing) we anxiously search for reasons and answers to problems. Myths probably arose partly to relieve the anxiety caused by difficult questions. And we get particularly anxious in our need to explain or to explain away seemingly inexplicable human behaviour. It's an affront to our comfortable and consoling belief that humans are ultimately knowable if they behave as if they're not, so we try hanging labels on such problem-people or problem-behaviour until we find a label that will do to put the problem out of mind.

And hanging labels on people is a process that starts early. Not only in school or college reports on students ('capable but lazy'), which rarely if ever do justice to the complexity of the individual, but perhaps as early as in infancy parents tend to label their offspring with what seem like oddly adult descriptors or discriminators. Babies are much alike but it's consoling to claim that an infant is 'stubborn' or 'sensitive' as a way of conceptualising the separateness or specialness of the single infant. We make sense of the world by finding and labelling the differences.

Characters in books, in mainstream fiction anyway, are very much part of the process. Characters in fiction may seem 'lifelike' and 'real' in their dimensionality and that's why we identify with them, but a little reflection shows that textual characters are qualitatively unlike ourselves. Characters have a limited number of traits which they repeatedly exhibit in their actions and speech; they develop (if at all) in ways that are, if only in retrospect, understandable; they are consistent or at least understandably inconsistent. They are knowable, again if only by the end of the book. I'm not like that. Nor are you. We're infinitely various, changing all the time in different interactions with others, a rich and bewildering mix of behavioural habits, unknowable to others, probably to ourselves. The notion that we can be reduced to a small handful of traits is pretty absurd. So why do we eagerly consume fiction? Why do we believe in the 'reality' of fictional characters?

It's presumably because of what we've already suggested. We don't like the unknowable. We label to explain. We cheer ourselves up with the notion that the rest of the world can be adequately labelled even if we resent the idea that *we* can be. Fiction colludes in this consoling and flattering process.

But *Bartleby*, emphatically, doesn't. The story indeed seems specifically designed to challenge our need to explain away. Bartleby is the least knowable 'character' in nineteenth-century literature. In fact he's not a character in the traditional sense at all. He, rather famously, doesn't talk like one. (He prefers not to.) The others in the story would like him to be, in order to label and be comfortable with him, and the text leads the reader through a process of our trying to label him into knowability, but he resists all such attempts. In that sense, though on the face of it the least 'real-life' or 'lifelike' character imaginable, Bartleby is most fundamentally human, most like our conceptions of ourselves, unknowable in our proud and secret uniqueness. If (as we saw Morgann discovering in relation to Shakespeare) mainstream literature gives the illusion of depth to its characters by showing the reader most of what makes the character 'add up' to a character and letting the reader find the few remaining bits that complete the picture, Melville inverts this with Bartleby.

For there's no real 'characterisation'. There's a series of comically desperate words and phrases that try to account for him. These frequently flirt with the paradoxical or impossible, such as him writing 'palely', his face being 'leanly composed', his use of a 'flute-like' voice to convey 'mildly cadaverous' replies and his tendency to slide 'noiselessly' and to 'gently' disappear. There's only one tiny moment of apparently human ordinariness and nothing certain can be made of that either. It's when the lawyer is asking Bartleby to tell him '*anything*' about himself. He asks, then waits 'a considerable time for a reply, during which his countenance remained immovable, only there was the faintest conceivable tremor of the white attenuated mouth'.

The temptation to the reader is to guess at what lies unspoken behind that tremor. (It's characteristic of this brilliant story that that 'tremor' gets transferred to the lawyer later. When challenged to take responsibility for Bartleby he speaks 'with assumed tranquillity, but an inward tremor'.) Guessing, like clutching at straws, is what the lawyer and the reader are reduced to. All of the usual inferred or provided stuff of fictional characterisation (history, motivation, desire) is simply unavailable. We have to make it up for ourselves, to invent a massive and invisible substructure under that tremor, to make Bartleby more comfortably human. But if we could really know, as opposed to guess, it wouldn't perhaps be so comfortable. This is the subject of one of Emily Dickinson's poems, as we'll see in a later chapter, when she suggests that if we could work out the 'undeveloped Freight' behind every little utterance we'd 'crumble' with its weight ('Could mortal lip divine'). The lawyer is involved in the same process of inferring a massive but unavailable substructure somehow behind the available figure of

Bartleby when he says that Bartleby is 'a bit of wreck in the mid-Atlantic' and, later, 'the last column of some ruined temple'.

And the guessing or making up is what we do as we read, just as the lawyer had to. This novella has, unsurprisingly, attracted an enormous range of conflicting readings, attempts to explain Bartleby. Is he for instance mad, autistic, an unsocialised child, a ghost, a visionary anti-capitalist, a martyr, Christ? Has he, in the words of a character in a play by Samuel Beckett, never been properly born? Is it possible that the most revealing line is the early one about Bartleby's industrious working 'as if long famishing for something to copy' ? Apart from the painful irony in 'famishing' is there a sense in which Bartleby is trying to copy himself into socialisation – and gives up, realising its futility, whereas the rest of them and the rest of us keep on copying until we've got enough socialisation to be going on with?

An entertaining book by Dan McCall patiently surveys the critical literature and, quite rightly, decides that even the best of them are no more than violations of Bartleby's privacy and right to silence. But that doesn't deny our very human need to try to understand. Not to dismiss him as Ginger Nut does when he calls him 'a little *luny*' but, as the lawyer feels impelled, to try to reach and help him. And the lawyer is humanised in the process, feeling a quite new and radical fellow-feeling for another human, for what he admits is 'the first time in my life'. Equivalently, his language matures from its rather self-satisfied wordi-ness to a charged and direct simplicity.

And the challenge to the reader is to enlarge our sympathies in the same way. Perhaps, once we've reached the extraordinary last four words, we realise the limitations of explaining, when it comes to other people as opposed to fictional characters. The tentative 'explanation' that the lawyer offers in the novella's second of its three endings (if the last four words are the third), the rumour that Bartleby worked in the office where letters that fail to reach their intended recipients are sent for disposal, is not one that will do to label Bartleby or to explain him away and nor does the lawyer think so either. Not now.

What we can take from the bizarre and painful experience of *Bartleby* are some questions with far-reaching implications. Perhaps our readings of all texts will feel different after this one. For, as we've seen, what we take for granted in reading stories is up for challenge here – notions such as charac-terisation, making sense, coherence, endings that end by closing. Critics have used the term 'interrogative text' about fictions that ask more than they answer. Perhaps all texts are interrogative in the sense that they can or have to be read interrogatively. This one has to be. It makes the reader unusually responsible for the making of meaning. Critics call this area 'reader-response criticism' and we'll meet the issue again sharply in the chapter on *The Turn of the Screw*. Lennard Davis's *Resisting Novels* (London, Methuen, 1987) is, as its title suggests, a critique of the effects of novels and novel-reading, a critique equivalent to that mounted by *Bartleby* itself. Dan McCall's *The Silence of Bartleby* (Ithaca, Cornell University Press, 1989), mentioned above, is a rich and wide-ranging guide to the *Bartleby* 'industry' and contains a full version of the text itself. Penguin publish *Bartleby* in a volume with Melville's later *Billy Budd* (Harmondsworth, Penguin, 1970), which is fascinating to compare. Benjamin Britten's opera *Billy Budd* (1951) opens in a way that accidentally echoes the opening of *Bartleby*. Two modern films, again accidentally, shed intriguing light on *Bartleby*: these are *Being There* (1979), with Peter Sellers, and *Zelig* (1983), with Woody Allen.

12

DICKINSON'S POEMS
Women writing the inexpressible

This chapter presents eleven poems by Emily Dickinson (about 1865). A brief commentary invites you to think about expression and the inexpressible, about women's writing and men's editing, about the written and the spoken word.

There are two things that are more or less popularly known about Emily Dickinson. The first is that she was a recluse, never venturing outside the door in her strictly orthodox father's New England home. And the other is that at her death her sister found nearly 2,000 unpublished little poems in hand-stitched little books secreted among her personal effects, eccentrically punctuated and in other ways quite unlike the typical poetry of the period either in America or England. Like many popularly known facts these two facts are not entirely true.

There's a third fact I stumbled across yesterday. A fantastically gifted American forger called Mark Hofmann killed a number of people in the process of making and marketing his forgeries, among the most brilliant of which was the alleged manuscript of a hitherto unknown Emily Dickinson poem. The market was there, ready to pay enormous sums for this bit of unique Americana. The Dickinson legend is, like the Shakespeare legend, a matter of cultural heritage industry upkeep. There's money at stake, as well as images of poets, of women.

Here are eleven poems.

'*Speech*' – is a prank of *Parliament* –
'*Tears*' – a trick of the *nerve* –
But the Heart with the heaviest freight on –
Doesn't – always – move –

––––––––

By homely gift and hindered Words
The human heart is told
Of Nothing –
'Nothing' is the force
That renovates the World –

––––––––

Could mortal lip divine
The undeveloped Freight
Of a delivered syllable
'Twould crumble with the weight.

––––––––

There is no Silence in the Earth – so silent
As that endured
Which uttered, would discourage Nature
And haunt the World.

––––––––

The Brain, within its Groove
Runs evenly – and true –
But let a Splinter swerve –
'Twere easier for You –

To put a Current back –
When Floods have slit the Hills –
And scooped a Turnpike for Themselves
And trodden out the Mills –

––––––––

It's such a little thing to weep –
So short a thing to sigh –
And yet – by Trades – the size of *these*
We men and women die!

–––––––––

There's a certain Slant of light,
Winter Afternoons –
That oppresses, like the Heft
Of Cathedral Tunes –

Heavenly Hurt, it gives us –
We can find no scar,
But internal difference,
Where the Meanings, are –

None may teach it – Any –
'Tis the Seal Despair –
An imperial affliction
Sent us of the Air –

When it comes, the Landscape listens –
Shadows – hold their breath –
When it goes, 'tis like the Distance
On the look of Death –

–––––––––

The Heart asks Pleasure – first
And then – Excuse from Pain –
And then – those little Anodynes
That deaden suffering –

And then – to go to sleep –
And then – if it should be
The will of its Inquisitor
The privilege to die –

–––––––––

How slow the Wind –
how slow the sea –
how late their Feathers be!

———————

That Love is all there is,
Is all we know of Love;
It is enough, the freight should be
Proportioned to the groove.

———————

I stepped from Plank to Plank
A slow and cautious way
The Stars about my Head I felt
About my Feet the Sea.

I knew not but the next
Would be my final inch –
This gave me that precarious Gait
Some call Experience.

There are nearly 2,000 Dickinson poems and the business of choosing between them has always been a difficult issue. I've chosen poems that all point towards ideas of the unexpressed or inexpressible, that which lies outside normal discourse and communication, the notion that there's always something beyond expression. Expressiveness of this kind, a kind always shadowed by the unsayable, by silence, by loss, and by what's in the margins, can be seen as peculiarly the province of women's writing. But perhaps I'm only reflecting my tastes. There are other chapters in this book that reflect an interest in silences and margins, and *Bartleby* which we explored in the last chapter is an obvious example.

Feminist criticism has stressed that women's writing is forced to be interested in margins and silences, and has to speak in a kind of code, because of the oppressiveness of patriarchy, the fully voiced dominations of men and men's books. Male poets write full, whole poems, replete with presence. Dickinson, in Helen McNeil's words, 'is the

American poet of what is broken and absent' (McNeil, 1986, p. 9). Dickinson herself said that 'my Business is Circumference' (*Letters*, II, p. 413) and that her task is to 'Tell all the Truth but tell it slant' (in the poem with that first line). In the words of an influential book by Sandra Gilbert and Susan Gubar, women writers produce 'works whose surface designs conceal or obscure deeper, less accessible (and less socially acceptable) levels of meaning' (Gilbert and Gubar, 1979, p. 73). Dickinson's interest in what cannot be expressed, the rapt intensities of her fraught poems, their unspoken 'freight' (one of her key words), conveys an awareness of the socially controlled limits of female expression. In a later chapter (*The Yellow Wallpaper*) we'll meet a woman writer coming very painfully against those carefully policed and male-ordained limits.

A more recent critical insight that might be helpful here comes from the challenging and difficult work of Julia Kristeva. She argued that when infants grow into language what gets repressed is the endless free-flow of primary pulses, a kind of pre-language of undifferentiated pleasure, and being only part-successfully repressed it exerts later a kind of subversive pressure on language in the form of 'contradictions, meaninglessness, disruption, silences and absences' (I draw here on Toril Moi's account (Moi, 1985, p. 162)). This makes me think of *Bartleby* again. But it also makes me think of Emily Dickinson's poems, which seem to convey a longing to return to the freedom of pre-language. And, again in a later chapter, we'll meet with the work of Jean Rhys, a woman for whom 'every word I say has chains round its ankles'. Dickinson chose the rhythms of hymns and nursery-rhymes and riddles, and more or less dispensed with the usual poetic decorations of adjectives and adverbs, perhaps out of the same impulse towards the pre-social or the pre-linguistic. These poems are like spells.

In the history of Dickinson scholarship it's interesting that, by and large, the editors have been men and the best critics women. Perhaps that's only because the editing came earlier, but it still suggests a kind of difference of process and role, the men organising and shaping and policing, the women pushing the interpretation towards further horizons. The editing by men goes back to the beginning, with the few poems that did appear in Dickinson's lifetime being heavily altered by male editors. Editions that followed were not only altered but made to conform to sentimental notions of the themes of women's writing, with

244

editors grouping the poems under headings such as Friendship, Nature and so on.

It wasn't until 1955 that, through the work of another man, Thomas H. Johnson, the complete poems in the form that she left them were finally presented. In the following year *The Penguin Book of English Verse*, which we discussed in relation to Wyatt in the first chapter, presented its selection of eight. Perhaps the editor, or T.S. Eliot, if it was he who chose them, deliberately ignored the Johnson edition or perhaps he or they didn't know it. Whatever, the eight poems are in re-punctuated form, indeed a seemingly antiquated form with use of ', –' as in early nineteenth-century novels. And one of the eight ('She rose to his requirement') is about a dutiful wife taking on the 'honorable work' of looking after the 'requirement' of a man. Editors edit and choose.

Johnson presented the poems in the form that Dickinson left them. I thought of writing 'in the form that she intended them to be published' but I changed my mind. In fact, after years of teaching students that Dickinson's extraordinary punctuation – those electrically charged dashes, even at the ends of poems – is such a crucial part of the poems' meaning and impact, I've begun to think rather differently. The dashes clearly are such a crucial part but questions remain. If the poems had come out in that form in her lifetime what would Dickinson have been claiming in terms of authority and expressiveness? Wouldn't she, in effect, have been identifying herself as, or at least laying herself open to the male charge of being the eccentric, scatty, over-emotional, hysterical, uncontrolled and uncontrollable female, clearly in need of a male editor to sort her writing out? 'Spasmodic' and 'uncontrolled' were words used about her, indeed in a letter to her, by one male reader (McNeil, 1986, p. 104). The effect would surely have been to lessen the claim the poems implicitly make, a kind of Puritan or Quaker claim to tell the truth to others, as she saw it. But what choice did she have?

I'm not suggesting that editors should impose orthodox punctuation on these poems, or even that Dickinson should have done. What I mean is that these poems, in the form she left them, are as it were meta-poems, not drafts or unfinished but in a state of rarefied expressiveness, suspended between language and silence, between ink and voice. Perhaps the most appropriate response to Dickinson is to internalise her, to learn the poems by heart. I've found that's how they communicate over time, slowly releasing their energies like depth-charges in the mind. Like me, you may well have found that there are poets who, after you've been reading them for a while, suddenly start speaking with uncanny clarity, as if you've tuned to their wavelength or they have to yours. Dickinson's voice was like that for me. I think that this is the other sense in which Dickinson connects with the most primitive of impulses. She said 'my Business is to sing' (quoted in Dickinson, Faber edition, 1968, p. 10). She is a voice, a woman's voice writing in speech, the poems a drama of voice and – the dashes – silences, a voice speaking in what I think is the most compelling way I've ever read, or heard.

> The suggestion above is that all poetry feels different after reading or internalising Emily Dickinson. It's almost as if she reinvented the poem, made finally clear the nature of the poetic enterprise itself. She herself was deeply read in earlier literature, as well as mythology, the Bible and Shake-speare, and if you explore Keats and the Brontës in particular it should be apparent how uniquely she absorbed and transformed what she read. She also seems to invite connections with seventeenth-century Protestant poets like George Herbert. Her effect on later poets is, in the same way, both certain but difficult to demonstrate. William Carlos Williams called her his patron-saint. Thomas H. Johnson's multi-volume editions of the *Poems* (Cambridge, Mass., Harvard University Press, 1955) and the Letters (Cam-bridge, Mass., Harvard University Press, 1958) are the source of all good later editions. But it is still easy to find modern editions that re-punctuate the poems, as in the selection in *The Oxford Book of Short Poems* (Oxford, Oxford University Press, 1985). The original punctuation is retained in a good *Choice of Emily Dickinson's Verse*, which has a lively introduction by Ted Hughes (London, Faber and Faber, 1968). Helen McNeil's *Emily Dickinson* (London, Virago Press, 1986) is a strong and subtle study, with useful material on the Puritan tradition. Sandra Gilbert and Susan Gubar have a chapter on Dickin-son in *The Madwoman in the Attic* (New Haven, Yale University Press, 1979), and they and Julia Kristeva are discussed in Toril Moi's *Sexual/Textual Politics* (London, Methuen, 1985). There's a very suggestive moment in Salinger's *The Catcher in the Rye* (London, Hamish Hamilton, 1951) in which one character asks another who the best war poet was, Rupert Brooke or Emily Dickinson. The implicitly correct answer is Dickinson, the notion being her insights into the war within consciousness.

13

DICKENS'S
OUR MUTUAL FRIEND
Between men, education and law

This chapter presents extracts from Charles Dickens's *Our Mutual Friend* (1865). The extracts focus on the rivalry between two men for a woman. The commentary tries to draw out the ways in which the rivalry is both articulated and not articulated. Class-relations, male–male bondings and master–pupil relations are patterned closely in this narrative and find particular significance in the way the novel draws on the 'pupil-teacher' system which Victorian reformers had begun.

Dickens's *Our Mutual Friend* is his last complete novel and, for many, his most complex and challenging. One of its two love-stories is about which of two young men is going to love and also educate a young woman. The woman is the object and the goal of the plot but the relations between the men, one a lawyer and the other a schoolteacher, are so fraught that they seem self-sufficient, needing no object or goal.

The young woman is Lizzie Hexam, daughter of a scavenger along the Thames whom she assists. She is unselfishly devoted to her selfishly ungenerous younger brother Charley, who she hopes can escape from her own and her father's way of life. Charley, at 15, attracts the attention of his 26-year-old schoolmaster (himself once a pauper, like the Hexams), Bradley Headstone, a man who has fought hard and long to struggle to his current status. Bradley's ambitions for the ambitious Charley are to bring him up to be a schoolmaster like himself.

Shortly after the start of the novel Charley brings news of a waterside death to a young solicitor, Mortimer Lightwood. Mortimer is the novel's first sympathetic male character. He is witty, stylish and also a narrator-figure: he tells other dinner-party guests, and thus the reader, the background to the novel's crucial inheritance plot. Present in the scene during the party is Lightwood's friend from public school, a barrister called Eugene Wrayburn. The solicitor has little work put his way, the barrister none. When Eugene first sees Charley, he hears him speaking slightingly of Lizzie to Mortimer.

> The gloomy Eugene, with his hands in his pockets, had strolled in and assisted at the latter part of the dialogue; when the boy spoke these words slightingly of his sister, he took him roughly enough by the chin, and turned up his face to look at it.
>
> 'Well, I'm sure, sir!', said the boy, resisting; 'I hope you'll know me again.'
>
> (Book I, Ch. 3)

For want of anything else to do, Eugene goes with Mortimer to the Hexam household and sees Lizzie. Later in the novel Bradley Headstone advises Charley that he should have nothing to do with his sister, who is by now orphaned. Here is that passage; it includes the novel's first account of Bradley Headstone.

> 'So you want to go and see your sister, Hexam?'
>
> 'If you please, Mr Headstone.'
>
> 'I have half a mind to go with you. Where does your sister live?'
>
> 'Why, she is not settled yet, Mr Headstone. I'd rather you didn't see her till she is settled, if it was all the same to you.'
>
> 'Look here, Hexam.' Mr Bradley Headstone, highly certificated stipendiary schoolmaster, drew his right forefinger through one of the buttonholes of the boy's coat, and looked at it attentively. 'I hope your sister may be good company for you?'
>
> 'Why do you doubt it, Mr Headstone?'
>
> 'I did not say I doubted it.'
>
> 'No, sir; you didn't say so.'
>
> Bradley Headstone looked at his finger again, took it out of the buttonhole and looked at it closer, bit the side of it and looked at it again.
>
> 'You see, Hexam, you will be one of us. In good time you are sure to pass a creditable examination and become one of us. Then the question is —'

The boy waited so long for the question, while the schoolmaster looked at a new side of his finger, and bit it, and looked
at it again, that at length the boy repeated:

'The question is, sir – ?'

'Whether you had not better leave well alone.'

'Is it well to leave my sister alone, Mr Headstone?'

I do not say so, because I do not know. I put it to you. I ask
you to think of it. I want you to consider. You know how well
you are doing here.'

'After all, she got me here,' said the boy, with a struggle.

'Perceiving the necessity of it,' acquiesced the schoolmaster,
'and making up her mind fully to the separation. Yes.'

The boy, with a return of that former reluctance or struggle
or whatever it was, seemed to debate with himself. At length
he said, raising his eyes to the master's face:

'I wish you'd come with me and see her, Mr Headstone,
though she is not settled. I wish you'd come with me, and take
her in the rough, and judge her for yourself.'

'You are sure you would not like,' asked the schoolmaster, 'to
prepare her?'

'My sister Lizzie,' said the boy, proudly, 'wants no preparing, Mr Headstone. What she is, she is, and shows herself to be.
There's no pretending about my sister.'

His confidence in her, sat more easily upon him than the
indecision with which he had twice contended. It was his better nature to be true to her, if it were his worse nature to be
wholly selfish. And as yet the better nature had the stronger
hold.

'Well, I can spare the evening,' said the schoolmaster. 'I am
ready to walk with you.'

'Thank you, Mr Headstone. And I am ready to go.'

Bradley Headstone, in his decent black coat and waistcoat,
and decent white shirt, and decent formal black tie, and decent
pantaloons of pepper and salt, with his decent silver watch in
his pocket and its decent hair-guard round his neck, looked
a thoroughly decent young man of six-and-twenty. He was
never seen in any other dress, and yet there was a certain stiff-
ness in his manner of wearing this, as if there were a want of

adaptation between him and it, recalling some mechanics in their holiday clothes. He had acquired mechanically a great store of teacher's knowledge. He could do mental arithmetic mechanically, sing at sight mechanically, blow various wind instruments mechanically, even play the great church organ mechanically. From his early childhood up, his mind had been a place of mechanical stowage. The arrangement of his whole-sale warehouse, so that it might be always ready to meet the demands of retail dealers – history here, geography there, astronomy to the right, political economy to the left – natural history, the physical sciences, figures, music, the lower math ematics, and what not, all in their several places – this care had imparted to his countenance a look of care; while the habit of questioning and being questioned had given him a suspicious manner, or a manner that would be better described as one of lying in wait. There was a kind of settled trouble in the face. It was the face belonging to a naturally slow or inattentive intel-lect that had toiled hard to get what it had won, and that had to hold it now that it was gotten. He always seemed to be uneasy lest anything should be missing from his mental warehouse, and taking stock to assure himself.

Suppression of so much to make room for so much, had given him a constrained manner, over and above. Yet there was enough of what was animal, and of what was fiery (though smouldering), still visible in him, to suggest that if young Bradley Headstone, when a pauper lad, had chanced to be told off for the sea, he would not have been the last man in a ship's crew. Regarding that origin of his, he was proud, moody, and sullen, desiring it to be forgotten. And few people knew of it.

In some visits to the Jumble his attention had been attracted to this boy Hexam. An undeniable boy for a pupil-teacher; an undeniable boy to do credit to the master who should bring him on. Combined with this consideration, there may have been some thought of the pauper lad now never to be men-tioned. Be that how it might, he had with pains gradually worked the boy into his own school, and procured him some offices to discharge there, which were repaid with food and lodging. Such were the circumstances that had brought

together, Bradley Headstone and young Charley Hexam that
autumn evening.

(Book II, Ch. 1)

Like other 'realist' novelists, Dickens suggests here, in order to
achieve a kind of depth-effect, that Bradley is almost too difficult for
Dickens himself to understand clearly. Thus phrases like 'or a manner
that would be better described as' and thus the smuggling in of what is
clearly the key phrase ('though smouldering') in brackets, as if it's
unimportant. But you might also be struck by his very odd action –
when he 'drew his right forefinger through one of the buttonholes of the
boy's coat, and looked at it attentively', then biting it, twice, methodically – and how this first action with Charley takes us back to Eugene's
taking of Charley's chin and looking at his face, as if inspecting the boy
with lordly superiority. Later that evening Bradley, who has now met
Lizzie, and Charley are walking home. Here there's another odd
physical connection Bradley makes with Charley.

The master and the pupil walked on, rapidly and silently.
They had nearly crossed the bridge, when a gentleman came
coolly sauntering towards them, with a cigar in his mouth, his
coat thrown back, and his hands behind him. Something in the
careless manner of this person, and in a certain lazily arrogant
air with which he approached, holding possession of twice as
much pavement as another would have claimed, instantly
caught the boy's attention. As the gentleman passed the boy
looked at him narrowly, and then stood still, looking after him.

'Who is it that you stare after?' asked Bradley.

'Why!' said the boy, with a confused and pondering frown
upon his face, 'It *is* that Wrayburn one!'

Bradley Headstone scrutinized the boy as closely as the boy
had scrutinized the gentleman.

'I beg your pardon, Mr Headstone, but I couldn't help
wondering what in the world brought *him* here!'

Though he said it as if his wonder were past – at the same
time resuming the walk – it was not lost upon the master that
he looked over his shoulder after speaking, and that the same
perplexed and pondering frown was heavy on his face.

251

'You don't appear to like your friend, Hexam?'

'I DON'T like him,' said the boy.

'Why not?'

'He took hold of me by the chin in a precious impertinent way, the first time I ever saw him,' said the boy.

'Again, why?'

'For nothing. Or – it's much the same – because something I happened to say about my sister didn't happen to please him.'

'Then he knows your sister?'

'He didn't at that time,' said the boy, still moodily pondering

'Does now?'

The boy had so lost himself that he looked at Mr Bradley Headstone as they walked on side by side, without attempting to reply until the question had been repeated; then he nodded and answered, 'Yes, sir.'

'Going to see her, I dare say.'

'It can't be!' said the boy, quickly. 'He doesn't know her well enough. I should like to catch him at it!'

When they had walked on for a time, more rapidly than before, the master said, clasping the pupil's arm between the elbow and the shoulder with his hand:

'You were going to tell me something about that person. What did you say his name was?'

'Wrayburn. Mr Eugene Wrayburn. He is what they call a barrister, with nothing to do. The first time he came to our old place was when my father was alive. He came on business; not that it was *his* business – *he* never had any business – he was brought by a friend of his.'

'And the other times?'

'There was only one other time that I know of. When my father was killed by accident, he chanced to be one of the finders. He was mooning about, I suppose, taking liberties with people's chins; but there he was, somehow. He brought the news home to my sister early in the morning, and brought Miss Abbey Potterson, a neighbour, to help break it to her. He was mooning about the house when I was fetched home in the afternoon – they didn't know where to find me till my sister

could be brought round sufficiently to tell them – and then he
mooned away.'

'And is that all?'

'That's all, sir.'

Bradley Headstone gradually released the boy's arm, as if he
were thoughtful, and they walked on side by side as before.
After a long silence between them, Bradley resumed the talk.

'I suppose – your sister –' with a curious break both before
and after the words, 'has received hardly any teaching, Hexam?'

'Hardly any, sir.'

'Sacrificed, no doubt, to her father's objections. I remember
them in your case. Yet – your sister – scarcely looks or speaks
like an ignorant person.'

'Lizzie has as much thought as the best, Mr Headstone. Too
much, perhaps, without teaching. I used to call the fire at
home, her books, for she was always full of fancies – sometimes
quite wise fancies, considering – when she sat looking at it.'

'I don't like that,' said Bradley Headstone.

His pupil was a little surprised by this striking in with so
sudden and decided and emotional an objection, but took it as
a proof of the master's interest in himself.

(ibid.)

Bradley now plans to undertake Lizzie's education but is bitter and
frustrated, as is Charley, to discover that Eugene has independently
employed someone to do just that. All this time Mortimer has had no
knowledge of Eugene's interest in Lizzie, let alone his motives towards
her, and the reader is allowed not much more. But Mortimer senses
something different in his friend, to whom he was 'strongly attached'.
The great and explosive scene that follows starts with remarks on
Mortimer's strong attachment.

Mortimer laughed again, with his usual commentaries of
'How *can* you be so ridiculous, Eugene!' and 'What an absurd
fellow you are!' but when his laugh was out, there was something serious, if not anxious, in his face. Despite that perni-
cious assumption of lassitude and indifference, which had
become his second nature, he was strongly attached to his

friend. He had founded himself upon Eugene when they were yet boys at school; and at this hour imitated him no less, admired him no less, loved him no less, than in those departed days.

'Eugene,' said he, 'if I could find you in earnest for a minute, I would try to say an earnest word to you.'

'An earnest word?' repeated Eugene. 'The moral influences are beginning to work. Say on.'

'Well, I will,' returned the other, 'though you are not earnest yet.'

'In this desire for earnestness,' murmured Eugene, with the air of one who was meditating deeply, 'I trace the happy influences of the little flour-barrel and the coffee-mill. Gratifying.'

'Eugene,' resumed Mortimer, disregarding the light interruption, and laying a hand upon Eugene's shoulder, as he, Mortimer, stood before him seated on his bed, 'you are withholding something from me.'

Eugene looked at him, but said nothing.

'All this past summer, you have been withholding something from me. Before we entered on our boating vacation, you were as bent upon it as I have seen you upon anything since we first rowed together. But you cared very little for it when it came, often found it a tie and a drag upon you, and were constantly away. Now it was well enough half-a-dozen times, a dozen times, twenty times, to say to me in your own odd manner, which I know so well and like so much, that your disappearances were precautions against our boring one another; but of course after a short while I began to know that they covered something. I don't ask what it is, as you have not told me; but the fact is so. Say, is it not?'

'I give you my word of honour, Mortimer,' returned Eugene, after a serious pause of a few moments, 'that I don't know.'

'Don't know, Eugene?'

'Upon my soul, don't know. I know less about myself than about most people in the world, and I don't know.'

'You have some design in your mind?'

'Have I? I don't think I have.'

'At any rate, you have some subject of interest there which used not to be there?'

'I really can't say,' replied Eugene, shaking his head blankly, after pausing again to reconsider. 'At times I have thought yes; at other times I have thought no. Now, I have been inclined to pursue such a subject; now I have felt that it was absurd, and that it tired and embarrassed me. Absolutely, I can't say. Frankly and faithfully, I would if I could.'

So replying, he clapped a hand, in his turn, on his friend's shoulder, as he rose from his seat upon the bed, and said:

'You must take your friend as he is. You know what I am, my dear Mortimer. You know how dreadfully susceptible I am to boredom. You know that when I became enough of a man to find myself an embodied conundrum, I bored myself to the last degree by trying to find out what I meant. You know that at length I gave it up, and declined to guess any more. Then how can I possibly give you the answer that I have not discovered? The old nursery form runs, "Riddle-me-riddle-me-ree, p'raps you can't tell me what this may be?" My reply runs, "No. Upon my life, I can't."'

So much of what was fantastically true to his own knowledge of this utterly careless Eugene, mingled with the answer, that Mortimer could not receive it as a mere evasion. Besides, it was given with an engaging air of openness, and of special exemption of the one friend he valued, from his reckless indifference.

'Come, dear boy!' said Eugene. 'Let us try the effect of smoking. If it enlightens me at all on this question, I will impart unreservedly.'

They returned to the room they had come from, and, finding it heated, opened a window. Having lighted their cigars, they leaned out of this window, smoking, and looking down at the moonlight, as it shone into the court below.

'No enlightenment,' resumed Eugene, after certain minutes of silence. 'I feel sincerely apologetic, my dear Mortimer, but nothing comes.'

'If nothing comes,' returned Mortimer, 'nothing can come from it. So I shall hope that this may hold good throughout, and that there may be nothing on foot. Nothing injurious to you, Eugene, or –'

Eugene stayed him for a moment with his hand on his arm, while he took a piece of earth from an old flowerpot on the window-sill and dexterously shot it at a little point of light opposite; having done which to his satisfaction, he said, 'Or?'

'Or injurious to any one else.'

'How,' said Eugene, taking another little piece of earth, and shooting it with great precision at the former mark, 'how injurious to any one else?'

'I don't know.'

'And,' said Eugene, taking, as he said the word, another shot, 'to whom else?'

'I don't know.'

Checking himself with another piece of earth in his hand, Eugene looked at his friend inquiringly and a little sus-piciously. There was no concealed or half-expressed meaning in his face.

'Two belated wanderers in the mazes of the law,' said Eugene, attracted by the sound of footsteps, and glancing down as he spoke, 'stray into the court. They examine the door-posts of number one, seeking the name they want. Not finding it at number one, they come to number two. On the hat of wanderer number two, the shorter one, I drop this pellet. Hitting him on the hat, I smoke serenely, and become absorbed in contempla-tion of the sky.'

Both the wanderers looked up towards the window; but, after interchanging a mutter or two, soon applied themselves to the door-posts below. There they seemed to discover what they wanted, for they disappeared from view by entering at the doorway. 'When they emerge,' said Eugene, 'you shall see me bring them both down'; and so prepared two pellets for the purpose.

He had not reckoned on their seeking his name, or Light-wood's. But either the one or the other would seem to be in question, for now there came a knock at the door. 'I am on duty to-night,' said Mortimer, 'stay you where you are, Eugene.' Requiring no persuasion, he stayed there, smoking quietly, and not at all curious to know who knocked, until Mortimer spoke to him from within the room, and touched him. Then, drawing in his head, he found the visitors to be young Charley Hexam and the schoolmaster; both standing facing him, and both recognized at a glance.

'You recollect this young fellow, Eugene?' said Mortimer.

'Let me look at him,' returned Wrayburn, coolly. 'Oh, yes, yes. I recollect him!'

He had not been about to repeat that former action of taking him by the chin, but the boy had suspected him of it, and had thrown up his arm with an angry start. Laughingly, Wrayburn looked to Lightwood for an explanation of this odd visit.

'He says he has something to say.'

'Surely it must be to you, Mortimer.'

'So I thought, but he says no. He says it is to you.'

'Yes, I do say so,' interposed the boy. 'And I mean to say what I want to say, too, Mr Eugene Wrayburn!'

Passing him with his eyes as if there were nothing where he stood, Eugene looked on to Bradley Headstone. With consummate indolence, he turned to Mortimer, inquiring: 'And who may this other person be?'

'I am Charles Hexam's friend,' said Bradley; 'I am Charles Hexam's schoolmaster.'

'My good sir, you should teach your pupils better manners,' returned Eugene.

Composedly smoking, he leaned an elbow on the chimney-piece, at the side of the fire, and looked at the schoolmaster. It was a cruel look, in its cold disdain of him, as a creature of no worth. The schoolmaster looked at him, and that, too, was a cruel look, though of the different kind, that it had a raging jealousy and fiery wrath in it.

Very remarkably, neither Eugene Wrayburn nor Bradley Headstone looked at all at the boy. Through the ensuing dialogue, those two, no matter who spoke, or whom was addressed, looked at each other. There was some secret, sure perception between them, which set them against one another in all ways.

'In some high respects, Mr Eugene Wrayburn,' said Bradley, answering him with pale and quivering lips, 'the natural feelings of my pupils are stronger than my teaching.'

'In most respects, I dare say,' replied Eugene, enjoying his cigar, 'though whether high or low is of no importance. You have my name very correctly. Pray what is yours?'

'It cannot concern you much to know, but –'

'True,' interposed Eugene, striking sharply and cutting him short at his mistake, 'it does not concern me at all to know. I can say Schoolmaster, which is a most respectable title. You are right, Schoolmaster.'

It was not the dullest part of this goad in its galling of Bradley Headstone, that he had made it himself in a moment of incautious anger. He tried to set his lips so as to prevent their quivering, but they quivered fast.

'Mr Eugene Wrayburn,' said the boy, 'I want a word with you. I have wanted it so much, that we have looked out your address in the book, and we have been to your office, and we have come from your office here.'

'You have given yourself much trouble, Schoolmaster,' observed Eugene, blowing the feathery ash from his cigar. 'I hope it may prove remunerative.'

'And I am glad to speak,' pursued the boy, 'in presence of Mr Lightwood, because it was through Mr Lightwood that you ever saw my sister.'

For a mere moment, Wrayburn turned his eyes aside from the schoolmaster to note the effect of the last word on Mortimer, who, standing on the opposite side of the fire, as soon as the word was spoken, turned his face towards the fire and looked down into it.

'Similarly, it was through Mr Lightwood that you ever saw her again, for you were with him on the night when my father was found, and so I found you with her on the next day. Since then, you have seen my sister often. You have seen my sister oftener and oftener. And I want to know why?'

'Was this worth while, Schoolmaster?' murmured Eugene, with the air of a disinterested adviser. 'So much trouble for nothing? You should know best, but I think not.'

'I don't know, Mr Wrayburn,' answered Bradley, with his passion rising, 'why you address me –

'Don't you? said Eugene. 'Then I won't.'

He said it so tauntingly in his perfect placidity, that the respectable right-hand clutching the respectable hair-guard of the respectable watch could have wound it round his throat and strangled him with it. Not another word did Eugene deem it worth while to utter, but stood leaning his head upon his hand, smoking, and looking imperturbably at the chafing Bradley Headstone with his clutching right-hand, until Bradley was wellnigh mad.

'Mr Wrayburn,' proceeded the boy, 'we not only know this that I have charged upon you, but we know more. It has not yet come to my sister's knowledge that we have found it out, but we have. We had a plan, Mr Headstone and I, for my sister's education, and for its being advised and overlooked by Mr Headstone, who is a much more competent authority, whatever you may pretend to think, as you smoke, than you could produce, if you tried. Then, what do we find? What do we find, Mr Lightwood? Why, we find that my sister is already being taught, without our knowing it. We find that while my sister gives an unwilling and cold ear to our schemes for her advantage – I, her brother, and Mr Headstone, the most competent authority, as his certificates would easily prove, that could be produced – she is wilfully and willingly profiting by other schemes. Ay, and taking pains, too, for I know what such pains are. And so does Mr Headstone! Well! Somebody pays for this, is a thought that naturally occurs to us; who pays? We apply ourselves to find out, Mr Lightwood, and we find that your friend, this Mr Eugene Wrayburn, here, pays. Then I ask him what right has he to do it, and what does he mean by it, and how comes he to be taking such a liberty without my consent, when I am raising myself in the scale of society by my own exertions and Mr Headstone's aid, and have no right to have any darkness cast upon my prospects, or any imputation upon my respectability, through my sister?'

The boyish weakness of this speech, combined with its great selfishness, made it a poor one indeed. And yet Bradley

Headstone, used to the little audience of a school, and unused to the larger ways of men, showed a kind of exultation in it.

'Now I tell Mr Eugene Wrayburn,' pursued the boy, forced into the use of the third person by the hopelessness of addressing him in the first, 'that I object to his having any acquaintance at all with my sister, and that I request him to drop it altogether. He is not to take it into his head that I am afraid of my sister's caring for *him* –'

(As the boy sneered, the Master sneered, and Eugene blew off the feathery ash again.)

'But I object to it, and that's enough. I am more important to my sister than he thinks. As I raise myself, I intend to raise her; she knows that, and she has to look to me for her prospects. Now I understand all this very well, and so does Mr Headstone. My sister is an excellent girl, but she has some romantic notions; not about such things as your Mr Eugene Wrayburns, but about the death of my father and other matters of that sort. Mr Wrayburn encourages those notions to make himself of importance, and so she thinks she ought to be grateful to him, and perhaps even likes to be. Now I don't choose her to be grateful to him, or to be grateful to anybody but me, except Mr Headstone. And I tell Mr Wrayburn that if he don't take heed of what I say, it will be worse for her. Let him turn that over in his memory, and make sure of it. Worse for her!'

A pause ensued, in which the schoolmaster looked very awkward.

'May I suggest, Schoolmaster,' said Eugene, removing his fast-waning cigar from his lips to glance at it, 'that you can now take your pupil away.'

'And Mr Lightwood,' added the boy, with a burning face, under the flaming aggravation of getting no sort of answer or attention, 'I hope you'll take notice of what I have said to your friend, and of what your friend has heard me say, word by word, whatever he pretends to the contrary. You are bound to take notice of it, Mr Lightwood, for, as I have already mentioned, you first brought your friend into my sister's company, and but for you we never should have seen him. Lord knows none of us ever wanted him, any more than any of us will ever miss him. Now Mr Headstone, as Mr Eugene Wrayburn has been obliged to hear what I had to say, and couldn't help himself, and as I have said it out to the last word, we have done all we wanted to do, and may go.'

'Go down-stairs, and leave me a moment, Hexam,' he returned. The boy complying with an indignant look and as much noise as he could make, swung out of the room; and Lightwood went to the window, and leaned there, looking out.

'You think me of no more value than the dirt under your feet,' said Bradley to Eugene, speaking in a carefully weighed and measured tone, or he could not have spoken at all.

'I assure you, Schoolmaster,' replied Eugene, 'I don't think about you.'

'That's not true,' returned the other; 'you know better.'

'That's coarse,' Eugene retorted; 'but you *don't* know better.'

'Mr Wrayburn, at least I know very well that it would be idle to set myself against you in insolent words or overbearing manners. The lad who has just gone out could put you to shame in half-a-dozen branches of knowledge in half an hour, but you can throw him aside like an inferior. You can do as much by me, I have no doubt, beforehand.'

'Possibly,' remarked Eugene.

'But I am more than a lad,' said Bradley, with his clutching hand, 'and I WILL be heard, sir.'

'As a schoolmaster,' said Eugene, 'you are always being heard. That ought to content you.'

'But it does not content me,' replied the other, white with passion. 'Do you suppose that a man, in forming himself for the duties I discharge, and in watching and repressing himself daily to discharge them well, dismisses a man's nature?'

'I suppose you,' said Eugene, 'judging from what I see as I look at you, to be rather too passionate for a good school-master.' As he spoke, he tossed away the end of his cigar.

'Passionate with you, sir, I admit I am. Passionate with you, sir, I respect myself for being. But I have not Devils for my pupils.'

'For your Teachers, I should rather say,' replied Eugene.

'Mr Wrayburn.'

'Schoolmaster.'

'Sir, my name is Bradley Headstone.'

'As you justly said, my good sir, your name cannot concern me. Now, what more?'

'This more. Oh, what a misfortune is mine,' cried Bradley, breaking off to wipe the starting perspiration from his face as he shook head to foot, 'that I cannot so control myself as to appear a stronger creature than this, when a man who has not felt in all his life what I have felt in a day can so command himself!' He said it in a very agony, and even followed it with an errant motion of his hands as if he could have torn himself

Eugene Wrayburn looked on at him, as if he found him beginning to be rather an entertaining study.

'Mr Wrayburn, I desire to say something to you on my own part.'

'Come, come, Schoolmaster,' returned Eugene, with a languid approach to impatience as the other again struggled with himself; 'say what you have to say. And let me remind you that the door is standing open, and your young friend waiting for you on the stairs.'

'When I accompanied that youth here, sir, I did so with the purpose of adding, as a man whom you should not be permitted to put aside, in case you put him aside as a boy, that his instinct is correct and right.' Thus Bradley Headstone, with great effort and difficulty.

'Is that all?' asked Eugene.

'No, sir,' said the other, flushed and fierce. 'I strongly support him in his disapproval of your visits to his sister, and in his objection to your officiousness – and worse – in what you have taken upon yourself to do for her.'

'Is *that* all?' asked Eugene.

'No, sir. I determined to tell you that you are not justified in these proceedings, and that they are injurious to his sister.'

'Are you her schoolmaster as well as her brother's? – Or perhaps you would like to be?' said Eugene.

It was a stab that the blood followed, in its rush to Bradley Headstone's face, as swiftly as if it had been dealt with a dagger. 'What do you mean by that?' was as much as he could utter.

'A natural ambition enough,' said Eugene, coolly. 'Far be it from me to say otherwise. The sister – who is something too much upon your lips, perhaps – is so very different from all the associations to which she had been used, and from all the low obscure people about her, that it is a very natural ambition.'

'Do you throw my obscurity in my teeth, Mr Wrayburn?'

'That can hardly be, for I know nothing concerning it, Schoolmaster, and seek to know nothing.'

'You reproach me with my origin,' said Bradley Headstone; 'you cast insinuations at my bringing-up. But I tell you, sir, I have worked my way onward, out of both and in spite of both, and have a right to be considered a better man than you, with better reasons for being proud.'

'How I can reproach you with what is not within my knowledge, or how I can cast stones that were never in my hand, is a problem for the ingenuity of a schoolmaster to prove,' returned Eugene. 'Is *that* all?'

'No, sir. If you suppose that boy –'

'Who really will be tired of waiting,' said Eugene, politely.

'If you suppose that boy to be friendless, Mr Wrayburn, you deceive yourself. I am his friend, and you shall find me so.'

'And you will find *him* on the stairs,' remarked Eugene.

'You may have promised yourself, sir, that you could do what you chose here, because you had to deal with a mere boy, inexperienced, friendless, and unassisted. But I give you warning that this mean calculation is wrong. You have to do with a man also. You have to do with me. I will support him, and, if need be, require reparation for him. My hand and heart are in this cause, and are open to him.'

'And – quite a coincidence – the door is open,' remarked Eugene.

'I scorn your shifty evasions, and I scorn you,' said the schoolmaster. 'In the meanness of your nature you revile me with the meanness of my birth. I hold you in contempt for it. But if you don't profit by this visit, and act accordingly, you will find me as bitterly in earnest against you as I could be if I deemed you worth a second thought on my own account.'

With a consciously bad grace and stiff manner, as Wrayburn

looked so easily and calmly on, he went out with these words, and the heavy door closed like a furnace-door upon his red and white heats of rage.

'A curious monomaniac,' said Eugene. 'The man seems to believe that everybody was acquainted with his mother!'

Mortimer Lightwood being still at the window, to which he had in delicacy withdrawn, Eugene called to him, and he fell to slowly pacing the room.

'My dear fellow,' said Eugene, as he lighted another cigar, 'I fear my unexpected visitors have been troublesome. If as a set-off (excuse the legal phrase from a barrister at law) you would like to ask Tippins to tea, I pledge myself to make love to her.'

'Eugene, Eugene, Eugene,' replied Mortimer, still pacing the room, 'I am sorry for this. And to think that I have been so blind!'

'How blind, dear boy?' inquired his unmoved friend.

'What were your words that night at the river-side public-house?' said Lightwood, stopping. 'What was it that you asked me? Did I feel like a dark combination of traitor and pickpocket when I thought of that girl?'

'I seem to remember the expression,' said Eugene.

'How do *you* feel when you think of her just now?'

His friend made no direct reply, but observed, after a few whiffs of his cigar, 'Don't mistake the situation. There is no better girl in all this London than Lizzie Hexam. There is no better among my people at home; no better among your people.'

'Granted. What follows?'

'There,' said Eugene, looking after him dubiously as he paced away to the other end of the room, 'you put me again upon guessing the riddle that I have given up.'

'Eugene, do you design to capture and desert this girl?'

'My dear fellow, no.'

'Do you design to marry her?'

'My dear fellow, no.'

'Do you design to pursue her?'

'My dear fellow, I don't design anything. I have no design

whatever. I am incapable of designs. If I conceived a design, I should speedily abandon it, exhausted by the operation.'

'Oh Eugene, Eugene!'

'My dear Mortimer, not that tone of melancholy reproach, I entreat. What can I do more than tell you all I know, and acknowledge my ignorance of all I don't know! How does that little old song go, which, under pretence of being cheerful, is by far the most lugubrious I ever heard in my life?

> "Away with melancholy,
> Nor doleful changes ring
> On life and human folly,
> But merrily merrily sing
>   Fal la!"

Don't let us sing Fal la, my dear Mortimer (which is comparatively unmeaning), but let us sing that we give up guessing the riddle altogether.'

'Are you in communication with this girl, Eugene, and is what these people say true?'

'I concede both admissions to my honourable and learned friend.'

'Then what is to come of it? What are you doing? Where are you going?'

'My dear Mortimer, one would think the schoolmaster had left behind him a catechizing infection. You are ruffled by the want of another cigar. Take one of these, I entreat. Light it at mine, which is in perfect order. So! Now do me the justice to observe that I am doing all I can towards self-improvement, and that you have a light thrown on those household implements which, when you only saw them as in a glass darkly, you were hastily – I must say hastily – inclined to depreciate. Sensible of my deficiencies, I have surrounded myself with moral influences expressly meant to promote the formation of the domestic virtues. To those influences, and to the improving society of my friend from boyhood, commend me with your best wishes.'

'Ah, Eugene!' said Lightwood, affectionately, now standing

near him, so that they both stood in one little cloud of smoke;
'I would that you answered my three questions! What is to
come of it? What are you doing? Where are you going?'

'And my dear Mortimer,' returned Eugene, lightly fanning
away the smoke with his hand for the better exposition of his
frankness of face and manner, 'believe me, I would answer them
instantly if I could. But to enable me to do so, I must first have
found out the troublesome conundrum long abandoned. Here
it is. Eugene Wrayburn.' Tapping his forehead and breast.
'Riddle-me, riddle-me-ree, perhaps you can't tell me what this
may be? – No, upon my life I can't. I give it up!'

(Book II, Ch. 6)

One effect of that passage is that the reader, like Mortimer, wants to
flinch, get out of its forcefield. Mortimer has now become the confused
reader's representative, having yielded his narrative authority in the
mystery of Eugene's motives. The electric currents in play are not so
much flashing simply from one protagonist to another as creating a
series of criss-crossed and intertangled triangular patterns in the
space inhabited by those present. As we find ourselves shifting or
shifted around in our sympathies (they certainly must go to Lizzie, precisely because she's absent) the forcefield and its current change,
creating more and more entangled patterns.

The effect on the reader duplicates the tangled emotional forces
which have been displaced on to the conventional narrative of heterosexual rivalry. These forces would include visible and invisible and
socially acceptable and socially unacceptable sexual energies flowing
in a number of directions, all sharply qualified by the two narrative
structures in which they find themselves: antagonistic class-relations
and master–pupil relations.

Charley's resentment of Eugene has its roots in the elder man's
lordly inspection of his face, holding his chin like a connoisseur of
erotic art with a model or, which comes to much the same thing, a
public-school prefect with a pretty new-boy. It also suggests the dandy
with the boy-prostitute, and the class-implications of that are what
sharpens Charley's resentment. Bradley's first odd action with Charley
is an act of penetration followed by self-mutilation. His second, as they
are walking along, 'clasping the pupil's arm between the elbow and the

shoulder with his arm', and only gradually releasing the arm, is a gro-
tesque and awkward embrace. Bradley needs to assert to himself his
painfully acquired status by reinventing Charley as a model of himself.
Mortimer has invented himself as a model of Eugene. Bradley and
Charley share the pauper background. By raising Charley from it
Bradley can further obliterate its hated class-traces in himself.

Lizzie's ambitions and love are for Charley, not herself. Her rival-
benefactors ride roughshod over that delicacy by asserting their male
and class-positioned right to educate her into appropriate labour, which
would be a state of low but decent gentility. Their motivations are
mixed but in neither case unselfish like Lizzie's for Charley. And it gives
Eugene something to do. It's the insolent indifference of that that
propels Bradley into his fury of rivalry.

An important insight from modern theory, particularly the work of
Rene Girard, is that processes of psychological identification precede
those of desire. The common-sense view would suggest the opposite.
Identification with another person involves imitation, and desire can be
seen as being an imitation of another's desire, needing a trigger of
perceived rivalry as much as its notional goal in order to be launched. It
certainly feels like that when Bradley is suddenly propelled on his
destructive and self-destructive course when conscious of potential
rivalry in Eugene.

But there's also the sense that Bradley and Eugene are dark versions of each other, as much needing each other for pseudo-erotic
identification as locked against each other. Lizzie is the convenient
object upon whom they displace their mutual need. For their being
opposites and doubles to each other is articulated at every level, in
their speech, fluency, manner, bearing, movement, dress – and, most
painfully for Bradley, their upbringing, education, work and class. For
Dickens, education and the law were two crucial languages of social
control. Here he tightens a very tight knot with them. And the suggestion is that Dickens is himself tensed in processes of identification
and desire with Eugene and Bradley which are grounded in the class
differences between them. Thus the white heat of their encounter.

Bradley is self-educated and friendless. Eugene is public-school
educated, idolised and loved since school by Mortimer who models
himself on his idol, not least in their languid attitude towards employment. This may remind you, if you know *David Copperfield*, of

David's idolising of Steerforth at school. There's some guilty desire on Dickens's part in his representations of these idolising male bondings. Bradley wishes to have Charley modelled on him, in their painfully gained employment. Eugene does nothing, is cynical about his gentlemanly status, has money and leisure, wastes and dissipates the money he has, toys with the law which is boring but entertaining enough to let him in on scandals and murders. That is, the law is mildly glamorous and a necessary bore – carrying none of the oppressive dread that it meant to the young Dickens. Bradley desperately hangs on to the little that he has achieved, has no leisure to let up on his dogged work which is the totality of his life, is in deadly earnest. Critics have often pointed out that Bradley is definitively anal. I haven't seen it pointed out that Eugene, in the beginning of the great scene above, is, by dropping pellets of earth from the window, shitting on Bradley's protégé. Dickens toyed with calling Bradley 'Amos Deadstone'. Later in the novel Eugene amuses himself (again, it's something to do) by forcing Bradley to stalk him around London on enormously convoluted walks, in an image of mutual hunting – a hunting of each other and of nothing.

Charley is Bradley's 'pupil-teacher'. This was a system, instigated by educational reformers only eighteen years before Dickens wrote this novel, whereby promising students like Charley were paid to be attached to schoolteachers from whom they would learn their skills. Dickens may have been scathing about educational practices, here and in *Hard Times*, but he was fiercely driven by the need for humanitarian reforms and it's important not to underestimate the extent to which both Charley and Bradley are the products of serious social efforts at improving the educational system – and both carry the burden of their own strenuous efforts to climb with its help and with each other out of hopeless obscurity. This sense of burden and precariousness is sharply counterposed to the insolent easiness worn by Eugene and Mortimer, representatives of public-school privilege at its most exclusive. And its ease, its airiness is guiltily attractive to Dickens who seems to have invested some intensely personal stuff in his characterisation of the blocked Bradley.

The bond between Charley and Bradley, the publicly acceptable pupil–teacher relationship, is shadowed by Bradley's pseudo-erotic need for Charley which gets itself attached to Lizzie (the allowed goal).

Both Bradley and Eugene wish to be Lizzie's teacher; both are, in another sense, her pupils. Eugene taunts Bradley in this passage with the idea that the devils are his teachers not his pupils. Charley is also in a paradoxical pupil–teacher relationship with his sister. The Charley–Bradley bond is also a version of the Eugene–Mortimer relationship, where both parties are also in a pupil–teacher bond (Mortimer was the idoliser; now he is the moral guardian), and in which, being public-school and gentlemanly, the homoerotic connection is allowed some expression, as it isn't for the working-class Bradley and Charley. Mortimer elsewhere in the novel tells Eugene that he loves him. And the image of Mortimer, at the end of this extract, 'affectionately . . . standing near' Eugene, 'so that they both stood in one little cloud of smoke' is very expressive, particularly as leisurely cigar-smoking is itself so expressive of the class-differences that are etched deep in this passage. Eugene chain-smokes the cigars, conspicuously consuming their expensiveness, an oral pleasure that duplicates his self-pleasing spoken comments. It's noticeable that Dickens says of his replies to Bradley that they are 'returned', as if Eugene is enjoying a rather easy game of tennis. Bradley has smoke coming out of his ears instead.

And Lizzie? Her later impulse, understandably enough given the electrical storms generated by all this unexpressed and expressed emotional energy, is to escape, to run away. Let the men get on with it.

The chapter on this novel in Eve Sedgwick's *Between Men* (New York, Columbia University Press, 1985) explores what she calls the homosocial relations between the protagonists in much more subtle detail than is possible above. The introductory chapters in this excellent book are of great interest and worth exploring. Your readings in the nineteenth-century novel, with its strong drive towards heterosexual matchings, may well be affected by Sedgwick's argument that it's actually the male–male relations, in all their varieties, that form the inner dynamics of the text. Sedgwick's own work draws on Rene Girard, mentioned above, in his *Deceit, Desire and the Novel* (Baltimore, Johns Hopkins University Press, 1965). The pages on identification in Jonathan Culler's *Literary Theory: A Very Short Introduction* (Oxford, Oxford University Press, 1997) are particularly helpful. Peter Ackroyd's biography (London, Mandarin, 1994) is the most lively available.

14

CARROLL'S 'ALICE' BOOKS
Remembering the love-gift

Here you'll find extracts from Lewis Carroll's two 'Alice' books (1865, 1872). Starting from a question about our own memories of these books the commentary reaches a question that can be asked after considering the contexts of the books' composition and their disguised autobiographical elements: the question about the original Alice remembering Carroll, or not, and if so how and in what way.

What do you remember of Lewis Carroll's 'Alice' books if you haven't revisited them since childhood, and if you can forget the Disney version?

Students often recall comic set-pieces like the Hatter and March Hare's tea-party or the trial of the Knave of Hearts – scenes often used in children's theatre – and remember outrageously colourful figures like the furious ('off with his head') Queen and the Ugly Duchess. Readers sometimes remember Tenniel's illustrations more readily than the dialogue: the Cheshire Cat's funny-sinister grin (without the Cat) is perhaps more memorable than his funny-mad questions. Having established from Alice that the baby she was carrying had turned into a pig – ' "I thought it would," said the Cat, and vanished' – the Cat suddenly materialises again: ' "Did you say 'pig', or 'fig?" said the Cat.' (A friend of mine thinks that's the funniest thing in nineteenth-century literature.) And perhaps because of Disney, which like other films mixes the two together, we tend to forget that there are two quite separate books, *Alice's Adventures in Wonderland* and *Through the Looking-Glass*. In terms of plot it's easy to forget that *Wonderland*, in so far as it has a plot at all, drifts around Alice's need to get into a garden and that *Looking-Glass* is a game of chess in which Alice becomes a queen.

What children rarely, it seems, respond to or consequently remember is what adults often find most startling in these books: the repeated sense of identity-loss and nightmarish change and transformation, the casual cruelty and violence, the jokes about time, age, growing-up, death ('you're beginning to fade, you know', says a Rose to Alice). It's difficult, for instance, for adults to read the scene in *Wonderland* between Alice and the Caterpillar – with his sinister reading of her mind, his cool undermining of her sense of her self (' "You!" said the Caterpillar contemptuously. "Who are *you*?" '), his sardonic responses to her efforts to assert herself ('she said, very gravely, "I think you ought to tell me who *you* are first." "Why?" said the Caterpillar') – without thinking of interrogation and psychological torture. And the scene from *Looking-Glass* in which the Tweedle brothers accuse Alice of being 'only a sort of thing in his [the Red King's] dream' carries a very anxious charge, the notion that 'reality' has layers of real-ness that cancel each other out (' "I hope you don't suppose those are *real* tears?" Tweedledum interrupted in a tone of great contempt'), and that Alice would go out 'just like a candle' if the King were to wake.

It's not only Tweedledum and the Caterpillar who address Alice with contempt. Openly voiced contempt is very cutting and wounding and, for that reason, adults tend to be shy of it with each other and would never want to use it on a child. But perhaps such tones of voice and such notions of loss of self or of going out like a candle are what children take for granted in their everyday play. What we may find frightening are the horrors children routinely tame and domesticate. It could be said that the 'Alice' books, very like the first two books of *Gulliver's Travels* in this respect, are like an elaborate child's game in which the child-protagonist imagines him or herself as the pseudo-adult having to keep in order an unruly set of creatures who, in their turn, exhibit the incomprehensible antics of the 'real' adult world.

What tends to get forgotten most readily from these extraordinary texts is the elaborate way in which Carroll frames them, their returnings to the real world, the poems he attaches to their beginnings and endings. These two texts have been endlessly framed and re-positioned in our culture since their appearance but it was Carroll himself who took most particular care over their frames. Here are some of those, with some thoughts on a submerged autobiographical context. First, the end of *Wonderland*, picking up the text from the climax to the Trial.

'Let the jury consider their verdict,' the King said, for about the twentieth time that day.

'No, no!' said the Queen. 'Sentence first – verdict afterwards.'

'Stuff and nonsense!' said Alice loudly. 'The idea of having the sentence first!'

'Hold your tongue!' said the Queen, turning purple.

'I won't!' said Alice.

'Off with her head!' the Queen shouted at the top of her voice. Nobody moved.

'Who cares for *you?*' said Alice (she had grown to her full size by this time). 'You're nothing but a pack of cards!'

At this the whole pack rose up into the air, and came flying down upon her; she gave a little scream, half of fright and half of anger, and tried to beat them off, and found herself lying on the bank, with her head in the lap of her sister, who was gently brushing away some dead leaves that had fluttered down from the trees upon her face.

'Wake up, Alice dear!' said her sister. 'Why, what a long sleep you've had!'

'Oh, I've had such a curious dream!' said Alice. And she told her sister, as well as she could remember them, all these strange Adventures of hers that you have just been reading about; and, when she had finished, her sister kissed her, and said 'It *was* a curious dream, dear, certainly; but now run in to your tea: it's getting late.' So Alice got up and ran off, thinking while she ran, as well she might, what a wonderful dream it had been.

But her sister sat still just as she left her, leaning her head on her hand, watching the setting sun, and thinking of little Alice and all her wonderful Adventures, till she too began dreaming after a fashion, and this was her dream:–

First, she dreamed about little Alice herself: once again the tiny hands were clasped upon her knee, and the bright eager eyes were looking up into hers – she could hear the very tones of her voice, and see that queer little toss of her head to keep back the wandering hair that *would* always get into her eyes – and still as she listened, or seemed to listen, the whole place around her became alive with the strange creatures of her little sister's dream.

The long grass rustled at her feet as the White Rabbit hurried by – the frightened Mouse splashed his way through the neighbouring pool – she could hear the rattle of the teacups as the March Hare and his friends shared their never-ending meal, and the shrill voice of the Queen ordering off her unfortunate guests to execution – once more the pig-baby was sneezing on the Duchess's knee, while plates and dishes crashed around it – once more the shriek of the Gryphon, the squeaking of the Lizard's slate-pencil, and the choking of the suppressed guinea-pigs, filled the air, mixed up with the distant sob of the miserable Mock Turtle.

So she sat on, with closed eyes, and half believed herself in Wonderland, though she knew she had but to open them again, and all would change to dull reality – the grass would be only rustling in the wind, and the pool rippling to the waving of the reeds – the rattling teacups would change to tinkling sheep-bells, and the Queen's shrill cries to the voice of the shepherd-boy – and the sneeze of the baby, the shriek of the Gryphon, and all the other queer noises, would change (she knew) to the confused clamour of the busy farm-yard – while the lowing of the cattle in the distance would take the place of the Mock Turtle's heavy sobs.

Lastly, she pictured to herself how this same little sister of hers would, in the after-time, be herself a grown woman; and how she would keep, through all her riper years, the simple and loving heart of her childhood; and how she would gather about her other little children, and make *their* eyes bright and eager with many a strange tale, perhaps even with the dream of Wonderland of long ago; and how she would feel with all their simple sorrows, and find a pleasure in all their simple joys, remembering her own child-life, and the happy summer days.

THE END

The end of *Wonderland* sets up a chain or a sequence across which the story, the text, is passed – first to Alice's rather oddly maternal sister, whose telescoped version of the adventure is like a speeded-up replay against a real-world screen, to Alice as an adult, to her passing it on to other children. What's suggestive about this chain is the idea of the text as a love-gift being passed, unbroken and sacred, somehow outside or protected from the world of time and change and death. That painful world – the 'dull reality' which Alice's sister is conscious of behind her day-dreaming – is intimated in the passage. It's dead leaves that Alice finds herself brushing away when she 'wakes' (the story started in the heat of high summer so the year has 'died' during its telling); gentle stress is placed twice on the sobs of the Mock Turtle; and, most tellingly perhaps, Alice's maturity is referred to as her 'riper' years 'in the after-time' which suggests both picking and dying. But the text will hold fast and young through the generations, even if Alice doesn't. The effect is of a gift that can never be fully or finally given over, of Carroll never quite being able to let go, of being ever-present somehow in an endless process of passing it on, a folding and refolding of the text through leaves of time.

'Love-gift' is the word Carroll uses himself. This is in the poem that the reader of the two 'Alice' books comes across next, after turning from *Wonderland* to *Looking-Glass*. Actually, immediately before the poem and the *Looking-Glass* title-page is a frontispiece illustration – of the White Knight, about whom more below. It's true that the two books were written and published separately, six years apart, but we're so used to the format of the two being together in one volume that the poem attached to the start of *Looking-Glass* acts like a hinge to them both. This is reinforced by the fact that this poem refers back to the boat-trip on the Thames during which Carroll told the real Alice the beginnings of what became *Wonderland*, the tale told then as 'A simple chime, that served to time / The rhythm of our rowing'. Perhaps we're meant to hear there an echo of another enchanted, suspended garden-time that we met in an earlier chapter of this book, Marvell's 'Bermudas'. On Tennyson's advice, 'Bermudas' had been included in Palgrave's massively popular *Golden Treasury*, published four years before *Wonderland*.

> Child of the pure unclouded brow
> And dreaming eyes of wonder!

274

Though time be fleet, and I and thou
 Are half a life asunder,
Thy loving smile will surely hail
The love-gift of a fairy-tale.

I have not seen thy sunny face,
 Nor heard thy silver laughter:
No thought of me shall find a place
 In thy young life's hereafter –
Enough that now thou wilt not fail
To listen to my fairy-tale.

A tale begun in other days,
 When summer suns were glowing –
A simple chime, that served to time
 The rhythm of our rowing –
Whose echoes live in memory yet,
Though envious years would say 'forget.'

Come, hearken then, ere voice of dread,
 With bitter tidings laden,
Shall summon to unwelcome bed
 A melancholy maiden!
We are but older children, dear,
Who fret to find our bedtime near.

Without, the frost, the blinding snow,
 The storm-wind's moody madness –
Within, the firelight's ruddy glow.
And childhood's nest of gladness.
The magic words shall hold thee fast:
Thou shalt not heed the raving blast.

And, though the shadow of a sigh
 May tremble through the story,
For 'happy summer days' gone by,
 And vanish'd summer glory –
It shall not touch, with breath of bale,
The pleasance of our fairy-tale.

'No thought of me shall find a place / In thy young life's hereafter.' Is this a plea expecting the answer – of course, I'll remember you? Emotional blackmail? In any case, her 'life's hereafter' is phrased in such a way, again, as to suggest that Alice's maturity is death. And is the voice of dread summoning 'to unwelcome bed / A melancholy maiden' just mother or nanny ordering the child to bed? The phrasing again suggests another possibility; it suggests the virginal bride trembling in fearful anticipation on the threshold of the honeymoon bed. An unwelcome dread of an idea – for whom? But, again, the 'magic words' of the text will 'hold thee fast', in a clasp that somehow and for ever will keep Alice from the wind's 'moody madness', from age and marriage, from leaving this 'nest' in which the love-gift is always being told.

'Though the shadow of a sigh / May tremble through the story.' Carroll's melancholic love, for which the love-gift is the only possible manifestation, sighs in a shadowy way through both these texts: through the Mock Turtle whose lament is 'once . . . I was a real Turtle' and whose tears, like Alice's according to the Tweedles, are suspected as not even being real (according to the Gryphon 'it's all his fancy, that: he hasn't got no sorrow'); and, most poignantly, through the '*very unhappy*' insect in *Looking-Glass* who wants Alice to make the jokes for a change. It was William Empson, in his classic essay on these texts, who first suggested the muted autobiographical representation in this strange passage. Here it is. Alice has found herself in a train among an odd assortment of passengers.

> Alice couldn't see who was sitting beyond the Beetle, but a hoarse voice spoke next. 'Change engines—' it said, and there it choked and was obliged to leave off.
>
> 'It sounds like a horse,' Alice thought to herself. And an extremely small voice, close to her ear, said ·You might make a joke on that – something about "horse" and "hoarse," you know.·
>
> Then a very gentle voice in the distance said, 'She must be labeled "Lass, with care," you know—'
>
> And after that other voices went on ('What a number of people there are in the carriage!' thought Alice), saying 'She must go by post, as she's got a head on her—' 'She must be sent as a message by the telegraph—' 'She must draw the train herself the rest of the way—,' and so on.

But the gentleman dressed in white paper leaned forwards and whispered in her ear, 'Never mind what they all say, my dear, but take a return-ticket every time the train stops.'

'Indeed I shan't!' Alice said rather impatiently. 'I don't belong to this railway journey at all – I was in a wood just now – and I wish I could get back there!'

'You might make a joke on *that*,' said the little voice close to her ear: 'something about "you *would* if you could," you know.'

'Don't tease so,' said Alice, looking about in vain to see where the voice came from. 'If you're so anxious to have a joke made, why don't you make one yourself?'

The little voice sighed deeply. It was *very* unhappy, evidently, and Alice would have said something pitying to comfort it, 'if it would only sigh like other people!' she thought. But this was such a wonderfully small sigh, that she wouldn't have heard it at all, if it hadn't come *quite* close to her ear. The consequence of this was that it tickled her ear very much, and quite took off her thoughts from the unhappiness of the poor little creature.

'I know you are a friend,' the little voice went on: 'a dear friend, and an old friend. And you won't hurt me, though I *am* an insect.'

'What kind of insect?' Alice inquired, a little anxiously. What she really wanted to know was, whether it could sting or not, but she thought this wouldn't be quite a civil question to ask.

'What, then you don't—' the little voice began, when it was drowned by a shrill scream from the engine, and everybody jumped up in alarm, Alice among the rest.

Then the passage breaks the spell – as if the subject is too painful – and the insect is materialised into a giant gnat who now speaks 'carelessly' and 'in a careless tone' – that is, like typical *Wonderland* or *Looking-Glass* creatures.

It was always Carroll who told the jokes, made up the games and the puzzles for the endless entertainment of Alice and others. Unhappy and socially inept with adults, Carroll's one source of happiness was the company of small girls. The wish that they, for once, could tell the jokes, be on a footing with him, even a kind of parent to him, is poignant enough, but the notion that they might hurt him – by being bored or unamused? by growing up? – and the painful question hanging in the air at 'what, then you don't –' (know who I am? what I feel? that I'd never hurt you? that I love you? that my love would never hurt you?) are signs of anxiety from which the text just has to step away.

But it's the White Knight, the last new figure Alice meets, chosen to be pictured on the title-page, with his zany and silly inventions and his incapacity to do even the one thing knights might be expected to be able to do (ride a horse), who is more obviously a representation of Carroll himself. Here he is, first, being 'certainly . . . *not* a good rider'.

Whenever the horse stopped (which it did very often), he fell off in front; and, whenever it went on again (which it generally did rather suddenly), he fell off behind. Otherwise he kept on pretty well, except that he had a habit of now and then falling off sideways; and, as he generally did this on the side on which Alice was walking, she soon found that it was the best plan not to walk *quite* close to the horse.

'I'm afraid you've not had much practice in riding,' she ventured to say, as she was helping him up from his fifth tumble.

The Knight looked very much surprised, and a little offended at the remark. 'What makes you say that?' he asked, as he scrambled back into the saddle, keeping hold of Alice's hair with one hand, to save himself from falling over on the other side.

'Because people don't fall off quite so often, when they've had much practice.'

'I've had plenty of practice,' the Knight said very gravely: 'plenty of practice!'

Alice could think of nothing better to say than 'Indeed?' but she said it as heartily as she could. They went on a little way in silence after this, the Knight with his eyes shut, muttering to himself, and Alice watching anxiously for the next tumble.

'The great art of riding,' the Knight suddenly began in a loud voice, waving his right arm as he spoke, 'is to keep—' Here the sentence ended as suddenly as it had begun, as the Knight fell heavily on the top of his head exactly in the path where Alice was walking. She was quite frightened this time, and said in an anxious tone, as she picked him up, 'I hope no bones are broken?'

'None to speak of,' the Knight said, as if he didn't mind breaking two or three of them. 'The great art of riding, as I was saying, is – to keep your balance properly. Like this, you know—'

He let go the bridle, and stretched out both his arms to show Alice what he meant, and this time he fell flat on his back, right under the horse's feet.

'Plenty of practice!' he went on repeating, all the time that Alice was getting him on his feet again. 'Plenty of practice!'

'It's too ridiculous!' cried Alice, losing all her patience this time. 'You ought to have a wooden horse on wheels, that you ought!'

'Does that kind go smoothly?' the Knight asked in a tone of great interest, clasping his arms round the horse's neck as he spoke, just in time to save himself from tumbling off again.

'Much more smoothly than a live horse,' Alice said, with a little scream of laughter, in spite of all she could do to prevent it.

'I'll get one,' the Knight said thoughtfully to himself. 'One or two – several.'

There was a short silence after this, and then the Knight went on again. 'I'm a great hand at inventing things. Now, I daresay you noticed, the last time you picked me up, that I was looking rather thoughtful?'

'You *were* a little grave,' said Alice.

'Well, just then I was inventing a new way of getting over a gate – would you like to hear it?'

'Very much indeed,' Alice said politely.

'I'll tell you how I came to think of it,' said the Knight. 'You see, I said to myself "The only difficulty is with the feet: the *head* is high enough already." Now, first I put my head on the top of the gate – then the head's high enough – then I stand on my head – then the feet are high enough, you see – then I'm over, you see.'

'Yes, I suppose you'd be over when that was done,' Alice said thoughtfully: 'but don't you think it would be rather hard?'

'I haven't tried it yet,' the Knight said, gravely; 'so I can't tell for certain – but I'm afraid it *would* be a little hard.'

He looked so vexed at the idea, that Alice changed the subject hastily. 'What a curious helmet you've got!' she said cheerfully. 'Is that your invention too?'

The Knight looked down proudly at his helmet, which hung from the saddle. 'Yes,' he said; 'but I've invented a better one than that – like a sugar-loaf. When I used to wear it, if I fell off the horse, it always touched the ground directly. So I had a *very* little way to fall, you see – But there *was* the danger of falling *into* it, to be sure. That happened to me once – and the worst of it was, before I could get out again, the other White Knight came and put it on. He thought it was his own helmet.'

The Knight looked so solemn about it that Alice did not dare to laugh. 'I'm afraid you must have hurt him,' she said in a trembling voice, 'being on the top of his head.'

'I had to kick him, of course,' the Knight said, very seriously. 'And then he took the helmet off again – but it took hours and hours to get me out. I was as fast as – as lightning, you know.'

'But that's a different kind of fastness,' Alice objected.

The Knight shook his head. 'It was all kinds of fastness with me, I can assure you!' he said. He raised his hands in some excitement as he said this, and instantly rolled out of the saddle, and fell headlong into a deep ditch.

Alice ran to the side of the ditch to look for him. She was rather startled by the fall, as for some time he had kept on very well, and she was afraid that he really *was* hurt this time. However, though she could see nothing but the soles of his feet, she was much relieved to hear that he was talking on in his usual tone. 'All kinds of fastness,' he repeated: 'but it was careless of him to put another man's helmet on – with the man in it, too.'

'How *can* you go on talking so quietly, head downwards?' Alice asked, as she dragged him out by the feet, and laid him in a heap on the bank.

The Knight looked surprised at the question. 'What does it matter where my body happens to be?' he said. 'My mind goes on working all the same. In fact, the more head-downwards I am, the more I keep inventing new things.'

'Now the cleverest thing of the sort that I ever did,' he went on after a pause, 'was inventing a new pudding during the meat-course.'

'In time to have it cooked for the next course?' said Alice. 'Well, that *was* quick work, certainly!'

'Well, not the *next* course,' the Knight said in a slow thoughtful tone: 'no, certainly not the next *course.*'

'Then it would have to be the next day. I suppose you wouldn't have two pudding-courses in one dinner?'

'Well, not the *next* day,' the Knight repeated as before: 'not the next *day*. In fact,' he went on, holding his head down, and his voice getting lower and lower, 'I don't believe that pudding ever *was* cooked! In fact, I don't believe that pudding ever *will* be cooked! And yet it was a very clever pudding to invent.'

'What did you mean it to be made of?' Alice asked, hoping to cheer him up, for the poor Knight seemed quite low-spirited about it.

'It began with blotting-paper,' the Knight answered with a groan.

'That wouldn't be very nice, I'm afraid—'

'Not very nice *alone*,' he interrupted, quite eagerly: 'but you've no idea what a difference it makes, mixing it with other things – such as gunpowder and sealing-wax. And here I must leave you.' They had just come to the end of the wood.

Alice could only look puzzled: she was thinking of the pudding.

'You are sad,' the Knight said in an anxious tone: 'let me sing you a song to comfort you.'

'Is it very long?' Alice asked, for she had heard a good deal of poetry that day.

'It's long,' said the Knight, 'but it's very, *very* beautiful. Everybody that hears me sing it – either it brings the *tears* into their eyes, or else—'

'Or else what?' said Alice, for the Knight had made a sudden pause.

'Or else it doesn't, you know. The name of the song is called "*Haddocks' Eyes*."'

'Oh, that's the name of the song, is it?' Alice said, trying to feel interested.

'No, you don't understand,' the Knight said, looking a little vexed. 'That's what the name is *called*. The name really *is* "*The Aged Aged Man*."'

'Then I ought to have said "That's what the *song* is called"?' Alice corrected herself.

'No, you oughtn't: that's quite another thing! The *song* is called "*Ways And Means*": but that's only what it's *called*, you know!'

'Well, what *is* the song, then?' said Alice, who was by this time completely bewildered.

'I was coming to that,' the Knight said. 'The song really *is* "*A-sitting On A Gate*": and the tune's my own invention.'

So saying, he stopped his horse and let the reins fall on its neck: then, slowly beating time with one hand, and with a faint smile lighting up his gentle foolish face, as if he enjoyed the music of his song, he began.

Of all the strange things that Alice saw in her journey Through The Looking-Glass, this was the one that she always remembered most clearly. Years afterwards she could bring the whole scene back again, as if it had been only yesterday – the mild blue eyes and kindly smile of the Knight – the setting sun gleaming through his hair, and shining on his armour in a blaze of light that quite dazzled her – the horse quietly moving about, with the reins hanging loose on his neck, cropping the grass at her feet – and the black shadows of the forest behind – all this she took in like a picture, as, with one hand shading her eyes, she leant against a tree, watching the strange pair, and listening, in a half-dream, to the melancholy music of the song.

'But the tune *isn't* his own invention,' she said to herself: 'it's "*I give thee all, I can no more*."' She stood and listened very attentively, but no tears came into her eyes.

[. . .]

As the Knight sang the last words of the ballad, he gathered up the reins, and turned his horse's head along the road by which they had come. 'You've only a few yards to go,' he said, 'down the hill and over that little brook, and then you'll be a Queen— But you'll stay and see me off first?' he added as Alice turned with an eager look in the direction to which he pointed. 'I shan't be long. You'll wait and wave your handkerchief when I get to that turn in the road! I think it'll encourage me, you see.'

'Of course I'll wait,' said Alice: 'and thank you very much for coming so far – and for the song – I liked it very much.'

'I hope so,' the Knight said doubtfully: 'but you didn't cry so much as I thought you would.'

So they shook hands, and then the Knight rode slowly away into the forest. 'It won't take long to see him *off*, I expect,' Alice said to herself, as she stood watching him. 'There he goes! Right on his head as usual! However, he gets on again pretty easily – that comes of having so many things hung round the horse—' So she went on talking to herself, as she watched the horse walking leisurely along the road, and the Knight tumbling off, first on one side and then on the other. After the fourth or fifth tumble he reached the turn, and then she waved her handkerchief to him, and waited till he was out of sight.

The White Knight is different from the others in the 'Alice' books. He treats Alice with unusual courtesy ('in a friendly tone') – that is, more normally than the others. And his manner of speaking has none of their usual abrupt or disconcerting inconsequence. If 'contemptuously' is the adverb we associate with the usual inhabitants of *Wonderland* and *Looking-Glass*, this gentle-faced and mild-eyed man speaks 'gravely', 'thoughtfully', 'very seriously' and 'in an anxious tone'. He also makes Alice 'anxious' on his behalf, not only for his safety but 'hoping to cheer him up'. That is, the two of them are relating to each other. And despite its mad comedy what the knight does in terms of action – falling off his horse in front of Alice – is, bizarrely, an interaction full of expressive suggestion. Alice's adventures started with a long fall (down the rabbit-hole) and it seems clear that all the changes in her size and the jokes about age carry anxiety about children having to fall from innocence to experience. Is the knight doing it for her? Proving it doesn't hurt much (no bones broken to speak of)? And falling at the beautiful princess's feet in comic replays of the romantic hero? Whatever, the passage contains Carroll's saddest-funniest joke, a joke different in kind from all the other jokes (which tend to be wordplay), the knight 'very gravely' saying he's had 'plenty of practice' at riding. Or at falling.

The clearest expression of the special place the White Knight holds in the emotional landscape of these texts is the portrait painted (it's like a picture, as Carroll says himself) as the knight starts his song. (The excerpt above omits the actual song for reasons of space.) Even the punctuation is unusual, the phrases suspended across a chain of dashes. It's the only time in either text that the frame is, as it were, broken. The forward projection to the 'years afterwards' in which Alice remembers this scene 'most clearly' may contain the same unstated note of pleading that we found in the poem. And Alice listening 'in a half-dream' almost 'dazzled' by the knight whom the scene transfigures from funny old fool to romantic-chivalric hero – keeping Alice from 'the black shadows of the forest behind' and for a few seconds more before she becomes a queen – is, unlike anywhere else in the texts, in a state of perfect, still suspension.

Here's the poem which ends *Looking-Glass*. I think it should speak for itself.

> A boat, beneath a sunny sky
> Lingering onward dreamily
> In an evening of July –
>
> Children three that nestle near,
> Eager eye and willing ear,
> Pleased a simple tale to hear –
>
> Long has paled that sunny sky:
> Echoes fade and memories die:
> Autumn frosts have slain July.
>
> Still she haunts me, phantomwise,
> Alice moving under skies
> Never seen by waking eyes.

Children yet, the tale to hear,
Eager eye and willing ear,
Lovingly shall nestle near.

In a Wonderland they lie,
Dreaming as the days go by,
Dreaming as the summers die:

Ever drifting down the stream –
Lingering in the golden gleam –
Life, what is it but a dream?

THE END

Hugh Haughton's edition of the 'Alice' books (Harmondsworth, Penguin, 1998) is particularly good: it includes Carroll's original version of *Wonderland* with his own illustrations. Worth seeking out is Martin Gardner's more whimsical but fascinating edition (2nd edition, Harmondsworth, Penguin, 1970). The William Empson essay, 'The Child as Swain', is in his *Some Versions of Pastoral* (1935; reprinted Harmondsworth, Penguin, 1995). The endnote to the next chapter, on Wilde's *The Happy Prince*, considers the impossibility of the innocent text. The most poignant evocation of what seems so important in these books – the idea of the love-gift – comes not in an essay but in *Dream-Child*, a wonderful TV film written by Dennis Potter which tells the story of the elderly woman who was the real Alice travelling to America to receive an honorary degree.

15

WILDE'S *THE HAPPY PRINCE*

Sex and politics in the fairy-tale

In this chapter we meet a famous and popular 'fairy-tale', Oscar Wilde's *The Happy Prince* (1888). Derived partly from the equally popular fairy-tales of Hans Christian Andersen, Wilde's tale also lends itself to considerations of sexual representations and to political analysis, both in terms of what the tale suggests and in the light of the political events of its time. We'll consider sex and politics in the commentary which starts by looking at the ending, which many have found problematic.

Here is *The Happy Prince*.

The Happy Prince

High above the city, on a tall column, stood the statue of the Happy Prince. He was gilded all over with thin leaves of fine gold, for eyes he had two bright sapphires, and a large red ruby glowed on his sword-hilt.

He was very much admired indeed. 'He is as beautiful as a weathercock,' remarked one of the Town Councillors who wished to gain a reputation for having artistic tastes; 'only not quite so useful,' he added, fearing lest people should think him unpractical, which he really was not.

'Why can't you be like the Happy Prince?' asked a sensible mother of her little boy who was crying for the moon. 'The Happy Prince never dreams of crying for anything.'

'I am glad there is someone in the world who is quite happy,' muttered a disappointed man as he gazed at the wonderful statue.

'He looks just like an angel,' said the Charity Children as

they came out of the cathedral in their bright scarlet cloaks and their clean white pinafores.

'How do you know?' said the Mathematical Master, 'you have never seen one.'

'Ah! but we have, in our dreams,' answered the children; and the Mathematical Master frowned and looked very severe, for he did not approve of children dreaming.

One night there flew over the city a little Swallow. His friends had gone away to Egypt six weeks before, but he had stayed behind, for he was in love with the most beautiful Reed. He had met her early in the spring as he was flying down the river after a big yellow moth, and had been so attracted by her slender waist that he had stopped to talk to her.

'Shall I love you?' said the Swallow, who liked to come to the point at once, and the Reed made him a low bow. So he flew round and round her, touching the water with his wings, and making silver ripples. This was his courtship, and it lasted all through the summer.

'It is a ridiculous attachment,' twittered the other Swallows; 'she has no money, and far too many relations'; and indeed the river was quite full of Reeds. Then, when the autumn came they all flew away.

After they had gone he felt lonely, and began to tire of his lady-love. 'She has no conversation,' he said, 'and I am afraid that she is a coquette, for she is always flirting with the wind.' And certainly, whenever the wind blew, the Reed made the most graceful curtseys. 'I admit that she is domestic,' he continued, 'but I love travelling, and my wife, consequently, should love travelling also.'

'Will you come away with me?' he said finally to her, but the Reed shook her head, she was so attached to her home.

'You have been trifling with me,' he cried. 'I am off to the Pyramids. Good-bye!' and he flew away.

All day long he flew, and at night-time he arrived at the city. 'Where shall I put up?' he said; 'I hope the town has made preparations.'

Then he saw the statue on the tall column.

'I will put up there,' he cried; 'it is a fine position, with plenty of fresh air.' So he alighted just between the feet of the Happy Prince.

'I have a golden bedroom' he said softly to himself as he looked round, and he prepared to go to sleep; but just as he was putting his head under his wing a large drop of water fell on him. 'What a curious thing!' he cried; 'there is not a single cloud in the sky, the stars are quite clear and bright, and yet it is raining. The climate in the north of Europe is really dreadful. The Reed used to like the rain, but that was merely her selfishness.'

Then another drop fell.

'What is the use of a statue if it cannot keep the rain off?' he said; 'I must look for a good chimney-pot,' and he determined to fly away.

But before he had opened his wings, a third drop fell, and he looked up, and saw — Ah! what did he see?

The eyes of the Happy Prince were filled with tears, and tears were running down his golden cheeks. His face was so beautiful in the moonlight that the little Swallow was filled with pity.

'Who are you?' he said.

'I am the Happy Prince.'

'Why are you weeping then?' asked the Swallow; 'you have quite drenched me.'

'When I was alive and had a human heart,' answered the statue, 'I did not know what tears were, for I lived in the Palace of Sans-Souci, where sorrow is not allowed to enter. In the daytime I played with my companions in the garden, and in the evening I led the dance in the Great Hall. Round the garden ran a very lofty wall, but I never cared to ask what lay beyond it, everything about me was so beautiful. My courtiers called me the Happy Prince, and happy indeed I was, if pleasure be happiness. So I lived, and so I died. And now that I am dead they have set me up here so high that I can see all the ugliness and all the misery of my city, and though my heart is made of lead yet I cannot choose but weep.'

'What! is he not solid gold?' said the Swallow to himself. He was too polite to make any personal remarks out loud.

'Far away,' continued the statue in a low musical voice, 'far away in a little street there is a poor house. One of the windows is open, and through it I can see a woman seated at a table. Her face is thin and worn, and she has coarse, red hands, all pricked by the needle, for she is a seamstress. She is embroidering passion-flowers on a satin gown for the loveliest of the Queen's maids-of-honour to wear at the next Court-ball. In a bed in the corner of the room her little boy is lying ill. He has a fever, and is asking for oranges. His mother has nothing to give him but river water, so he is crying. Swallow, Swallow, little Swallow, will you not bring her the ruby out of my sword-hilt? My feet are fastened to this pedestal and I cannot move.'

'I am waited for in Egypt,' said the Swallow. 'My friends are flying up and down the Nile, and talking to the large lotus-flowers. Soon they will go to sleep in the tomb of the great King. The King is there himself in his painted coffin. He is wrapped in yellow linen, and embalmed with spices. Round his neck is a chain of pale green jade, and his hands are like withered leaves.'

'Swallow, Swallow, little Swallow,' said the Prince, 'will you not stay with me for one night, and be my messenger? The boy is so thirsty, and the mother so sad.'

'I don't think I like boys,' answered the Swallow. 'Last summer, when I was staying on the river, there were two rude boys, the miller's sons, who were always throwing stones at me. They never hit me, of course; we swallows fly far too well for that, and besides, I come of a family famous for its agility; but still, it was a mark of disrespect.'

But the Happy Prince looked so sad that the little Swallow was sorry. 'It is very cold here,' he said; 'but I will stay with you for one night, and be your messenger.'

'Thank you, little Swallow,' said the Prince.

So the Swallow picked out the great ruby from the Prince's sword, and flew away with it in his beak over the roofs of the town.

He passed by the cathedral tower, where the white marble angels were sculptured. He passed by the palace and heard the sound of dancing. A beautiful girl came out on the balcony with her lover. 'How wonderful the stars are,' he said to her, 'and how wonderful is the power of love!'

'I hope my dress will be ready in time for the State-ball,' she answered; 'I have ordered passion-flowers to be embroidered on it; but the seamstresses are so lazy.'

He passed over the river, and saw the lanterns hanging to the masts of the ships. He passed over the Ghetto, and saw the old Jews bargaining with each other, and weighing out money in copper scales. At last he came to the poor house and looked in. The boy was tossing feverishly on his bed, and the mother had fallen asleep, she was so tired. In he hopped, and laid the great ruby on the table beside the woman's thimble. Then he flew gently round the bed, fanning the boy's forehead with his wings. 'How cool I feel!' said the boy, 'I must be getting better': and he sank into a delicious slumber.

Then the Swallow flew back to the Happy Prince, and told him what he had done. 'It is curious,' he remarked, 'but I feel quite warm now, although it is so cold.'

'That is because you have done a good action,' said the Prince. And the little Swallow began to think, and then he fell asleep. Thinking always made him sleepy.

When day broke he flew down to the river and had a bath. 'What a remarkable phenomenon!' said the Professor of Ornithology as he was passing over the bridge. 'A swallow in winter!' And he wrote a long letter about it to the local newspaper. Everyone quoted it, it was full of so many words that they could not understand.

'To-night I go to Egypt,' said the Swallow, and he was in high spirits at the prospect. He visited all the public monuments, and sat a long time on top of the church steeple. Wherever he went the Sparrows chirruped, and said to each other, 'What a distinguished stranger!' so he enjoyed himself very much.

When the moon rose he flew back to the Happy Prince. 'Have you any commissions for Egypt?' he cried; 'I am just starting.'

'Swallow, Swallow, little Swallow,' said the Prince, 'will you not stay with me one night longer?'

'I am waited for in Egypt,' answered the Swallow. 'To-morrow my friends will fly up to the Second Cataract. The river-horse couches there among the bulrushes, and on a great granite house sits the God Memnon. All night long he watches the stars, and when the morning star shines he utters one cry of joy, and then he is silent. At noon the yellow lions come down to the water's edge to drink. They have eyes like green beryls, and their roar is louder than the roar of the cataract.'

'Swallow, Swallow, little Swallow,' said the Prince, 'far away across the city I see a young man in a garret. He is leaning over a desk covered with papers, and in a tumbler by his side there is a bunch of withered violets. His hair is brown and crisp, and his lips are red as a pomegranate, and he has large and dreamy eyes. He is trying to finish a play for the Director of the Theatre, but he is too cold to write any more. There is no fire in the grate, and hunger has made him faint.'

'I will wait with you one night longer,' said the Swallow, who really had a good heart. 'Shall I take him another ruby?'

'Alas I have no ruby now,' said the Prince; 'my eyes are all that I have left. They are made of rare sapphires, which were brought out of India a thousand years ago. Pluck out one of them and take it to him. He will sell it to the jeweller, and buy firewood, and finish his play.'

'Dear Prince,' said the Swallow, 'I cannot do that'; and he began to weep.

'Swallow, Swallow, little Swallow,' said the Prince, 'do as I command you.'

So the Swallow plucked out the Prince's eye, and flew away to the student's garret. It was easy enough to get in, as there was a hole in the roof. Through this he darted, and came into the room. The young man had his head buried in his hands, so he did not hear the flutter of the bird's wings, and when he looked up he found the beautiful sapphire lying on the withered violets.

'I am beginning to be appreciated,' he cried; 'this is from some great admirer. Now I can finish my play,' and he looked quite happy.

The next day the Swallow flew down to the harbour. He sat

on the mast of a large vessel and watched the sailors hauling big chests out of the hold with ropes. 'Heave a-hoy!' they shouted as each chest came up. 'I am going to Egypt!' cried the Swallow, but nobody minded, and when the moon rose he flew back to the Happy Prince.

'I am come to bid you good-bye,' he cried.

'Swallow, Swallow, little Swallow,' said the Prince, 'will you not stay with me one night longer?'

'It is winter,' answered the Swallow, 'and the chill snow will soon be here. In Egypt the sun is warm on the green palm-trees, and the crocodiles lie in the mud and look lazily about them. My companions are building a nest in the Temple of Baalbec, and the pink and white doves are watching them, and cooing to each other. Dear Prince, I must leave you, but I will never forget you, and next spring I will bring you back two beautiful jewels in place of those you have given away. The ruby shall be redder than a red rose, and the sapphire shall be as blue as the great sea.'

'In the square below,' said the Happy Prince, 'there stands a little match-girl. She has let her matches fall in the gutter, and they are all spoiled. Her father will beat her if she does not bring home some money, and she is crying. She has no shoes or stockings, and her little head is bare. Pluck out my other eye, and give it to her, and her father will not beat her.'

'I will stay with you one night longer,' said the Swallow, 'but I cannot pluck out your eye. You would be quite blind then.'

'Swallow, Swallow, little Swallow,' said the Prince, 'do as I command you.'

So he plucked out the Prince's other eye, and darted down with it. He swooped past the match-girl, and slipped the jewel into the palm of her hand. 'What a lovely bit of glass!' cried the little girl; and she ran home, laughing.

Then the Swallow came back to the Prince. 'You are blind now,' he said, 'so I will stay with you always.'

'No, little Swallow,' said the poor prince, 'you must go away to Egypt.'

'I will stay with you always,' said the Swallow, and he slept at the Prince's feet.

All the next day he sat on the Prince's shoulder, and told him stories of what he had seen in strange lands. He told him of the red ibises, who stand in long rows on the banks of the Nile, and catch goldfish in their beaks; of the Sphinx, who is as old as the world itself, and lives in the desert, and knows everything; of the merchants, who walk slowly by the side of their camels and carry amber beads in their hands; of the King of the Mountains of the Moon, who is as black as ebony, and worships a large crystal; of the great green snake that sleeps in a palm-tree, and has twenty priests to feed it with honey-cakes; and of the pygmies who sail over a big lake on large flat leaves, and are always at war with the butterflies.

'Dear little Swallow,' said the Prince, 'you tell me of marvellous things, but more marvellous than anything is the suffering of men and of women. There is no Mystery so great as Misery. Fly over my city, little Swallow, and tell me what you see there.'

So the Swallow flew over the great city, and saw the rich making merry in their beautiful houses, while the beggars were sitting at the gates. He flew into dark lanes, and saw the white faces of starving children looking out listlessly at the black streets. Under the archway of a bridge two little boys were lying in one another's arms to try and keep themselves warm. 'How hungry we are!' they said. 'You must not lie here,' shouted the watchman, and they wandered out into the rain.

Then he flew back and told the Prince what he had seen.

'I am covered with fine gold,' said the Prince, 'you must take it off, leaf by leaf, and give it to my poor; the living always think that gold can make them happy.'

Leaf after leaf of the fine gold the Swallow picked off, till the Happy Prince looked quite dull and grey. Leaf after leaf of the fine gold he brought to the poor, and the children's faces grew rosier, and they laughed and played games in the street. 'We have bread now!' they cried.

Then the snow came, and after the snow came the frost. The streets looked as if they were made of silver, they were so bright and glistening; long icicles like crystal daggers hung down from the eaves of the houses, everybody went about in furs, and the little boys wore scarlet caps and skated on the ice.

The poor little Swallow grew colder and colder, but he would not leave the Prince, he loved him too well. He picked up crumbs outside the baker's door when the baker was not looking, and tried to keep himself warm by flapping his wings.

But at last he knew that he was going to die. He had just enough strength to fly up to the Prince's shoulder once more. 'Good-bye, dear Prince!' he murmured, 'will you let me kiss your hand?'

'I am glad that you are going to Egypt at last, little Swallow,' said the Prince, 'you have stayed too long here; but you must kiss me on the lips, for I love you.'

'It is not to Egypt that I am going,' said the Swallow. 'I am going to the House of Death. Death is the brother of Sleep, is he not?'

And he kissed the Happy Prince on the lips, and fell down dead at his feet.

At that moment a curious crack sounded inside the statue, as if something had broken. The fact is that the leaden heart had snapped right in two. It certainly was a dreadfully hard frost.

Early the next morning the Mayor was walking in the square below in company with the Town Councillors. As they passed the column he looked up at the statue: 'Dear me! how shabby the Happy Prince looks!' he said.

'How shabby, indeed!' cried the Town Councillors, who always agreed with the Mayor; and they went up to look at it.

'The ruby has fallen out of his sword, his eyes are gone, and he is golden no longer,' said the Mayor; 'in fact, he is little better than a beggar!'

'Little better than a beggar,' said the Town Councillors.

'And here is actually a dead bird at his feet!' continued the Mayor. 'We must really issue a proclamation that birds are not to be allowed to die here.' And the Town Clerk made a note of the suggestion.

So they pulled down the statue of the Happy Prince. 'As he is no longer beautiful he is no longer useful,' said the Art Professor at the University.

Then they melted the statue in a furnace, and the Mayor held a meeting of the Corporation to decide what was to be done with the metal. 'We must have another statue, of course,' he said, 'and it shall be a statue of myself.'

'Of myself,' said each of the Town Councillors, and they quarrelled. When I last heard of them they were quarrelling still.

'What a strange thing!' said the overseer of the workmen at the foundry. 'This broken lead heart will not melt in the furnace. We must throw it away.' So they threw it on a dust-heap where the dead Swallow was also lying.

'Bring me the two most precious things in the city,' said God to one of His Angels; and the Angel brought Him the leaden heart and the dead bird.

'You have rightly chosen,' said God, 'for in my garden of Paradise this little bird shall sing for evermore, and in my city of gold the Happy Prince shall praise me.'

You might first be struck by yet another problem ending. This one looks stuck on, as if Wilde felt obliged to give the tale, ostensibly for children, a happy ending with its conventionalised Christian formula. You might like to try the experiment of stopping the tale in as many places as you can in the last paragraphs. A surprising number of such endings 'work', if often rather bleakly or comically, and perhaps 'work' more convincingly than the actual ending. Melville's penultimate paragraph in *Bartleby* offered, as we saw, an 'explanation' that seems designed to explain inadequately, to invite us to reject it. Wilde's last paragraph seems more of an escape-clause, a bid for respectability. But it depends where you're coming from, and readers used to coming to children's fairy-tales with the expectation of orthodox Christian endings would presumably be happy here at the sudden change of tone and perspective, and with the rather oddly proprietorial God ('will sing in my garden . . . will praise me').

If it is a bid for respectability why might that have been considered necessary? One answer might lie in the sexual politics of the tale. Another simple experiment is to ask yourself how the tale would have been different if the swallow had been a girl-swallow. Or we might look at the way heterosexuality is represented in this tale. There are, for such a short text, a remarkable number of single parents where, presumably, relations have broken down. And the romantic couple on the palace balcony are a surprise. Readers usually expect the comment about the lovely stars and the wonderful power of love to be attached with 'she said to him' but it's 'he said to her', inverting the usual stereotypes of the manly male and the romantic female. Not only that but, in a particularly sharp and even brutal piece of manipulation by Wilde, the beautiful girl is shown to be not only unromantic, and not only materialistic and callous, but her coldly aggressive remark 'the seamstresses are so lazy' cruelly contradicts what we ourselves know to be the case, because we've met the poor and suffering seamstress with the sick son, working on this girl's dress. So this relationship presumably will break down and it will be the woman's fault, because she's a – well, choose your own term of abuse.

And there's another romantic young male, the playwright in his garret. The crisp brown hair, dreamy eyes and pomegranate lips belong more, one might have thought, to Mills and Boon-style Victorian romances than children's fairy-tale, but there's a particular antecedent here, I think: a famous painting by Henry Wallis from about 1855 of the young poet-forger Chatterton who, taking his own life at 18 after his forgeries were exposed, became an icon of romantic frustration and sublime agony in the period before Wilde. Wilde adulated his work and his memory. And Wallis's painting would have had currency as a gay icon. The playwright presumes that the jewel is a 'gift from some great admirer'. Er, gender of this admirer?

The other heterosexual relationship is the swallow's with the reed. This too breaks down because the female lets the male down or isn't up to it: the reed is too 'attached' to her female domesticity. So the swallow, who was at first identified as just one of the boys but became separated because he fell in love, moves on again. And this time he moves on to the Happy Prince and the deeper love and deeper self-knowledge he discovers through him, the love which reveals the completed 'character' of the swallow who, as it were, has now grown up.

His journey is, in miniature, what the protagonists of mainstream nineteenth-century novels undergo. An effect of depth is suggested by what happens to the swallow, his development or growth made more plausible by being placed in a context in which the other characters stay static.

And the swallow's journey – an internalised one while his companions are on their more regular migrationary journey to the exotic east – has been from being one of the boys, to first love and its disappointment, to real love and its fulfilment. When I was a schoolboy I was told that homosexual feelings were a phase one goes through on the great march forward towards heterosexuality and marriage. (Or words to that effect.) Wilde has inverted the story, again. The swallow moves from the adolescent infatuation of heterosexual love (where the female lets him down) to the real thing, the true love that is homoeroticism. And it's so true and so spiritual that it can only end in death.

And – though whether Wilde intended this any more than he specifically intended to represent his own sexual agenda is uncertain – the story of the swallow's progress is like a gay version of *Romeo and Juliet*, in which Romeo moves from being one of the boys, to infatuation, to the real thing. So Wilde's remarkable little story, with its highly partisan presentation of heterosexuality, uses a powerfully orthodox model to effect an implicit legitimising and spiritualising of homoerotic love. Implicit but not overt, and thus the more persuasive.

We started with the Christian ending and now we've met *Romeo and Juliet*. Also intertextually at work in the tale is an even more famous story, one that sheds light on the odd ending. For the Happy Prince is clearly a Christ figure, sacrificing himself for his people, as if from his cross. The mix of homoeroticism and the dying Christ is a heady mix. But it has a long, if subversive, tradition, with roots in the literary-sexual underground. A tale for children?

The political morality of the tale looks, at first, more straightforward and, again, in tune with the prince as a Christ figure. The tale is clearly coming from the political left, with its cruel and greedy rich and its suffering poor – particularly its suffering children. The tale powerfully conveys to its young readers that society is constructed along unfair lines and that something must be done.

But is that quite what is being said? There are two very strange things the Happy Prince says towards the end, and readers often notice their strangeness. The first is the bizarrely capitalised 'there is no Mystery so great as Misery'. This, in effect, blurs the political message by mystifying it, turning something that is perfectly explainable – the gap between rich and poor – into a Mystery. There was, for instance, nothing at all mysterious about the fact that the number of children living in poverty in Britain climbed from 9 per cent to 25 per cent in the 1980s and early 1990s: it was a direct and predictable result of specific social policies put in place by the Conservative government of the time. And the thing about Mysteries, especially capitalised ones, is that they resist explanation and therefore remove from everyone the responsibility of trying to understand and improve the situation. If it's a Mystery there's no point thinking or doing anything about it. Mystification is politically very useful in maintaining the status quo.

And the other odd thing the Happy Prince says relates closely to that. His tone for the first and last time changes when he says: 'the living always think that gold can make them happy'. World-weary bitterness? Wry sarcasm? Whatever, being out of line with the rest of what he says, like all such moments of interesting contradiction in texts, it repays close attention. The sentiment presupposes that the living are wrong, that gold – as the prince knows – will not make them happy. This is equivalent to our saying to a beggar, just as we hand over a coin: 'here you are, mate; spending it on booze won't make you happy, you know, but here's a sign of my caring anyway'. It's the liberal middle-class bind but it makes the giver feel better. Something in the Happy Prince's tone conveys the equivalent condescension. The gold won't make the poor happy but give it to them anyway.

But in a further contradiction the gold does make the poor happy and, wonder to behold, it also solves the poverty problem at a stroke. The poor have bread, and 'everyone went around in furs'. Everyone. The politics of this gesture of giving, the tone with which the giving is offered, and its result are deeply contradictory and thus a sign of liberal anxiety.

Wilde wrote about this issue elsewhere. You'll see that he views altruism, the charitable impulse towards the 'task of remedying the evils' of poverty and starvation, as a sentimental prolonging of the disease and not a cure. Such 'remedies are part of the disease'. Here's what he said a few lines from the opening of his *The Soul of Man Under Socialism*.

The Soul of Man Under Socialism

The majority of people spoil their lives by an unhealthy and exaggerated altruism – are forced, indeed, so to spoil them.

They find themselves surrounded by hideous poverty, by hideous ugliness, by hideous starvation. It is inevitable that they should be strongly moved by all this. The emotions of man are stirred more quickly than man's intelligence; and as I pointed out some time ago in an article on the function of criticism, it is much more easy to have sympathy with suffering than it is to have sympathy with thought. Accordingly, with admirable, though misdirected intentions, they very seriously and very sentimentally set themselves to the task of remedying the evils that they see. But their remedies do not cure the disease: they merely prolong it. Indeed, their remedies are part of the disease.

They try to solve the problem of poverty, for instance, by keeping the poor alive; or, in the case of a very advanced school, by amusing the poor.

But this is not a solution; it is an aggravation of the difficulty. The proper aim is to try and reconstruct society on such a basis that poverty will be impossible. And the altruistic virtues have really prevented the carrying out of this aim. Just as the worst slave-owners were those who were kind to their slaves, and so prevented the horror of the system being realised by those who suffered from it, and understood by those who contemplated it, so, in the present state of things in England, the people who do most harm are the people who try to do most good; and at last we have had the spectacle of men who have really studied the problem and know the life – educated men who live in the East End – coming forward and imploring the community to restrain its altruistic impulses of charity, benevolence, and the like. They do so on the ground that such charity degrades and demoralises. They are perfectly right. Charity creates a multitude of sins. There is also this to be said. It is immoral to use private property in order to alleviate the horrible evils that result from the institution of private property. It is both immoral and unfair.

That was published in 1891. *The Happy Prince* was published in May 1888 (though written a couple of years earlier). You'll remember that the third and last individualised figure to receive the prince's altruistic gift was a match-girl. The year 1888 saw the first successful results of a newly concentrated mass movement of radicals and socialists in London following the brutal police suppression of a large demonstration in November 1887. The first manifestation of this new movement was the Bryant and May match-girls' strike of May 1888. The conditions of their work also prompted Annie Besant's article 'White Slavery in London'. A major dock strike of 1889 led within a year to 200,000 unskilled workers joining the newly formed unions. In 1892 Engels hailed the transformation of London's East End from 'that immense haunt of human misery' to its 'organisation of the great mass of "unskilled" workers' (quoted in Morton, *A People's History of England*, p. 452). Wilde's position in both 1888 and 1891 seems equivocal and his criticism of the impulse towards charity raises some difficult questions. His match-girl is a lone street-seller with a brutal father from whom the prince's charitable gift (which she mistakes for glass) protects her; in the month of the tale's publication organised women match-makers revolted against the brutality of their working conditions and their male employers in a move designed to help 'reconstruct society on such a basis that poverty will be impossible'.

You might respond to the apparent contradiction or critique of the Happy Prince's charitable altruism in Wilde's essay by arguing that a children's fairy-tale would be an inappropriate place to show how we should 'reconstruct society on such a basis that poverty will be impossible'. Or that the Prince is not just a Victorian do-gooder but Christ showing the charity that is love. But the tale does mount a subtly powerful argument for wholesale reconstruction of existing arrangements – in its sexual politics and the implicit elevation and sanctification of homoerotic love. The existing sexual arrangements carried very different attitudes towards gay relations, particularly cross-class relations, as in *The Happy Prince*. Wilde not only knew that but seems to have wish-fulfilled society's revenge on his subversion of those arrangements in the plot of this painfully prophetic tale.

Teachers and lecturers are fond of saying that 'there's no such thing as an innocent text: it's only the reading that can be innocent'. Even as adults we can choose to read as innocently as we like. But an act of writing is an act of intervention in a real world. Fairy-tales may, largely, have innocent readers but their histories are deeply implicated in social history. The definitive guide to the social histories of fairy-tales is Jack Zipes, whom we met in relation to

Wordsworth in an earlier chapter. His readings of *The Happy Prince* are in his *Fairy Tales and the Art of Subversion* (London, Heinemann, 1983) and *When Dreams Came True* (London, Routledge, 1999). In one obvious way adult readers bring a necessarily adult perspective to their reading of this tale: they can hardly avoid their knowledge of Wilde's fall from grace in his trials and imprisonment (the fate so oddly predicted in the prince's story). Wilde's best biographer is Richard Ellman (London, Hamish Hamilton, 1987). The most vivid evocation of the trials is a double-cassette audio dramatisation with an enormous and star-studded cast – that is, with Martin Jarvis brilliantly playing all the roles. Wilde's fairy-tale *The Selfish Giant*, also in the *Complete Shorter Fiction* (Oxford, Oxford University Press, 1980), incorporates its Christian dimension in a more integrated way and its old man/little boy love is difficult, again, to read innocently.

16

GILMAN'S *THE YELLOW WALLPAPER*
The woman's body, hysteria, intertextuality

In this chapter we meet, in its entirety, Charlotte Perkins Gilman's *The Yellow Wallpaper* (1892). The commentary places the story in three linked contexts: its relations with earlier classic fiction; its fascination with the female body, as perceived by men; and its place in the history of the treatment of female hysteria.

The Yellow Wallpaper

It is very seldom that mere ordinary people like John and myself secure ancestral halls for the summer.

A colonial mansion, a hereditary estate, I would say a haunted house and reach the height of romantic felicity – but that would be asking too much of fate!

Still I will proudly declare that there is something queer about it.

Else, why should it be let so cheaply? And why have stood so long untenanted?

John laughs at me, of course, but one expects that.

John is practical in the extreme. He has no patience with faith, an intense horror of superstition, and he scoffs openly at any talk of things not to be felt and seen and put down in figures.

John is a physician, and *perhaps* – (I would not say it to a living soul, of course, but this is dead paper and a great relief to my mind) – *perhaps* that is one reason I do not get well faster.

You see, he does not believe I am sick! And what can one do?

If a physician of high standing, and one's own husband,

302

assures friends and relatives that there is really nothing the matter with one but temporary nervous depression – a slight hysterical tendency – what is one to do?

My brother is also a physician, and also of high standing, and he says the same thing.

So I take phosphates or phosphites – whichever it is – and tonics, and air and exercise, and journeys, and am absolutely forbidden to 'work' until I am well again.

Personally, I disagree with their ideas.

Personally, I believe that congenial work, with excitement and change, would do me good.

But what is one to do?

I did write for a while in spite of them; but it *does* exhaust me a good deal – having to be so sly about it, or else meet with heavy opposition.

I sometimes fancy that in my condition, if I had less opposition and more society and stimulus – but John says the very worst thing I can do is to think about my condition, and I confess it always makes me feel bad.

So I will let it alone and talk about the house.

The most beautiful place! It is quite alone, standing well back from the road, quite three miles from the village. It makes me think of English places that you read about, for there are hedges and walls and gates that lock, and lots of separate little houses for the gardeners and people.

There is a *delicious* garden! I never saw such a garden – large and shady, full of box-bordered paths, and lined with long grape-covered arbors with seats under them.

There were greenhouses, but they are all broken now.

There was some legal trouble, I believe, something about the heirs and co-heirs; anyhow, the place has been empty for years.

That spoils my ghostliness, I am afraid, but I don't care – there is something strange about the house – I can feel it.

I even said so to John one moonlight evening, but he said what I felt was a draught, and shut the window.

I get unreasonably angry with John sometimes. I'm sure I never used to be so sensitive. I think it is due to this nervous condition.

But John says if I feel so I shall neglect proper self-control; so I take pains to control myself – before him, at least, and that makes me very tired.

I don't like our room a bit. I wanted one downstairs that opened onto the piazza and had roses all over the window, and such pretty old-fashioned chintz hangings! But John would not hear of it.

He said there was only one window and not room for two beds, and no near room for him if he took another.

He is very careful and loving, and hardly lets me stir without special direction.

I have a schedule prescription for each hour in the day; he takes all care from me, and so I feel basely ungrateful not to value it more.

He said we came here solely on my account, that I was to have perfect rest and all the air I could get. 'Your exercise depends on your strength, my dear,' said he, 'and your food somewhat on your appetite; but air you can absorb all the time.' So we took the nursery at the top of the house.

It is a big, airy room, the whole floor nearly, with windows that look all ways, and air and sunshine galore. It was nursery first, and then playroom and gymnasium, I should judge, for the windows are barred for little children, and there are rings and things in the walls.

The paint and paper look as if a boys' school had used it. It is stripped off – the paper – in great patches all around the head of my bed, about as far as I can reach, and in a great place on the other side of the room low down. I never saw a worse paper in my life. One of those sprawling, flamboyant patterns committing every artistic sin.

It is dull enough to confuse the eye in following, pro-nounced enough constantly to irritate and provoke study, and when you follow the lame uncertain curves for a little distance they suddenly commit suicide – plunge off at outrageous angles, destroy themselves in unheard-of contradictions.

The color is repellent, almost revolting: a smouldering unclean yellow, strangely faded by the slow-turning sunlight.

It is a dull yet lurid orange in some places, a sickly sulphur tint in others.

No wonder the children hated it! I should hate it myself if I had to live in this room long.

There comes John, and I must put this away – he hates to have me write a word.

We have been here two weeks, and I haven't felt like writing before, since that first day.

I am sitting by the window now, up in this atrocious nursery, and there is nothing to hinder my writing as much as I please, save lack of strength.

John is away all day, and even some nights when his cases are serious.

I am glad my case is not serious!

But these nervous troubles are dreadfully depressing.

John does not know how much I really suffer. He knows there is no reason to suffer, and that satisfies him.

Of course it is only nervousness. It does weigh on me so not to do my duty in any way!

I meant to be such a help to John, such a real rest and comfort, and here I am a comparative burden already!

Nobody would believe what an effort it is to do what little I am able – to dress and entertain, and order things.

It is fortunate Mary is so good with the baby. Such a dear baby!

And yet I *cannot* be with him, it makes me so nervous.

I suppose John never was nervous in his life. He laughs at me so about this wallpaper!

At first he meant to repaper the room, but afterward he said that I was letting it get the better of me, and that nothing was worse for a nervous patient than to give way to such fancies.

He said that after the wallpaper was changed it would be the heavy bedstead, and then the barred windows, and then that gate at the head of the stairs, and so on.

'You know the place is doing you good,' he said, 'and really, dear, I don't care to renovate the house just for a three months' rental.'

'Then do let us go downstairs,' I said. 'There are such pretty rooms there.'

Then he took me in his arms and called me a blessed little goose and said he would go down to the cellar, if I wished, and have it whitewashed into the bargain.

But he is right enough about the beds and windows and things.

It is as airy and comfortable a room as anyone need wish, and, of course, I would not be so silly as to make him uncomfortable just for a whim.

I'm really getting quite fond of the big room, all but that horrid paper.

Out of one window I can see the garden – those mysterious deep-shaded arbors, the riotous old-fashioned flowers, and bushes and gnarly trees.

Out of another I get a lovely view of the bay and a little private wharf belonging to the estate. There is a beautiful shaded lane that runs down there from the house. I always fancy I see people walking in these numerous paths and arbors, but John has cautioned me not to give way to fancy in the least. He says that with my imaginative power and habit of story-making, a nervous weakness like mine is sure to lead to all manner of excited fancies, and that I ought to use my will and good sense to check the tendency. So I try.

I think sometimes that if I were only well enough to write a little it would relieve the press of ideas and rest me.

But I find I get pretty tired when I try.

It is so discouraging not to have any advice and companionship about my work. When I get really well, John says we will ask Cousin Henry and Julia down for a long visit; but he says he would as soon put fireworks in my pillow-case as to let me have those stimulating people about now.

I wish I could get well faster.

But I must not think about that. This paper looks to me as if it *knew* what a vicious influence it had!

There is a recurrent spot where the pattern lolls like a broken neck and two bulbous eyes stare at you upside down.

I get positively angry with the impertinence of it and the

everlastingness. Up and down and sideways they crawl, and those absurd unblinking eyes are everywhere. There is one place where two breadths didn't match, and the eyes go all up and down the line, one a little higher than the other.

I never saw so much expression in an inanimate thing before, and we all know how much expression they have! I used to lie awake as a child and get more entertainment and terror out of blank walls and plain furniture than most children could find in a toy-store.

I remember what a kindly wink the knobs of our big old bureau used to have, and there was one chair that always seemed like a strong friend.

I used to feel that if any of the other things looked too fierce I could always hop into that chair and be safe.

The furniture in this room is no worse than inharmonious, however, for we had to bring it all from downstairs. I suppose when this was used as a playroom they had to take the nursery things out, and no wonder! I never saw such ravages as the children have made here.

The wallpaper, as I said before, is torn off in spots, and it sticketh closer than a brother – they must have had perseverance as well as hatred.

Then the floor is scratched and gouged and splintered, the plaster itself is dug out here and there, and this great heavy bed, which is all we found in the room, looks as if it had been through the wars.

But I don't mind it a bit – only the paper.

There comes John's sister. Such a dear girl as she is, and so careful of me! I must not let her find me writing.

She is a perfect and enthusiastic housekeeper, and hopes for no better profession. I verily believe she thinks it is the writing which made me sick!

But I can write when she is out, and see her a long way off from these windows.

There is one that commands the road, a lovely shaded winding road, and one that just looks off over the country. A lovely country, too, full of great elms and velvet meadows.

This wallpaper has a kind of sub-pattern in a different shade, a particularly irritating one, for you can only see it in certain lights, and not clearly then.

But in the places where it isn't faded and where the sun is just so – I can see a strange, provoking, formless sort of figure that seems to skulk about behind that silly and conspicuous front design.

There's sister on the stairs!

Well, the Fourth of July is over! The people are all gone, and I am tired out. John thought it might do me good to see a little company, so we just had Mother and Nellie and the children down for a week.

Of course I didn't do a thing. Jennie sees to everything now.

But it tired me all the same.

John says if I don't pick up faster he shall send me to Weir Mitchell in the fall.

But I don't want to go there at all. I had a friend who was in his hands once, and she says he is just like John and my brother, only more so!

Besides, it is such an undertaking to go so far.

I don't feel as if it was worthwhile to turn my hand over for anything, and I'm getting dreadfully fretful and querulous.

I cry at nothing, and cry most of the time.

Of course I don't when John is here, or anybody else, but when I am alone.

And I am alone a good deal just now. John is kept in town very often by serious cases, and Jennie is good and lets me alone when I want her to.

So I walk a little in the garden or down that lovely lane, sit on the porch under the roses, and lie down up here a good deal.

I'm getting really fond of the room in spite of the wallpaper. Perhaps *because* of the wallpaper.

It dwells in my mind so!

I lie here on this great immovable bed – it is nailed down, I believe – and follow that pattern about by the hour. It is as good as gymnastics, I assure you. I start, we'll say, at the bottom, down in the corner over there where it has not been touched, and I determine for the thousandth time that

I *will* follow that pointless pattern to some sort of a conclusion.

I know a little of the principle of design, and I know this thing was not arranged on any laws of radiation, or alternation, or repetition, or symmetry, or anything else that I ever heard of.

It is repeated, of course, by the breadths, but not otherwise.

Looked at in one way, each breadth stands alone; the bloated curves and flourishes – a kind of 'debased Romanesque' with delirium tremens – go waddling up and down in isolated columns of fatuity.

But, on the other hand, they connect diagonally, and the sprawling outlines run off in great slanting waves of optic horror, like a lot of wallowing sea-weeds in full chase.

The whole thing goes horizontally, too, at least it seems so, and I exhaust myself trying to distinguish the order of its going in that direction.

They have used a horizontal breadth for a frieze, and that adds wonderfully to the confusion.

There is one end of the room where it is almost intact, and there, when the crosslights fade and the low sun shines directly upon it, I can almost fancy radiation after all – the interminable grotesque seems to form around a common center and rush off in headlong plunges of equal distraction.

It makes me tired to follow it. I will take a nap, I guess.

I don't know why I should write this.

I don't want to.

I don't feel able.

And I know John would think it absurd. But I *must* say what I feel and think in some way – it is such a relief!

But the effort is getting to be greater than the relief.

Half the time now I am awfully lazy, and lie down ever so much. John says I mustn't lose my strength, and has me take cod liver oil and lots of tonics and things, to say nothing of ale and wine and rare meat.

Dear John! He loves me very dearly, and hates to have me sick. I tried to have a real earnest reasonable talk with him the other day, and tell him how I wish he would let me go and make a visit to Cousin Henry and Julia.

But he said I wasn't able to go, nor able to stand it after I got there; and I did not make out a very good case for myself, for I was crying before I had finished.

It is getting to be a great effort for me to think straight. Just this nervous weakness, I suppose.

And dear John gathered me up in his arms, and just carried me upstairs and laid me on the bed, and sat by me and read to me till it tired my head.

He said I was his darling and his comfort and all he had, and that I must take care of myself for his sake, and keep well.

He says no one but myself can help me out of it, that I must use my will and self-control and not let any silly fancies run away with me.

There's one comfort – the baby is well and happy, and does not have to occupy this nursery with the horrid wallpaper.

If we had not used it, that blessed child would have! What a fortunate escape! Why, I wouldn't have a child of mine, an impressionable little thing, live in such a room for worlds.

I never thought of it before, but it is lucky that John kept me here after all; I can stand it so much easier than a baby, you see.

Of course I never mention it to them any more – I am too wise – but I keep watch for it all the same.

There are things in that wallpaper that nobody knows about but me, or ever will.

Behind that outside pattern the dim shapes get clearer every day.

It is always the same shape, only very numerous.

And it is like a woman stooping down and creeping about behind that pattern. I don't like it a bit. I wonder – I begin to think – I wish John would take me away from here!

It is so hard to talk with John about my case, because he is so wise, and because he loves me so.

But I tried it last night.

It was moonlight. The moon shines in all around just as the sun does.

I hate to see it sometimes, it creeps so slowly, and always comes in by one window or another.

John was asleep and I hated to waken him, so I kept still and watched the moonlight on that undulating wallpaper till I felt creepy.

The faint figure behind seemed to shake the pattern, just as if she wanted to get out.

I got up softly and went to feel and see if the paper *did* move, and when I came back John was awake.

'What is it, little girl?' he said. 'Don't go walking about like that – you'll get cold.'

I thought it was a good time to talk, so I told him that I really was not gaining here, and that I wished he would take me away.

'Why, darling!' said he. 'Our lease will be up in three weeks, and I can't see how to leave before.

'The repairs are not done at home, and I cannot possibly leave town just now. Of course, if you were in any danger, I could and would, but you really are better, dear, whether you can see it or not. I am a doctor, dear, and I know. You are gaining flesh and color, your appetite is better, I feel really much easier about you.'

'I don't weigh a bit more,' said I, 'nor as much; and my appetite may be better in the evening when you are here but it is worse in the morning when you are away!'

'Bless her little heart!' said he with a big hug. 'She shall be as sick as she pleases! But now let's improve the shining hours by going to sleep, and talk about it in the morning!'

'And you won't go away?' I asked gloomily.

'Why, how can I, dear? It is only three weeks more and then we will take a nice little trip of a few days while Jennie is getting the house ready. Really, dear, you are better!'

'Better in body perhaps –' I began, and stopped short, for he sat up straight and looked at me with such a stern, reproachful look that I could not say another word.

'My darling,' said he; 'I beg of you, for my sake and for our child's sake, as well as for your own, that you will never for one instant let that idea enter your mind! There is nothing so

311

dangerous, so fascinating, to a temperament like yours. It is a false and foolish fancy. Can you not trust me as a physician when I tell you so?'

So of course I said no more on that score, and we went to sleep before long. He thought I was asleep first, but I wasn't, and lay there for hours trying to decide whether that front pattern and the back pattern really did move together or separately.

On a pattern like this, by daylight, there is a lack of sequence, a defiance of law, that is a constant irritant to a normal mind.

The color is hideous enough, and unreliable enough, and infuriating enough, but the pattern is torturing.

You think you have mastered it, but just as you get well under way in following, it turns a back-somersault and there you are. It slaps you in the face, knocks you down, and tramples upon you. It is like a bad dream.

The outside pattern is a florid arabesque, reminding one of a fungus. If you can imagine a toadstool in joints, an interminable string of toadstools, budding and sprouting in endless convolutions – why, that is something like it.

That is, sometimes!

There is one marked peculiarity about this paper, a thing nobody seems to notice but myself, and that is that it changes as the light changes.

When the sun shoots in through the east window – I always watch for that first long, straight ray – it changes so quickly that I never can quite believe it.

That is why I watch it always.

By moonlight – the moon shines in all night when there is a moon – I wouldn't know it was the same paper.

At night in any kind of light, in twilight, candlelight, lamplight, and worst of all by moonlight, it becomes bars! The outside pattern, I mean, and the woman behind it is as plain as can be.

I didn't realize for a long time what the thing was that showed behind, that dim sub-pattern, but now I am quite sure it is a woman.

By daylight she is subdued, quiet. I fancy it is the pattern that keeps her so still. It is so puzzling. It keeps me quiet by the hour.

I lie down ever so much now. John says it is good for me, and to sleep all I can.

Indeed he started the habit by making me lie down for an hour after each meal.

It is a very bad habit, I am convinced, for you see, I don't sleep.

And that cultivates deceit, for I don't tell them I'm awake – oh, no!

The fact is I am getting a little afraid of John.

He seems very queer sometimes, and even Jennie has an inexplicable look.

It strikes me occasionally, just as a scientific hypothesis, that perhaps it is the paper!

I have watched John when he did not know I was looking, and come into the room suddenly on the most innocent excuses, and I've caught him several times *looking at the paper*! And Jennie too. I caught Jennie with her hand on it once.

She didn't know I was in the room, and when I asked her in a quiet, a very quiet voice, with the most restrained manner possible, what she was doing with the paper, she turned around as if she had been caught stealing, and looked quite angry – asked me why I should frighten her so!

Then she said that the paper stained everything it touched, that she had found yellow smooches on all my clothes and John's and she wished we would be more careful!

Did not that sound innocent? But I know she was studying that pattern, and I am determined that nobody shall find it out but myself!

Life is very much more exciting now than it used to be. You see, I have something more to expect, to look forward to, to watch. I really do eat better, and am more quiet than I was.

John is so pleased to see me improve! He laughed a little the other day, and said I seemed to be flourishing in spite of my wallpaper.

I turned it off with a laugh. I had no intention of telling him it was *because* of the wallpaper – he would make fun of me. He might even want to take me away.

I don't want to leave now until I have found it out. There is a week more, and I think that will be enough.

I'm feeling ever so much better!

I don't sleep much at night, for it is so interesting to watch developments; but I sleep a good deal during the daytime.

In the daytime it is tiresome and perplexing.

There are always new shoots on the fungus, and new shades of yellow all over it. I cannot keep count of them, though I have tried conscientiously.

It is the strangest yellow, that wallpaper! It makes me think of all the yellow things I ever saw – not beautiful ones like buttercups, but old, foul, bad yellow things.

But there is something else about that paper – the smell! I noticed it the moment we came into the room, but with so much air and sun it was not bad. Now we have had a week of fog and rain, and whether the windows are open or not, the smell is here.

It creeps all over the house.

I find it hovering in the dining-room, skulking in the parlor, hiding in the hall, lying in wait for me on the stairs.

It gets into my hair.

Even when I go to ride, if I turn my head suddenly and surprise it – there is that smell!

Such a peculiar odor, too! I have spent hours in trying to analyze it, to find what it smelled like.

It is not bad – at first – and very gentle, but quite the subtlest, most enduring odor I ever met.

In this damp weather it is awful. I wake up in the night and find it hanging over me.

It used to disturb me at first. I thought seriously of burning the house – to reach the smell.

But now I am used to it. The only thing I can think of that it is like is the *color* of the paper! A yellow smell.

314

There is a very funny mark on this wall, low down, near the mop-board. A streak that runs round the room. It goes behind every piece of furniture, except the bed, a long, straight, even *smooch*, as if it had been rubbed over and over.

I wonder how it was done and who did it, and what they did it for. Round and round and round – round and round and round – it makes me dizzy!

I really have discovered something at last.

Through watching so much at night, when it changes so, I have finally found out.

The front pattern *does* move – and no wonder! The woman behind shakes it!

Sometimes I think there are a great many women behind, and sometimes only one, and she crawls around fast, and her crawling shakes it all over.

Then in the very bright spots she keeps still, and in the very shady spots she just takes hold of the bars and shakes them hard.

And she is all the time trying to climb through. But nobody could climb through that pattern – it strangles so; I think that is why it has so many heads.

They get through and then the pattern strangles them off and turns them upside down, and makes their eyes white!

If those heads were covered or taken off it would not be half so bad.

I think that woman gets out in the daytime!

And I'll tell you why – privately – I've seen her!

I can see her out of every one of my windows!

It is the same woman, I know, for she is always creeping, and most women do not creep by daylight.

I see her in that long shaded lane, creeping up and down. I see her in those dark grape arbors, creeping all around the garden.

I see her on that long road under the trees, creeping along, and when a carriage comes she hides under the blackberry vines.

I don't blame her a bit. It must be very humiliating to be caught creeping by daylight!

I always lock the door when I creep by daylight. I can't do it at night, for I know John would suspect something at once.

And John is so queer now that I don't want to irritate him. I wish he would take another room! Besides, I don't want anybody to get that woman out at night but myself.

I often wonder if I could see her out of all the windows at once.

But, turn as fast as I can, I can only see out of one at one time.

And though I always see her, she *may* be able to creep faster than I can turn! I have watched her sometimes away off in the open country, creeping as fast as a cloud shadow in a high wind.

If only that top pattern could be gotten off from the under one! I mean to try it, little by little.

I have found out another funny thing, but I shan't tell it this time! It does not do to trust people too much.

There are only two more days to get this paper off, and I believe John is beginning to notice. I don't like the look in his eyes.

And I heard him ask Jennie a lot of professional questions about me. She had a very good report to give.

She said I slept a good deal in the daytime.

John knows I don't sleep very well at night, for all I'm so quiet!

He asked me all sorts of questions, too, and pretended to be very loving and kind.

As if I couldn't see through him!

Still, I don't wonder he acts so, sleeping under this paper for three months.

It only interests me, but I feel sure John and Jennie are affected by it.

Hurrah! This is the last day, but it is enough. John is to stay in town over night, and won't be out until this evening.

Jennie wanted to sleep with me – the sly thing; but I told her I should undoubtedly rest better for a night all alone.

That was clever, for really I wasn't alone a bit! As soon as it was moonlight and that poor thing began to crawl and shake the pattern, I got up and ran to help her.

I pulled and she shook. I shook and she pulled, and before morning we had peeled off yards of that paper.

A strip about as high as my head and half around the room.

And then when the sun came and that awful pattern began to laugh at me, I declared I would finish it today!

We go away tomorrow, and they are moving all my furniture down again to leave things as they were before.

Jennie looked at the wall in amazement, but I told her merrily that I did it out of pure spite at the vicious thing.

She laughed and said she wouldn't mind doing it herself, but I must not get tired.

How she betrayed herself that time!

But I am here, and no person touches this paper but Me – not *alive*!

She tried to get me out of the room – it was too patent! But I said it was so quiet and empty and clean now that I believed I would lie down again and sleep all I could, and not to wake me even for dinner – I would call when I woke.

So now she is gone, and the servants are gone, and the things are gone, and there is nothing left but that great bedstead nailed down, with the canvas mattress we found on it.

We shall sleep downstairs tonight, and take the boat home tomorrow.

I quite enjoy the room, now it is bare again.

How those children did tear about here!

This bedstead is fairly gnawed!

But I must get to work.

I have locked the door and thrown the key down into the front path.

I don't want to go out, and I don't want to have anybody come in, till John comes.

I want to astonish him.

I've got a rope up here that even Jennie did not find. If that woman does get out, and tries to get away, I can tie her!

But I forgot I could not reach far without anything to stand on!

This bed will *not* move!

I tried to lift and push it until I was lame, and then I got so angry I bit off a little piece at one corner – but it hurt my teeth.

Then I peeled off all the paper I could reach standing on the floor. It sticks horribly and the pattern just enjoys it! All those strangled heads and bulbous eyes and waddling fungus growths just shriek with derision!

I am getting angry enough to do something desperate. To jump out of the window would be admirable exercise, but the bars are too strong even to try.

Besides I wouldn't do it. Of course not. I know well enough that a step like that is improper and might be misconstrued.

I don't like to *look* out of the windows even – there are so many of those creeping women, and they creep so fast.

I wonder if they all come out of that wallpaper as I did?

But I am securely fastened now by my well-hidden rope – you don't get *me* out in the road there!

I suppose I shall have to get back behind the pattern when it comes night, and that is hard!

It is so pleasant to be out in this great room and creep around as I please!

I don't want to go outside. I won't, even if Jennie asks me to.

For outside you have to creep on the ground, and everything is green instead of yellow.

But here I can creep smoothly on the floor, and my shoulder just fits in that long smooch around the wall, so I cannot lose my way.

Why, there's John at the door!

It is no use, young man, you can't open it!

How he does call and pound!

Now he's crying to Jennie for an axe.

It would be a shame to break down that beautiful door!

'John, dear!' said I in the gentlest voice. 'The key is down by the front steps, under a plantain leaf!'

That silenced him for a few moments.

Then he said, very quietly indeed, 'Open the door, my darling!'

'I can't,' said I. 'The key is down by the front door under a plantain leaf!' And then I said it again, several times, very gently and slowly, and said it so often that he had to go and see, and he got it of course, and came in. He stopped short by the door.

'What is the matter?' he cried. 'For God's sake, what are you doing!'

I kept on creeping just the same, but I looked at him over my shoulder.

'I've got out at last,' said I, 'in spite of you and Jane. And I've pulled off most of the paper, so you can't put me back!'

Now why should that man have fainted? But he did, and right across my path by the wall, so that I had to creep over him every time!

And that leaves most readers, particularly men, very uncomfortable.

This astonishing story is something of a cult-classic in America, like *Bartleby*, with which it might be seen to share some anxious ideas about supposed normalities. And like *Bartleby*, but even more like the text in the next chapter, James's *The Turn of the Screw*, it is a story exploring the creative inventiveness of 'abnormal' minds. Notions of madness hover with worrying persistence over many of the texts in this volume, like the smell in this story that clings everywhere. Emily Dickinson was described by a sympathetic male-reader as half-crazed. The Cheshire Cat blandly tells Alice that she's mad, that we're all mad. And women are, or are in danger of being, institutionalised in plays by Williams and Beckett discussed below. Or – perhaps it's not worrying, this madness, but liberating. The woman in this story, after all, in one sense, emerges into freedom at the end.

To start at the end, with a problem. Problems in texts are usually productive places to think but some problems yield more productive thinkings than others. Readers often leave this story with what might or might not be a niggling question that they almost feel awkward about asking. So we'll ask it. Who's the 'Jane' at the end ('I've got out at last . . . in spite of you and Jane')? The narrator herself, named at last in a moment of split consciousness by the woman who is now outside her old oppressed identity? Her sister-in-law Jennie, named incorrectly in the narrator's confusion or triumph, or correctly but more formally (Jane and Jennie being the same name at the time in America?), the formality marking the narrator's increased independence and defiance of 'womanly' intimacy?

These routes out of the apparent problem are variously productive. But there's another. And that's the possibility that 'Jane' evokes another Jane, a fictional one, Jane Eyre. In that case the woman at the end is or becomes or is equivalent, by narrative affiliation, to Bertha Mason, the first Mrs Rochester, the 'madwoman in the attic', the dark Double or Other, that projected male fear of the unmanning and unknowable female that critics have found throughout mainstream literature. (And Bertha's story is told in *Wide Sargasso Sea* by Jean Rhys, one of whose other novels is excerpted in Chapter 20.)

After all, this story takes pains to establish itself in an 'untenanted' mansion with a 'queer' feel about it, a colonial house with its 'hereditary' history – that is, an English history. An old decayed Englishness clings to the house as it does to the story, specifically so when the narrator, towards the end, contemplates burning the house down, which, of course, is what Bertha does. John's patronising attitude to his wife is duplicated almost word for word in Rochester's attempt to argue that what Jane had seen in her room was not Bertha but 'the creature of an over-stimulated brain . . . I must be careful of you, my treasure: nerves like yours were not made for rough handling' (Chapter XXV). And it's possible to hear echoes of Jane Eyre's childhood imprisonment in the Red Room (Chapter II) where she imagines ghostly oppressions.

There's a sense that this apparently slight and 'nervous' text has beneath it a massive submerged substructure of English-European fiction and, by extension, colonial oppression – an oppression equivalent to that exercised over the narrator by her doctor-husband. I'm struck by the equivalent situation in *Cat on a Hot Tin Roof* (also discussed in a later chapter): there the American plantation-mansion is loaded down in its cellar by rotting junk, relics of valuables bought up on a tour of the old Europe. By 'becoming' Bertha rather than Jane Eyre the narrator is reversing the usual narrative pattern of the dark Other being conquered by the heroine, typically in marriage. The slight and nervous American child-wife becomes the powerful woman of the old haunted European world – or perhaps it's that she transcends the old European model, by tearing off and tearing up the irritatingly expressive old writings of that culture and releasing the free woman held in those chains of old novels, releasing what Dickinson called 'Ourself behind ourself, concealed' ('One need not be a chamber').

But her victory, of course, is or may be seen as only partial. Attached to her rope and on all fours, though maybe no longer biting and tearing at her prison, she is an image of woman as chained animal. Or of Americanism for ever enslaved in the dead and imprisoning institutions of European culture. Or of a woman imprisoned in marriage from the outset and denied access to her baby (they've told her she's in a nursery, of all grim ironies, but the barred windows, the rings in the wall and the nailed-down bed suggest something more frightening) and only able to achieve freedom by going mad and regressing to animality. But, still, a victory and freedom of a kind. It's the husband who faints at the end and it's she who creeps 'over him every time' (having earlier 'felt creepy' looking at the slow-creeping moonlight). And the text that she has produced is a material product of her own, a textual victory, an expressive voice and a history achieved on the 'dead paper' which she had to hide from men, like the 'Dead Letter Office' where Bartleby tried to be human. If Bartleby, at least at first, tries to write (copy) himself into being socially human, the woman here, like Dickinson, has to hide the writing in which she expresses self – and that, too, returns us to Charlotte Brontë and others who had to write as if they weren't women.

This is to look at the story as a peculiarly fraught example of inter-textuality, to locate its anxieties and the ambivalence of its ending in its semi-conscious entanglement in a network of famous or oppressive other texts. A connected way of reading it is to locate its energies and anxieties at the level of the woman's body. That, after all, is where the story is contested. It's her body as well as her mind that the doctor-husband is 'curing' or 'caring for' in his regime of repression. It's her inability to write (writing is her 'work'), to exercise, to nurse her baby, that imprisons her. Her bodily activity and power are disallowed in the repression of her writing, speech, health, sanity, all in the name of her 'nervous depression – a slight hysterical tendency'. For it's clear that this intensely able woman (a repressed novelist) is disabled by the treatment which causes her symptoms in the first place, or at least, if she's post-natally depressed, exacerbates them. The sister-in-law Jennie (in a very unsisterly diagnosis) thinks it's her writing that made her ill.

It's striking how a very expressive bodily disgust is conveyed by the obsessively described obsessiveness of the wallpaper's colour and patterns. It's 'repellent, almost revolting; a smouldering unclean yellow', 'dull yet lurid . . . a sickly sulphur', 'it makes me think of . . . old foul, bad yellow things', and its patterns are like a 'fungus . . . an interminable string of toadstools, budding and sprouting', its 'waddling fungus growths'. And there are 'yellow smooches' that stain everything, as well as the 'long, straight, even smooch, as if it had been rubbed over and over' into which she eventually fits her shoulder in her last creepings round the room. And, most expressively of all, there's the smell which 'creeps . . . hovering . . . skulking . . . hanging over me', 'the subtlest, most enduring odor I ever met'.

The context to be suggested here (as confirmed in an essay by Mary Jacobus, which draws on a book by Jane Gallop) is that the paper's colour, shape and smell evoke the female body and its genitals as seen, imagined, smelled and feared by men. It's as if the woman has internalised male-hysterical fear of the woman's body, its 'unclean', 'bad yellow' smell (the creepiness first came to her from the moon – menstrually?). And it's even as if she's enacting the male terror-fantasy of the sexually self-satisfying woman, doing without men (fitting in her 'straight, even *smooch*, as if it had been rubbed over and over'). The hysteria, that is, comes from the man, not the woman, but the sexual politics is set up in such a way that the hysterical symptoms can only be displaced, self-punishingly, on to the woman herself. But, again, it can be read as a vindicating freedom as well as self-punishment.

The third and last of the contexts I want to put to work here is the most straightforward and it's the source of a positive note on which to end. The name of the doctor, Weir Mitchell, with whom the husband threatens his wife, belonged to a very real and bodily figure. Weir Mitchell invented the 'rest-cure' which he used in cases of so-called hysteria, the 'female malady' which literary historians have explored and described for us, and it's this rest-cure that the narrator here endures at John's hands – and which Charlotte Perkins Gilman endured herself at Mitchell's hands. She almost went mad. She recovered by writing, and among other stories she wrote this. She sent Mitchell a copy. He didn't acknowledge it. But, through a third party, Gilman subsequently learned that he'd indeed read it, been very affected by it – and had changed his practices because of it.

Texts are interventions in social processes. But they don't usually intervene as tellingly and productively as this.

Sandra Gilbert and Susan Gubar's classic study *The Madwoman in the Attic* (New Haven, Yale University Press, 1979) has had a powerful influence in feminist criticism. Its importance and its impact are discussed in Toril Moi's *Sexual/Textual Politics* (London, Methuen, 1985). You may well find that *The Yellow Wallpaper* affects your reading of earlier nineteenth-century literature generally, as well as two writers we've met in this book, Emily Brontë and Emily Dickinson. Another classic of literary critical-history referred to above is Elaine Showalter's *The Female Malady* (London, Virago Press, 1987), a study of the treatment of hysteria. The body in literature is a topic with wide-ranging implications. The Mary Jacobus essay referred to above is 'An Unnecessary Maze of Sign-Reading' in her *Reading Woman* (London, Methuen, 1986). She draws on Jane Gallop's *Feminism and Psychoanalysis: The Daughter's Seduction* (London, Macmillan, 1982). Jacobus's important essay 'The Difference of View', in *Women Writing and Writing About Women* (London, Croom Helm, 1979) which she edited, is also in Catherine Belsey and Jane Moore's *The Feminist Reader* (2nd edition, London, Macmillan, 1997), which is an excellent collection with an extremely helpful introduction, glossary and annotated list of further reading.

17

JAMES'S *THE TURN OF THE SCREW*
Desire in loss and the reader-response

In this chapter we'll be reading the first part of Henry James's *The Turn of the Screw* (1898). The commentary comes largely from a psychoanalytic point of view, exploring notions of desire and displacement. It is suggested that love, language and interpretation are all shadowed by dissatisfaction and loss, and that James's story demonstrates the painful interactions between them. The issue of interpretation leads us to so-called 'reader-response criticism'.

Here's a frightening story, for many readers one of the most frightening ever. It's the story of a governess and the two young and orphaned children she's employed to look after in a large country-house called Bly. Her employer, their uncle in London, gives her sole responsibility and tells her never to bother him with anything. There's a housekeeper at Bly, Mrs Grose, and some servants. And what's frightening is that there may be two other figures at Bly. And even more frightening is the possibility that there may not be.

At the outset of *The Turn of the Screw* we're at a Christmas gathering where ghost-stories are being told. Douglas, a man of about 60, has a story – 'beyond everything. Nothing at all that I know touches it' – which he, rather reluctantly, is prepared to share. It's the story of the governess. She herself told him the story, some ten years after the events it describes, when he was a student and when she was his own sister's governess. He liked her 'extremely'. Years later, before she died, she wrote the story down and sent it to him. Years later again, Douglas sends the manuscript to the narrator when he (Douglas) knows he's dying. And the narrator makes a transcript. The published text, we're led to believe, derives from that transcript. The title was chosen by the narrator, not Douglas.

We start with the governess's first impressions of Flora, the girl in her charge, her subsequent meeting with Flora's older brother Miles and response to his being asked to leave his school, and the first of her uncanny encounters.

I was carried triumphantly through the following hours by my introduction to the younger of my pupils. The little girl who accompanied Mrs Grose appeared to me on the spot a creature so charming as to make it a great fortune to have to do with her. She was the most beautiful child I had ever seen, and I afterwards wondered that my employer had not told me more of her. I slept little that night – I was too much excited; and this astonished me too, I recollect, remained with me, adding to my sense of the liberality with which I was treated. The large, impressive room, one of the best in the house, the great state bed, as I almost felt it, the full, figured draperies, the long glasses in which, for the first time, I could see myself from head to foot, all struck me – like the extraordinary charm of my small charge – as so many things thrown in. It was thrown in as well, from the first moment, that I should get on with Mrs Grose in a relation over which, on my way, in the coach, I fear I had rather brooded. The only thing indeed that in this early outlook might have made me shrink again was the clear circumstance of her being so glad to see me. I perceived within half an hour that she was so glad – stout, simple, plain, clean, wholesome woman – as to be positively on her guard against showing it too much. I wondered even then a little why she should wish not to show it and that, with reflection, with suspicion, might of course have made me uneasy.

But it was a comfort that there could be no uneasiness in a connexion with anything so beatific as the radiant image of my little girl, the vision of whose angelic beauty had probably more than anything else to do with the restlessness that, before morning, made me several times rise and wander about my room to take in the whole picture and prospect; to watch, from my open window, the faint summer dawn, to look at such portions of the rest of the house as I could catch, and to listen, while, in the fading dusk, the first birds began to twitter, for

the possible recurrence of a sound or two, less natural and not
without, but within, that I had fancied I heard. There had been
a moment when I believed I recognized, faint and far, the cry of
a child; there had been another when I found myself just consciously starting as at the passage, before my door, of a light
footstep. But these fancies were not marked enough not to be
thrown off, and it is only in the light, or the gloom, I should
rather say, of other and subsequent matters that they now
come back to me. To watch, teach, 'form' little Flora would too
evidently be the making of a happy and useful life. It had been
agreed between us downstairs that after this first occasion I
should have her as a matter of course at night, her small white
bed being already arranged, to that end, in my room. What I
had undertaken was the whole care of her, and she had
remained, just this last time, with Mrs Grose only as an effect
of our consideration for my inevitable strangeness and her natural timidity. In spite of this timidity – which the child herself, in the oddest way in the world, had been perfectly frank
and brave about, allowing it, without a sign of uncomfortable
consciousness, with the deep, sweet serenity indeed of one of
Raphael's holy infants, to be discussed, to be imputed to her
and to determine us – I felt quite sure she would presently like
me. It was part of what I already liked Mrs Grose herself for,
the pleasure I could see her feel in my admiration and wonder
as I sat at supper with four tall candles and with my pupil, in a
high chair and a bib, brightly facing me, between them, over
bread and milk. There were naturally things that in Flora's
presence could pass between us only as prodigious and gratified
looks, obscure and roundabout allusions.

'And the little boy – does he look like her? Is he too so very
remarkable?'

One wouldn't flatter a child. 'Oh Miss, *most* remarkable. If
you think well of this one!' – and she stood there with a plate in
her hand, beaming at our companion, who looked from one of
us to the other with placid heavenly eyes that contained
nothing to check us.

'Yes; if I do –?'

'You *will* be carried away by the little gentleman!'

'Well, that, I think, is what I came for – to be carried away. I'm afraid, however,' I remember feeling the impulse to add, 'I'm rather easily carried away. I was carried away in London!'

I can still see Mrs Grose's broad face as she took this in. 'In Harley Street?'

'In Harley Street.'

'Well, Miss, you're not the first – and you won't be the last.'

'Oh, I've no pretension,' I could laugh, 'to being the only one. My other pupil, at any rate, as I understand, comes back tomorrow?'

'Not tomorrow – Friday, Miss. He arrives, as you did, by the coach, under care of the guard, and is to be met by the same carriage.'

I forthwith expressed that the proper as well as the pleasant and friendly thing would be therefore that on the arrival of the public conveyance I should be in waiting for him with his little sister; an idea in which Mrs Grose concurred so heartily that I somehow took her manner as a kind of comforting pledge – never falsified, thank heaven! – that we should on every question be quite at one. Oh, she was glad I was there!

What I felt the next day was, I suppose, nothing that could be fairly called a reaction from the cheer of my arrival; it was probably at the most only a slight oppression produced by a fuller measure of the scale, as I walked round them, gazed up at them, took them in, of my new circumstances. They had, as it were, an extent and mass for which I had not been prepared and in the presence of which I found myself, freshly, a little scared as well as a little proud. Lessons, in this agitation, certainly suffered some delay; I reflected that my first duty was, by the gentlest arts I could contrive, to win the child into the sense of knowing me. I spent the day with her out of doors; I arranged with her, to her great satisfaction, that it should be she, she only, who might show me the place. She showed it step by step and room by room and secret by secret, with droll, delightful, childish talk about it and with the result, in half an hour, of our becoming immense friends. Young as she was, I was struck, throughout our little tour, with her confidence and courage with the way, in empty chambers and dull corridors, on

crooked staircases that made me pause and even on the summit of an old machicolated square tower that made me dizzy,
her morning music, her disposition to tell me so many more
things than she asked, rang out and led me on. I have not
seen Bly since the day I left it, and I dare say that to my
older and more informed eyes it would now appear sufficiently contracted. But as my little conductress, with her
hair of gold and her frock of blue, danced before me round
corners and pattered down passages, I had the view of a castle
of romance inhabited by a rosy sprite, such a place as would
somehow, for diversion of the young idea, take all colour
out of storybooks and fairy-tales. Wasn't it just a storybook
over which I had fallen a-doze and a-dream? No; it was a big,
ugly, antique, but convenient house, embodying a few features
of a building still older, half replaced and half utilized, in
which I had the fancy of our being almost as lost as a handful of
passengers in a great drifting ship. Well, I was, strangely, at
the helm!

2

This came home to me when, two days later, I drove over with
Flora to meet, as Mrs Grose said, the little gentleman; and all
the more for an incident that, presenting itself the second evening, had deeply disconcerted me. The first day had been, on the
whole, as I have expressed, reassuring; but I was to see it wind
up in keen apprehension. The postbag, that evening – it came
late – contained a letter for me, which, however, in the hand of
my employer, I found to be composed but of a few words
enclosing another, addressed to himself, with a seal still
unbroken. 'This, I recognize, is from the head-master, and the
head-master's an awful bore. Read him, please; deal with him;
but mind you don't report. Not a word. I'm off!' I broke the
seal with a great effort – so great a one that I was a long time
coming to it; took the unopened missive at last up to my room
and only attacked it just before going to bed. I had better have
let it wait till morning, for it gave me a second sleepless night.
With no counsel to take, the next day, I was full of distress; and

it finally got so the better of me that I determined to open myself at least to Mrs Grose.

'What does it mean? The child's dismissed his school.'

She gave me a look that I remarked at the moment; then, visibly, with a quick blankness, seemed to try to take it back. 'But aren't they all –?'

'Sent home – yes. But only for the holidays. Miles may never go back at all.'

Consciously, under my attention, she reddened. 'They won't take him?'

'They absolutely decline.'

At this she raised her eyes, which she had turned from me; I saw them fill with good tears. 'What has he done?'

I hesitated; then I judged best simply to hand her my letter – which, however, had the effect of making her, without taking it, simply put her hands behind her. She shook her head sadly. 'Such things are not for me, Miss.'

My counsellor couldn't read! I winced at my mistake, which I attenuated as I could, and opened my letter again to repeat it to her; then, faltering in the act and folding it up once more, I put it back in my pocket. 'Is he really *bad*?'

The tears were still in her eyes. 'Do the gentlemen say so?'

'They go into no particulars. They simply express their regret that it should be impossible to keep him. That can have only one meaning.' Mrs Grose listened with dumb emotion; she forbore to ask me what this meaning might be; so that, presently, to put the thing with some coherence and with the mere aid of her presence to my own mind, I went on: 'That he's an injury to the others.'

At this, with one of the quick turns of simple folk, she suddenly flamed up. 'Master Miles! – *him* an injury?'

There was such a flood of good faith in it that, though I had not yet seen the child, my very fears made me jump to the absurdity of the idea. I found myself, to meet my friend the better, offering it, on the spot, sarcastically. 'To his poor little innocent mates!'

'It's too dreadful,' cried Mrs Grose, 'to say such cruel things! Why, he's scarce ten years old.'

'Yes, yes; it would be incredible.'

She was evidently grateful for such a profession. 'See him, Miss, first. *Then* believe it!' I felt forthwith a new impatience to see him; it was the beginning of a curiosity that, for all the next hours, was to deepen almost to pain. Mrs Grose was aware, I could judge, of what she had produced in me, and she followed it up with assurance. 'You might as well believe it of the little lady. Bless her,' she added the next moment – '*look* at her!'

I turned and saw that Flora, whom, ten minutes before, I had established in the schoolroom with a sheet of white paper, a pencil and a copy of nice 'round O's', now presented herself to view at the open door. She expressed in her little way an extraordinary detachment from disagreeable duties, looking at me, however, with a great childish light that seemed to offer it as a mere result of the affection she had conceived for my person, which had rendered necessary that she should follow me. I needed nothing more than this to feel the full force of Mrs Grose's comparison, and, catching my pupil in my arms, covered her with kisses in which there was a sob of atonement.

None the less, the rest of the day, I watched for further occasion to approach my colleague, especially as, towards evening, I began to fancy she rather sought to avoid me. I overtook her, I remember, on the staircase; we went down together, and at the bottom I detained her, holding her there with a hand on her arm. 'I take what you said to me at noon as a declaration that *you've* never known him to be bad.'

She threw back her head; she had clearly, by this time, and very honestly, adopted an attitude. 'Oh, never known him – I don't pretend *that*!'

I was upset again. 'Then you *have* known him –?'

'Yes indeed, Miss, thank God!'

On reflection I accepted this. 'You mean that a boy who never is –?'

'Is no boy for *me*!'

I held her tighter. 'You like them with the spirit to be naughty?' Then keeping pace with her answer, 'So do I!' I eagerly brought out. But not to the degree to contaminate –'

'To contaminate?' – my big word left her at a loss.

I explained it. 'To corrupt.'

She stared, taking my meaning in; but it produced in her an odd laugh. 'Are you afraid he'll corrupt *you?*' She put the question with such a fine bold humour that, with a laugh, a little silly doubtless, to match her own, I gave way for the time to the apprehension of ridicule.

But the next day, as the hour for my drive approached, I cropped up in another place. 'What was the lady who was here before?'

'The last governess? She was also young and pretty – almost as young and almost as pretty, Miss, even as you.'

'Ah, then, I hope her youth and her beauty helped her!' I recollect throwing off. 'He seems to like us young and pretty!'

'Oh, he *did*,' Mrs Grose assented: 'it was the way he liked everyone!' She had no sooner spoken indeed than she caught herself up. 'I mean that's *his* way – the master's.'

I was struck. 'But of whom did you speak first?'

She looked blank, but she coloured. 'Why, of *him*.'

'Of the master?'

'Of who else?'

There was so obviously no one else that the next moment I had lost my impression of her having accidentally said more than she meant; and I merely asked what I wanted to know. 'Did *she* see anything in the boy –?'

'That wasn't right? She never told me.'

I had a scruple, but I overcame it. 'Was she careful – particular?'

Mrs Grose appeared to try to be conscientious. 'About some things – yes.'

'But not about all?'

Again she considered. 'Well, Miss – she's gone. I won't tell tales.'

'I quite understand your feeling,' I hastened to reply; but I thought it, after an instant, not opposed to this concession to pursue: 'Did she die here?'

'No – she went off.'

I don't know what there was in this brevity of Mrs Grose's that struck me as ambiguous. 'Went off to die?' Mrs Grose

looked straight out of the window, but I felt that, hypothetic-
ally, I had a right to know what young persons engaged for Bly
were expected to do. 'She was taken ill, you mean, and went
home?'

'She was not taken ill, so far as appeared, in this house. She
left it, at the end of the year, to go home, as she said, for a short
holiday, to which the time she had put in had certainly given
her a right. We had then a young woman – a nursemaid who
had stayed on and who was a good girl and clever; and *she* took
the children altogether for the interval. But our young lady
never came back, and at the very moment I was expecting her I
heard from the master that she was dead.'

I turned this over. 'But of what?'

'He never told me! But please, Miss,' said Mrs Grose, 'I must
get to my work.'

3

Her thus turning her back on me was fortunately not, for my
just preoccupations, a snub that could check the growth of our
mutual esteem. We met, after I had brought home little Miles,
more intimately than ever on the ground of my stupefaction,
my general emotion: so monstrous was I then ready to pronounce it that such a child as had now been revealed to me
should be under an interdict. I was a little late on the scene,
and I felt, as he stood wistfully looking out for me before the
door of the inn at which the coach had put him down, that I
had seen him, on the instant, without and within, in the great
glow of freshness, the same positive fragrance of purity, in
which I had, from the first moment, seen his little sister. He
was incredibly beautiful, and Mrs Grose had put her finger on
it: everything but a sort of passion of tenderness for him was
swept away by his presence. What I then and there took him to
my heart for was something divine that I have never found to
the same degree in any child – his indescribable little air of
knowing nothing in the world but love. It would have been
impossible to carry a bad name with a greater sweetness of
innocence, and by the time I had got back to Bly with him I

remained merely bewildered – so far, that is, as I was not outraged – by the sense of the horrible letter locked up in my room, in a drawer. As soon as I could compass a private word with Mrs Grose I declared to her that it was grotesque.

She promptly understood me. 'You mean the cruel charge –?'

'It doesn't live an instant. My dear woman, *look* at him!'

She smiled at my pretension to have discovered his charm. 'I assure you, Miss, I do nothing else! What will you say, then?' she immediately added.

'In answer to the letter?' I had made up my mind. 'Nothing.'

'And to his uncle?'

I was incisive. 'Nothing.'

'And to the boy himself?'

I was wonderful. 'Nothing.'

She gave with her apron a great wipe to her mouth. 'Then I'll stand by you. We'll see it out.'

'We'll see it out!' I ardently echoed, giving her my hand to make it a vow.

She held me there a moment, then whisked up her apron again with her detached hand. 'Would you mind, Miss, if I used the freedom –'

'To kiss me? No!' I took the good creature in my arms and, after we had embraced like sisters, felt still more fortified and indignant.

This, at all events, was for the time: a time so full that, as I recall the way it went, it reminds me of all the art I now need to make it a little distinct. What I look back at with amazement is the situation I accepted. I had undertaken, with my companion, to see it out, and I was under a charm, apparently, that could smooth away the extent and the far and difficult connexions of such an effort. I was lifted aloft on a great wave of infatuation and pity. I found it simple, in my ignorance, my confusion, and perhaps my conceit, to assume that I could deal with a boy whose education for the world was all on the point of beginning. I am unable even to remember at this day what proposal I framed for the end of his holidays and the resumption of his studies. Lessons with me indeed, that charming summer, we all had a theory that he was to have; but I now feel that, for weeks, the lessons must have been rather my own. I learnt something – at first certainly – that had not been one of the teachings of my small, smothered life; learnt to be amused, and even amusing, and not to think for the morrow. It was the first time, in a manner, that I had known space and air and freedom, all the music of summer and all the mystery of nature. And then there was consideration – and consideration was sweet. Oh, it was a trap – not designed, but deep – to my imagination, to my delicacy, perhaps to my vanity; to whatever, in me, was most excitable. The best way to picture it all is to say that I was off my guard. They gave me so little trouble – they were of a gentleness so extraordinary. I used to speculate – but even this with a dim disconnectedness – as to how the rough future (for all futures are rough!) would handle them and might bruise them. They had the bloom of health and happiness; and yet, as if I had been in charge of a pair of little grandees, of princes of the blood, for whom everything, to be right, would have to be enclosed and protected, the only form that, in my fancy, the after-years could take for them was that of a romantic, a really royal extension of the garden and the park. It may be, of course, above all, that what suddenly broke into this gives the previous time a charm of stillness – that hush in which something gathers or crouches. The change was actually like the spring of a beast.

In the first weeks the days were long; they often, at their finest, gave me what I used to call, my own hour, the hour when, for my pupils, tea-time and bed-time having come and gone, I had, before my final retirement, a small interval alone. Much as I liked my companions, this hour was the thing in the day I liked most; and I liked it best of all when, as the light faded – or rather, I should say, the day lingered and the last calls of the last birds sounded, in a flushed sky, from the old trees – I could take a turn into the grounds and enjoy, almost with a sense of property that amused and flattered me, the beauty and dignity of the place. It was a pleasure at these moments to feel myself tranquil and justified; doubtless, perhaps, also to reflect that by my discretion, my quiet good sense and general high propriety, I was giving pleasure – if he ever thought of it! – to the person to whose pressure I had responded. What I was doing was what he had earnestly hoped and directly asked of me, and that I *could*, after all, do it proved even a greater joy than I had expected. I dare say I fancied myself, in short, a remarkable young woman and took comfort in the faith that this would more publicly appear. Well, I needed to be remarkable to offer a front to the remarkable things that presently gave their first sign.

It was plump, one afternoon, in the middle of my very hour: the children were tucked away and I had come out for my stroll. One of the thoughts that, as I don't in the least shrink now from noting, used to be with me in these wanderings was that it would be as charming as a charming story suddenly to meet someone. Someone would appear there at the turn of a path and would stand before me and smile and approve. I didn't ask more than that – I only asked that he should *know*; and the only way to be sure he knew would be to see it, and the kind light of it, in his handsome face. That was exactly present to me – by which I mean the face was – when, on the first of these occasions, at the end of a long June day, I stopped short on emerging from one of the plantations and coming into view of the house. What arrested me on the spot – and with a shock much greater than any vision had allowed for – was the sense that my imagination had, in a flash, turned real. He did stand there! – but high up, beyond the lawn and at the very top of the tower to which, on that first morning, little Flora had conducted me. This tower was one of a pair – square, incongruous, crenelated structures – that were distinguished, for some reason, though I could see little difference, as the new and the old. They flanked opposite ends of the house and were probably architectural absurdities, redeemed in a measure indeed by not being wholly disengaged nor of a height too pretentious, dating, in their gingerbread antiquity, from a romantic revival that was already a respectable past. I admired them, had fancies about them, for we could all profit in a degree, especially when they loomed through the dusk, by the grandeur of their actual battlements; yet it was not at such an elevation that the figure I had so often invoked seemed most in place.

It produced in me, this figure, in the clear twilight, I remember, two distinct gasps of emotion, which were, sharply, the shock of my first and that of my second surprise. My second was a violent perception of the mistake of my first: the man who met my eyes was not the person I had precipitately supposed. There came to me thus a bewilderment of vision of which, after these years, there is no living view that I can hope to give. An unknown man in a lonely place is a permitted object of fear to a young woman privately bred; and the figure that faced me was – a few more seconds assured me – as little anyone else I knew as it was the image that had been in my mind. I had not seen it in Harley Street – I had not seen it anywhere. The place, moreover, in the strangest way in the world, had, on the instant, and by the very fact of its appearance, become a solitude. To me at least, making my statement here with a deliberation with which I have never made it, the whole feeling of the moment returns. It was as if, while I took in – what I did take in – all the rest of the scene had been stricken with death. I can hear again, as I write, the intense hush in which the sounds of evening dropped. The rooks stopped cawing in the golden sky and the friendly hour lost, for the minute, all its voice. But there was no other change in nature, unless indeed it were a change that I saw with a stranger sharpness. The gold was still in the sky, the clearness in the air, and the man who looked at me over the battlements was as definite as a picture in a frame. That's how I thought, with extraordinary quickness, of each person that he might have been and that he was not. We were confronted across our distance quite long enough for me to ask myself with intensity who then he was and to feel, as an effect of my inability to say, a wonder that in a few instants more became intense.

The great question, or one of these, is, afterwards, I know, with regard to certain matters, the question of how long they have lasted. Well, this matter of mine, think what you will of it, lasted while I caught at a dozen possibilities none of which made a difference for the better, that I could see, in there having been in the house – and for how long, above all? – a person of whom I was in ignorance. It lasted while I just bridled a little with the sense that my office demanded that there should be no such ignorance and no such person. It lasted while this visitant, at all events – and there was a touch of the strange freedom, as I remember, in the sign of familiarity of his wearing no hat – seemed to fix me, from his position, with just the question, just the scrutiny through the fading light, that his own presence provoked. We were too far apart to call to each other, but there was a moment at which, at shorter range, some challenge between us, breaking the hush, would have been the right result of our straight mutual stare. He was in one of the angles, the one away from the house, very erect, as it struck me, and with both hands on the ledge. So I saw him as I see the letters I form on this page; then, exactly, after a minute, as if to add to the spectacle, he slowly changed his place – passed, looking at me hard all the while, to the opposite corner of the platform. Yes, I had the sharpest sense that during this transit he never took his eyes from me, and I can see at this moment the way his hand, as he went, passed from one of the crenelations to the next. He stopped at the other corner, but less long, and even as he turned away still markedly fixed me. He turned away; that was all I knew.

Deciding that an 'intrusion' has taken place and that 'we should surely see no more of him' the governess busies herself for some days in the charm of the children.

I remember feeling with Miles in especial as if he had had, as it were, no history. We expect of a small child a scant one, but there was in this beautiful little boy something extraordinarily sensitive, yet extraordinarily happy, that, more than in any creature of his age I have seen, struck me as beginning anew each day. He had never for a second suffered. I took this as a direct disproof of his having really been chastised. If he had been wicked he would have 'caught' it, and I should have caught it by the rebound – I should have found the trace. I found nothing at all and he was therefore an angel. He never spoke of his school, never mentioned a comrade or a master; and I, for my part, was quite too much disgusted to allude to them. Of course I was under the spell, and the wonderful part is that, even at the time, I perfectly knew I was. But I gave myself up to it; it was an antidote to any pain, and I had more pains than one. I was in receipt in these days of disturbing letters from home, where things were not going well. But with my children, what things in the world mattered? That was the question I used to put to my scrappy retirements. I was dazzled by their loveliness.

There was a Sunday – to get on – when it rained with such force and for so many hours that there could be no procession to church; in consequence of which, as the day declined, I had arranged with Mrs Grose that, should the evening show improvement, we would attend together the late service. The rain happily stopped, and I prepared for our walk, which, through the park and by the good road to the village, would be a matter of twenty minutes. Coming down stairs to meet my colleague in the hall, I remembered a pair of gloves that had required three stitches and that had received them – with a publicity perhaps not edifying – while I sat with the children at their tea, served on Sundays, by exception, in that cold, clean temple of mahogany and brass, the 'grown-up' dining-room. The gloves had been dropped there, and I turned in to recover them. The day was grey enough, but the afternoon light still lingered, and it enabled me, on crossing the threshold, not only to recognize, on a chair near the wide window, then closed, the articles I wanted, but to become aware of a person on the other side of the window and looking straight in. One step into the room had sufficed; my vision was instantaneous; it was all there. The person looking straight in was the person who had already appeared to me. He appeared thus again with I won't say greater distinctness, for that was impossible, but with a nearness that represented a forward stride in our intercourse and made me, as I met him, catch my breath and turn cold. He was the same – he was the same, and seen, this time, as he had been seen before, from the waist up, the window, though the dining-room was on the ground-floor, not going down to the terrace on which he stood. His face was close to the glass, yet the effect of this better view was, strangely, only to show me how intense the former had been. He remained but a few seconds – long enough to convince me he also saw and recognized; but it was as if I had been looking at him for years and had known him always. Something, however, happened this time that had not happened before; his stare into my face, through the glass and across the room, was as deep and hard as then, but it quitted me for a moment during which I could still watch it, see it fix successively several other things. On the spot there came to me the added shock of a certitude that it was not for me he had come there. He had come for someone else.

The flash of this knowledge – for it was knowledge in the midst of dread – produced in me the most extraordinary effect, started, as I stood there, a sudden vibration of duty and courage. I say courage because I was beyond all doubt already far gone. I bounded straight out of the door again, reached that of the house, got, in an instant, upon the drive, and, passing along the terrace as fast as I could rush, turned a corner and came full in sight. But it was in sight of nothing now – my visitor had vanished. I stopped, I almost dropped, with the real relief of this; but I took in the whole scene – I gave him time to reappear. I call it time, but how long was it? I can't speak to the purpose today of the duration of these things. That kind of measure must have left me: they couldn't have lasted as they actually appeared to me to last. The terrace and the whole place, the lawn and the garden beyond it, all I could see of the park, were empty with a great emptiness. There were shrubberies and big trees, but I remember the clear assurance I felt that none of them concealed him. He was there or was not there: not there if I didn't see him. I got hold of this; then, instinctively, instead of returning as I had come, went to the window. It was confusedly present to me that I ought to place myself where he had stood. I did so; I applied my face to the pane and looked, as he had looked, into the room. As if, at this moment, to show me exactly what his range had been, Mrs Grose, as I had done for himself just before, came in from the hall. With this I had the full image of a repetition of what had already occurred. She saw me as I had seen my own visitant; she pulled up short as I had done; I gave her something of the shock that I had received. She turned white, and this made me ask myself if I had blanched as much. She stared, in short, and retreated on just *my* lines, and I knew she had then passed out and come round to me and that I should presently meet her. I remained where I was, and while I waited I thought of more things than one. But there's only one I take space to mention. I wondered why *she* should be scared.

5

Oh, she let me know as soon as, round the corner of the house, she loomed again into view. 'What in the name of goodness is the matter –?' She was now flushed and out of breath.

I said nothing till she came quite near. 'With me?' I must have made a wonderful face. 'Do I show it?'

'You're as white as a sheet. You look awful.'

I considered; I could meet on this, without scruple, any innocence. My need to respect the bloom of Mrs Grose's had dropped, without a rustle, from my shoulders, and if I wavered for the instant it was not with what I kept back. I put out my hand to her and she took it; I held her hard a little, liking to feel her close to me. There was a kind of support in the shy heave of her surprise. 'You came for me for church, of course, but I can't go.'

'Has anything happened?'

'Yes. You must know now. Did I look very queer?'

'Through this window? Dreadful!'

'Well,' I said, 'I've been frightened.' Mrs Grose's eyes expressed plainly that *she* had no wish to be, yet also that she knew too well her place not to be ready to share with me any marked inconvenience. Oh, it was quite settled that she *must* share! 'Just what you saw from the dining-room a minute ago was the effect of that. What *I* saw – just before – was much worse.'

Her hand tightened. 'What was it?'

'An extraordinary man. Looking in.'

340

'What extraordinary man?'

'I haven't the least idea.'

Mrs Grose gazed round us in vain. Then where is he gone?'

'I know still less.'

'Have you seen him before?'

'Yes – once. On the old tower.'

She could only look at me harder. 'Do you mean he's a stranger?'

'Oh, very much!'

'Yet you didn't tell me?'

'No – for reasons. But now that you've guessed –'

Mrs Grose's round eyes encountered this charge. 'Ah, I haven't guessed!' she said very simply. 'How can I if *you* don't imagine?'

'I don't in the very least.'

'You've seen him nowhere but on the tower?'

'And on this spot just now.'

Mrs Grose looked round again. 'What was he doing on the tower?'

'Only standing there and looking down at me.'

She thought a minute. 'Was he a gentleman?'

I found I had no need to think. 'No.' She gazed in deeper wonder. 'No.'

'Then nobody about the place? Nobody from the village?'

'Nobody – nobody. I didn't tell you, but I made sure.'

She breathed a vague relief: this was, oddly, so much to the good. It only went indeed a little way. 'But if he isn't a gentleman –'

'What *is* he? He's a horror.'

'A horror?'

'He's – God help me if I know *what* he is!'

Mrs Grose looked round once more; she fixed her eyes on the duskier distance, then, pulling herself together, turned to me with abrupt inconsequence. 'It's time we should be at church.'

'Oh, I'm not fit for church!'

'Won't it do you good?'

'It won't do *them* –!' I nodded at the house.

'The children?'

'I can't leave them now.'

'You're afraid –?'

I spoke boldly. 'I'm afraid of *him*.'

Mrs Grose's large face showed me, at this, for the first time, the far-away faint glimmer of a consciousness more acute: I somehow made out in it the delayed dawn of an idea I myself had not given her and that was as yet quite obscure to me. It comes back to me that I thought instantly of this as something I could get from her; and I felt it to be connected with the desire she presently showed to know more. 'When was it – on the tower?'

'About the middle of the month. At this same hour.'

'Almost at dark,' said Mrs Grose.

'Oh no, not nearly. I saw him as I see you.'

'Then how did he get in?'

'And how did he get out?' I laughed. 'I had no opportunity to ask him! This evening, you see,' I pursued, 'he has not been able to get in.'

'He only peeps?'

'I hope it will be confined to that!' She had now let go my hand; she turned away a little. I waited an instant; then I brought out: 'Go to church. Good-bye. I must watch.'

Slowly she faced me again. 'Do you fear for them?'

We met in another long look. 'Don't *you*?' Instead of answering she came nearer to the window and, for a minute, applied her face to the glass. 'You see how he could see,' I meanwhile went on.

She didn't move. 'How long was he here?'

'Till I came out. I came to meet him.'

Mrs Grose at last turned round, and there was still more in her face. '*I* couldn't have come out.'

'Neither could I!' I laughed again. 'But I did come. I have my duty.'

'So have I mine,' she replied; after which she added: 'What is he like?'

'I've been dying to tell you. But he's like nobody.'

'Nobody?' she echoed.

'He has no hat.' Then seeing in her face that she already, in this, with a deeper dismay, found a touch of picture, I quickly added stroke to stroke. 'He has red hair, very red, close-curling, and a pale face, long in shape, with straight, good features and little, rather queer whiskers that are as red as his hair. His eyebrows are, somehow, darker; they look particularly arched and as if they might move a good deal. His eyes are sharp, strange – awfully; but I only know clearly that they're rather small and very fixed. His mouth's wide, and his lips are thin, and except for his little whiskers he's quite clean-shaven. He gives me a sort of sense of looking like an actor.'

'An actor!' It was impossible to resemble one less, at least, than Mrs Grose at that moment.

'I've never seen one, but so I suppose them. He's tall, active, erect,' I continued, 'but never – no, never! – a gentleman.'

My companion's face had blanched as I went on; her round eyes started and her mild mouth gaped. 'A gentleman?' she gasped, confounded, stupefied: 'a gentleman *he*?'

'You know him then?'

She visibly tried to hold herself. 'But he *is* handsome?'

I saw the way to help her. 'Remarkably!'

'And dressed –?'

'In somebody's clothes. They're smart, but they're not his own.'

She broke into a breathless affirmative groan. 'They're the master's!'

I caught it up. 'You *do* know him?'

She faltered but a second. 'Quint!' she cried.

'Quint?'

'Peter Quint – his own man, his valet, when he was here!'

'When the master was?'

Gaping still, but meeting me, she pieced it all together. 'He never wore his hat, but he did wear – well, there were waistcoats missed! They were both here – last year. Then the master went, and Quint was alone.'

I followed, but halting a little. 'Alone?'

'Alone with *us*.' Then, as from a deeper depth, 'In charge,' she added.

'And what became of him?'

She hung fire so long that I was still more mystified. 'He went too,' she brought out at last.

'Went where?'

Her expression, at this, became extraordinary. 'God knows where! He died.'

'Died?' I almost shrieked.

She seemed fairly to square herself, plant herself more firmly to utter the wonder of it. 'Yes. Mr Quint is dead.'

The governess and Mrs Grose (who 'had seen nothing, not the shadow of a shadow') talk into the night.

Perfectly can I recall now the particular way strength came to me before we separated for the night. We had gone over and over every feature of what I had seen.

'He was looking for someone else, you say – someone who was not you?'

'He was looking for little Miles.' A portentous clearness now possessed me. '*That's* whom he was looking for.'

'But how do you know?'

'I know, I know, I know!' My exaltation grew. 'And *you* know, my dear!'

She didn't deny this, but I required, I felt, not even so much telling as that. She resumed in a moment, at any rate: 'What if *he* should see him?'

'Little Miles? That's what he wants!'

She looked immensely scared again. 'The child?'

'Heaven forbid! The man. He wants to appear to *them*.' That he might was an awful conception, and yet, somehow, I could keep at bay; which, moreover, as we lingered there, was what I succeeded in practically proving. I had an absolute certainty that I should see again what I had already seen, but something within me said that by offering myself bravely as the sole sub-ject of such experience, by accepting, by inviting, by sur-mounting it all, I should serve as an expiatory victim and guard the tranquillity of my companions. The children, in especial, I should thus fence about and absolutely save. I recall one of the last things I said that night to Mrs Grose.

'It does strike me that my pupils have never mentioned –'

She looked at me hard as I musingly pulled up. 'His having been here and the time they were with him?'

'The time they were with him, and his name, his presence, his history, in any way.'

'Oh, the little lady doesn't remember. She never heard or knew.'

'The circumstances of his death?' I thought with some intensity. 'Perhaps not. But Miles would remember – Miles would know.'

'Ah, don't try him!' broke from Mrs Grose.

I returned her the look she had given me. 'Don't be afraid.' I continued to think. 'It *is* rather odd.'

'That he has never spoken of him?'

'Never by the least allusion. And you tell me they were "great friends"?'

'Oh, it wasn't *him*!' Mrs Grose with emphasis declared. 'It was Quint's own fancy. To play with him, I mean – to spoil him.' She paused a moment; then she added: 'Quint was much too free.'

This gave me, straight from my vision of his face – *such* a face! – a sudden sickness of disgust 'Too free with *my* boy?'

'Too free with everyone!'

I forbore, for the moment, to analyse this description further than by the reflection that a part of it applied to several of the members of the household, of the half-dozen maids and men who were still of our small colony. But there was everything, for our apprehension, in the lucky fact that no discomfortable legend, no perturbation of scullions, had ever, within anyone's memory, attached to the kind old place. It had neither bad name nor ill fame, and Mrs Grose, most apparently, only desired to cling to me and to quake in silence. I even put her, the very last thing of all, to the test. It was when, at midnight, she had her hand on the schoolroom door to take leave. 'I have it from you then – for it's of great importance – that he was definitely and admittedly bad?'

'Oh, not admittedly. *I* knew it – but the master didn't.'

'And you never told him?'

'Well, he didn't like tale-bearing – he hated complaints. He was terribly short with anything of that kind, and if people were all right to *him* –'

'He wouldn't be bothered with more?' This squared well enough with my impression of him: he was not a trouble-loving gentleman, nor so very particular perhaps about some of the company *he* kept. All the same, I pressed my interlocutress. 'I promise you *I* would have told!'

She felt my discrimination. 'I dare say I was wrong. But, really, I was afraid.'

'Afraid of what?'

'Of things that man could do. Quint was so clever – he was so deep.'

I took this in still more than, probably, I showed. 'You weren't afraid of anything else? Not of his effect –?'

'His effect?' she repeated with a face of anguish and waiting while I faltered.

'On innocent little precious lives. They were in your charge.'

'No, they were not in mine!' she roundly and distressfully returned. 'The master believed in him and placed him here because he was supposed not to be well and the country air so good for him. So he had everything to say. Yes' – she let me have it – 'even about *them*.'

'Them – that creature?' I had to smother a kind of howl. 'And you could bear it?'

'No. I couldn't – and I can't now!' And the poor woman burst into tears.

A week passes during which the governess learns that Quint had, apparently, died from falling drunk down an icy slope.

I scarce know how to put my story into words that shall be a credible picture of my state of mind; but I was in these days literally able to find a joy in the extraordinary flight of heroism the occasion demanded of me. I now saw that I had been asked for a service admirable and difficult; and there would be a greatness in letting it be seen – oh, in the right quarter! – that I could succeed where many another girl might have failed. It was an immense help to me – I confess I rather applaud myself as I look back! – that I saw my service so strongly and so simply. I was there to protect and defend the little creatures in the world the most bereaved and the most lovable, the appeal of whose helplessness had suddenly become only too explicit, a deep, constant ache of one's own committed heart. We were cut off, really, together; we were united in our danger. They had nothing but me, and I – well, I had *them*. It was in short a magnificent chance. This chance presented itself to me in an image richly material. I was a screen – I was to stand before them. The more I saw, the less they would. I began to watch them in a stifled suspense, a disguised excitement that might well, had it continued too long, have turned to something like madness. What saved me, as I now see, was that it turned to something else altogether. It didn't last as suspense – it was superseded by horrible proofs. Proofs, I say, yes – from the moment I really took hold.

This moment dated from an afternoon hour that I happened to spend in the grounds with the younger of my pupils alone. We had left Miles indoors, on the red cushion of a deep window-seat; he had wished to finish a book, and I had been glad to encourage a purpose so laudable in a young man whose only defect was an occasional excess of the restless. His sister, on the contrary, had been alert to come out, and I strolled with her half an hour, seeking the shade, for the sun was still high and the day exceptionally warm. I was aware afresh, with her, as we went, of how, like her brother, she contrived – it was the charming thing in both children – to let me alone without appearing to drop me and to accompany me without appearing to surround. They were never importunate and yet never list-less. My attention to them all really went to seeing them amuse themselves immensely without me: this was a spectacle they seemed actively to prepare and that engaged me as an active admirer. I walked in a world of their invention – they had no occasion whatever to draw upon mine; so that my time was taken only with being, for them, some remarkable person or thing that the game of the moment required and that was merely, thanks to my superior, my exalted stamp, a happy and highly distinguished sinecure. I forget what I was on the present occasion; I only remember that I was something very important and very quiet and that Flora was playing very hard. We were on the edge of the lake, and, as we had lately begun geography, the lake was the Sea of Azof.

Suddenly, in these circumstances, I became aware that, on the other side of the Sea of Azof, we had an interested spectator. The way this knowledge gathered in me was the strangest thing in the world – the strangest, that is, except the very much stranger in which it quickly merged itself. I had sat down with a piece of work – for I was something or other that could sit – on the old stone bench which overlooked the pond; and in this position I began to take in with certitude, and yet without direct vision, the presence, at a distance, of a third person. The old trees, the thick shrubbery, made a great and pleasant shade, but it was all suffused with the brightness of the hot, still hour. There was no ambiguity in anything; none whatever, at least, in the conviction I from one moment to another found myself forming as to what I should see straight before me and across the lake as a consequence of raising my eyes. They were attached at this juncture to the stitching in which I was engaged, and I can feel once more the spasm of my effort not to move them till I should so have steadied myself as to be able to make up my mind what to do. There was an alien object in view – a figure whose right of presence I instantly, passionately questioned. I recollect counting over perfectly the possibilities, reminding myself that nothing was more natural, for instance, than the appearance of one of the men about the place, or even of a messenger, a postman or a tradesman's boy, from the village. That reminder had as little effect on my practical certitude as I was conscious – still even without looking – of its having upon the character and attitude of our visitor. Nothing was more natural than that these things should be the other things that they absolutely were not.

Of the positive identity of the apparition I would assure myself as soon as the small clock of my courage should have ticked out the right second; meanwhile, with an effort that was already sharp enough, I transferred my eyes straight to little Flora, who, at the moment, was about ten yards away. My heart had stood still for an instant with the wonder and terror of the question whether she too would see; and I held my breath while I waited for what a cry from her, what some sudden innocent sign either of interest or of alarm, would tell me. I waited, but nothing came; then, in the first place – and there is something more dire in this, I feel, than in anything I have to relate – I was determined by a sense that, within a minute, all sounds from her had previously dropped; and, in the second, by the circumstance that, also within the minute, she had, in her play, turned her back to the water. This was her attitude when I at last looked at her – looked with the confirmed conviction that we were still, together, under direct personal notice. She had picked up a small flat piece of wood, which happened to have in it a little hole that had evidently suggested to her the idea of sticking in another fragment that might figure as a mast and make the thing a boat. This second morsel, as I watched her, she was very markedly and intently attempting to tighten in its place. My apprehension of what she was doing sustained me so that after some seconds I felt I was ready for more. Then I again shifted my eyes – I faced what I had to face.

7

I got hold of Mrs Grose as soon after this as I could; and I can give no intelligible account of how I fought out the interval. Yet I still hear myself cry as I fairly threw myself into her arms: 'They *know* – it's too monstrous: they know, they know!'

'And what on earth –?' I felt her incredulity as she held me.

'Why, all that *we* know – and heaven knows what else besides!' Then, as she released me, I made it out to her, made it out perhaps only now with full coherency even to myself. 'Two hours ago, in the garden' – I could scarce articulate – 'Flora *saw*!'

Mrs Grose took it as she might have taken a blow in the stomach. 'She has told you?' she panted.

'Not a word – that's the horror. She kept it to herself! The child of eight, *that* child!' Unutterable still, for me, was the stupefaction of it.

Mrs Grose, of course, could only gape the wider. 'Then how do you know?'

'I was there – I saw with my eyes: saw that she was perfectly aware.'

'Do you mean aware of *him*?'

'No – of *her*.' I was conscious as I spoke that I looked prodigious things, for I got the slow reflection of them in my companion's face. 'Another person – this time; but a figure of quite as unmistakable horror and evil: a woman in black, pale and dreadful – with such an air also, and such a face! – on the other side of the lake. I was there with the child – quiet for the hour; and in the midst of it she came.'

'Came how – from where?'

'From where they come from! She just appeared and stood there – but not so near.'

'And without coming nearer?'

'Oh, for the effect and the feeling, she might have been as close as you!'

My friend, with an odd impulse, fell back a step. 'Was she someone you've never seen?'

'Yes. But someone the child has. Someone *you* have.' Then, to show how I had thought it all out: 'My predecessor – the one who died.'

'Miss Jessel?'

'Miss Jessel. You don't believe me?' I pressed.

She turned right and left in her distress. 'How can you be sure?'

This drew from me, in the state of my nerves, a flash of impatience. 'Then ask Flora – *she's* sure!' But I had no sooner spoken than I caught myself up. 'No, for God's sake, *don't*! She'll say she isn't – she'll lie!'

Mrs Grose was not too bewildered instinctively to protest. 'Ah, how *can* you?'

'Because I'm clear. Flora doesn't want me to know.'

'It's only then to spare you.'

'No, no – there are depths, depths! The more I go over it, the more I see in it, and the more I see in it the more I fear. I don't know what I *don't* see – what I *don't* fear!'

Mrs Grose tried to keep up with me. 'You mean you're afraid of seeing her again?'

'Oh no; that's nothing – now!' Then I explained. 'It's of *not* seeing her.'

But my companion only looked wan. 'I don't understand you'.

'Why, it's that the child may keep it up – and that the child assuredly *will* – without my knowing it.'

At the image of this possibility Mrs Grose for a moment collapsed, yet presently to pull herself together again, as if from the positive force of the sense of what, should we yield an inch, there would really be to give way to. 'Dear, dear – we must keep our heads! And after all, if she doesn't mind it –!' She even tried a grim joke. 'Perhaps she likes it!'

'Likes *such* things – a scrap of an infant!'

'Isn't it just a proof of her blessed innocence?' my friend bravely inquired.

She brought me, for the instant, almost round. 'Oh, we must clutch at *that* – we must cling to it! If it isn't a proof of what you say, it's a proof of – God knows what! For the woman's a horror of horrors.'

Mrs Grose, at this, fixed her eyes a minute on the ground; then at last raising them, 'Tell me how you know,' she said.

'Then you admit it's what she was?' I cried.

'Tell me how you know,' my friend simply repeated.

'Know? By seeing her! By the way she looked.'

'At you, do you mean – so wickedly?'

'Dear me, no – I could have borne that. She gave me never a glance. She only fixed the child.'

Mrs Grose tried to see it. 'Fixed her?'

'Ah, with such awful eyes!'

She stared at mine as if they might really have resembled them. 'Do you mean of dislike?'

'God help us, no. Of something much worse.'

'Worse than dislike?' – this left her indeed at a loss.

'With a determination – indescribable. With a kind of fury of intention.'

I made her turn pale. 'Intention?'

'To get hold of her.' Mrs Grose – her eyes just lingering on mine – gave a shudder and walked to the window; and while she stood there looking out I completed my statement. '*That's* what Flora knows.'

After a little, she turned round. 'The person was in black, you say?'

'In mourning – rather poor, almost shabby. But – yes – with extraordinary beauty.' I now recognized to what I had at last, stroke by stroke, brought the victim of my confidence, for she quite visibly weighed this. 'Oh, handsome – very, very,' I insisted; 'wonderfully handsome. But infamous.'

She slowly came back to me. 'Miss Jessel – *was* infamous.' She once more took my hand in both her own, holding it as tight as if to fortify me against the increase of alarm I might draw from this disclosure. 'They were both infamous,' she finally said.

So, for a little, we faced it once more together; and I found absolutely a degree of help in seeing it now so straight. 'I appreciate,' I said, 'the great decency of your not having hitherto spoken; but the time has certainly come to give me the whole thing.' She appeared to assent to this, but still only in silence; seeing which I went on: 'I must have it now. Of what did she die? Come, there was something between them.'

'There was everything.'

'In spite of the difference –?'

'Oh, of their rank, their condition' – she brought it woefully out. '*She* was a lady.'

I turned it over; I again saw. 'Yes – she was a lady.'

'And he so dreadfully below,' said Mrs Grose.

I felt that I doubtless needn't press too hard, in such company, on the place of a servant in the scale; but there was nothing to prevent an acceptance of my companion's own measure of my predecessor's abasement. There was a way to deal with that, and I dealt; the more readily for my full vision – on the evidence – of our employer's late clever, good-looking 'own man'; impudent, assured, spoiled, depraved. 'The fellow was a hound.'

Mrs Grose considered as if it were perhaps a little a case for a sense of shades. 'I've never seen one like him. He did what he wished.'

'With *her?*'

'With them all.'

It was as if now in my friend's own eyes Miss Jessel had again appeared. I seemed at any rate, for an instant, to see their evocation of her as distinctly as I had seen her by the pond; and I brought out with decision: 'It must have been also what *she* wished!'

Mrs Grose's face signified that it had been indeed, but she said at the same time: 'Poor woman – she paid for it!'

'Then you do know what she died of?' I asked.

'No – I know nothing. I wanted not to know; I was glad enough I didn't; and I thanked heaven she was well out of this!'

'Yet you had, then, your idea – '

'Of her real reason for leaving? Oh yes – as to that. She couldn't have stayed. Fancy it here – for a governess! And afterwards I imagined – and I still imagine. And what I imagine is dreadful.'

'Not so dreadful as what *I* do,' I replied; on which I must have shown her – as I was indeed but too conscious – a front of miserable defeat. It brought out again all her compassion for me, and at the renewed touch of her kindness my power to resist broke down. I burst, as I had, the other time, made her burst, into tears; she took me to her motherly breast, and my lamentation overflowed. 'I don't do it!' I sobbed in despair; 'I don't save or shield them! It's far worse than I dreamed – they're lost!'

The rest, as they say, has to be read to be believed – or, crucially, not believed, for it's clear that this is either a classic ghost-story with real ghosts or, more worryingly, that it isn't. Henry James's famously serpent-like sentences are phrased in such a way that more or less everything the governess says, thinks, sees, hears could go either way. And the same could be said of everything Mrs Grose and the children say. So either the ghosts are real or the governess is seeing things – that is, not seeing anything but imagining the projected fears of her own overworked mind. Obsessive, hysterical, mad, the definitive unreliable narrator? Or a reliable reporter? And if an obsessive-hysteric, why?

To return to the beginning, it's striking how one of the very few quite certain things that Douglas establishes is that this is, in at least a sense, a love-story. When Douglas says that the governess had never told her story before, the company wonder why. Douglas fixes the narrator with a look and says: 'You'll easily judge . . . *you* will.' At this the narrator, returning his fixed look, says: 'I see. She was in love.' Douglas laughs. 'You *are* acute. Yes, she was in love. That is she had been.' When one of the listeners, Mrs Griffin, asks who the governess was in love with, Douglas says that 'the story won't tell . . . not in any literal, vulgar way'. Well, does it? One obvious candidate for who she's in love with is her handsome and charming employer. Douglas himself, just before starting the story, seems to agree with the suggestion that 'the beauty' of the governess's 'passion' was that she only saw this man twice. And in the opening pages the governess herself happily admits to a romantic infatuation with him, focused on a desire to please him and to be acknowledged in her desire. But Douglas has said that 'the story *won't* tell' of her love in any literal way and her feelings for her employer are literal and obvious enough, even to Mrs Grose.

But she is in love. And the challenge to 'acute' readers, like the male narrator but not, apparently, like Mrs Griffin, is to assess that love and its object or objects. What are the other possibilities that Douglas might have meant, less literal or vulgar? In love with Peter Quint or Quint in the guise of his master? When the figure on the tower is first seen, the governess mistakes him for her employer about whom she's been romantically musing, day-dreaming an encounter with the 'kind light' of his smile and approving looks. Then: 'my imagination . . . turned real. He did stand there!' After a moment of bewildered double-vision she realises that she's looking at someone 'very erect' who 'seemed to fix me . . . looking at me hard . . . and even as he turned away still markedly fixed me'. It's odd how this fixing duplicates the mutually fixing looks shared between Douglas and the narrator when the governess being in love is first discussed. I'm also reminded of Hamlet's father's ghost who 'fixed his eyes . . . constantly' on the terrified guards. Whatever, the words evoke a sexually threatening presence, the dark other or double to the 'kind light' of the governess's employer. The governess later describes him as 'looking like an actor' and wearing borrowed (his master's?) clothes.

In that later description, the physical details – his 'red hair, very red, close-curling' – evoke (as recent essays have shown) the stereotypical cad, the sexually rapacious villain of Victorian culture as much as they evoke a 'real' man – the kind of villain the governess is reading about when we see her reading Fielding's *Amelia*. One possibility is that Quint is a projection of the sexual power the governess longs to submit to but can only fear and repress. In her fear she externalises and demonises him. Then Miss Jessel may be a projected, dark other version of herself (the stereotypical 'fallen woman') and the Quint/Jessel relationship the repressed double to hers with her employer. And, by the same logic, the 'joy' she finds in the 'heroism' of her role as a 'screen' to protect the children from the dark couple (like Carroll's White Knight keeping Alice from the dark forest) could be a self-deluding projection of her own obsessive-possessive feelings for the children. (She finds herself standing in for Quint when she repeats his stare through the window, frightening Mrs Grose.) For the children may be the object of her love in a way that is both obvious to her and not – for she may love them as substitutes for darker and more adult relations. And the dark powers she assumes Quint and Jessel have over the children could be projections of the actual but repressed desires she has for them. 'I don't do it!' sobs the governess at the end of this extract.

Or she's in love with herself. A nice detail has her noticing, on her arrival at Bly, the mirrors in her room, 'the long glasses in which, for the first time, I could see myself from head to foot'. Here's the Narcissus story again. Young and hitherto sheltered in a 'small, smothered life' (the word 'smothered' will come to haunt this text), she's suddenly given power, control, autonomy, a sense of self and value, the experience of 'being amused, and even amusing', a sense of her bodily desirability – but along with a kind of in-built frustration because the children are so self-sufficient and because her need for approval is blocked by her employer. Desire is off its rein and (perhaps this is the best way of putting it) has no object, no objective, so it veers uncontrollably across the text as a series of frustrated substitutes, tangled in wilder and more desperate imaginative notions. We've reached the point in the text when she paranoiacally assumes that the children know everything and cruelly collude with the 'ghosts' at her expense. Love is like that. Especially love where the object is more imagined than real. It's an acutely painful, self-inturned narcissism. It's like an endless stumbling from one inadequate goal to another. But if love is like that the same might be said of language and of interpretation.

Modern psychoanalytic theory argues that both desire and language are structured as chains of always inadequate substitutes, always doomed to pursue illusionary goals – the goals of wholeness, of absolute meaning, of completed fulfilment. This is what the infant-self emerges into when, after the crucial and wounding loss of whole identifying oneness with the mother, it enters the realm of language and other signifying systems. Our extract from *The Turn of the Screw* ends with the governess sobbing on Mrs Grose's 'motherly breast', a cry of loss, the loss that shadows all our desires and needs.

What's so suggestive about this chilling tale is that it's not just the governess's desire but language and interpretation too that seem set here in a chain of endlessly receding mirrors. The issues are interconnected. This is established from the outset, in the framings of the narrative with which we began, for the way the story, in its spoken and written forms, is handed on seems almost like a neurotic or obsessive process, one defined by muted and incomplete suggestion, half-formed or unspoken desire – between the governess and Douglas, between Douglas and the narrator. I mustn't spoil the ending but I can add that the opening idea of the story being handed on across an obscure chain of desire is duplicated much later when we hear more of why Miles was asked to leave his school. The process of handing on the story as love-gift is also what we found in Carroll's 'Alice' books. Carroll and the governess have exactly this in common: the obsessive-neurotic fear of losing children to maturity. (This is also the psychic mechanism that drives Holden Caulfield in Salinger's *The Catcher in the Rye*.)

The story that reaches us through these mutedly desiring intermediaries may be one in which the governess chases receding mirrors of her own illusionary, delusionary, displaced desires, finding them everywhere apart from where they originate, in her repressed self. But it's also one where the reader is forced to undergo the challenge, equivalent to the challenge the governess feels she has set for herself or had set for her, of creating the meaning out of a chain of teasingly suggestive signs. That is, like the governess, it's we who write and create, using 'imagination' to make 'real' sense, connecting the chain together for the illusion of wholeness – and frightening the wits out of ourselves as we do so. (And the process of making meaning from the pattern is, of course, exactly what happens in *The Yellow Wallpaper*.) And we're happy to do so because we too are on a chain of desire, the pleasure of reading and of making.

A school of criticism called reader-response criticism focuses on the role of the reader in directing the meaning-making processes of reading. It may be applied to all texts, but *The Turn of the Screw* demands it in an unprecedentedly pure way. The 'meaning' of the text is, precisely, the reading the reader reads, the story we make from the signs on the narrative surface. We are united with the governess in that activity, though our stories may not be the same as hers. The scene by the lake at the end of this extract where Flora is playing with her makeshift boat has no single unique 'meaning' lying inside ready to be taken out. Meaning never works like that. Meaning is always a process and a transaction. But here the process is 'acute'. Who exactly is turning the screws when the 'mast' being fixed in the 'hole' is read suggestively? That is James's uncanny skill, almost frightening itself, in making us write our own ghost-story – or something even more frightening than that.

One of the best volumes in the Case Studies in Contemporary Criticism series is Peter G. Beidler's collection on *The Turn of the Screw* (Boston, Bedford Books, 1995). It prints the text and contains impressive critical essays written from a variety of critical viewpoints, all of which illuminate this endlessly fascinating story. Benjamin Britten's opera (1954) is a version very much worth seeking out. A strong collection of reader-response essays (including two on *The Yellow Wallpaper*) is in *Readers and Reading*, edited by Andrew Bennett (Harlow, Longman, 1995). The psychoanalytic approach above is influenced by the work of Jacques Lacan. He is notoriously difficult and thus best approached through the help of others. A good introduction is by Malcolm Bowie in John Sturrock's *Structuralism and Since* (Oxford, Oxford University Press, 1979). Jane Gallop's *The Daughter's Seduction* (see last endnote, p. 323) is Lacanian in its emphasis. The psychoanalytic study of texts is very much part of the critical mainstream now and it has a long history. Elizabeth Wright's *Psychoanalytic Criticism* (London, Methuen, 1984) is a clear guide. Freud couldn't have found the Oedipal complex without reading it in *Hamlet*.

18

CONRAD'S *THE SECRET AGENT*

Journeying into political vision

This and the next chapter could be read as a pair but don't need to be. They are both extracts from novels set in cities in the first decades of the twentieth century and they both describe journeys. The commentary explores them in the way their sharply differing languages and styles shape the narratives of change, escape and struggle, and in the way they draw on and develop the idea of the journey, a recurrent motif in literary culture. The extract here is from Joseph Conrad's *The Secret Agent* (1907) and it provides us with more material about people, like Bartleby, whose strangeness proves to be a source of insight.

Here is a little less than half of Chapter 8 of *The Secret Agent*. It's almost a self-contained episode in the novel's elaborate plot which we won't be needing to deal with here. It concerns the decision of an old lady to avoid becoming a burden on her daughter's family with whom she has hitherto lived. Her daughter Winnie fails to appreciate the unselfishness of her mother's motives. The two women travel in this episode to an almshouse provided by a charity. They travel by horse and carriage. And along with Mrs Winnie Verloc and Mrs Verloc's mother goes Winnie's younger brother Stevie. Stevie is 'a little peculiar' and 'absent-minded'. That is, Stevie is what used to be called simple.

Winnie, with her hat on, silent behind her mother's back, went on arranging the collar of the old woman's cloak. She got her handbag, an umbrella, with an impassive face. The time had come for the expenditure of the sum of three-and-sixpence on what might well be supposed the last cab drive of Mrs. Verloc's mother's life. They went out at the shop door.

The conveyance awaiting them would have illustrated the proverb that 'truth can be more cruel than caricature', if such a proverb existed. Crawling behind an infirm horse, a metropolitan hackney carriage drew up on wobbly wheels and with a maimed driver on the box. This last peculiarity caused some embarrassment. Catching sight of a hooked iron contrivance protruding from the left sleeve of the man's coat, Mrs. Verloc's mother lost suddenly the heroic courage of these days. She really couldn't trust herself. 'What do you think, Winnie?' She hung back. The passionate expostulations of the big-faced cabman seemed to be squeezed out of a blocked throat. Leaning over from his box, he whispered with mysterious indignation. What was the matter now? Was it possible to treat a man so? His enormous and unwashed countenance flamed red in the muddy stretch of the street. Was it likely they would have given him a licence, he inquired desperately, if—

The police constable of the locality quieted him by a friendly glance; then addressing himself to the two women without marked consideration, said:

'He's been driving a cab for twenty years. I never knew him to have an accident.'

'Accident!' shouted the driver in a scornful whisper.

The policeman's testimony settled it. The modest assemblage of seven people, mostly under age, dispersed. Winnie followed her mother into the cab. Stevie climbed on the box. His vacant mouth and distressed eyes depicted the state of his mind in regard to the transactions which were taking place. In the narrow streets the progress of the journey was made sensible to those within by the near fronts of the houses gliding past slowly and shakily, with a great rattle and jingling of glass, as if about to collapse behind the cab; and the infirm horse, with the harness hung over his sharp backbone flapping very loose about his thighs, appeared to be dancing mincingly on his toes with infinite patience. Later on, in the wider space of Whitehall, all visual evidences of motion became imperceptible. The rattle and jingle of glass went on indefinitely in front of the long Treasury building – and time itself seemed to stand still.

At last Winnie observed: 'This isn't a very good horse.'

Her eyes gleamed in the shadow of the cab straight ahead, immovable. On the box, Stevie shut his vacant mouth first, in order to ejaculate earnestly: 'Don't.'

The driver, holding high the reins twisted around the hook, took no notice. Perhaps he had not heard. Stevie's breast heaved.

'Don't whip.'

The man turned slowly his bloated and sodden face of many colours bristling with white hairs. His little red eyes glistened with moisture. His big lips had a violet tint. They remained closed. With the dirty back of his whip-hand he rubbed the stubble sprouting on his enormous chin.

'You mustn't,' stammered out Stevie violently. 'It hurts.'

'Mustn't whip,' queried the other in a thoughtful whisper, and immediately whipped. He did this, not because his soul was cruel and his heart evil, but because he had to earn his fare. And for a time the walls of St. Stephen's, with its towers and pinnacles, contemplated in immobility and silence a cab that jingled. It rolled too, however. But on the bridge there was a commotion. Stevie suddenly proceeded to get down from the box. There were shouts on the pavement, people ran forward, the driver pulled up, whispering curses of indignation and astonishment. Winnie lowered the window, and put her head out, white as a ghost. In the depths of the cab, her mother was exclaiming, in tones of anguish: 'Is that boy hurt? Is that boy hurt?'

Stevie was not hurt, he had not even fallen, but excitement as usual had robbed him of the power of connected speech. He could do no more than stammer at the window: 'Too heavy. Too heavy.' Winnie put out her hand on to his shoulder.

'Stevie! Get up on the box directly, and don't try to get down again.'

'No. No. Walk. Must walk.'

In trying to state the nature of that necessity he stammered himself into utter incoherence. No physical impossibility stood in the way of his whim. Stevie could have managed easily to keep pace with the infirm, dancing horse without getting out of breath. But his sister withheld her consent decisively. 'The idea! Who ever heard of such a thing! Run after a cab!' Her mother, frightened and helpless in the depths of the conveyance, entreated:

'Oh, don't let him, Winnie. He'll get lost. Don't let him.'

'Certainly not. What next! Mr. Verloc will be sorry to hear of this nonsense, Stevie, I can tell you. He won't be happy at all.'

The idea of Mr. Verloc's grief and unhappiness acting as usual powerfully upon Stevie's fundamentally docile disposition, he abandoned all resistance, and climbed up again on the box, with a face of despair.

The cabby turned at him his enormous and inflamed countenance truculently. 'Don't you go for trying this silly game again, young fellow.'

After delivering himself thus in a stern whisper, strained almost to extinction, he drove on, ruminating solemnly. To his mind the incident remained somewhat obscure. But his intellect, though it had lost its pristine vivacity in the benumbing years of sedentary exposure to the weather, lacked not independence or sanity. Gravely he dismissed the hypothesis of Stevie being a drunken young nipper.

Inside the cab the spell of silence, in which the two women had endured shoulder to shoulder the jolting, rattling, and jingling of the journey, had been broken by Stevie's outbreak. Winnie raised her voice.

'You've done what you wanted, Mother. You'll have only yourself to thank for it if you aren't happy afterwards. And I don't think you'll be. That I don't. Weren't you comfortable enough in the house? Whatever people'll think of us – you throwing yourself like this on a Charity?'

'My dear,' screamed the old woman earnestly above the noise, 'you've been the best of daughters to me. As to Mr. Verloc – there—'

Words failing her on the subject of Mr. Verloc's excellence, she turned her old tearful eyes to the roof of the cab. Then she averted her head on the pretence of looking out of the window, as if to judge of their progress. It was insignificant, and went on close to the curbstone. Night, the early dirty night, the sinister, noisy, hopeless and rowdy night of South London, had overtaken her on her last cab drive. In the gas-light of the low-fronted shops her big cheeks glowed with an orange hue under a black and mauve bonnet.

Mrs. Verloc's mother's complexion had become yellow by the effect of age and from a natural predisposition to bilious-ness, favoured by the trials of a difficult and worried exist-ence, first as wife, then as widow. It was a complexion that under the influence of a blush would take on an orange tint. And this woman, modest indeed but hardened in the fires of adversity, of an age, moreover, when blushes are not expected, had positively blushed before her daughter. In the privacy of a four-wheeler, on her way to a charity cottage (one of a row) which by the exiguity of its dimensions and the simplicity of its accommodation, might well have been devised in kindness as a place of training for the still more straitened circumstances of the grave, she was forced to hide from her own child a blush of remorse and shame.

[. . .]

The cab rattled, jingled, jolted; in fact, the last was quite extraordinary. By its disproportionate violence and magnitude it obliterated every sensation of onward movement; and the effect was of being shaken in a stationary apparatus like a medieval device for the punishment of crime, or some very new-fangled invention for the cure of a sluggish liver. It was extremely distressing; and the raising of Mrs. Verloc's mother's voice sounded like a wail of pain.

'I know, my dear, you'll come to see me as often as you can spare the time. Won't you?'

'Of course,' answered Winnie shortly, staring straight before her.

And the cab jolted in front of a steamy, greasy shop in a blaze of gas and in the smell of fried fish.

The old woman raised a wail again.

'And, my dear, I must see that poor boy every Sunday. He won't mind spending the day with his old mother—'

Winnie screamed out stolidly:

'Mind! I should think not. That poor boy will miss you

something cruel. I wish you had thought a little of that, Mother.'

Not think of it! The heroic woman swallowed a playful and inconvenient object like a billiard ball, which had tried to jump out of her throat. Winnie sat mute for a while, pouting at the front of the cab, then snapped out, which was an unusual tone with her:

'I expect I'll have a job with him at first, he'll be that restless—'

'Whatever you do, don't let him worry your husband, my dear.'

Thus they discussed on familiar lines the bearings of a new situation. And the cab jolted. Mrs. Verloc's mother expressed some misgivings. Could Stevie be trusted to come all that way alone? Winnie maintained that he was much less 'absent-minded' now. They agreed as to that. It could not be denied. Much less – hardly at all. They shouted at each other in the jingle with comparative cheerfulness. But suddenly the maternal anxiety broke out afresh. There were two omnibuses to take, and a short walk between. It was too difficult! The old woman gave way to grief and consternation.

Winnie stared forward.

'Don't you upset yourself like this, Mother. You must see him, of course.'

'No, my dear. I'll try not to'.

She mopped her streaming eyes.

'But you can't spare the time to come with him, and if he should forget himself and lose his way and somebody spoke to him sharply, his name and address may slip his memory and he'll remain lost for days and days—'

The vision of a workhouse infirmary for poor Stevie – if only during inquiries – wrung her heart. For she was a proud woman. Winnie's stare had grown hard, intent, inventive.

'I can't bring him to you himself myself every week,' she cried. 'But don't you worry, Mother. I'll see to it that he don't get lost for long.'

They felt a peculiar bump; a vision of brick pillars lingered before the rattling windows of the cab; a sudden cessation of atrocious jolting and uproarious jingling dazed the two women. What had happened? They sat motionless and scared in the profound stillness, till the door came open, and a rough, strained whispering was heard:

'Here you are!'

A range of gabled little houses, with one dim yellow window on the ground floor, surrounded the dark open space of a grass plot planted with shrubs and railed off from the patchwork of lights and shadows in the wide road, resounding with the dull rumble of traffic. Before the door of one of these tiny houses – one without a light in the little downstairs window – the cab had come to a standstill. Mrs. Verloc's mother got out first, backwards, with a key in her hand. Winnie lingered on the flagstone path to pay the cabman. Stevie, after helping to carry inside a lot of small parcels, came out and stood under the light of a gas-lamp belonging to the Charity. The cabman looked at the pieces of silver, which, appearing very minute in his big, grimy palm, symbolized the insignificant results which reward the ambitious courage and toil of a mankind whose day is short on this earth of evil.

He had been paid decently – four one-shilling pieces – and he contemplated them in perfect stillness, as if they had been the surprising terms of a melancholy problem. The slow transfer of that treasure to an inner pocket demanded much laborious groping in the depths of decayed clothing. His form was squat and without flexibility. Stevie, slender, his shoulders a little up, and his hands thrust deep in the side pockets of his warm overcoat, stood at the edge of the path, pouting.

The cabman, pausing in his deliberate movements, seemed struck by some misty recollection.

'Oh! 'Ere you are, young fellow,' he whispered. 'You'll know him again – won't you?'

Stevie was staring at the horse, whose hind quarters appeared unduly elevated by the effect of emaciation. The little stiff tail seemed to have been fitted in for a heartless joke; and at the other end the thin, flat neck, like a plank covered with old horse-hide, drooped to the ground under the weight of an enormous bony head. The ears hung at different angles, negligently; and the macabre figure of that mute dweller on the earth steamed straight up from ribs and backbone in the muggy stillness of the air.

The cabman struck lightly Stevie's breast with the iron hook protruding from a ragged, greasy sleeve.

'Look 'ere, young fellow. 'Ow'd *you* like to sit behind this 'oss up to two o'clock in the morning p'raps?'

Stevie looked vacantly into the fierce little eyes with red-edged lids.

'He ain't lame,' pursued the other, whispering with energy. 'He ain't got no sore places on 'im. 'Ere he is. 'Ow would *you* like—'

His strained, extinct voice invested his utterance with a character of vehement secrecy. Stevie's vacant gaze was changing slowly into dread.

'You may well look! Till three and four o'clock in the morning. Cold and 'ungry. Looking for fares. Drunks.'

His jovial purple cheeks bristled with white hairs; and like Virgil's Silenus, who, his face smeared with the juice of berries, discoursed of Olympian God to the innocent shepherds of Sicily, he talked to Stevie of domestic matters and the affairs of men whose sufferings are great and immortality by no means assured.

'I am a night cabby, I am,' he whispered, with a sort of boastful exasperation. 'I've got to take out what they will blooming well give me at the yard. I've got my missus and four kids at 'ome.'

The monstrous nature of that declaration of paternity seemed to strike the world dumb. A silence reigned, during which the flanks of the old horse, the steed of apocalyptic misery, smoked upwards in the light of the charitable gas-lamp.

The cabman grunted, then added in his mysterious whisper:

'This ain't an easy world.'

Stevie's face had been twitching for some time, and at last his feelings burst out in their usual concise form.

'Bad! Bad!'

His gaze remained fixed on the ribs of the horse, self-conscious and sombre, as though he were afraid to look about him at the badness of the world. And his slenderness, his rosy lips and pale, clear complexion, gave him the aspect of a delicate boy, not withstanding the fluffy growth of golden hair on his cheeks. He pouted in a scared way like a child. The cabman, short and broad, eyed him with his fierce little eyes that seemed to smart in a clear and corroding liquid.

"Ard on 'osses, but dam' sight 'arder on poor chaps like me,' he wheezed just audibly.

'Poor! Poor!' stammered out Stevie, pushing his hands deeper into his pockets with convulsive sympathy. He could say nothing; for the tenderness to all pain and misery, the desire to make the horse happy and the cabman happy, had reached the point of a bizarre longing to take them to bed with him. And that, he knew, was impossible. For Stevie was not mad. It was, as it were, a symbolic longing; and at the same time it was very distinct, because springing from experience, the mother of wisdom. Thus when as a child he cowered in a dark corner scared, wretched, sore, and miserable with the black, black misery of his soul, his sister Winnie used to come along, and carry him off to bed with her, as into a heaven of consoling peace. Stevie, though apt to forget mere facts, such as his name and address, for instance, had a faithful memory of sensations. To be taken into a bed of compassion was the supreme remedy, with the only one disadvantage of being difficult of application on a large scale. And looking at the cabman, Stevie perceived this clearly because he was reasonable.

The cabman went on with his leisurely preparations as if Stevie had not existed. He made as if to hoist himself on the box, but at the last moment from some obscure motive, perhaps merely from disgust with carriage exercise, desisted. He approached instead the motionless partner of his labours, and stooping to seize the bridle, lifted up the big, weary head to the height of his shoulder with one effort of his right arm, like a feat of strength.

'Come on,' he whispered secretly.

Limping, he led the cab away. There was an air of austerity in this departure, the scrunched gravel of the drive crying out under the slowly turning wheels, the horse's lean thighs moving with ascetic deliberation away from the light into the obscurity of the open space bordered dimly by the pointed roofs and the feebly shining windows of the little almshouses. The plaint of the gravel travelled slowly all round the drive. Between the lamps of the charitable gate-way the slow cortège reappeared lighted up for a moment, the short, thick man limping busily, with the horse's head held aloft in his fist, the lank animal walking in stiff and forlorn dignity, the dark, low box on wheels rolling behind comically with an air of waddling. They turned to the left. There was a pub down the street, within fifty yards of the gate.

Stevie, left alone beside the private lamp-post of the Charity, his hands thrust deep into his pockets, glared with vacant sulkiness. At the bottom of his pockets his incapable weak hands were clinched hard into a pair of angry fists. In the face of anything which affected directly or indirectly his morbid dread of pain, Stevie ended by turning vicious. A magnanimous indignation swelled his frail chest to bursting, and caused his candid eyes to squint. Supremely wise in knowing his own powerlessness, Stevie was not wise enough to restrain his passions. The tenderness of his universal charity had two phases as indissolubly joined and connected as the reverse and obverse sides of a medal. The anguish of immoderate compassion was succeeded by the pain of an innocent but pitiless rage. Those two states expressing themselves outwardly by the same signs of futile bodily agitation, his sister Winnie soothed his excitement without ever fathoming its twofold character. Mrs. Verloc wasted no portion of this transient life in seeking for fundamental information. This is a sort of economy having all the appearances and some of the advantages of prudence. Obviously it may be good for one not to know too much. And such a view accords very well with constitutional indolence.

On that evening on which it may be said that Mrs. Verloc's mother having parted for good from her children had also departed this life, Winnie Verloc did not investigate her brother's psychology. The poor boy was excited, of course. After once more assuring the old woman on the threshold that she would know how to guard against the risk of Stevie losing himself for very long on his pilgrimages of filial piety, she took her brother's arm to walk away. Stevie did not even mutter to himself, but with the special sense of sisterly devotion developed in her earliest infancy, she felt that the boy was very much excited indeed. Holding tight to his arm, under the appearance of leaning on it, she thought of some words suitable to the occasion.

'Now, Stevie, you must look well after me at the crossings, and get first into the bus, like a good brother.'

This appeal to manly protection was received by Stevie with his usual docility. It flattered him. He raised his head and threw out his chest.

'Don't be nervous, Winnie. Mustn't be nervous! Bus all right,' he answered in a brusque slurring stammer partaking of the timorousness of a child and the resolution of a man. He advanced fearlessly with the woman on his arm, but his lower lip dropped. Nevertheless, on the pavement of the squalid and wide thoroughfare whose poverty in all the amenities of life stood foolishly exposed by a mad profusion of gas-lights, their resemblance to each other was so pronounced as to strike the casual passers-by.

Before the doors of the public-house at the corner, where the profusion of gas-light reached the height of positive wickedness, a four-wheeled cab standing by the curbstone with no one on the box, seemed cast out into the gutter on account of irremediable decay. Mrs. Verloc recognized the conveyance. Its aspect was so profoundly lamentable, with such a perfection of grotesque misery and weirdness of macabre details as if it were the Cab of Death itself, that Mrs. Verloc, with that ready compassion of a woman for a horse (when she is not sitting behind him), exclaimed vaguely:

'Poor brute!'

Hanging back suddenly, Stevie inflicted an arresting jerk upon his sister.

'Poor! Poor!' he ejaculated appreciatively. 'Cabman poor too. He told me himself.'

The contemplation of the infirm and lonely steed overcame him. Jostled, but obstinate, he would remain there, trying to express the view newly opened to his sympathies of the human and equine misery in close association. But it was very difficult. 'Poor brute, poor people!' was all he could repeat. It did not seem forcible enough, and he came to a stop with an angry splutter: 'Shame!' Stevie was no master of phrases, and perhaps for that very reason his thoughts lacked clearness and precision. But he felt with greater completeness and some profundity. That little word contained all his sense of indignation and horror at one sort of wretchedness having to feed upon the anguish of the other – at the poor cabman beating the poor horse in the name, as it were, of his poor kids at home. And Stevie knew what it was to be beaten. He knew it from experience. It was a bad world. Bad! Bad!

Mrs. Verloc, his only sister, guardian, and protector, could not pretend to such depths of insight. Moreover, she had not experienced the magic of the cabman's eloquence. She was in the dark as to the inwardness of the word 'Shame'. And she said placidly:

'Come along, Stevie. You can't help that.'

The docile Stevie went along; but now he went along without pride, shamblingly, and muttering half words, and even words that would have been whole if they had not been made up of halves that did not belong to each other. It was as though he had been trying to fit all the words he could remember to his sentiments in order to get some sort of corresponding idea. And, as a matter of fact, he got it at last. He hung back to utter it at once.

'Bad world for poor people.'

Directly he had expressed that thought he became aware that it was familiar to him already in all its consequences. This circumstance strengthened his conviction immensely, but also augmented his indignation. Somebody, he felt, ought to be punished for it – punished with great severity. Being no sceptic, but a moral creature, he was in a manner at the mercy of his righteous passions.

'Beastly!' he added concisely.

It was clear to Mrs. Verloc that he was greatly excited.

'Nobody can help that,' she said. 'Do come along. Is that the way you're taking care of me?'

Stevie's dawning recognition of brutal social realities is delivered to us here by means of the alienating effect of his being 'simple'. The result is a sharp political critique, equivalent to the way Bartleby's refusal to function by the usual social rules estranges those rules and conventions. Stevie's newly awakened and furious social insight is at least partly comic, particularly in his wanting to take the cabby and the horse to his bed, but the comedy sharpens the social critique yet further, for it's as if Conrad's narrative voice, which is somewhere between playful and sardonic, teases the reader with the easy option of being patronisingly amused with Stevie.

The narrative voice here is remarkable. The notion of the omniscient narrator, the third-party narrator who knows everything and unfolds the narrative as if it's happening in real-time and yet also with god-like authority, is a paradox that grew up at the same time as the realist novel itself. But there is something inherently comic in the convention and Conrad seems to have stylised his voice here deliberately to tip it into comedy. The style is poised and urbane and, above all, knowing. It's as if the narrative and its assumed reader are positioned in a class above the protagonists and we have to negotiate the irony and assess the true anger in the passage.

But the very physicality and rawness of Stevie's responses, his bodily anguish, insist that we can't sustain any class superiority. Stevie, perhaps like Bartleby, seems to be missing a usual human layer, the one which limits our susceptibility to the pain of others. His 'simplicity' allows him more direct access to that pain, just as his simple language, struggling to articulate at all, articulates the situation ('bad world for poor people') with such force. This is the power of the implied critique. It's the child's pure and direct emotional responsiveness which adulthood and cultural socialisation blunt and redirect into safer responses. Stevie's vision is like Blake's in its radical and childlike simplicity and Blake was considered mad. Stevie is like a holy fool, a figure granted a particularly pure form of visionary understanding, like King Lear's Fool. Perhaps Gulliver in Book Four of his travels becomes a holy fool.

Thus also the significance of the scene's location and the role of Mrs Verloc, here as elsewhere. The city-scape, like Manhattan in *Bartleby*, is peopled with figures of alienated normality, like the cabby for whom the pressures of everyday life mean he can't engage with Stevie's feelings for his horse, and like Winnie whose attitude of not looking too closely into things is not just a result of laziness or stupidity, or even a result of her husband's peculiar business dealings, but an exact and very typical response to the sheer awfulness of everyday life all around her, as around us. To think outside oneself is always pain. If we're not like the sardonic narrator in this passage, the temptation is to be like Winnie, to avert our eyes, to be typically middle-class. We explored the problems in that position in the chapter on Wilde's *The Happy Prince*.

Thus also the importance of the journey-motif. It's remarkable how many literary texts use versions of the journey as their narrative structure. But perhaps it's not that remarkable in so far as we routinely conceptualise our own lives as journeys or quests. The comforting thing about journeys and quests is that journeys tend to get somewhere and quests tend to find what is lost. It has been recognised that many folk-tales are quests to re-unite lost members of families and that such a narrative has very deep and extensive social and psychological roots. (As usual Jack Zipes is the authority here.) This passage from *The Secret Agent* plays subtle variations on the idea. Winnie's mother is breaking up the family unit for the unselfish goal of further bonding the remaining three members. Her goal is to retire to the margins, in the interests of the younger generation, a typical folk-tale formula.

But what we also have here is an example of journeying simultaneously literal and figurative. Again, this has a long and distinguished literary pedigree, and again it reflects the way we consider our own life-histories. Indeed, perhaps all literary journeys are both literal and figurative, operating on both the horizontal plane – in time and in place – and the vertical plane – inwards and internal. *King Lear* is a clear case. The protagonists journey to Dover and its cliffs, the edge of England and the world, while simultaneously journeying into their selves. The journey into the heart of human darkness is most memorably narrated by Conrad himself in his *Heart of Darkness*. So just as Winnie, her mother and Stevie are literally journeying to the almshouse, Stevie is journeying on the vertical plane to the raw and painful insights that we have explored above. Again, it's like *The Happy Prince*, where the swallow sets off on a literal and horizontal journey only to discover that he's actually on an internal and vertical journey within. James Joyce's story

'Araby' in his *Dubliners* works in the same way. Such stories, which operate literally and figuratively at the same time, are allegories. The cabby and his horse are literal enough for Stevie to want to take them to bed with him, but they're figurative too, like the cab (a 'Cab of Death itself'), as Conrad suggests by making them seem like creatures of some other-world mythology, the cabby as 'Virgil's Silenus' and the horse a 'steed of apocalyptic misery'. The allegory also positions the cabby as a kind of Charon, the ferryman who conveyed the dead over the river of oblivion. We hear no more of Winnie's mother. But Stevie has, in effect, woken up.

We are not dealing here with the complex plot of this novel but I need to say that Stevie's internal journey, which is his new accession to ideas of class and power, is a crucial development. It becomes, and Stevie becomes, a useful thing, a commodity. That is, the working-class Stevie having, as it were, become revolutionarised here becomes a pawn in a very different game where the rules, unknown to him, are being written from a very great deal higher up the social hierarchy. In terms of both journey and class-consciousness it's a very terrible story.

As usual in this book I hope you've seen enough here to want to read the whole novel. This chapter has contexts that we've seen coincide: the vision-ary insights afforded to an 'odd' or 'simple' character who, though odd, becomes our representative; the relations between the narrative language and Stevie's language; and the notion of journeys without and within. There's a very concentrated and challenging essay on the problematic politics of this novel in Terry Eagleton's *Against the Grain* (London, Verso, 1986). As the title suggests, the novel is, partly, a thriller about double and triple agents, police investigation and high politics and thus can interestingly be read alongside other late nineteenth- and early twentieth-century police and detective thrillers by, for instance, Wilkie Collins and Conan Doyle. Conrad's stylised and polished language has often been discussed in terms of the surprising fact that English was not even his mother-tongue (he was born in Poland). It's remarkable that the writer of the most stylish and polished novels in English from the second half of the twentieth century (regrettably absent from this book) was also not a native English speaker – the Russian-born Vladimir Nabokov.

19

GREEN'S *LIVING*
The working class in modernism and the search for the father

This chapter could be read in conjunction or comparison with the last but doesn't need to be. It presents an extract from Henry Green's *Living* (1929), an account of a young couple journeying from one city to another in 1929. The commentary invites you to think about the extract in the light of representations of working-class life, issues of regionalism and modernism in novels both in and out of the canon, and the searching for family and for escape.

Bert Jones and Lily Gates want a better life than that offered by factory-life and near-poverty in Birmingham. Lily is the one who, despite her guilty sense of the men in her home who depend on her, pressures Bert to make the move. So they do. In this extract (which is edited to focus closely on their story) they journey from Birmingham, where they live and work, to Liverpool where Bert's parents live. They plan to borrow money from his parents in order to emigrate to Canada. Bert Jones doesn't in fact know where his parents currently live but he hasn't told Lily yet.

18

When Lily got to station, bag in hand, she was so tired with strain of walking through streets seeing in each man or woman she passed someone who would ask her where she was going off to with a bag on Sunday morning, and at the first, leaving home like she had — all those lies and the way she crept downstairs had so tired her that she could hardly see who were standing on the platform. Whether were any there she knew. She said in mind she was in such a state now she did not mind if there was someone who'd see her. She put bag down and there, when she looked up again, was Mr. Jones. In his hand was bouquet of tulips.

'Why, what 'ave you got there?'

'I stopped by the cemetery and bought 'em.'

'Whatever did you bring those for?' she said, 'Yes, what for?', growing hysterical. 'Why I nearly fainted away. Oh Bert, 'ow could you?'

'Why, what's the matter? I thought . . .'

'And me thinkin' 'ow I could make myself less conspicuous, yes, and then there you are with a great bunch of flowers on the station platform, why whatever will they think?'

'Think? Oo'll think? What's it matter what they think?'

'You stand where you are while I 'ave a look round your shoulder.'

Trembling, breathing deeply, she peered round his shoulder at those who were to travel with them. She stood by shoulder of the arm below which hung the tulips, his head bent over hers as she peered round and this movement repeated in her knee which was bent over heads of the tulips as they hung. She had on silk stockings today.

She gave up looking at the travellers. She looked now at the tulips.

'Where'll you put them?'

'Where will I put them?' He raised them up till they were upright as they grew.

'Do not!' she said and snatched at his wrist and turned them upside down.

'Oo's being conspicuous now?'

'You go and leave them in the Gentlemen.'

'Leave 'em in the lavatory?'

'Yes, what are you lookin' at me for, we can't take them with us what's come over you, yes, leave 'em in there. Why, at every station the train stopped we'd 'ave porters lookin' in at the window and wondering.'

'Well what's it matter if they do wonder, what do they know?'

'O Bert I do wish I 'adn't come.'

'All right,' he said, 'if that's the way you feel I'll leave 'em

there.' He went off to do this. Looking at her shoes she thought
in mind why you see they'd telegraph back, telegraphs being
free between themselves so to speak, they'd telegraph back
along the line: – seen a young lady with a boy and tulips,
something's up evidently, do the police want 'em, like that,
yes, O why had he bought them? Look at those people on the
platform now watching him going. – But they were not watching him, being too disgusted at having to travel on a Sunday to
notice anything but themselves.

When he came back without the tulips she breathed easier
for it and began to feel for her hair under brim of hat. He was
bewildered.

But they were not long without their tulips. Like old stage
joke they were brought to them by lavatory attendant. As he
gave them to Mr. Jones, who did not resist, he said:

'You'm be by the banks of the river Nile, mister,' he said. 'I
sees you forget 'em out of the corner of me eye from where I was
in the office, and I daint stay longer'n to put me coat on before I
was after you.'

Miss Gates turned and walked off to end of platform furthest
from where other passengers stood.

'You'll 'ave the missus create at you my lad,' he said, 'if you go
hon forgetting.' He turned and started back. 'Maybe, again, you'll
forget 'erself,' he said, more to himself than to Mr. Jones, turning
prophetic. Mr. Jones went after Miss Gates. Now again tulips
hung down bobbing along, thumping against calves of his legs
under plum coloured suit he wore. When he got to her she said:

'I come over bad.'

'Sit on the seat then.'

They sat there.

'Give 'em to me dear,' she said then, suddenly reckless, 'I
don't care and it's a shame to hold 'em the way you are,' and she
took them and rocked them in her arms. He smiled and for a
moment had great relief. (For he wanted badly to go to the
lavatory and having to leave the tulips had not given him time
to have one. Now he could not go back, because of the lavatory
attendant. His mind was fixed on possibility of train being
corridor train.) At this moment train came in.

As on platform suddenly then she had stopped being afraid to meet someone she knew, now in the compartment, empty but for themselves – and, being Sunday, it was not corridor train, – she put tulips on the rack and they did not worry her any more. Now one or two, their heads drooping through meshes of the rack, wobbled at them when train drew out of station.

They sat side by side. Now it was all over she folded eyelids down over her eyes. He thought Derby would be the next stop where there'd be any wait worth calling by the name. Other stations they'd just stop, look out, and be off again.

Tulips, tulips she remembered time of infinite happiness in a cinema when a film was on about tulips. Not about tulips, but tulips came in.

This train stopped at next station. Man came into their compartment. He was working man. They both looked at him, not speaking, and he looked at them and all 3 turned eyes away from each other's eyes. Then he looked again at Mr. Jones and when train started again he said 'Excuse me won' cher but would your name be Pinks?' Mr. Jones said no, his name weren't Pinks. This man said Pinks had a double in him then, they might be twin brothers for all you could tell the difference between them. 'Excuse my asking you like that,' he said and he noticed suddenly tulips on rack above his head, – (he was sitting opposite to them). He had to lean his head back to see them properly and when he did Lily winked at Mr. Jones. Then, bringing his face down to them, again all 3 turned eyes away from each other's eyes.

Lily looked to see if that man should smile but he did not and thought it unobservant in him not to smile at meaning of those tulips. Then she was surprised because Mr. Jones had winked at this man and jerked with his head to other side of the compartment. Both of them went over there, leaving her by herself, and Bert began whispering to him. Miss Gates did not know what to make of it.

They came into next station and stopped. This man got out. As he got out she heard him say to Mr. Jones no, he wouldn't get real chance before Derby. As he went away she plainly heard him say well he hoped it would come out all right for him. She was amazed.

'What'll come out all right for you?' she said and Bert said it was nothing.

'You didn't take 'im into the corner away from me for nothing.'

'I just wanted to ask 'im something.'

'O it's something now is it, instead of being nothing? Ain't supposed to know.'

'Well no, you ain't, that is . . .'

'Why ain't I supposed to know?'

'There weren't anything in it Lil, it was only I . . . I won't tell yer.'

'You will!'

'I won't.'

But she looked so miserable then that he explained. He went red in the face when she began to laugh at him. 'Ah, but I'm not laughing,' he said and she laughed and discussed ways and means with him. They could find no way out. 'Kiss me Bert,' she said but that was no good as he said he could not, the way he was feeling now. Somehow this delighted her. Their journey, at last, was beginning. Every minute they were further from Birmingham and everything harassing was away behind them now. And they were getting near to Derby.

When train drew into Derby station he ran out of the train and she leant out of the window. When he came back all smiles she opened door for him from where she was on the inside, and once he was in she put hands on his shoulders and pushed him down onto the seat. She sat down across his legs and kissed him.

Then she got down and sat by his side. Train started again. Now at last, she thought in mind, this journey is begun. He kissed her.

But it's not like that. While she expected to be happy she was not and Mr. Jones could only think of what they would do when they got to Liverpool.

For as racing pigeon fly in the sky, always they go round

above house which provides for them or, if loosed at a distance from that house then they fly straight there, so her thoughts would not point away long from house which had provided for her.

With us it is not only food, as possibly it is for pigeon, but if we are for any length of time among those who love us and whom we love too, then those people become part of ourselves.

As, in Yorkshire, the housewives on a Sunday will go out, in their aprons, carrying a pigeon and throw this one up and it will climb in spirals up in the air, then, when it has reached a sufficient height it will drop down plumb into the apron she holds out for it, so Miss Gates, in her thoughts and when these ever threatened to climb up in air, was always coming bump back again to Mr. Craigan. And again, as when we set off impetuously sometimes then all at once we have to stop as suddenly just how little we are rushing off for becomes apparent to us, so, now first excitement was over, for first time it was plain to her just what she was after. She wanted to better herself and she wanted a kid.

At home was Mr. Craigan with no more work in him, and her father, and Mr. Dale. For some years Mr. Dale's life had been part of hers and she thought in mind how she was mostly Mr. Dale's life.

We do not want a thing so very badly all the time: just now she didn't, now she came to think on it, particularly want children.

Mr. Craigan, what would he do without her? And in his illness who'd look after him? And wasn't a bird in hand worth 2 in the bush? Who'd say if they'd be any better off wherever they were going.

Mr. Jones jogged at her arm. What was she thinking of, he thought, she was so silent now? Nodding to window he said:

'Black Country.'

She looked out of window. It was the Black Country. Now series of little hills followed one on the heels of another. Small houses. Lots of smoke.

Train began to slow down. She did hate the country anyway really. You couldn't say anything for this bit but that were lots of towns in it.

Mr. Jones then said, wondering still what she could be thinking about.

'Black Country courtship.'

She looked out at once. When she had heard word 'courtship' just now and for some time past heart had tugged at her breathing.

She saw man and girl walking up winding path which had been made up a slag heap. Man was dressed in dark suit with a white stock for collar and wore bowler hat, high crowned. But it was the girl's clothes interested Miss Gates.

Her clothes were so much exactly what she liked that seeing her walking there, it might have been her twin. Not that she could see her face, but it was just what Miss Gates liked in clothes. And she who had been saving to go to Canada where they wore those things you saw in movie pictures, wide hats and blue shirts! Though the older women did dress more ordinary. But O it was so safe and comfortable what that girl was wearing. Temptation clutched at her. She put forefinger to her mouth. She hoped for train to go on. Train stopped. She could not take eyes away from looking at those two, O it was so safe and comfortable to be walking on this slag heap. For where was she going herself? Where would they walk themselves when they got out there. Miss Gates felt she didn't want to walk any place where she hadn't walked before. Or to wear any clothes but what that girl and she liked, and that only where would be others who liked those clothes looking out of train windows or from the roads, wherever they might be.

Looking at her Mr. Jones saw she was dreaming. He thought this was a funny way to start off on life's journey, but then women, he thought in mind, were funny things. He relapsed back into his own worries. Fact was his parents had not written to him for 3 years. They'd be able to put her up for a night or 2 till he got the licence and he and Lily got married before they went off. Why hadn't Lily liked to get married in Brum. Anyway was no hanky panky about her, it was marry or nothing with her, and that's the way any responsible chap looks at it he thought in mind.

But that was the trouble, suppose he cold not find parents. He knew they had changed shop they had managed, and lived over, for another. They had written to say they would write from their new address, but they never had. Suppose the people at the old address did not know where his home had gone. It made you bad to think of it. And his aunt, her who was wife of the lodge-keeper not far from tram terminus, she hadn't had word of them, not since long before he had. He hadn't told Lily, had kept it from her. He'd have to tell her, it wouldn't be right if he didn't tell her. He'd say, just as they were drawing into Liverpool, how he didn't know their address just yet as they'd changed houses and he'd lost letter when they'd written to tell him, but he and she would go to the old address and ask. Made you look foolish when you told all that was on your mind and then there was nothing in it. Yes, that's what he'd say and besides they'd find them, the people who'd taken over their shop would be bound to know where they'd gone.

Now everything which before had seemed terrible to her, like how if she stayed in Birmingham she would get like all the other women, and Bert the same as all other men, never any better off – only poorer, now this to her put on appearance of the great comfort. But now at the same time she put this from her mind. Wheeling turning her thoughts took on formation ducks have or aeroplanes when they are flying, both of them. She had come so far. She could not go back. 'Yes, I can't go back now,' she said in mind. Blindly her hand stumbled to get in crook of his arm, (for she did not look at him), and crept through like water seeping and round his arm. He turned and kissed her. Then he turned back and watched those 2 on the slag heap.

They sat. The train was still. She looked at shoes on her feet, he at those 2 standing on the slag heap above. Her arm was round his arm. She put head on his shoulder, their hair whispered together, both had yellow hair. Train moved on now, smoothly, like water the land glided past outside. He rested his head on hers where it rested on his shoulder. So their heads inclined one to the other, so their breathing fell in one with the other, so they took breath together in one breath as they had been, once before in night. Her arm through his arm felt his body breathe with hers and then her life was deep and strong to her like she couldn't remember feeling before. He did not notice, for he worried yet.

[. . .]

They sat in railway carriage side by side. Now she had drawn back from him.

He was so sure they would find his parents when they got to Liverpool that he was making plans now of what they would do in Canada, of how well they would do. Again was first day outside, another fine evening. They stopped at station and he let down the window to let country air in onto air they had brought with them from Birmingham, but Lily asked him to close it. He thought how nervous she seemed but then it was only natural in a woman starting on life's journey.

Miss Gates was very nervous. She kept herself by force now, as it might be, from thinking of Mr. Craigan. She was now wondering how she could ever happen to be in this railway carriage. Bert seemed like stranger to her, and in these strange stations. And the night air that was coming up, it couldn't be healthy in these parts. But she was frightened, O yes. Night was coming in, she was frightened of this night. In strange house. Not in her own bed. Her underclothes she was now wearing were strange to her, she had made them for this. No, they couldn't have had that window open, it wasn't safe.

Then, – he was so confident he brought it out by the way like, – he told her how he did not know his parents' address. He told her what they would do.

'Why did you tell me?'

'I 'ad to tell you, love. I wouldn't 'ave been right.'

'But we'll find them shan't we Bert?'

'Of course we will.'

'Then why put ideas into my 'ead. Now I feel frightened,' she said.

He put his arms about her shoulders. He poked his face blindly round in her hair. Strength of his arms about her made her feel safer but all the same her thoughts turned round and round this new thing now, in images. She lay limp against him. She saw them in streets, it getting darker, and they walking and walking till there'd be nowhere they could go. Being with his parents, well it was decent, it wasn't the last word on what they were going to do, she could still then go back to Birmingham, she hadn't burnt her boats as they say. But being alone with him, well there you were. She wondered if she could yet go back, even if his people were in Liverpool. She thought they'd just got to be in Liverpool.

Just then train came into a station and stopped. Mr. Jones took arms from off her and looked out of window. Noise of loud voices came from towards them along platform, one man said ''Ere Charley this'd do,' another, 'No Ed let's go farther along.' Terrified Miss Gates watched bit of platform through the window and wooden paling behind it on which was nailed advertisement for Pears Soap. Next that was advertisement for Liverpool paper. Behind road outside was pink house and the sky in bars of red and black. She watched this space most intently. 9 men came into it. They looked into this carriage, she saw one man with white face who had bright green muffler. That was bad luck about, seeing green like that. They went by, she heard 'ere you are – get in 'ere Sid – of course there ain't no bloody corridor one said. Good thing, there wasn't a corridor now, even if it had caused a bit of bother before. Then she remembered these men had been carrying musical instrument cases. She thought what would they have been up to on a Sunday, think, on a Sunday. She did feel so nervous. Porter ran up laughing and said through window to these men how he hoped they were all right. Then he said, walking along by side of train which was now moving, how he did not think the folks down this way would forget them coming for some time yet. The men were all laughing.

This dance band had been hired by vicar to play hymn tunes in church service, for every Sunday now his church was empty and he would do anything to have it full. He had given them tea and while he had gone off to take his evening service and to find the church quite full again, not even standing room, these

9 men had come and caught this train back to Liverpool where they lived and worked.

This Sunday had been unusual Sunday for them, by now they were quite worked up. 3 sat in racks, 6 about on the seats. One said to come on and have a tune. As he took saxophone out of case this turned red in sunset light. Pianist said what'll I do? Someone said he could raise his ugly voice. As they got instruments out of the cases they laughed each one to himself, alone, they played a little separately to tune these instruments. Then they all looked at one man. This one did not seem to move yet all at once suddenly they all slipped into playing, all 9 of them, pianist played on cushions of the seat, they were one, no more 9 of them, one now.

What more could have been wanted to fit in so with Mr. Jones' happy feelings? In wonderment he listened. He got up. Forgetting Lily he opened window to listen better to them and hung head out.

'Bert' screamed Miss Gates. She jumped up and pulled at his shoulders.

When he came in again she said: 'whatever were you doing that for? Why a bridge might 'ave come and cut your head off and where would I be then?'

Sharp air of evening rushed in on them. She pulled window up. He sat down and when window was up he drew her down onto his knees. He said had she been scared? He kissed her. But she got down from his knees. She listened to tune they were playing with distrust. She trembled.

As he listened beat of that music, so together, made everything in the world brother to him. As he listened and they played he expanded in his feeling and looking back in his memory for something he might express this by he put arms round Lily. He said:

'In our iron foundry at our place there was a chap used to sing 'E 'ad a wonderful voice, what you might call a really fine voice, you know love what I mean. Last time I 'eard him sing 'e went on all day. D'you know what it was? 'Is wife 'ad given 'im a son the night before.' He kissed Miss Gates. 'All the chaps used to come round when he sang.'

Again she lay limp in his arms, distraught. Kids, I don't want 'em she cried in mind.

Pianist sang. He was tenor. He sang:

'Your eyes are my eyes
My heart looks through'

Horror. She looked past Mr. Jones' head which was pressing against her head and there was Liverpool beginning. She hated it. Factories. Poor quarters. More and more of them.

She got up and tidied herself by the glass. Her face even frightened her.

So when they got into station and got out she said in mind it was all he could do to walk.

'Aren't you going to take the flowers,' he said laughing

'What are you talking of?' she said. 'Leave 'em in there for Christ's sake.'

19

[. . .]

They had come on tram to outskirts of Liverpool. They were walking in the direction back in now. They looked for address of shop. Mr. Jones knew his way. Smell of the sea was at her, forcing itself on her.

They had been on edge of the Residential District. They were coming now to blinded shops. Roads were broader, lighter by a little. Here was dropsical fatness of shopkeepers' paunches, when they got to address they were looking for they knocked one up. Early to bed early to rise this one's motto. In nightshirt he came to window above. He leaned paunch out over window frame, he let his weight sink on it, bulging. If they'd wait two minutes he would get address for them where their parents had moved and in his place at window showed curling papers like bobbins. Whining voice came from inside of that room – 'what is it ma? Ma, ma, who's there ma, what is it?' His wife poked her nose over window frame. Lily saw nose, one eye, curling papers.

'Well now' said fat shopkeeper they met afterwards squirming along in shadows of the street looking for a bit of fun – these courting couples in the doorways y'know, y'know you can see a bit o' fun o' nights – 'well now' he said, 'it's Mulgrave Street you want is it?' He told them, shopkeeper they had knocked up hadn't been able to tell them way to address he had given them and Mr. Jones did not know that part of town it was in. Dropsically fat, hatpin little eyes, shopkeeper watched Miss Gates as he told them. Something up here. That gal looked frightened out of her life. But that young chap was up to a bit o' fun. Didn't know how to start with 'er, that's 'ow it looked. Yum yum he felt in huge belly, um yum.

Now first that feeling which had soaked all through about Mr. Jones, how everything, everything was wonderful, she was the sweetest girl in the world and wouldn't the old people be glad to see her, now first that feeling ebbed and died in him. He was afraid for her as now they were going into poorer quarter of the town, streets were getting now to be the streets of ports, darkness of waters looked now to be flowing over into these streets. He did not know the way, but he knew they were going towards the docks. He had seen in his mind their coming to that shop and those there telling him to go back the way he had come with Miss Gates, to go back in direction of the Residential District. In his heart picture had warmed him of his bringing Lily to quiet respectable shop in a quiet decent street. He had thought out two ways of turning off her surprise and admiration when she saw so much prosperity. 'It's simple,' was one thing he was going to say, 'it's simple but the old folks knows what's comfortable.' One thing he had always feared, and that was effect his father would have on Miss Gates and now, as they walked further, and the streets were poorer and poorer streets, it was his father he suspected as having thrown his ma's prosperity away.

Ship's syren sounded, wailing, and with a great pang Miss Gates thought a factory buzzer at this time of the night, it couldn't be nightshift at this time of the night, O she did feel afraid. And that man they had asked their way of, his eyes! How dark it was getting! Well she just wouldn't look any more

if it only made her shivery, she just wouldn't notice anything
more. But it didn't happen often, did it, that all you thought of
worst came to pass. But then she thought it wasn't quite so
bad, they'd not expected to find them first go off. All the same,
these streets! Well, she wouldn't look that's all.

[. . .]

So Miss Gates did not look at anything. She just followed
Mr. Jones.

They went by public house. Man played on instrument,
which was kind of xylophone, laid flat in the doorway. As the
air sweats on metal so little balls of notes this man made hung
on smell of stale beer which was like a slab outside the door.
Man playing on this instrument was on his knees, and trunk of
his body bent over it, head almost touched ground on other
side of this flat instrument. Mr. Jones saw position that man
was in. He'd never seen one like it. Feeling of uneasiness grew
up in him.

They were now in working class streets. Doors stood open.
Miss Gates heard voices talking dialect strange to her. But she
shut her ears to this, though it gave her slight feeling of comfort. She was so tired with walking. She got more and more
blank.

Mr. Jones took tighter grip on bag he was carrying, (his own
he had left at railway station). They were getting into the
dockers' quarter. He did not like it. But this was Mulgrave St.
And this was No. 439. He knocked on the door. Miss Gates
stood, she did not look up. He knocked. Door was opened by
man in his shirt sleeves. He was a stranger to Mr. Jones. He
told them where his parents had gone was a ½ mile further on
and then they'd shifted from there so he'd heard though he
couldn't say where they'd gone. He'd better go there, he said,
and the people there might tell him. Miss Gates heard this and
did not think at all, except she thought once it would have to
finish some time. Mr. Jones was frightened now. Man shut door
on him and he stood frightened. Street was dark.

Street was dark. Miss Gates felt something in the street
looking out, looking out then it was gone. Then it was back
again. Where was Bert, had he gone? She looked up quickly

but of course he was there. But street was dark. She got much more frightened and was rigid with it for 2 moments. Again something looked and was gone. And again. She felt no, after looking up to see if Bert was there she wouldn't look up again to see what that was. There it was. She had to look. No she wouldn't. She had to, so she looked. It was searchlight from the lighthouse, it stroked over sky and was gone. With great pang she wondered what that was doing there. Then she decided that was what came from looking up. She would not look up again. They began walking again. She was blank, blank. Again it came along the sky.

Mr. Jones watched, watched everything but Lil. He did not like to look at her. He thought of his parents, what could have brought them to this part? He was ashamed. What they would do now he couldn't say. What would come of it if the next address didn't know where they'd gone. What'd he do with Lil.

Once before when their relations one with the other had come to a point, he had seen it like he was setting job up on a lathe, the foreman looking on and others in the shop watching him. Job was difficult, he'd been in two minds to begin or not. Now he was alone, lathe was stopped, he was alone. Job was going wrong. If he went now, and he would never come back, chances were they could work that bit in again for now he thought this ending was like the finish of all what you might call dreams. Anything a bit out of the way and he couldn't do it. He blamed himself. What was the good in trying to better yourself when you couldn't hold a better job. Now if he went on with this bit on the lathe he would hopelessly spoil it. Now, he thought, if he went on with Lily, and his parents weren't there or in a bad way, he couldn't ask her to take on any wife's life in this town, the ordinary kind of life anywhere, when she'd come out to get on in the world. Better she went back to Mr. Craigan which had money of his own.

For if he could not find father and mother who then would give them money for their passage. Besides it was like taking Lil on false pretences to take her to this. Smelling of the sea like this street did, it wasn't respectable, apart from the people that lived in it. He was afraid then she might not be able to go on, who had walked so far already this evening. He hardly dared look at her. Dragging a little behind, face turned down towards the ground, he thought she looked all one way, skint. He thought it was no wonder, but then this would be the address.

He stopped. Lily stopped. Door of this house was open, man he did not know sat on chair just by it. Mr. Jones said in low voice so Lily would not hear, did a man called Jones live here at one time? This man said yes but he and his wife had gone and had left no address. 'Would you be connected with the family?' he said. Mr. Jones said 'Yes.' 'Well then,' this man said, he believed there'd been a bit of trouble but he couldn't say for sure and said goodnight to Mr. Jones. For looking at Lily he took her for daft, and he decided he did not want to be mixed up in this, for it looked funny to his mind's eye.

Mr. Jones said, 'it ain't much further to go now Lil,' and went off again. She followed a little behind. He was so ashamed he did not like to come near her to help her. He only went slower as he was afraid her strength might give up any time now. He thought her blankness he saw to look at her, was her hating him.

He had remembered great tall street which should be near to them to the west. Trams ran down it. He leads her there.

They get there. It is bright with street lamps. He was sure now was nothing but to leave her get home, if he went with her it might all begin again, he might not be able to let her alone. Here they were in this tall street. He stopped by lamp post where trams stopped. She stopped. Then he sees she is crying quietly. He comes close to her and she leans a little on him. He stood so for a bit then he said, 'Lil, here's your bag.' Without thinking, she was all blank, she reached down to pick it up. She looks up to him then. But he was running away down this street. She picked up bag and began to run after him, still not realising and like obediently, like small children run, in steps, not strides. She put forefinger in her mouth. She could not see distinctly so did not see him turn down alley way. (When he got into dark court at end of this alley he crouches down in a corner beyond cone of light which falls in front of it.) He looks back over his shoulder but she had not seen him turn, she is still trotting. Tear drops off her chin. Then she saw a policeman and no Bert. She stopped. Tram drew up there which was another stopping place for trams. Woman that was there and had seen her face said quickly come in on the tram dear. She got on. Policeman turned away.

I think the last paragraph of that is as painful in its quiet immediacy as anything from English fiction between the wars. The shift into and out of the present tense is particularly deft and poignant, suggesting as it does a point of view that is trying to retain the conventions of third-person narrative but slips as if desperately into a reliving of the story in the present, the narrator living it with them, wanting to help like the woman at the tram-stop, not being able to, having to turn away like the policeman in the last sentence.

Henry Green's *Living* is, many think, his finest and strongest novel. It is one of the very few inter-war novels to register working-class life in unsentimentalised, felt sensation. Its story of Bert Jones and Lily Gates and their journey through the intimidating city, from poor to poorer addresses, enacting for Lily a nightmare of deeper and deeper entrapment rather than the escape she'd been hoping for, is as we've just seen quite uncannily acute, funny, tender and, at this extract's close and as Lily becomes in effect an abandoned and lost child, almost too painful to read.

So I hope the following fact comes as a surprise. *Living* has only just now been republished in Britain after many years in which it has been unavailable. It was out of print when I drafted this chapter and has never been a widely read novel. The comment made by a reader of the outline plan for the current volume, querying the inclusion of Green, is typical: 'Henry Green is great but who reads him?'

The question as to why *Living* has not been regularly in print since 1929, unlike say the novels of his friend and contemporary Evelyn Waugh – who incidentally reviewed *Living* very favourably when it came out – is worth thinking about and it returns us to the question of the canon which we last met when discussing Milton's reputation in the twentieth century. *Living* is experimental in its language and style, a style that is entirely his own and also one which in its daring transgressions associates Green with more famous modernist writers like Joyce and Eliot. But the function of the style is, of course, to give us in as unmediated a form as possible the idioms and the feelings and the thoughts of his protagonists. In that respect the style works in exactly the opposite way to the lofty and sardonic tone that we saw Conrad use in his presentation of Stevie in the last chapter. That is, Green's style and his evocation of working-class lives are indissoluble. And *Living* is in language and subject regional, not metropolitan; it is specific and localised in its dialect and its interest in working conditions, not generalised or mythologised in the way that Joyce mythologises his Dublin and his Irishisms in *Ulysses*. That is to say, we can't soften the blow of the end of this extract by subjecting it to any large-scale mythological reading. Bert and Lily are, as if obstinately, ordinary and what happens here is an appallingly ordinary failure. That said, you might have noticed, if you know Joyce's 'Eveline' in *Dubliners*, a probable source for Bert and Lily's story.

The combination of ungeneralisable regionalism, working-class lives, and experimental language is perhaps enough to ensure that *Living* has only had a tangential place in the canon. Exactly the same may be said, and for the same reasons, of another masterpiece from just a few years later, Lewis Grassic Gibbon's trilogy *A Scots Quair* (1932–4) in which Scottish working-class history is bruisingly delivered in uncompromisingly rich and vividly regional language. This too is usually out of print. Literary culture, and the opinion-formers who police it, have always preferred the values and conventions of London metropolitan life or, at a push, Dublin and Paris with their highly self-conscious artistic-literary traditions. And the tradition in the English novel is to represent the working class by sentimentalising or sensationalising or mystifying their lives. Green and Grassic Gibbon refuse any of those options.

In this respect there's a moment in George Orwell's *The Road to Wigan Pier* (1937) that is worth putting beside our extract from *Living*. Green and Orwell were both from upper middle-class families. Green's real name was Henry Yorke and he worked in the Birmingham factory owned by his industrialist father. Orwell set out to tell the true conditions in which the working class in the north of England lived and worked. Dickens went to Preston for the same investigative reasons before he wrote *Hard Times*. It's suggestive that both Orwell and Dickens ignored or suppressed what they actually saw and met – that is, sensible and radical working-class activists working together.

Orwell takes a train towards the beginning of *Wigan Pier*, having had enough of the Brookers family with whom he'd been staying. The Brookers had sons and daughters ' "at Canada", as Mrs Brooker used to put it', and only one son – 'a large pig-like young man' – remained. Orwell left because 'the place was beginning to depress me', what with Mr Brooker peeling potatoes 'with quite such an air of brooding resentment' and Mrs Brooker 'lying on her sofa, a soft mound of fat and self-pity, saying the same things over and over again'. So 'the train bore me away, through the monstrous scenery of slag-heaps, chimneys, piled scap-iron, foul canals, paths of cindery mud criss-crossed by the prints of clogs'. And as the train moves on Orwell sees something.

> As we moved slowly through the outskirts of the town we passed row after row of little grey slum houses running at right angles to the embankment. At the back of one of the houses a young woman was kneeling on the stones, poking a stick up the leaden waste-pipe which ran from the sink inside and which I suppose was blocked. I had time to see everything about her – her sacking apron, her clumsy clogs, her arms reddened by the cold. She looked up as the train passed, and I was almost near enough to catch her eye. She had a round pale face, the usual exhausted face of the slum girl who is twenty-five and looks forty, thanks to miscarriages and drudgery; and it wore, for the second in which I saw it, the most desolate, hopeless expression I have ever seen. It struck me then that we are mistaken when we say that 'It isn't the same for them as it would be for us,' and that people bred in the slums can imagine nothing but the slums. For what I saw in her face was not the ignorant suffering of an animal. She knew well enough what was happening to her – understood as well as I did how dreadful a destiny it was to be kneeling there in the bitter cold, on the slimy stones of a slum backyard, poking a stick up a foul drain-pipe.

(Harmondsworth, Penguin, 1962, pp. 16–17)

The presumptiveness of that, the way Orwell from the comfort of his train dares presume and appropriate this young woman's life-history, a 'usual' history of 'miscarriages and drudgery', leaves a sourer taste even than that left by his treatment of the Brookers. The contrast with Lily in her train, so poignantly identifying with the woman walking 'so safe and comfortable' on the slag heap, and worrying about Canada, could hardly be more striking.

One of the saddest sentences in the *Living* extract conveys Bert's worries about the 'effect his father would have on Miss Gates' and his suspicion that his father had 'thrown his ma's prosperity away'. I said above that there's little incentive to read this journey mythologically, as we did in the last chapter, but it does seem intriguing that this journey at least resembles the folk-motif mentioned in the last chapter, the son seeking his father, either in order to re-unite the fragmented family or for the younger generation to confront and supplant the older. As Bert travels more and more desperately in search, it's as if his parents are running away from him, as he in effect runs away from Lily. The son–father quest is a narrative that seems to get told repeatedly in the period from about 1930 and it prompts reflections on the relationship between the generations after the catastrophes of the First World War.

Writers of Green's age would have been about 14 at the end of the war and thus subject to the sense of being the generation-after. As in Evelyn Waugh's *Vile Bodies* (1930), which shows the influence of *Living*, there's a sense of a need for the hero-father, an adult getting adulthood right after the appalling wastages on the battlefields. Both Bert and Lily have fathers that fail to meet that need. Bert's has presumably squandered the family money and Lily's is drunken and abusive. And that failure leads directly to the frustrations and abandonments faced by the young. A generation frustrated in its longing for a father is a generation susceptible to fascism. In a very pointed moment during Bert and Lily's journey to Liverpool, Mr Craigan, Lily's substitute-father, is seen worrying about her, restlessly unable to read Dickens's *Little Dorrit* (the classic tale of imprisoned hopes) and preparing to listen to the radio to 'see what they were doing now in Berlin'. But he fails to do that either.

Berlin in 1929 saw serious riots, clashes between communists and the police (leaving seventeen dead in two days in May), and the city declared under a state of siege. Communists and Nazis later confronted each other in armed street battles. This is the most immediate context in which the search for the father and the consequent escape to Canada have such significance. Literature in the 1930s and early

1940s is a literature haunted above all by the rise of fascism and the need to escape, to cross borders, to confront father-figures or father-lands. A highly allegorical novel from 1941, Rex Warner's remarkable *The Aerodrome* (also rarely in print), weaves together the story of a fascist or police-state take-over in rural England with the narrator's confused discovery of his two fathers and his eventual and comforting rejection of the biological-fascist father for the loving version of father-land in old England. Samuel Beckett's *Watt* (written in 1944) presents in comic form a son-figure, Watt, frustrated in his attempt to get to know or even see a father-figure, Mr Knott. And this is the period in which popular films like Disney's *Pinocchio* (1940) rewrite the folk-tale to turn it into the comforting story of a boy becoming real by finding and saving his father from 'a whale of a whale', in effect from history. But Bert and Lily are stranded, estranged from each other, abandoned and parentless, and Lily becomes a child.

Fathers and sons discovering their love for each other and thus saving the family from itself is something we'll meet in the later chapter on Tennessee Williams. Arthur Miller's plays circle around the father–son issue and he once said that all his work was written against fascism. Valentine Cunningham's studies of the literature of the 1930s are exemplary, particularly his *British Writers of the Thirties* (Oxford, Oxford University Press, 1988) which has an extensive bibliography. Raymond Williams's short book on Orwell (expanded edition, London, Fontana, 1984) is the best thing of its kind. There's some discussion of Green, Grassic Gibbon, Warner, Beckett, Orwell, Waugh and others in the present writer's 'The Novel in the 1930s and 1940s' in *The Twentieth Century*, edited by Martin Dodsworth (Harmondsworth, Penguin, 1994): this also discusses the novels of Jean Rhys, one of which is featured in the next chapter of this book.

RHYS'S *GOOD MORNING, MIDNIGHT*

Women in colonialism and framed in exhibition

This chapter presents extracts from Jean Rhys's *Good Morning, Midnight* (1939). The commentary invites you to consider the text in a number of inter-related ways: in the light of colonialism and its repressed stories; women as commodities and exhibits; the Paris Great Exhibition of 1937; the connections between the lives and works of Jean Rhys and Emily Dickinson.

Good Morning, Midnight is the last novel Jean Rhys wrote and published before she dropped out of literary history. Her reappearance many years later with *Wide Sargasso Sea*, her famous 'prequel' to *Jane Eyre*, was, for all intents and purposes, like a return from the dead. But it's *Good Morning, Midnight*, published on the eve of the Second World War, which tells the story of a return from the dead. It's the bitter-comic story of a woman (Sasha), on the eve of middle age ('but I've never been young') and scarred by her past entanglements with men, and with the world generally, returning from a kind of death in London, to a kind of life in Paris, where much of her recent life's sad history has been spent. And, as Sasha says, 'it hurts when you have been dead to come alive'. In Paris, negotiating at once the city's painfully associative memories and the men whom she magnetically both attracts and resists, Sasha attempts something between a renewal of and a revenge on her life. This is the most disquieting of Rhys's pre-war texts; it's also, many would argue, her single most distinguished novel. But given its radical sexual politics it's not altogether surprising that the War (in Rhys's words) 'killed' it.

What follows is three extracts. The first is from the novel's opening pages. The second is a flashback to a scene in which Sasha, in her earlier life in Paris, is working in a prestigious Parisian clothes-salon.

And the third is at the novel's centre, a long reminiscence from a painter, whom Sasha visits with a Russian friend, about a neighbour of his when he lived in London. 'Luminal', in the first line below, is a sleeping-draught.

I take some more luminal, put the light out and sleep at once.

I am in the passage of a tube station in London. Many people are in front of me; many people are behind me. Everywhere there are placards printed in red letters: This Way to the Exhibition, This Way to the Exhibition. But I don't want the way to the exhibition – I want the way out. There are passages to the right and passages to the left, but no exit sign. Everywhere the fingers point and the placards read: This Way to the Exhibition. . . . I touch the shoulder of the man walking in front of me. I say: 'I want the way out.' But he points to the placards and his hand is made of steel. I walk along with my head bent, very ashamed, thinking: 'Just like me – always wanting to be different from other people.' The steel finger points along a long stone passage. This Way – This Way – This Way to the Exhibition. . . .

Now a little man, bearded, with a snub nose, dressed in a long white night-shirt, is talking earnestly to me. 'I am your father,' he says. 'Remember that I am your father.' But blood is streaming from a wound in his forehead. 'Murder,' he shouts, 'murder, murder.' Helplessly I watch the blood streaming. At last my voice tears itself loose from my chest. I too shout: 'Murder, murder, help, help,' and the sound fills the room. I wake up and a man in the street outside is singing the waltz from *Les Saltimbanques*. 'C'est l'amour qui flotte dans l'air à ronde,' he sings.

I believe it's a fine day, but the light in this room is so bad that you can't be sure. Outside on the landing you can't see at all unless the electric light is on. It's a large landing, cluttered up from morning to night with brooms, pails, piles of dirty sheets and so forth – the wreckage of the spectacular floors below.

The man who has the room next to mine is parading about as

usual in his white dressing-gown. Hanging around. He is like
the ghost of the landing. I am always running into him.

He is as thin as a skeleton. He has a bird-like face and
sunken, dark eyes with a peculiar expression, cringing, ingrati-
ating, knowing. What's he want to look at me like that for? . . .
He is always wearing a dressing-gown – a blue one with black
spots or the famous white one. I can't imagine him in street
clothes.

'Bonjour.'

'Bonjour,' I mutter. I don't like this damned man. . . .

And here's Sasha, in her earlier Paris days, as a clothes-salon
receptionist.

. . . It was a large white-and-gold room with a dark-polished
floor. Imitation Louis Quinze chairs, painted screens, three or
four elongated dolls, beautifully dressed, with charming and
malicious oval faces.

Every time a customer arrived, the commissionaire touched
a bell which rang just over my head. I would advance towards
the three steps leading down to the street-door and stand
there, smiling a small, discreet smile. I would say 'Good afternoon, madame. . . . Certainly, madame,' or 'Good afternoon,
madame. Mademoiselle Mercédès has had your telephone
message and everything is ready,' or 'Certainly, madame. . . .
Has madame a vendeuse?'

Then I would conduct the customer to the floor above, where
the real activities of the shop were carried on, and call for
Mademoiselle Mercédès or Mademoiselle Henriette or Madame
Perron, as the case might be. If I forgot a face or allotted a new
customer to a saleswoman out of her turn, there was a row.

There was no lift in this shop. That's why I was there. It was
one of those dress-houses still with a certain prestige – anyhow
among the French – but its customers were getting fewer and
fewer.

I had had the job for three weeks. It was dreary. You couldn't
read; they didn't like it. I would feel as if I were drugged,
sitting there, watching those damned dolls, thinking what a

success they would have made of their lives if they had been women. Satin skin, silk hair, velvet eyes, sawdust heart – all complete. I used to envy the commissionaire, because at least he could watch the people passing in the street. On the other hand, he had to stand up all the time. Yes, perhaps I had rather be myself than the commissionaire.

There was always a very strong smell of scent. I would pretend that I could recognize the various scents. Today it's L'Heure Bleue; yesterday it was Nuits de Chine. . . . The place also smelt of the polish on the floor, the old furniture, the dolls' clothes.

The shop had a branch in London, and the boss of the London branch had bought up the whole show. Every three months or so he came over to the French place and it was rumoured that he was due to arrive on a certain day. What's he like? Oh, he's the real English type. Very nice, very, very chic, the real English type, le businessman. . . . I thought: 'Oh, my God, I know what these people mean when they say the real English type.'

. . . He arrives. Bowler-hat, majestic trousers, oh-my-God expression, ha-ha eyes – I know him at once. He comes up the steps with Salvatini behind him, looking very worried. (Salvatini is the boss of our shop.) Don't let him notice me, don't let him look at me. Isn't there something you can do so that nobody looks at you or sees you? Of course, you must make your mind vacant, neutral, then your face also becomes vacant, neutral – you are invisible.

No use. He comes up to my table.

'Good morning, good morning, Miss –'

'Mrs Jansen,' Salvatini says.

Shall I stand up or not stand up? Stand up, of course. I stand up.

'Good morning.'

I smile at him.

'And how many languages do you speak?'

He seems quite pleased. He smiles back at me. Affable, that's the word. I suppose that's why I think it's a joke.

'One,' I say, and go on smiling.

Now, what's happened? . . . Oh, of course. . . .

'I understand French quite well.'

He fidgets with the buttons on his coat.

'I was told that the receptionist spoke French and German fluently,' he says to Salvatini.

'She speaks French,' Salvatini says. 'Assez bien, assez bien.'

Mr Blank looks at me with lifted eyebrows.

'Sometimes,' I say idiotically.

Of course, sometimes, when I am a bit drunk and am talking to somebody I like and know, I speak French very fluently indeed. At other times I just speak it. And as to that, my dear sir, you've got everything all wrong. I'm here because I have a friend who knows Mr Salvatini's mistress, and Mr Salvatini's mistress spoke to Mr Salvatini about me, and the day that he saw me I wasn't looking too bad and he was in a good mood. Nothing at all to do with fluent French and German, dear sir, nothing at all. I'm here because I'm here because I'm here. And just to prove to you that I speak French, I'll sing you a little song about it: 'Si vous saviez, si vous saviez, si vous saviez comment ça se fait.'

For God's sake, I think, pull yourself together.

I say: 'I speak French fairly well. I've been living in Paris for eight years.'

No, he's suspicious now. Questions short and sharp.

'How long have you been working here?'

'About three weeks.'

'What was your last job?'

'I worked at the Maison Chose in the Place Vendôme.'

'Oh, really, you worked for Chose, did you? You worked for Chose.' His voice is more respectful. 'Were you receptionist there?'

'No,' I say. 'I worked as a mannequin.'

'You worked as a mannequin?' Down and up his eyes go, up and down. 'How long ago was this?' he says.

How long ago was it? Now, everything is a blank in my head – years, days, hours, everything is a blank in my head. How long ago was it? I don't know.

'Four, nearly five, years ago.'

'How long did you stay there?'

398

'About three months,' I say.

He seems to be waiting for further information.

'And then I left,' I say in a high voice. (Decidedly this is one of my good days. This is one of the days when I say everything right.)

'Oh, you left?'

'Yes, I left.'

Yes, my dear sir, I left. I got bored and I walked out on them. But that was four, nearly five, years ago and a lot can happen in five years. I haven't the slightest intention of walking out on you, I can assure you of that. And I hope you haven't the slightest intention of – And just the thought that you may have the slightest intention of – makes my hands go cold and my heart beat.

'Have you worked anywhere else since then?'

'Well, no. No, I haven't.'

'I see,' he says. He waves backwards and forwards like a tall tree that is going to fall on me. Then he makes a sound like 'Hah', and goes off into a room at the back, followed by Salvatini.

Well, this has gone badly, there's no disguising it. It has gone as badly as possible. It couldn't have gone worse. But it's over. Now he'll never notice me again; he'll forget about me.

[. . .]

Salvatini puts his head out of the door behind me and says: 'Mr Blank wants to see you.'

I at once make up my mind that he wants to find out if I can speak German. All the little German I know flies out of my head. Jesus, Help me! Ja, ja, nein, nein, was kostet es, Wien ist eine sehr schöne Stadt, Buda-Pest auch ist sehr schön, ist schön, mein Herr, ich habe meinen Blumen vergessen, aus meinen grossen Schmerzen, homo homini lupus, aus meinen grossen Schmerzen mach ich die kleinen Lieder, homo homini lupus (I've got that one, anyway), aus meinen grossen Schmerzen homo homini doh ré mi fah soh la ti doh. . . .

He is sitting at the desk, writing a letter. I stand there. He is sure to notice how shabby my shoes are.

Salvatini looks up, gives me a furtive smile and then looks away again.

Come on, stand straight, keep your head up, smile. . . . No, don't smile. If you smile, he'll think you're trying to get off with him. I know his type. He won't give me the benefit of a shadow of a doubt. Don't smile then, but look eager, alert, attentive. . . . Run out of the door and get away. . . . You fool, stand straight, look eager, alert, attentive. . . . No, look here, he's doing this on purpose. . . . Of course he isn't doing it on purpose. He's just writing a letter. . . . He is, he is. He's doing it on purpose. I know it, I feel it. I've been standing here for five minutes. This is impossible.

'Did you wish to see me, Mr Blank?'

He looks up and says sharply: 'Yes, yes, what is it? What do you want? Wait a minute, wait a minute.'

At once I know. He doesn't want me to talk German, he's going to give me the sack. All right then, hurry up, get it over. . . .

Nothing. I just stand there. Now panic has come on me. My hands are shaking, my heart is thumping, my hands are cold. Fly, fly, run from these atrocious voices, these abominable eyes. . . .

He finishes his letter, writes a line or two on another piece of paper and puts it into an envelope.

'Will you please take this to the kise?'

Take this to the kise. . . . I look at Salvatini. He smiles encouragingly.

Mr Blank rattles out: 'Be as quick as you can, Mrs – er – please. Thank you very much.'

I turn and walk blindly through a door. It is a lavatory. They look sarcastic as they watch me going out by the right door.

I walk a little way along the passage, then stand with my back against the wall.

This is a very old house – two old houses. The first floor, the shop proper, is modernized. The showrooms, the fitting-rooms, the mannequins' room. . . . But on the ground floor are the workrooms and offices and dozens of small rooms, passages that don't lead anywhere, steps going up and steps going down.

Kise – kise. . . . It doesn't mean a thing to me. He's got me into such a state that I can't imagine what it can mean.

Now, no panic. This envelope must have a name on it. . . . Monsieur L. Grousset.

Somewhere in this building is a Monsieur L. Grousset. I have got to take this letter to him. Easy. Somebody will tell me where his room is. Grousset, Grousset. . . .

I turn to the right, walk along another passage, down a flight of stairs. The workrooms. . . . No, I can't ask here. All the girls will stare at me. I shall seem such a fool.

I try another passage. It ends in a lavatory. The number of lavatories in this place, c'est inoui. . . . I turn the corner, find myself back in the original passage and collide with a strange young man. He gives me a nasty look.

'Could you tell me, please, where I can find Monsieur Grousset?'

'Connais pas,' the young man says.

After this it becomes a nightmare. I walk up stairs, past doors, along passages – all different, all exactly alike. There is something very urgent that I must do. But I don't meet a soul and all the doors are shut.

This can't go on. Shall I throw the damned thing away and forget all about it?

'What you must do is this,' I tell myself: 'You must go back and say – quite calmly – "I'm very sorry, but I didn't understand where you wanted me to take this note." '

I knock. He calls out: 'Come in.' I go in.

He takes the note from my hand. He looks at me as if I were a dog which had presented him with a very, very old bone. (Say something, say something. . . .)

'I couldn't find him.'

'But how do you mean you couldn't find him? He must be there.'

'I'm very sorry. I didn't know where to find him.'

'You don't know where to find the cashier – the counting-house?'

'La caisse,' Salvatini says – helpfully, but too late.

But if I tell him that it was the way he pronounced it

that confused me, it will seem rude. Better not say anything. . . .

'Well, don't you know?'

'Yes, I do. Oh yes, I do know.'

That is to say, I knew this morning where the cashier's office is. It isn't so far from the place where we put our hats and coats. But I don't know a damned thing now. . . . Run, run away from their eyes, run from their voices, run. . . .

We stare at each other. I breathe in deeply and breathe out again.

'Extraordinary,' he says, very slowly, 'quite extraordinary. God knows I'm used to fools, but this complete imbecility. . . . This woman is the biggest fool I've ever met in my life. She seems to be half-witted. She's hopeless. . . . Well, isn't she?' he says to Salvatini.

Salvatini makes a rolling movement of his head, shoulders and eyes, which means; 'I quite agree with you. Deplorable, deplorable.' Also: 'She's not so bad as you think.' Also: 'Oh, my God, what's all this about? What a day, what a day! When will it be over?' Anything you like, Salvatini's shrug means.

Not to cry in front of this man. Tout, mais pas ça. Say something. . . . No, don't say anything. Just walk out of the room.

'No, wait a minute,' he says. 'You'd better take that note along. You do know who to take it to now, don't you? The cashier.'

'Yes.'

He stares at me. Something else has come into his eyes. He knows how I am feeling – yes, he knows.

'Just a hopeless, helpless little fool, aren't you?' he says. Jovial? Bantering? On the surface, yes. Underneath? No, I don't think so.

'Well, aren't you?'

'Yes, yes, yes, yes. Oh, yes.'

I burst into tears. I haven't even got a handkerchief.

'Dear me,' Mr Blank says.

'Allons, allons,' Salvatini says. 'Voyons. . . .'

I rush away from them into a fitting-room. It is hardly ever used. It is only used when the rooms upstairs are full. I shut the door and lock it.

I cry for a long time – for myself, for the old woman with the bald head, for all the sadness of this damned world, for all the fools and all the defeated. . . .

In this fitting-room there is a dress in one of the cupboards which has been worn a lot by the mannequins and is going to be sold off for four hundred francs. The saleswoman has promised to keep it for me. I have tried it on; I have seen myself in it. It is a black dress with wide sleeves embroidered in vivid colours – red, green, blue, purple. It is my dress. If I had been wearing it I should never have stammered or been stupid.

Now I have stopped crying. Now I shall never have that dress. Today, this day, this hour, this minute I am utterly defeated. I have had enough.

Now the circle is complete. Now, strangely enough, I am no longer afraid of Mr Blank. He is one thing and I am another. He knew me right away, as soon as he came in at the door. And I knew him. . . .

I go into the other room, this time without knocking. Salvatini has gone. Mr Blank is still writing letters. Is he making dates with all the girls he knows in Paris? I bet that's what he is doing.

He looks at me with distaste. Plat du jour – boiled eyes, served cold. . . .

Well, let's argue this out, Mr Blank. You, who represent Society, have the right to pay me four hundred francs a month. That's my market value, for I am an inefficient member of Society, slow in the uptake, uncertain, slightly damaged in the fray, there's no denying it. So you have the right to pay me four hundred francs a month, to lodge me in a small, dark room, to clothe me shabbily, to harass me with worry and monotony and unsatisfied longings till you get me to the point when I blush at a look, cry at a word. We can't all be happy, we can't all be rich, we can't all be lucky – and it would be so much less fun if we were. Isn't it so, Mr Blank? There must be the dark background to show up the bright colours. Some must cry so that

403

the others may be able to laugh the more heartily. Sacrifices are necessary. . . . Let's say that you have this mystical right to cut my legs off. But the right to ridicule me afterwards because I am a cripple – no, that I think you haven't got. And that's the right you hold most dearly, isn't it? You must be able to despise the people you exploit. But I wish you a lot of trouble, Mr Blank, and just to start off with, your damned shop's going bust. Alleluia! Did I say all this? Of course I didn't. I didn't even think it.

I say that I'm ill and want to go. (Get it in first.) And he says he quite agrees that it would be the best thing. 'No regrets,' he says, 'no regrets.'

And there I am, out in the Avenue Marigny, with my month's pay – four hundred francs. And the air so sweet, as it can only be in Paris. It is autumn and the dry leaves are blowing along. Swing high, swing low, swing to and fro. . . .

And, finally, back in Sasha's present again, here is her painter-friend's story of his London neighbour.

We drink more tea. The stove has quite gone out and it is very cold, but they don't seem to notice it. I am glad of my coat. I think I ought to ask to see his pictures, but he is in a flow of talk which I can't interrupt. He is relating an experience he had in London.

'Oh, you've lived in London?'

'Yes, I was there for a time, but I didn't stay long – no. But I got a fine suit,' he says. 'I looked quite an Englishman from the neck down. I was very proud. . . . I had a room near Notting Hill Gate. Do you know it?'

'Oh yes, I know it.'

'A very comfortable room. But one night this happened. Talking about weeping – I still think of it. . . . I was sitting by the fire, when I heard a noise as if someone had fallen down outside. I opened the door and there was a woman lying full-length in the passage, crying. I said to her: "What's the matter?" She only went on crying. "Well," I thought, "it's nothing to do with me." I shut the door firmly. But still I could hear

her. I opened the door again and I asked her: "What is it? Can I
do anything for you?" She said: "I want a drink."'

'Exactly like me,' I say. 'I cried, and I asked for a drink.' He
certainly likes speechifying, this peintre. Is he getting at me?

'No, no,' he says. 'Not like you at all.'

He goes on: 'I said to her "Come in if you wish. I have some
whisky." She wasn't a white woman. She was half-negro – a
mulatto. She had been crying so much that it was impossible to
tell whether she was pretty or ugly or young or old. She was
drunk too, but that wasn't why she was crying. She was crying
because she was at the end of everything. There was that sound
in her sobbing which is quite unmistakable – like certain
music. . . . I put my arm round her, but it wasn't like putting
your arm round a woman. She was like something that has
turned into stone. She asked again for whisky. I gave it to her,
and she started a long story, speaking sometimes in French,
sometimes in English, when of course I couldn't understand
her very well. She came from Martinique, she said, and she had
met this monsieur in Paris, the monsieur she was with on the
top floor. Everybody in the house knew she wasn't married to
him, but it was even worse that she wasn't white. She said that
every time they looked at her she could see how they hated her,
and the people in the streets looked at her in the same way. At
first she didn't mind – she thought it comical. But now she had
got so that she would do anything not to see people. She told
me she hadn't been out, except after dark, for two years. When
she said this I had an extraordinary sensation, as if I were
looking down into a pit. It was the expression in her eyes. I
said: "But this monsieur you are living with, what about him?"
"Oh, he is very Angliche, he says I imagine everything." I
asked if he didn't find it strange that she never went out. But
she said No, he thought it quite natural. She talked for a long
time about this monsieur. It seemed that she stayed with him
because she didn't know where else to go, and he stayed with
her because he liked the way she cooked. All this sounds a little
ridiculous, but if you had seen this woman you'd understand
why it is I have never been able to forget her. I said to her:
"Don't let yourself get hysterical, because if you do that it's the

end." But it was difficult to speak to her reasonably, because I had all the time this feeling that I was talking to something that was no longer quite human, no longer quite alive.'

'It's a very sad story,' I say. 'I'm sure you were kind to her.'

'But that's just it. I wasn't. She told me that that afternoon she'd felt better and wanted to go out for a walk. "Even though it wasn't quite dark," she said. On the way out she had met the little girl of one of the other tenants. This house was one of those that are let off in floors. There were several families living in it. She said to the little girl: "Good afternoon. . . ." It was a long story, and of course, as I said, I couldn't understand everything she said to me. But it seemed that the child had told her that she was a dirty woman, that she smelt bad, that she hadn't any right in the house. "I hate you and I wish you were dead," the child said. And after that she had drunk a whole bottle of whisky and there she was, outside my door. Well, what can you say to a story like that? I knew all the time that what she wanted was that I should make love to her and that it was the only thing that would do her any good. But alas, I couldn't. I just gave her what whisky I had and she went off, hardly able to walk. . . . There were two other women in the house. There was one with a shut, thin mouth and a fat one with a bordel laugh. I must say I never heard them speaking to the Martiniquaise, but they had cruel eyes, both of them. . . . I didn't much like the way they looked at me, either. . . . But perhaps all women have cruel eyes. What do you think?'

I say: 'I think most human beings have cruel eyes.' That rosy, wooden, innocent cruelty. I know.

'When I passed her on the stairs next day I said good morning, but she didn't answer me. . . . Once I saw the child putting her tongue out at the poor creature. Only seven or eight, and yet she knew so exactly how to be cruel and who it was safe to be cruel to. One must admire Nature. . . . I got an astonishing hatred of the house after that. Every time I went in it was as if I were walking into a wall – one of those walls where people are built in, still alive. I've never forgotten this. Seriously, all the time I was in London, I felt as if I were being suffocated, as if a large derrière was sitting on me.'

'Well, some people feel that way and other people, of course, don't. It all depends.'

In that last extract, within the layers of narrative, is a very raw story of a woman from Martinique brought from Paris to London by a very 'Angliche' monsieur as his mistress, hated by neighbours and now 'at the end of everything'. But, as we found with Shakespeare's Cressida, getting unmediated access to the feelings of this woman is problematic, because of the layers and the framings between the reader and the woman. The problem is equivalent also to our difficulty of access to Bertha Mason, the 'dark other' from the colonies secreted in the European big house. We last met this notion when thinking about *The Yellow Wallpaper*. The woman in this extract is never named and we hear no more about her. But she's at the centre of Sasha's novel and she's, in effect, an unfreed sex-slave, half-black and therefore presumably a descendant of both slave and slave-owner, neither really French nor English but compelled to tell her story to someone who 'of course . . . couldn't understand her very well'. Called 'dirty' she can't, like Bertha Mason, leave her room till after dark. (The incident is set at least twenty years before mass immigration and subsequent mass race-hatred in London.) The contrast with the Virginian Frank Barber, the freed slave in Dr Johnson's household a hundred and fifty years earlier in the same city, could hardly be more demeaning. To recover her story is equivalent to the difficulty of telling the story of colonial oppression itself.

The representation here of the drunk and embarrassing figure, making an exhibition of herself, both in need of and ill-handled by men (the painter assumes she wants sex but she clearly just needs human warmth), is also a version of Sasha, as she partly recognises, and, yet further from the narrative, a version of Jean Rhys. Rhys was a white Dominican and as a child she encountered inverse prejudice from the black children she loved and admired. The hatred of the white children in this passage is another reversal. As a child Jean Rhys wanted to be black. There's a wry and ironic self-portrait in this passage. The effect of this, and of Sasha's identification with the woman, paradoxically makes the recovery of the woman's own story, the post-colonial reading, harder still. Sasha, for instance, only sees her in European terms, a fellow-victim ('exactly like me'), though that is something and it's

407

better than the painter's attitude. The framings exert a pressure of only partial understandings, as in the only dubiously sympathetic narrative of the painter. The framing-process is confirmed when, after his story, Sasha and Delmar try to arrange the painter's canvases into a make-shift exhibition. The canvases resist. 'They curl up; they don't want to go into frames.' This, too, is a wry self-recognition for Sasha, for whom not being exhibited and framed is so crucial. But the woman from Martinique is now forgotten.

Sasha's refusal to be an exhibit and inability to avoid turning herself into one ('just like me – always wanting to be different from other people') are established from the start. Her experience has a general force, for women in the period, the 1920s and 1930s, as now. The dream-sequence in the first pages features an 'Exhibition' in London to which Sasha desperately wants not to have to go (to see nothing; not to be seen) because she wants 'the way out' from the 'passage in a tube station' instead. Passages to the right and to the left, and no exit, convey the anxious political choices of the late thirties. And in Sasha's dream there's also a powerful claustrophobia conveyed by the press of people, the passages, the placards, and no way out. The scene in the bowels of Mr Blank's shop is the equivalent nightmare – and an image of bodily suffocation is conveyed in the painter's story of the woman from Martinique, where being in London is described as 'being suffocated, as if a large derrière was sitting on me'.

But it's the steel-handed man pointing inexorably in the dream that carries the sexual-political urgency. It suggests that Sasha's panic-driven need to control and organise her life, her routines, is haunted by the knowledge that such control and sense of direction are not hers but in the hands of men. In Emily Dickinson power has a face of steel.

The episode with Mr Blank is prototypical in its cruelty. For what does this blank of a thug want with Sasha apart from a display of male sexual-sadistic power, reducing her to a whimpering animal? Why, after all, does he summon her to his office? The ostensible reason, to deliver a message to the cashier, is preposterous. The effect is more like a cruel ritual, a circus act that she has to perform for him, to be his exhibition. And the woman's response, in her social and financial dependencies, is cruelly limited. The precariousness of Sasha's self-image is focused on that dress she'd been promised cheap. So it's with an appalling appropriateness that, faced with Mr Blank's cold aggression, Sasha runs to cry in the fitting-room where 'her' dress hangs. And it's then that she delivers what is the angriest, most elementally powerful political critique in Rhys's novels, a brilliantly bitter denunciation of male economic power. But: 'Did I say all this? Of course I didn't. I didn't even think it.' Addressed to a space filled more with Sasha's and our mute frustrations than with speaking people, it is as if addressed from that fitting-room, to that dress.

Good Morning, Midnight suddenly, and for Rhys very uncharacteristically, throws us a date. 'It is late October 1937.'

The Paris International Exposition of the Arts and Technology of Modern Life, intended to demonstrate unity between the fifty-two contributing countries, opens in June 1937, overshadowed by strikes, unrest and the increasingly tense international situation. The exhibition's Russian and German pavilions, on both sides of the Trocadéro, are clear expressions of ideological confrontation, and bad art. The largest painting in the world, Dufy's *La Fée Electricité*, is in the Palace of Light, the exhibition's centrepiece, with its 23-foot-long spark, also the largest in the world, regularly lighting up above water.

And a few months later Paris sees another international exhibition: the Surrealist Exhibition at the Beaux-Arts Gallery. This is entered through 'Surrealist Street', a corridor where twenty mannequins are exhibited. Man Ray's is a weeping woman shedding large crystal tears; André Masson's has its head imprisoned in a wicker cage. The central hall has softly rippled folds in one of which is a pond covered with dead leaves. In the corners are four oversized beds. Salvador Dali is expected to grace the opening but he's gone to London to meet Freud and share notes on paranoia with Jacques Lacan. October 1937 is equidistant between the openings of these two landmark exhibitions.

The precision of the date invites us to situate these extracts, Sasha's nightmare about the Exhibition especially, at a particular juncture of empty triumphalisms, as well as on the brink of war. Here are the aggressively competing egos of imperialist systems defacing the Paris skyline; the blinding faith in technological advance; high culture's routine dependence on images of women as submissive commodities, emblems of male desire. Machines crush in Jean Rhys. In late October 1937 the machine is careering out of control, on many fronts simultaneously. Paris is flailing about, trying to celebrate, trying to forget the lessons of the past and ignore what it knows is the European future.

The novel's Paris is topographically exact in its verisimilitude but in an eerie way it's empty, a Paris uneasily full of strangers encountering each other, like Sasha and the painter, in eerily functionless chance, empty of normal residents doing normal things.

Sasha's personal anxiety is to forget and ignore. And Jean Rhys in 1937 has her own grim statistic to celebrate, forget, or ignore. It is exactly thirty years since she arrived in England from Dominica – Sasha has 'no name, no face, no country' – and that was the moment when Rhys became so crucially a stranger, so much more acutely a stranger than she was before as a white Creole and to her own mother. Carole Angier, at the close of her exhaustive biography, urges the determining importance of the 'failure of the relation between mother and child' in Rhys's personality (Angier, 1992, p. 657).

There is one literary affiliation towards which *Good Morning, Midnight* directs the reader from the moment the book is picked up. The novel's title is the first line of an Emily Dickinson poem, one published for the first time only in 1929. The decision so to name the novel is unlikely to have been random.

Why Dickinson? It is the voice of lone, embattled sanity in a world gone mad which Sasha struggles to articulate, and which speaks with a kind of whispered intensity in Dickinson, as in a letter where she says 'pardon my sanity in a world insane'. And Dickinson and Rhys connect so often at the level of obsessively repeated concerns, not least in the way they both communicate language's state of hopeless compromise, the near-impossibility of the most important, urgent things being communicated at all. 'Did I say all this? . . . I didn't even think it.' For the heart 'with the heaviest freight on' (the heart is a 'heavy jagged weight' for Sasha) 'doesn't – always – move – '.

Dickinson's poetry was, as we saw in the chapter on Dickinson, only presented accurately and in full in 1955. For Rhys to name a novel from Dickinson's work as early as 1939 may have been an act of modernist solidarity with a writer who did without so much, notably men. The solitudes and resiliences of the lone consciousness are the site where meaning is generated and fought over in both these writers. At first, and perhaps even now, patronised as eccentric and over-emotional women, writing on and about being on the edges of the social and literary mainstreams, their work then redefined those mainstreams, became paradigms of an enlarged, more challenging model of literature. And in their defiance of convention and decorum they retain their considerable power to disconcert. And of Jean Rhys's pre-war novels this is especially the case with *Good Morning, Midnight*, the most urgently contemporary, as well as the most historicised of her books.

I should add that its ending is the most disturbing thing I know from this period.

Carol Angier's biography of Jean Rhys (revised edition, Harmondsworth, Penguin, 1992) tells the astonishing story in exhaustive detail. Helen Carr's short study (Plymouth, Northcote House, 1996) is clear and very helpful. There's some debate about whether it's right to think of Rhys as a feminist writer. But feminism is complex and multiple. Toril Moi's *Sexual/Textual Politics* (London, Methuen, 1985) outlines the crucial differences in feminist criticism. The introduction to *The Feminist Reader* (2nd edition, London, Macmillan, 1997) is a lucid survey and it emphasises the important connections between feminist and post-colonial criticism. The *Reader* prints Gayatri Chakravorty Spivack's 'Three Women's Texts and a Critique of Imperialism' which brings together *Jane Eyre*, *Frankenstein* and Jean Rhys's *Wide Sargasso Sea*. Selma James's *The Ladies and the Mammies* (Bristol, Falling Wall Press, 1993) is an eloquent bringing together of Jane Austen and Jean Rhys. *The Post-Colonial Studies Reader*, edited by Bill Ashcroft, Gareth Griffiths and Helen Tiffin (London, Routledge, 1995) is a wide-ranging and important collection. It prints part of the Spivack essay.

21

WILLIAMS'S DRAMA
Realism in the theatre, policing the allowable on stage and in film

This chapter presents, side by side, playscript and filmscript extracts from two plays by Tennessee Williams. The related contexts are issues of 'realism' and characterisation in the theatre and questions of what is allowable in terms of representation on stage and on film.

There are a number of American plays from the late 1940s and early 1950s in which a crucial and formative sequence of events happens not on stage but before the curtain goes up. The play's protagonists have to undergo a process of recognition or rediscovery of this story. It has to be re-presented and re-narrated. The effects of the original events, and the consequent effects of their revisiting, are what drive the play's emotional intensities. Coming to terms or failing to come to terms with this burden in the past is what characters have to struggle with.

Although this device goes back to ancient Greek theatre it perhaps had its purest expression in the later plays of Henrik Ibsen with their pioneering 'realism'. The effect seems designed to give theatre something of the illusionary three-dimensions and inwardness that we associate with the great European novels earlier in the century. By shifting the balance of characterisation so that some of the most formative material is in a character's past, to be recovered during stage-time, the playwright gives the illusion of depth as well as meeting the expectations of audiences familiar with a model of psychology (of character-making and of the buried past) that itself was becoming dominant in this period, most obviously from the work of Freud.

This is, anyway, what we find in plays like Tennessee Williams's *A Streetcar Named Desire* (1947) and *Cat on a Hot Tin Roof* (1955) and

412

Arthur Miller's *Death of a Salesman* (1949) and *The Crucible* (1952). The innovation, in *Salesman* and *Streetcar* particularly, was to put Ibsenic realism to work expressionistically, such that staging and presentation techniques act as an extension of the stresses felt by the protagonists in their stories – as in an expressionist painting like Munch's *The Scream*.

Two crucially problematic pre-play stories get painfully revisited in the two Williams plays. These stories haunt two of the loneliest figures in mid-twentieth century drama, a man of 27 and a woman of 30. We'll look at these stories and see what happens when they move from the stage to the big screen.

Brick is 27, an ex-football player and ex-sports commentator. He is an alcoholic and, following a drunken fall, is hobbling on a crutch. He lives with, but in effect separately from, his wife Maggie (the Cat of the title). Their living together is subject to conditions which Brick has imposed. These include not sleeping together and not talking about certain subjects. One subject in particular Maggie finds it difficult to avoid. She needs to talk about it. In the last stages of Act One of *Cat on a Hot Tin Roof* she makes herself say it, though Brick is manically trying to stop her, physically threatening her with his crutch. Here is the extract, from the playscript. The child who appears at the end is one of Gooper's children. Gooper is Brick's brother, eight years older. Maggie is talking 'as if to herself'.

> I've thought a whole lot about it and now I know when I made my mistake. Yes, I made my mistake when I told you the truth about that thing with Skipper. Never should have confessed it, a fatal error, tellin' you about that thing with Skipper.
>
> BRICK: Maggie, shut up about Skipper. I mean it, Maggie; you got to shut up about Skipper.
>
> MARGARET: You ought to understand that Skipper and I –
>
> BRICK: You don't think I'm serious, Maggie? You're fooled by the fact that I am saying this quiet? Look, Maggie. What you're doing is a dangerous thing to do. You're – you're – you're – foolin' with something that – nobody ought to fool with.
>
> MARGARET: This time I'm going to finish what I have to say

to you. Skipper and I made love, if love you could call it, because it made both of us feel a little bit closer to you. You see, you son of a bitch, you asked too much of people, of me, of him, of all the unlucky poor damned sons of bitches that happen to love you, and there was a whole pack of them, yes, there was a pack of them besides me and Skipper, you asked too goddam much of people that loved you, you – superior creature! – you godlike being! – And so we made love to each other to dream it was you, both of us! Yes, yes, yes! Truth, truth! What's so awful about it? I like it, I think the truth is – yeah! I shouldn't have told you. . . .

BRICK [*holding his head unnaturally still and uptilted a bit*]: It was Skipper that told me about it. Not you, Maggie.

MARGARET: I told you!

BRICK: After he told me!

MARGARET: What does it matter who –?

[*Brick turns suddenly out upon the gallery and calls:*]

BRICK: Little girl! Hey, little girl!

LITTLE GIRL [*at a distance*]: What, Uncle Brick?

BRICK: Tell the folks to come up! – Bring everybody upstairs!

MARGARET: I can't stop myself! I'd go on telling you this in front of them all, if I had to!

BRICK: Little girl! Go on, go on, will you? Do what I told you, call them!

MARGARET: Because it's got to be told and you, you! – you never let me!

[*She sobs, then controls herself, and continues almost calmly.*]

It was one of those beautiful, ideal things they tell about in the Greek legends, it couldn't be anything else, you being you, and that's what made it so sad, that's what made it so awful, because it was love that never could be carried through to anything satisfying or even talked about plainly. Brick, I tell you, you got to believe me, Brick, I *do* understand all about it! I – I think it was – *noble*! Can't you tell I'm sincere when I say I respect it? My only point, the only point that I'm making, is life has got to be allowed to continue even after the *dream* of life is – all – over. . . .

[*Brick is without his crutch. Leaning on furniture, he crosses to*

414

pick it up as she continues as if possessed by a will outside herself:]

Why I remember when we double-dated at college, Gladys Fitzgerald and I and you and Skipper, it was more like a date between you and Skipper. Gladys and I were just sort of tagging along as if it was necessary to chaperone you! – to make a good public impression –

BRICK [*turns to face her, half lifting his crutch*]: Maggie, you want me to hit you with this crutch? Don't you know I could kill you with this crutch?

MARGARET: Good Lord, man, d' you think I'd care if you did?

BRICK: One man has one great good true thing in his life. One great good thing which is true! – I had friendship with Skipper. – You are naming it dirty!

MARGARET: I'm not naming it dirty! I am naming it clean.

BRICK: Not love with you, Maggie, but friendship with Skipper was that one great true thing, and you are naming it dirty!

MARGARET: Then you haven't been listenin', not understood what I'm saying! I'm naming it so damn clean that it killed poor Skipper! – You two had something that had to be kept on ice, yes, incorruptible, yes! – and death was the only icebox where you could keep it. . . .

BRICK: I married you, Maggie. Why would I marry you, Maggie, if I was –?

MARGARET: Brick, don't brain me yet, let me finish! – I know, believe me I know, that it was only Skipper that harboured even any *unconscious* desire for anything not perfectly pure between you two! – Now let me skip a little. You married me early that summer we graduated out of Ole Miss, and we were happy, weren't we, we were blissful, yes, hit heaven together ev'ry time that we loved! But that fall you an' Skipper turned down wonderful offers of jobs in order to keep on bein' football heroes – pro-football heroes. You organized the Dixie Stars that fall, so you could keep on bein' team-mates for ever! But somethin' was not right with it! – *Me included!* – between you. Skipper began hittin' the bottle . . . You got a spinal injury – couldn't play the Thanksgivin' game in Chicago,

415

watched it on TV from a traction bed in Toledo. I joined
Skipper. The Dixie Stars lost because poor Skipper was drunk.
We drank together that night all night in the bar of the
Blackstone and when cold day was comin' up over the Lake
an' we were comin' out drunk to take a dizzy look at it, I said,
'SKIPPER! STOP LOVIN' MY HUSBAND OR TELL HIM
HE'S GOT TO LET YOU ADMIT IT TO HIM!' – one way
or another!

HE SLAPPED ME HARD ON THE MOUTH! – then
turned and ran without stopping once, I am sure, all the way
back into his room at the Blackstone. . . .

– When I came to his room that night, with a little scratch
like a shy little mouse at his door, he made that pitiful, inef-
fectual little attempt to prove that what I had said wasn't
true. . . .

[*Brick strikes at her with his crutch, a blow that shatters the
gemlike lamp on the table.*]

– In this way, I destroyed him, by telling him truth that he
and his world which he was born and raised in, yours and his
world, had told him could not be told!

– From then on Skipper was nothing at all but a receptacle
for liquor and drugs. . . .

– *Who shot cock-robin? I with my –*

[*She throws back her head with tight shut eyes.*]

– *merciful arrow!*

[*Brick strikes at her; misses.*]

Missed me! – Sorry, – I'm not tryin' to whitewash my
behaviour, Christ, no! Brick, I'm not good. I don't know why
people have to pretend to be good, nobody's good. The rich or
the well-to-do can afford to respect moral patterns, conventional moral patterns, but I could never afford to, yeah,
but – I'm honest! Give me credit for just that, will you *please*?
– Born poor, raised poor, expect to die poor unless I manage to
get us something out of what Big Daddy leaves when he dies
of cancer! But Brick?! – *Skipper is dead! I'm alive!* Maggie the
cat is –

[*Brick hops awkwardly forward and strikes at her again with
his crutch.*]

– *alive! I am alive! I am . . .*

[*He hurls the crutch at her, across the bed she took refuge
behind, and pitches forward on the floor as she completes her
speech.*]

– *alive!*

[*A little girl, Dixie, bursts into the room, wearing an Indian
war bonnet and firing a cap pistol at Margaret and shouting:
'Bang, bang, bang!'*]

       *Laughter downstairs floats through the open hall door. Mar-
garet had crouched gasping to bed at child's entrance. She now
rises and says with cool fury:*]

Little girl, your mother or someone should teach you –
[*gasping*] – to knock at a door before you come into a room.
Otherwise people might think that you – lack – good
breeding. . . .

DIXIE: Yanh, yanh, yanh, what is Uncle Brick doin' on th'
floor?

BRICK: I tried to kill your Aunt Maggie, but I failed – and I
fell. Little girl, give me my crutch so I can get up off th' floor.

MARGARET: Yes, give your uncle his crutch, he's a cripple,
honey, he broke his ankle last night jumping hurdles on the
high school athletic field!

DIXIE: What were you jumping hurdles for, Uncle Brick?

BRICK: Because I used to jump them, and people like to do
what they used to do, even after they've stopped being able to
do it. . . .

MARGARET: That's right, that's your answer, now go away,
little girl.

[*Dixie fires cap pistol at Margaret three times.*]

Stop, you stop that, monster! You little no-neck monster!

[*She seizes the cap pistol and hurls it through gallery doors.*]

DIXIE [*with a precocious instinct for the cruellest thing*]: You're
jealous! – You're just jealous because you can't have babies!

[*She sticks out her tongue at Margaret as she sashays past her
with her stomach stuck out, to the gallery. Margaret slams the
gallery doors and leans panting against them. There is a pause.
Brick has replaced his spilt drink and sits, faraway, on the
great four-poster bed.*]

417

MARGARET: You see? – they gloat over us being childless, even in front of their five little no-neck monsters!

[*Pause. Voices approach on the stairs.*]

Brick? – I've been to a doctor in Memphis, a – a gynaecologist. . . .

I've been completely examined, and there is no reason why we can't have a child whenever we want one. And this is my time by the calendar to conceive. Are you listening to me? Are you? Are you LISTENING TO ME!

BRICK: Yes. I hear you, Maggie.

[*His attention returns to her inflamed face.*]

– But how in hell on earth do you imagine – that you're going to have a child by a man that can't stand you?

MARGARET: That's a problem that I will have to work out.

[*She wheels about to face the hall door.*]

Here they come!

[*The lights dim.*]

CURTAIN

There's the buried story, revealed rather earlier than in some plays. At least it's Maggie's version of it. And she's hardly a neutral witness. But the story she tells here, and even more perhaps Brick's response to it and indeed her own interpretative spin on it (how she presents the two men), are very difficult to assess and not only because he's trying to knock her into silence. An audience, anyway, pieces together a narrative in which three people are entangled and where the motives for two of them sleeping together are rather surprising. The nature of the relationship between Brick and Skipper, and Brick's degree of self-knowledge about it and about himself generally, are clear or opaque, depending on where you're sitting. Skipper is now dead. It's usual to infer that Brick and Maggie's dysfunctional relations and his alcoholism are the result.

One small but odd item in the narrative is Brick's insistence that Skipper told him about the affair before Maggie did. This puzzles Maggie and us. It's explained or sort-of explained (its exact content remains uncertain) in Act Two when Brick tells his version, with its different emphases, in a painful exchange with his father. Big Daddy thinks he's been given a positive bill of health from the clinic. In fact, he has advanced and terminal cancer but, so far, he hasn't been told. What Maggie called a law of silence – the one Brick put on the subject of Skipper – applies to his cancer too. But, as Maggie says, 'silence about a thing just magnifies it. It grows and festers in silence, becomes malignant.' This is their dialogue as it reaches its climax. (A long stage-direction is taken out and kept back for later.) Big Daddy is speaking.

> *You* I *do* like for some reason, did always have some kind of real feeling for – affection – respect – yes, always. . . .
>
> You and being a success as a planter is all I ever had any devotion to in my whole life! – and that's the truth. . . .
>
> I don't know why, but it is!
>
> *I've* lived with mendacity! – Why can't *you* live with it? Hell, you *got* to live with it, there's nothing *else* to *live* with except mendacity, is there?
>
> BRICK: Yes, sir. Yes, sir, there is something else that you can live with!
>
> BIG DADDY: What?
>
> BRICK: [*lifting his glass*]: This! – Liquor. . . .
>
> BIG DADDY: That's not living, that's dodging away from life.
>
> BRICK: I want to dodge away from it.
>
> BIG DADDY: Then why don't you kill yourself, man?
>
> BRICK: I like to drink . . .
>
> BIG DADDY: Oh, God, I can't talk to you. . . .
>
> BRICK: I'm sorry, Big Daddy.
>
> BIG DADDY: Not as sorry as I am. I'll tell you something. A little while back when I thought my number was up –
>
> [*This speech should have torrential pace and fury.*]
>
> – before I found out it was just this – spastic – colon. I thought about you. Should I or should I not, if the jig was up, give you this place when I go – since I hate Gooper an' Mae an' know that they hate me, and since all five same monkeys are little Maes an' Goopers. – And I thought, No! – Then I thought, Yes! – I couldn't make up my mind. I hate Gooper and his five same monkeys and that bitch Mae! Why should I turn over twenty-eight thousand acres of the richest land this side of the valley Nile to not my kind? – But why in hell, on the other hand, Brick – should I subsidize a goddam fool on the bottle?

419

– Liked or not liked, well, maybe even – *loved!* – Why should I do that? – Subsidize worthless behaviour? Rot? Corruption?

BRICK [*smiling*]: I understand.

BIG DADDY: Well, if you do, you're smarter than I am, God damn it, because I don't understand. And this I will tell you frankly. I didn't make up my mind at all on that question and still to this day I ain't made out no will! – Well, now I don't *have* to. The pressure is gone. I can just wait and see if you pull yourself together or if you don't.

BRICK: That's right, Big Daddy.

BIG DADDY: You sound like you thought I was kidding.

BRICK [*rising*]: No, sir, I know you're not kidding.

BIG DADDY: But you don't care –?

BRICK [*hobbling toward the gallery door*]: No, sir, I don't care. . . . Now how about taking a look at your birthday fireworks and getting some of that cool breeze off the river?

[*He stands in the gallery doorway as the night sky turns pink and green and gold with successive flashes of light.*]

BIG DADDY: WAIT! – Brick. . . .

[*His voice drops. Suddenly there is something shy, almost tender, in his restraining gesture.*]

Don't let's – leave it like this, like them other talks we've had, we've always – talked around things, we've – just talked around things for some rutten reason, I don't know what, it's always like something was left not spoken, something avoided because neither of us was honest enough with the – other. . . .

BRICK: I never lied to you, Big Daddy.

BIG DADDY: Did I ever to *you?*

BRICK: No, sir. . . .

BIG DADDY: Then there is at least two people that never lied to each other.

BRICK: But we've never *talked* to each other.

BIG DADDY: We can *now.*

BRICK: Big Daddy, there don't seem to be anything much to say.

BIG DADDY: You say that you drink to kill your disgust with lying.

BRICK: You said to give you a reason.

420

BIG DADDY: Is liquor the only thing that'll kill this disgust?

BRICK: Now. Yes.

BIG DADDY: But not once, huh?

BRICK: Not when I was still young an' believing. A drinking man's someone who wants to forget he isn't still young an' believing.

BIG DADDY: Believing what?

BRICK: Believing. . . .

BIG DADDY: Believing *what?*

BRICK [*stubbornly evasive*]: Believing . . .

BIG DADDY: I don't know what the hell you mean by believing and I don't think you know what you mean by believing, but if you still got sports in your blood, go back to sports announcing and –

BRICK: Sit in a glass box watching games I can't play? Describing what I can't do while players do it? Sweating out their disgust and confusion in contests I'm not fit for? Drinkin' a coke, half bourbon, so I can stand it? That's no goddam good any more, no help – time just outran me, Big Daddy – got there first . . .

BIG DADDY: I think you're passing the buck.

BRICK: You know many drinkin' men?

BIG DADDY [*with a slight, charming smile*]: I have known a fair number of that species.

BRICK: Could any of them tell you why he drank?

BIG DADDY: Yep, you're passin' the buck to things like time and disgust with 'mendacity' and – crap! – if you got to use that kind of language about a thing, it's ninety-proof bull, and I'm not buying any.

BRICK: I had to give you a reason to get a drink!

BIG DADDY: You started drinkin' when your friend Skipper died.

[*Silence for five beats. Then Brick makes a startled movement, reaching for his crutch.*]

BRICK: What are you suggesting?

BIG DADDY: I'm suggesting nothing.

[*The shuffle and clop of Brick's rapid hobble away from his father's steady, grave attention.*]

– But Gooper an' Mae suggested that there was something not right exactly in your –

BRICK: [*stopping short downstage as if backed to a wall*]: 'Not right'?

BIG DADDY: Not, well, exactly *normal* in your friendship with –

BRICK: They suggested that, too? I thought that was Maggie's suggestion.

[. . .]

[*The following scene should be played with great concentration, with most of the power leashed but palpable in what is left unspoken.*]

Who else's suggestion is it, is it *yours?* How many others thought that Skipper and I were –

BIG DADDY [*gently*]: Now, hold on, hold on a minute, son. – I knocked around in my time.

BRICK: What's that got to do with –

BIG DADDY: I said 'Hold on!' – I bummed, I bummed this country till I was –

BRICK: Whose suggestion, who else's suggestion is it?

BIG DADDY: Slept in hobo jungles and railroad Y's and flop-houses in all cities before I –

BRICK: Oh, *you* think so, too, you call me your son and a queer. Oh! Maybe that's why you put Maggie and me in this room that was Jack Straw's and Peter Ochello's, in which that pair of old sisters slept in a double bed where both of 'em died!

BIG DADDY: *Now just don't go throwing rocks at* –

[*Suddenly Reverend Tooker appears in the gallery doors, his head slightly, playfully, fatuously cocked, with a practised clergyman's smile, sincere as a bird-call blown on a hunter's whistle, the living embodiment of the pious, conventional lie.*

Big Daddy gasps a little at this perfectly timed, but incongruous, apparition.]

– What're you looking for, Preacher?

REVEREND TOOKER: The gentlemen's lavatory, ha ha! – heh, heh. . . .

BIG DADDY [*with strained courtesy*]: – Go back out and walk down to the other end of the gallery, Reverend Tooker, and use the bathroom connected with my bedroom, and if you can't find it, ask them where it is!

REVEREND TOOKER: Ah, thanks.

[*He goes out with a deprecatory chuckle.*]

BIG DADDY: It's hard to talk in this place . . .

BRICK: Son of a –!

BIG DADDY [*leaving a lot unspoken*]: – I seen all things and understood a lot of them, till 1910. Christ, the year that – I had worn my shoes through, hocked my – I hopped off a yellow dog freight car half a mile down the road, slept in a wagon of cotton outside the gin – Jack Straw an' Peter Ochello took me in. Hired me to manage this place which grew into this one. – When Jack Straw died – why, old Peter Ochello quit eatin' like a dog does when its master's dead, and died, too!

BRICK: Christ!

BIG DADDY: I'm just saying I understand such –

BRICK [*violently*]: Skipper is dead. I have not quit eating!

BIG DADDY: No, but you started drinking.

[*Brick wheels on his crutch and hurls his glass across the room shouting.*]

BRICK: YOU THINK SO, TOO?

BIG DADDY: *Shhh!*

[*Footsteps run on the gallery. There are women's calls.*

Big Daddy goes toward the door.]

Go 'way! – Just broke a glass. . . .

[*Brick is transformed, as if a quiet mountain blew suddenly up in volcanic flame.*]

BRICK: You think so, too? You think so, too? You think me an' Skipper did, did, did! – *sodomy!* – together?

BIG DADDY: Hold –!

BRICK: That what you –

BIG DADDY: – *ON* – a minute!

BRICK: You think we did dirty things between us, Skipper an' –

BIG DADDY: Why are you shouting like that? Why are you –

BRICK: – Me, is that what you think of Skipper, is that –

BIG DADDY: – so excited? I don't think nothing. I don't know nothing. I'm simply telling you what –

BRICK: You think that Skipper and me were a pair of dirty old
men?

BIG DADDY: Now that's –

BRICK: Straw? Ochello? A couple of –

BIG DADDY: Now just –

BRICK: – ducking sissies? Queers? Is that what you –

BIG DADDY: Shhh.

BRICK: – think?

> [*He loses his balance and pitches to his knees without noticing the pain. He grabs the bed and drags himself up.*]

BIG DADDY: Jesus! – Whew. . . . Grab my hand!

BRICK: Naw, I don't want your hand. . . .

BIG DADDY: Well, I want yours. Git up!

> [*He draws him up, keeps an arm about him with concern and affection.*]

You broken out in a sweat! You're panting like you'd run a
race with –

BRICK [*freeing himself from his father's hold*]: Big Daddy, you
shock me, Big Daddy, you, you – *shock* me! Talkin' so –

> [*He turns away from his father.*]

– casually! – about a – thing like that . . .

– Don't you know how people *feel* about things like that?
How, how *disgusted* they are by things like that? Why, at Ole
Miss when it was discovered a pledge to our fraternity,
Skipper's and mine, did a, *attempted* to do a, unnatural thing
with –

We not only dropped him like a hot rock! – We told him to
git off the campus, and he did, he got! – All the way to –

> [*He halts, breathless.*]

BIG DADDY: – Where?

BRICK: North Africa, last I heard!

BIG DADDY: Well, I have come back from further away than
that, I have just now returned from the other side of the
moon, death's country, son, and I'm not easy to shock by
anything here.

> [*He comes downstage and faces out.*]

Always, anyhow, lived with too much space around me to be
infected by ideas of other people. One thing you can grow on a

big place more important than cotton! – is *tolerance!* – I grown it.

[*He returns toward Brick.*]

BRICK: Why can't exceptional friendship, *real, real, deep, deep friendship!* between two men be respected as something clean and decent without being thought of as –

BIG DADDY: It can, it is, for God's sake.

BRICK: – *Fairies.* . . .

[*In his utterance of this word, we gauge the wide and profound reach of the conventional mores he got from the world that crowned him with early laurel.*]

BIG DADDY: I told Mae an' Gooper –

BRICK: Frig Mae and Gooper, frig all dirty lies and liars! – Skipper and me had a clean, true thing between us! – had a clean friendship, practically all our lives, till Maggie got the idea you're talking about. Normal? No! – It was too rare to be normal, any true thing between two people is too rare to be normal. Oh, once in a while he put his hand on my shoulder or I'd put mine on his, oh, maybe even, when we were touring the country in pro-football an' shared hotel-rooms we'd reach across the space between the two beds and shake hands to say goodnight, yeah, one or two times we –

BIG DADDY: Brick, nobody thinks that that's not normal!

BRICK: Well, they're mistaken, it was! It was a pure an' true thing an' that's not normal.

[*They both stare straight at each other for a long moment. The tension breaks and both turn away as if tired.*]

BIG DADDY: Yeah, it's – hard t' – talk. . . .

BRICK: All right, then, let's – let it go. . . .

BIG DADDY: Why did Skipper crack up? Why have you?

[*Brick looks back at his father again. He has already decided, without knowing that he has made this decision, that he is going to tell his father that he is dying of cancer. Only this could even the score between them: one inadmissible thing in return for another.*]

BRICK [*ominously*]: All right. You're asking for it, Big Daddy. We're finally going to have that real true talk you wanted. It's too late to stop it, now, we got to carry it through and cover every subject.

[*He hobbles back to the liquor cabinet.*]

Uh-huh.

[*He opens the ice bucket and picks up the silver tongs with slow admiration of their frosty brightness.*]

Maggie declares that Skipper and I went into pro-football after we left 'Ole Miss' because we were scared to grow up . . .

[*He moves downstage with the shuffle and clop of a cripple on a crutch. As Margaret did when her speech became 'recitative', he looks out into the house, commanding its attention by his direct, concentrated gaze – a broken, 'tragically elegant' figure telling simply as much as he knows of 'the Truth':*]

– Wanted to – keep on tossing – those long, long! – high, high! – passes that – couldn't be intercepted except by time, the aerial attack that made us famous! And so we did, we did, we kept it up for one season, that aerial attack, we held it high! – Yeah, but –

– that summer, Maggie, she laid the law down to me, said, Now or never, and so I married Maggie. . . .

BIG DADDY: How was Maggie in bed?

BRICK [*wryly*]: Great! the greatest!

[*Big Daddy nods as if he thought so.*]

She went on the road that fall with the Dixie Stars. Oh, she made a great show of being the world's best sport. She wore a – wore a – tall bearskin cap! A shako, they call it, a dyed moleskin coat, a moleskin coat dyed red! – Cut up crazy! Rented hotel ballrooms for victory celebrations, wouldn't cancel them when it – turned out – defeat. . . .

MAGGIE THE CAT! Ha ha!

[*Big Daddy nods.*]

– But Skipper, he had some fever which came back on him which doctors couldn't explain and I got that injury – turned out to be just a shadow on the X-ray plate – and a touch of bursitis. . . .

I lay in a hospital bed, watched our games on TV, saw Maggie on the bench next to Skipper when he was hauled out of a game for stumbles, fumbles! – Burned me up the way she

hung on his arm! – Y'know, I think that Maggie had always
felt sort of left out because she and me never got any closer
together than two people just get in bed, which is not much
closer than two cats on a – fence humping. . . .

So! She took this time to work on poor dumb Skipper. He
was a less than average student at Ole Miss, you know that,
don't you?! – Poured in his mind the dirty, false idea that
what we were, him and me, was a frustrated case of that ole
pair of sisters that lived in this room, Jack Straw and Peter
Ochello! – He, poor Skipper, went to bed with Maggie to
prove it wasn't true, and when it didn't work out, he thought
it *was* true! – Skipper broke in two like a rotten stick –
nobody ever turned so fast to a lush – or died of it so
quick. . . .

– Now are you satisfied?

[*Big Daddy has listened to this story, dividing the grain from
the chaff. Now he looks at his son.*]

BIG DADDY: Are *you* satisfied?

BRICK: With what?

BIG DADDY: That half-ass story!

BRICK: What's half-ass about it?

BIG DADDY: Something's left out of that story. What did you
leave out?

[*The phone has started ringing in the hall. As if it reminded
him of something, Brick glances suddenly toward the sound and
says:*]

BRICK: Yes! – I left out a long-distance call which I had from
Skipper, in which he made a drunken confession to me and on
which I hung up! – last time we spoke to each other in our
lives. . . .

[*Muted ring stops as someone answers phone in a soft, indistinct
voice in hall.*]

BIG DADDY: You hung up?

BRICK: Hung up. Jesus! Well –

BIG DADDY: Anyhow now! – we have tracked down the lie
with which you're disgusted and which you are drinking to
kill your disgust with, Brick. You been passing the buck. This
disgust with mendacity is disgust with yourself.

You! – dug the grave of your friend and kicked him in it! – before you'd face truth with him!

BRICK: *His* truth, not *mine!*

BIG DADDY: His truth, okay! But you wouldn't face it with him!

BRICK: Who *can* face truth? Can *you?*

BIG DADDY: Now don't start passin' the rotten buck again, boy!

BRICK: *How about these birthday congratulations, these many, many happy returns of the day, when ev'rybody but you knows there won't be any!*

> [*Whoever has answered the hall phone lets out a high, shrill laugh; the voice becomes audible saying: 'no, no, you got it all wrong! Upside down! Are you crazy?'*
>
> *Brick suddenly catches his breath as he realizes that he has made a shocking disclosure. He hobbles a few paces, then freezes, and without looking at his father's shocked face, says:*]

Let's, let's – go out, now, and –

> [*Big Daddy moves suddenly forward and grabs hold of the boy's crutch like it was a weapon for which they were fighting for possession.*]

BIG DADDY: Oh, no, no! No one's going out! What did you start to say?

BRICK: I don't remember.

BIG DADDY: 'Many happy returns when they know there won't be any'?

BRICK: Aw, hell, Big Daddy, forget it. Come on out on the gallery and look at the fireworks they're shooting off for your birthday. . . .

BIG DADDY: First you finish that remark you were makin' before you cut off. 'Many happy returns when they know there won't be any'? Ain't that what you just said?

BRICK: Look, now. I can get around without that crutch if I have to but it would be a lot easier on the furniture an' glassware if I didn' have to go swinging along like Tarzan of th' –

BIG DADDY: FINISH WHAT YOU WAS SAYIN'!

> [*An eerie green glow shows in sky behind him.*]

BRICK: [*sucking the ice in his glass, speech becoming thick*]: Leave

428

th' place to Gooper and Mae an' their five little same little monkeys. All I want is –

BIG DADDY: 'LEAVE TH' PLACE,' did you say?

BRICK: [*vaguely*]: All twenty-eight thousand acres of the richest land this side of the valley Nile.

BIG DADDY: Who said I was 'leaving the place' to Gooper or anybody? This is my sixty-fifth birthday! I got fifteen years or twenty years left in me! I'll outlive *you!* I'll bury you an' have to pay for your coffin!

BRICK: Sure. Many happy returns. Now let's go watch the fireworks, come on, let's –

BIG DADDY: Lying, have they been lying? About the report from th' – clinic. Did they, did they – find something? – *Cancer.* Maybe?

BRICK: Mendacity is a system that we live in. Liquor is one way out an' death's the other . . .

> [*He takes the crutch from Big Daddy's loose grip and swings out on the gallery, leaving the doors open.*
>
> *A song, 'Pick a Bale of Cotton', is heard.*]

MAE [*appearing in door*]: Oh, Big Daddy, the field-hands are singin' fo' you!

BIG DADDY [*shouting hoarsely*]: BRICK! BRICK!

MAE: He's outside drinkin', Big Daddy.

BIG DADDY: *BRICK!*

> [*Mae retreats, awed by the passion of his voice. Children call Brick in tones mocking Big Daddy. His face crumbles like broken yellow plaster about to fall into dust.*
>
> *There is a glow in the sky. Brick swings back through the doors, slowly, gravely, quite soberly.*]

BRICK: I'm sorry, Big Daddy. My head don't work any more and it's hard for me to understand how anybody could care if he lived or died or was dying or cared about anything but whether or not there was liquor left in the bottle and so I said what I said without thinking. In some ways I'm no better than the others, in some ways worse because I'm less alive. Maybe it's being alive that makes them lie, and being almost *not* alive makes me sort of accidentally truthful – I don't know but – anyway – we've been friends . . .

— And being friends is telling each other the truth . . .
     [*There is a pause.*]
You told *me!* I told *you!*
     [*A child rushes into the room and grabs a fistful of fire-cracker, and runs out again.*]
CHILD [*screaming*]: Bang, bang, bang, bang, bang, bang, bang, bang, bang!
BIG DADDY [slowly and passionately]: CHRIST – DAMN – ALL – LYING SONS OF – LYING BITCHES!
     [*He straightens at last and crosses to the inside door. At the door he turns and looks back as if he had some desperate question he couldn't put into words. Then he nods reflectively and says in a hoarse voice:*]
Yes, all liars, all liars, all lying dying liars!
     [*This is said slowly, slowly, with a fierce revulsion. He goes on out.*]
— Lying! Dying! Liars!
     [*His voice dies out. There is the sound of a child being slapped. It rushes, hideously bawling, through room and out the hall door.*
     Brick remains motionless as the lights dim out and the curtain falls.]

CURTAIN

Again it's difficult to know what we're meant to make of Brick and Skipper. Brick's manic over-defensiveness and denial-displacement (*you're* naming it dirty), here as with Maggie, and the violence of the reaction to the college student who made a pass at Skipper or Brick (surely a massive over-reaction, even for the time) look like desperate tactics. 'Oh, once in a while he put his hand on my shoulder or I'd put mine on his, oh, maybe even, when we were touring the country in pro-football an' shared hotel-rooms we'd reach across the space between the two beds and shake hands to say goodnight, yeah, one or two times we –.' The tone and rhythm say as much as the words here. And, like Alice's gnat in *Through the Looking-Glass*, the uncompleted sentence hangs full of suggestion. But who is doing the interrupting or censoring here?

Is it that Brick can't be more explicit because there's nothing to be explicit about? Or because he didn't then and doesn't now realise his own feelings? Or because he does but can't talk about them to his father (or anyone else)? Or because he does realise and could express them but it's Williams who can't because of repressive conventions in the theatre in 1955? Or is it because Williams himself just doesn't 'know' Brick fully, either because he's too close to him (the play certainly treats Brick very gently) or because he's resisting doing what writers usually do – simplifying and clarifying at the expense of psychological complexity? This is the long stage direction that belongs where you'll find '[. . .]' above. Does it help?

> [*Brick's detachment is at last broken through. His heart is accelerated; his forehead sweat-beaded; his breath becomes more rapid and his voice hoarse. The thing they're discussing, timidly and painfully on the side of Big Daddy, fiercely, violently on Brick's side, is the inadmissible thing that Skipper died to disavow between them. The fact that if it existed it had to be disavowed to 'keep face' in the world they lived in, may be at the heart of the 'mendacity' that Brick drinks to kill his disgust with. It may be the root of his collapse. Or maybe it is only a single manifestation of it, not even the most important. The bird that I hope to catch in the net of this play is not the solution of one man's psychological problem. I'm trying to catch the true quality of experience in a group of people, that cloudy, flickering, evanescent – fiercely charged! – interplay of live human beings in the thundercloud of a common crisis. Some mystery should be left in the revelation of character in a play, just as a great deal of mystery is always left in the revelation of character in life, even in one's own character to himself. This does not absolve the playwright of his duty to observe and probe as clearly and deeply as he legitimately can: but it should steer him away from 'pat' conclusions, facile definitions which make a play just a play, not a snare for the truth of human experience.*]

This is elusive, even evasive, but it does convey a recognition that characters in texts should resist full 'revelation', that texts shouldn't provide facile solutions but instead cast a 'snare' for the 'fiercely charged interplay of live human beings'. It's a model of characterisation perhaps at odds with the device we started with – that of having a secret narrative to be recovered, one that will 'explain'. And the other characters in the play are characterised more conventionally. It may be that Williams is special-pleading, in recognition that Brick's knowability is radically uncertain, and perhaps that it doesn't 'work'. We met this issue, this problem of characterisation, with Melville's Bartleby, where conventional 'explanations' for unknowability are offered only to be resisted. But Bartleby's absolute unknowability seems to 'work'.

Act Three exists in two forms, both unsatisfactory, for contracting reasons. One thing was that the director Elia Kazan objected to the first version because (among other reasons) he thought that Brick should change fundamentally as a result of the dialogue with his father. Williams, unsurprisingly in the light of that stage direction, disagreed, arguing that Brick's 'moral paralysis' was a 'root thing in his tragedy' and that no single conversation, 'however revelatory, ever effects so immediate an effect in the heart or even conduct of a person in Brick's state of spiritual disrepair' (Williams's note to the Broadway version of Act Three, in Penguin edition, 1976, p. 107). Was it even 'revelatory' for Brick anyway? Does Brick really learn anything at the end of Act Two? But Williams did, if crudely and unconvincingly, soften Brick's cold indifference to Maggie in the second version of Act Three and, unlike in the first version where all he does is drink and sing to himself and where the ending is frustratingly open, there's an implausible possibility that Brick and Maggie will live together happily and have children (thus beating Gooper to the estate). This is the version as first performed on Broadway. So much for Brick's rooted moral paralysis and spiritual disrepair. And in both versions the 'festering' issue of Brick's sexuality has, along with any further discussion of Skipper, been magicked away.

The problem of the two endings and the problem of Brick and Skipper's sexuality were, together, unresolved and perhaps unresolvable enough to allow the scriptwriters of the 1958 film version (not Williams) the most free of free hands. The results are startling.

In the equivalent of Act One Brick doesn't allow Maggie to tell anything much of her version of the pre-play story apart from a very brief mention of something in a hotel-room and about Skipper being a no-good person. The audience presumably thinks an affair took place. And instead of the second half of the Brick–Big Daddy dialogue the film has an extraordinary three-way discussion. This is it.

BIG DADDY: What was going on between you and Skipper?

MARGARET: Well, you see, Big Daddy . . .

BRICK: Well, come on, Maggie, you wanted to tell truth upstairs. Go on now, tell him.

MARGARET: Skipper didn't like me.

BRICK: Why Maggie, why didn't Skipper like you?

MARGARET: You know he was against us getting married.

BRICK: Why Maggie?

MARGARET: 'Cos it meant less freedom for you.

BRICK: Freedom to do what, Maggie?

MARGARET: Freedom to run from town to town, playing, always running, football practice –

BRICK: Nobody forced you to come along with us.

MARGARET: I didn't expect to spend my honeymoon in the locker-room with the boys.

BRICK: Since when did the smell of a man ever injure your sensitive feelings?

MARGARET: Football, baby, the idea of football smelled, especially the notions of a professional team. Why, he didn't need a team of his own, he could have gotten a spot on any pro-team in the country. You organised your own team on account of Skipper –

BRICK: You're a liar –

MARGARET: On account of he wasn't good enough to make it on his own.

BRICK: Professional football, Maggie, is a business.

MARGARET: A business of making money?

BRICK: Yeah, money, the stuff your dreams are made of.

MARGARET: Why, the Dixie Stars never made a nickel, not from the first day to the last. It wasn't the money, it was the cheers, he lapped them up.

BRICK: Sure, the cheers didn't mean anything to me. But they meant something to you, didn't they? They shut you out and that's what you hated, being shut out.

MARGARET: Not by the boys, baby, by you, by the man I worshipped. That's why I hated Skipper.

BRICK: You hated him so much, you got him drunk and went to bed with him. [*Long pause*]

BIG DADDY: Well, is that true?

MARGARET: Oh, Big Daddy, you don't think I ravished a football hero? [*Pause*]

BRICK: Skipper was drunk.

MARGARET: So are you, most of the time. I don't seem to make out so well with you.

BRICK: Are you . . . Are you trying to say that nothing happened between you and Skipper?

MARGARET: You know what happened.

BRICK: I don't know what happened. I don't know, Maggie, I wasn't there, I couldn't play that Sunday, I wasn't in Chicago, I was in a hospital –

MARGARET: But Skipper played. Oh, he played all right, he played his first professional game without Brick. Tell Big Daddy what happened. Go on, tell him, you're a sports announcer. Give us a running account of the all-American bust. Tell Big Daddy how many times Skipper fumbled and stumbled and fell apart. On offence he was useless, on defence he was a coward. And it was all over. Chicago 47, Dixie Stars 0.

BRICK: Bad breaks.

MARGARET: No.

BRICK: An off day.

MARGARET: No baby. Without you, Skipper was nothing. Outside big, tough, confident. Inside, pure jelly. You saw the game on TV, you saw what happened.

BRICK: But I didn't see what happened in Skipper's hotel room. That little episode was not on TV. Go ahead, tell Big Daddy why you were in Skipper's room.

MARGARET: He was sick. [*Music starts*] Sick with drink and he wouldn't come out. He'd busted some furniture and the hotel manager said to stop him before he called the police. So I went to his room. I scratched on his door and begged him let me in. He was half crazy, violent and screaming one minute and weak and crying the next. And all the time scared stiff about you. So I said to him maybe it was time we forgot about football. Maybe he ought to get a job and let me and Brick alone. I thought he'd hit me. He just walked towards me with a funny kind of smile on his face. Then he did the strangest thing. He kissed me. That was the first time he'd ever touched me. Then I knew what I was going to do. I'd get rid of Skipper. I'd show Brick that that deep true friendship was a big lie. I'd prove it by showing that Skipper would make love to the wife of his best friend. He didn't need any coaxing. He was more than willing. He even seemed to have the same idea.

BRICK: You're just trying to whitewash it.

MARGARET: I'm not. I was just trying to win back my husband. It didn't matter how. I would have done anything. Even that. At the last second I got panicky. Supposing I lost you instead. Supposing you'd hate me instead of Skipper. So I ran. Nothing happened. I've tried to tell him a hundred times but he won't let me. Nothing happened.

BRICK: Hallelujah! Saint Maggie!

MARGARET: I wanted to get rid of Skipper. But not if it meant losing you. He blames me for Skipper's death. Maybe I got rid of Skipper. Skipper went out anyway. I didn't get rid of him at all. [*Long pause*] Isn't it an awful joke, honey? I lost you anyway.

BIG DADDY: You didn't talk to him again before he –

MARGARET: No. But Brick did.

BIG DADDY: How do you know they talked?

MARGARET: Skipper told me.

BIG DADDY: When?

MARGARET: When they put his poor broken body in the ambulance. I rode with him to the hospital. All the time he kept on saying 'Why did Brick hang up on me, why?' Why, Brick? [*Maggie leaves room*]

[. . .]

BIG DADDY: Why did you hang up on Skipper when he called you? Answer me. What did he say? Was it about him and Maggie?

BRICK: He said they'd made love.

435

BIG DADDY: And you believed him?

BRICK: Yes.

BIG DADDY: Then why haven't you thrown her out? Something's missing here. Now why did Skipper kill himself?

BRICK: 'Cos someone let him down. [*Pause. Music*] I let him down. When he called that night I couldn't make much sense out of it. There was one thing that was sure. Skipper was scared. Scared. What happened that day on the football field, that I'd blame him, scared that I'd walk out on him. Skipper afraid, I couldn't believe that. Inside he was real deep down scared and he broke like a rotten stick. He started crying 'I need you'. He kept adding 'help me, help me'. Me help him! How does one drowning man help another drowning man?

BIG DADDY: So you hung up on him.

BRICK: And then that phone started to ring again and it rang and it rang and it wouldn't stop ringing. And I lay in that hospital bed, I was unable to move or run from that sound and still it kept ringing louder and louder and the sound of that was like Skipper screaming for help. I couldn't pick it up . . .

BIG DADDY: So that's why he killed himself.

BRICK: Yup. Because I let him down. So that disgust with mendacity is really disgust with myself. And when I hear that click in my head I don't hear the sound of that phone ringing any more. And I can stop thinking. I'm ashamed, Big Daddy, that's why I'm a drunk. When I'm drunk I can stand myself.

Nothing happened. Maggie didn't commit adultery (and, unlike in the playscript, wasn't drunk when she, er, didn't). Skipper was not dependable and was nothing without Brick. Maggie was prepared to prove this to Brick but changed her mind when she realised the risk. Skipper lied – claiming to Brick that they had slept together – in order to break up the marriage. So the marriage broke for wholly artificial reasons, and thus can be repaired, surprise surprise. The film has neatly prepared for this, inventing a nice bit of early business in which Brick is seen hugging Maggie's bathrobe. Not only adultery but any question of sexuality between Brick and Skipper has simply been washed out of the text.

And what that allows for is the extra scene, half-way through the equivalent of Act Three, that the filmscript spirits out of the air – a scene between the suddenly sober Brick and his 'pa' (as he now calls him) in the cellar, facing his death. A completely new stretch of dialogue establishes that Brick's problem is not uncertain sexuality from having been over-idealised, 'crowned . . . with early laurel', devotedly doted on by both parents (this is one reading of the evidence in the playscript), but the opposite, that his dad hasn't loved him at all (or anyone) properly – because he loved possessions and power too much. Thus Brick, having no real father, had to rely too heavily on Skipper.

Brick's task in the cellar (after smashing it up a bit and breaking down) is to educate his father about love. This he does (not only now sober but a sudden moral authority) by reminding him that Big Daddy's own 'hobo' tramp of a father (cue banjo music) loved him and took him everywhere and left him something more important than possessions – love. Williams himself had inadvertently omitted to write about Big Daddy's father, instead giving him a dubious pair of pseudo-father figures in Straw and Ochello, about whom Brick is so suspiciously antagonistic. 'Yeah', says Big Daddy, in the film's educational climax, 'I loved him'. So father learns how to love son through recognising his own mutualised father-love and this in turn can allow Brick, at last, to express his own love for wife as well as father, to resume his marital relations, have a child, get the estate, etc.

A fine, upstanding film about fathers and sons, and families healed by fathers and sons discovering their mutual love. And it works because the playscript is too committed, for personal as well as institutional reasons, to sliding off and circling round its own most urgent and anxious need to speak. It's as if it's a gay play not allowing itself or not allowed to come out. So it moves on to Broadway and then into cinema, writing itself into the kind of text with the kind of 'pat' and 'facile' character-development that Williams doesn't really believe in.

* * *

In *Streetcar*, Blanche Dubois is 30 and wants to be younger. Like Brick, and for similar reasons, she's an alcoholic. She obsessively bathes. (Brick is in the shower when the play opens, accuses his wife and father of dirtying him and, without even noticing it, wipes Maggie's kiss off his mouth.) Blanche is staying with her sister Stella who, leaving home young to marry Stanley, has moved into a rough, urban and working-class environment quite different from the faded grandeur of the sisters' decayed family estate, Belle Reve. The play's names are always expressionistically suggestive. Blanche arrives at her sister's via a streetcar named Desire and one named Cemeteries. (The head of the school she teaches in is a Mr Graves.) Relations in the cramped little apartment between its three occupants are difficult from the start; between Blanche and Stanley they reach a terrible climax.

Like Brick, Blanche has problems with truth and with the past. But one man, Stanley's best friend Mitch, seems to fall happily into her embroidered version of her self and it is to this apparently sympathetic listener that she tells, without fabrication, her crucial burden-story, the events that, like the story of Brick and Skipper and Maggie, changed everything. She married young. And, as revealed in the first scene, 'the boy died'. The 1951 film, for which Williams had screenplay responsibility, sticks very much closer to the playscript than is the case with *Cat*. Let's reverse what we did with *Cat* and hear the filmscript version of this crucial scene, at the play's exact centre, first.

BLANCHE: He was a boy, just a boy, when I was a very young girl. When I was 16, I made the discovery – love. All at once and much, much too completely. It was like you suddenly turned a blinding light on something that had always been half in shadow, that's how it struck the world for me. But I was unlucky. Deluded. There was something about the boy, a nervousness, a tenderness, an uncertainty, and I didn't understand. I didn't understand why this boy, who wrote poetry, didn't seem to be able to do anything else. He lost every job. He came to me for help. I didn't know that. I didn't know anything except I loved him unendurably. At night I pretended to sleep. I heard him crying, crying, crying the way a lost child cries.

MITCH: I don't understand.

BLANCHE: No, no, neither did I. And that's why . . . [*pause*] I killed him.

MITCH: You . . .

BLANCHE: One night, we drove out to a place called Moon Lake Casino. We danced the Varsouviana. Suddenly in the middle of the dance the boy I had married broke away from me

and ran out of the casino. A few moments later – a shot! I ran
out – all did – all ran and gathered about the terrible thing at
the edge of the lake. He'd stuck the revolver into his mouth,
and fired. It was because – on the dancefloor – unable to stop
myself – I'd said – 'You're weak. I've lost respect for you. I
despise you.' And then the searchlight which had been turned
on the world was turned off again and never for one moment
since has there been any light that's stronger than this . . .

And that, for swathes of cinema audiences, presumably leaves a big
black hole. This key moment, offered indeed by Blanche as a key to
understanding her self in her present, has at its centre an absence, an
inexplicable gap. Where 'realism' in the theatre teaches us to expect
an explanation to an offered secret narrative – why her young husband
committed suicide – we have incomprehension. Is this because suicide
in 'real' life is often incomprehensible, or, in having multiple explanations, just can't be explained? Is this a Bartleby-like inexplicable
death? Or is it, as Big Daddy would say, that there's something missing
here? Here's the playscript version.

BLANCHE: He was a boy, just a boy, when I was a very young
girl. When I was sixteen, I made the discovery – love. All at
once and much, much too completely. It was like you suddenly turned a blinding light on something that had always
been half in shadow, that's how it struck the world for me.
But I was unlucky. Deluded. There was something different
about the boy, a nervousness, a softness and tenderness which
wasn't like a man's, although he wasn't the least bit
effeminate-looking – still – that thing was there. . . . He came
to me for help. I didn't know that. I didn't find out anything
till after our marriage when we'd run away and come back and
all I knew was I'd failed him in some mysterious way and
wasn't able to give the help he needed but couldn't speak of!
He was in the quicksands and clutching at me – but I wasn't
holding him out, I was slipping in with him! I didn't know
that. I didn't know anything except I loved him unendurably
but without being able to help him or help myself. Then
I found out. In the worst of all possible ways. By coming

439

suddenly into a room that I thought was empty – which wasn't empty, but had two people in it . . .

[*A locomotive is heard approaching outside. She claps her hands to her ears and crouches over. The headlight of the locomotive glares into the room as it thunders past. As the noise recedes she straightens slowly and continues speaking.*]

Afterwards we pretended that nothing had been discovered. Yes, the three of us drove out to Moon Lake Casino, very drunk and laughing all the way.

[*Polka music sounds, in a minor key faint with distance.*]

We danced the Varsouviana! Suddenly in the middle of the dance the boy I had married broke away from me and ran out of the casino. A few moments later – a shot!

[*The polka stops abruptly.*

BLANCHE *rises stiffly. Then the polka resumes in a major key.*]

I ran out – all did – all ran and gathered about the terrible thing at the edge of the lake! I couldn't get near for the crowding. Then somebody caught my arm. 'Don't go any closer! Come back! You don't want to see!' See? See what! Then I heard voices say – Allan! Allan! The Grey boy! He'd stuck the revolver into his mouth, and fired – so that the back of his head had been – blown away!

[*She sways and covers her face.*]

It was because – on the dance-floor – unable to stop myself – I'd suddenly said – 'I know! I know! You disgust me . . .' And then the searchlight which had been turned on the world was turned off again and never for one moment since has there been any light that's stronger than this – kitchen – candle. . . .

[MITCH *gets up awkwardly and moves towards her a little. The polka music increases.* MITCH *stands beside her.*]

MITCH [*drawing her slowly into his arms*]: You need somebody. And I need somebody, too. Could it be – you and me, Blanche?

[*She stares at him vacantly for a moment. Then with a soft cry huddles in his embrace. She makes a sobbing effort to speak but the words won't come. He kisses her forehead and her eyes and*]

*finally her lips. The polka tune fades out. Her breath is drawn
and released in long, grateful sobs.*]
BLANCHE: Sometimes – there's God – so quickly!

We get a name now, expressive as usual – the 'Grey' boy, neither one
thing nor the other. And we have some details oddly duplicating the
equivalent scene in *Cat*, the drunkenness, the scene by the lake, the
woman's bitter ultimatum-denunciation. And there was something
missing. It's the story of a gay boy who, as with Skipper, failed to prove
the heterosexual lie in bed with a woman – what Maggie called
Skipper's 'pitiful little attempt', what Blanche, in more coded and, for
Williams, self-censoring language, calls her not being 'able to give the
help he needed'. The self-censoring, even in this playscript, makes for
a telling of the events much less explicit than Maggie's. 'A room that I
thought was empty . . . but had two people in it': that's presumably two
young men in a bed.

But, despite the more veiled language, the guilt and sense of failure
and inadequacy that follow this death are clear as the source of
Blanche's present dependencies and vulnerabilities, her painful
insight about desire being death's opposite. As a revealed hidden
cause it has the clarity that Williams, perhaps, was resisting with Brick
(leaving 'mystery' in the 'revelation of character'). The *Streetcar* filmscript, faithful up to this point, muffles the issue into obscurity, forced
to do so from perceived external pressures. In *Cat* it was the opposite:
a playscript left, perhaps intentionally, muffled allowed the film to
invent a wholly new and clear moral fable. But in each case a crippling
inability to deal with forbidden sexuality is the root problem of the root
secret-narrative.

At the end of *Streetcar* Stanley rapes Blanche (when Stella is in
hospital having their baby). Lines in the playscript that point towards
this fact (the rape is, of course, not explicitly presented) include
Stanley's 'come to think of it – maybe you wouldn't be bad to – interfere
with . . . ' and his appalling, archetypical rapist's 'we've had this date
with each other from the beginning'. These are, again for institutional
reasons, cut from the film. The result is that the fact of the rape is
momentarily obscured – but, in a brilliant bit of film-making, the very
next shot is of the street being violently hosed down, which, as it were,
smuggles the fact back in at the level of figurative meaning, in that

poignant image of violent washing. In the last scene Mitch fights ineffectually with Stanley, and in the filmscript vital extra business and an extra line are added. The other men stare at Stanley in silent accusation for a long held moment until he says 'what are you looking at? I never once touched her.' This, again, retrospectively makes the rape certain and further removes sympathy for Stanley, isolated and defensively lying.

But it's the last moments of playscript and filmscript that diverge most startlingly and, in the contexts of what we have been exploring – issues of allowable representation on stage and in film and of ways of characterising – most suggestively. Blanche is taken away to an institution for the mad. Her sister knows what's happened between Blanche and Stanley but can't or won't let herself believe it. Here's the playscript.

> BLANCHE [*faintly*]: Ask her to let go of me.
>
> DOCTOR [*to the* MATRON]: Let go.
>
> > [*The* MATRON *releases her.* BLANCHE *extends her hands towards the* DOCTOR. *He draws her up gently and supports her with his arm and leads her through the portières.*]
>
> BLANCHE [*holding tight to his arm*]: Whoever you are – I have always depended on the kindness of strangers.
>
> > [*The poker players stand back as* BLANCHE *and the* DOCTOR *cross the kitchen to the front door. She allows him to lead her as if she were blind. As they go out on the porch,* STELLA *cries out her sister's name from where she is crouched a few steps upon the stairs.*]
>
> STELLA: Blanche! Blanche, Blanche!
>
> > [BLANCHE *walks on without turning, followed by the* DOCTOR *and the* MATRON. *They go around the corner of the building.*
> >
> > EUNICE *descends to* STELLA *and places the child in her arms. It is wrapped in a pale blue blanket.* STELLA *accepts the child, sobbingly.* EUNICE *continues downstairs and enters the kitchen where the men except for* STANLEY *are returning silently to their places about the table.* STANLEY *has gone out on the porch and stands at the foot of the steps looking at* STELLA.]

STANLEY [*a bit uncertainly*]: Stella?

    [*She sobs with inhuman abandon. There is something luxurious in her complete surrender to crying now that her sister is gone.*]

STANLEY [*voluptuously, soothingly*]: Now, honey. Now, love. Now, now love. [*He kneels beside her and his fingers find the opening of her blouse.*] Now, now, love. Now, love. . . .

    [*The luxurious sobbing, the sensual murmur fade away under the swelling music of the 'blue piano' and the muted trumpet.*]

STEVE: This game is seven-card stud.

CURTAIN

The end of the film is best described. Stanley reaches to Stella who says 'you touch me! Don't you ever touch me again.' She picks up her baby, starts to go in, changes her mind, says to herself 'I'm not going back in there again, not this time, never going back, never' and – accompanied by Stanley's off-camera shouts of 'hey, Stella!' – she leaves, running up to her friend's flat upstairs with that friend, Eunice, standing to let her in, in a pose suggesting a protective guard. And that pose is the last shot.

'Not this time'? After a scene of violence at Stanley's hands earlier in the play, Stella leaves for Eunice's – and then returns. This film-ending lends itself to more than a single reading. Either – she's left for good. Stanley's punishment is proper and appropriate. Blanche has, in effect, at last been believed. Wholesome morality prevails; wrong must not be allowed to prosper. Or – it's more open: she'll return as she did before, eventually. She's a woman who puts up with, even seems to thrive on, Stanley's violence. The two readings clearly come from different sexual-political positions, as well as answering to different preconceptions of what makes for successful endings and what makes for convincing character-development. But whatever else, the film-ending – whether it is hedging its bets or recording a feminist victory – makes one wonder how theatre audiences are meant to respond to Stanley securing everything, unreservedly, at the end of the playscript, and why theatre audiences, not film-goers, are allowed that response in the first place.

As with *Gulliver's Travels* and *Cat on a Hot Tin Roof*, we're clearly in the area of studio and producer pressures, the institution's fear of losing the big money. But the effect is what seems of sharpest interest. To return to our opening remarks, in the case of *Streetcar* (as with Miller's *Salesman*) the playscript is inhabiting, in its ending, a realism calculated to shock and upset with the impact of classical tragedy. It's Blanche's terrible defeat we're left with in the theatre, Stella's victory in the cinema. When texts of that kind collide with the pressures of big money, the market-place, and what perhaps is perceived as the optimism of mass audiences, the result is bound to be a set of problems.

The best-known plays of Ibsen and Miller will be familiar to some readers and notions of characterisation explored in this chapter will be worth considering in relation to those plays. It's worth looking back in this book to what Maurice Morgann said about Shakespeare's characters and to *Bartleby*. Problems in the film versions of written texts have been met in relation to *Gulliver's Travels* and *Wuthering Heights*: you may well have evidence from other sources about what films do to books. *The Color Purple* is one example; another is Disney's *Little Mermaid*, compared to Hans Christian Andersen's. The *Cat* filmscript's need to establish a network of mutualised father–son relations seems to show as much dependence on Miller's *Salesman* as anything in Williams. Williams's *Suddenly Last Summer* (1958, and there's a strong and faithful film (1959)) relates closely to issues in the two plays explored here.

22

HILL'S 'SEPTEMBER SONG'
The modern poet in history, the poem's right to exist

This chapter focuses on a celebrated poem by Geoffrey Hill, 'September Song' (1967). The commentary explores the poem's difficulty of utterance in the light of the moral and ethical issues it raises. These issues include the questioning of the right that poetry has traditionally claimed to address important social and cultural matters.

September Song
born 19.6.32 – deported 24.9.42

Undesirable you may have been, untouchable
you were not. Not forgotten
or passed over at the proper time.

As estimated, you died. Things marched,
sufficient, to that end.
Just so much Zyklon and leather, patented
terror, so many routine cries.

(I have made
an elegy for myself it
is true)

September fattens on vines. Roses
flake from the wall. The smoke
of harmless fires drifts to my eyes.

This is plenty. This is more than enough.

It often takes two or three readings of that for its subject-matter, and its subject, to reveal itself, themselves, to the reader. So here's one issue to start with: how and why does this poem deploy a kind of difficulty of utterance and exert a corresponding pressure over its readers as part of its making of meaning?

I need to assume now that you have responded to that difficult pressure and have moved, through how ever many readings it took you, to a position where the sheer awfulness – perhaps the unutterability – of the poem's matter and subject is clear to you. The process whereby you reached that stage was, perhaps, a little like a piecing together of clues or pieces of a jigsaw and, again perhaps, you might consider that appropriate to the poem's concern with bearing witness to and recovering an item of terrible historical fact. The clues or pieces of jigsaw, in the process of reading and re-reading, involve and indeed insist on you criss-crossing the poem, re-examining its fragments, moving backwards and forwards till the whole poem clicks together. That is, even more than with other difficult modern poems, you are compelled to keep working through and across it, to know it and to know its painful facts until that knowledge presses most violently and oppressively on the mind.

Readers assemble the evidence in their own way and at their own speed. Again, this is true of all readings of all poems but, again, it seems to have a pointed appropriateness to this poem: you need to make it yours, to appropriate it, in your own time. We'll return to this issue of personal appropriation of the poem later. The evidence? For some readers, it's the epigraph that first sets the alarm bells ringing: the dates, the odd movement from 'born' to 'deported' (worryingly not the expected 'departed'), the lack of capital letters suggesting the impersonal records of officialese and its evasions. For some it's the one capitalised word in the poem, if it is a word, the word 'Zyklon' which either demands an encyclopedia or dictionary or which students happen to know. For some it's the ferocious series of puns, virtually every word in the first seven lines that separately (most obviously 'passed over') and together convey a voice so full of the bitterest anger as to suggest something so beyond the ordinary that it has to be confronted at this level of intensity.

Whatever the order of the unfolding to the individual reader, we're clearly in the presence of a short poem of quite astonishing force and power, a poem or 'song' addressed to and about the 'routine' killing of a 10-year-old Jewish child in the Nazi gas-chambers. (Zyklon is the brand-name of the gas.) And the anger, bitterness and power reach their peak of ferocity in the terrible sixth and seventh lines where 'just' slides into 'just so much', where 'Zyklon' and 'leather' sit next to each other like two ends of a process, that process appallingly realised in the slide from 'leather' to 'patented' and, across the line, from 'patented' to 'terror'.

At which point the poem could easily have ended. It would have been, as that, the most powerful short literary response to the Holocaust. But it goes on, in two stages, first to the remarkable bracketed lines at the poem's centre (in terms of its five verses) where an 'I' suddenly speaks – to whom? – and then to a present-time evocation of Autumn, of ripeness or over-ripeness, of fattening as if (in terrible irony) for sacrifice, and of (now) 'harmless' bonfires.

The bracketed lines move the poem out into new areas of response and exert a different kind of difficulty. It's not now a matter of unpacking puns but of answering or rather speculating on the open vistas suggested by questions such as these: in what way can this poem be said to be an elegy (a lament) for the poet himself? Why is there a need to say that at all, and is that need qualified by being expressed in brackets? Why is it 'true' or rather why is the issue of the truth (of the elegy or of the making of it?) articulated here and not elsewhere in the poem? That is, does the assertion of the truth of the elegy or its making leave the question of the truth of the child and the child's death open or closed? If, indeed, the child was a child the truth of whose existence was known to the poet, how does that position the poet who has appropriated her/his story? And if the child is fictional, that is a generic figure standing for all the deaths of children in the gas-chambers, what does that make of issues of truthfulness?

'An elegy for myself'? The guilt of the survivor, of the surviving generation. Geoffrey Hill was born in 1932: does the poem depend on us knowing that? The guilt of the poet. Are the bracketed lines signalling painfully towards the idea that, faced with the brute facts of the Holocaust, poets and poetry can only be mute and marginal, that language (as George Steiner famously argued) became in effect unusable after the Holocaust? An elegy for the poet himself, in the sense of an elegy for poetry's decline in socio-cultural status in the later twentieth century, its new social and political functionlessness. Is this what the poem's punning last lines suggest? This is plenty, the season of plenty, and this poem is not only plenty but 'more than enough': the poet has said enough, or too much. And he has said enough or too much in a poem first published in 1967. It may be part of the poem's field of knowledge that the Arab–Israeli war of 1967, which it is now known almost led to super-power and even nuclear involvement, meant an upsurge of western consciousness about Jewish rights and Jewish history. An elegy that is true.

The suggestiveness of the bracketed lines in effect puts into question, into brackets, the entire post-Romantic notion of the central humanising function of the poet and of poetry. What can a poem do? What can ferociously angry words do? They bear witness, they remember, they force history on to the reader's consciousness – yes. But isn't there always, in that process, going to be the danger of the reader's attention being focused as much on the poet's performance and the reader's personally aroused feelings as on the facts of history, the poem's raw material which the poem and the poet and the reader have somehow appropriated? At the height of early Romanticism Coleridge famously scribbled a very worrying note in his 1796 Notebook (about which Hill has written): 'Poetry – excites us to artificial feelings – makes us callous to real ones.' Hill calls this note the 'appropriate epigraph' to 'that obsessive self-critical Romantic monologue in which eloquence and guilt are intertwined' (Hill, 1984, pp. 3–4).

This debate is a very live issue and so it should be. On the day I'm writing these words Britain's first permanent exhibition of the Holocaust is being opened by the Queen. On the simplest level, it's a matter of entitlement in the curriculum. The Holocaust must be taught, in whatever way. Holocaust-denial is a real phenomenon and it thrives on ignorance. But you'll probably know the anxieties that were caused by the Spielberg film *Schindler's List*: doesn't Hollywood, however well-intentioned, glamorise history, necessarily falsifying it or at least associating history with the general mythologising and fantasising that are the Hollywood film-industry? But, then, how do we mediate history at all, coming necessarily after it as we do? We can never occupy history in an unmediated way.

The debate can be put this way. For many years I've felt obliged, as a matter of student-entitlement, to teach this poem. It invariably delivers and 'works', often marking for students a literary experience quite unlike anything they'd encountered before. Occasionally students afterwards confess they knew nothing about the Holocaust before the class. But something feels not quite right, and I try to voice that doubt as part of the poem's own contexts, its own suggested self-critique, querying its own right to exist. What feels not quite right is the very success of the class-experience of the poem, the fact that a group of comfortable people are sitting around getting – well, getting our academic thrill from and with the poem, sharing almost in a spirit of mutual self-satisfaction in the poet's sensitively self-questioning doubts. And then we close our books. And perhaps the students write something and get rewarded for it. Or consider this fact and how you feel yourself responding to it. In the early 1980s the poster company Athena decided to add to its usual diet of selling cheap posters of Van Gogh's cornfields and the like, for people to hang on their walls, by selling framed poems artfully transcribed in the style of a scroll. One of these was (unless I dreamed it) 'September Song'.

* * *

Let's end by lowering the temperature a little and moving to other poems. It's certainly of interest that other poets, and Hill elsewhere, make poems out of the sense that modern poetry can only have marginal relations with the hard facts of history and politics, that poets can no longer automatically claim any social function, that the poet is a culturally minor figure selling negligible numbers of books. It's not as if contemporary poets are like Byron whose poem *Corsair* sold 10,000 copies – on its first *day* of publication. (At the same time, 1813–14, Jane Austen's *Pride and Prejudice* sold some 1,500 copies in its first six months.)

One poet who sells rather more than most is Tony Harrison, whose background was similar to Hill's though his poetry is Hill's opposite in its accessibility and colloquial language. In his long poem *v.* (1985), and in a number of short poems in his sequence *The School of Eloquence*, Harrison eloquently confronts himself with the notion that poems are middle-class products and that any claim by the poet that he's trying to give a voice to working-class concerns is sentimental self-deceit, and at best an attempt to make up for the guilt the poet feels for having abandoned his working roots. Harrison's alter-ego in *v.*, a football hooligan spraying graffiti on gravestones, puts it like this (the italics are in the original): '*A book, yer stupid cunt, 's not worth a fuck*' and '*Don't talk to me of fucking representing / the class yer were born into any more* [. . .] *Who needs / yer fucking poufy words. Ah write my own. / Ah've got mi work on show all over Leeds / like this UNITED 'ere on some sod's stone.*' And in his short poem 'Turns', Harrison gives a moving account of the death of his father, a man whose working-class pride insisted that 'he never begged. For nowt!' In sharpest contrast Harrison identifies the very act of his poetry-writing as 'opening my trap / to busk the class that broke him', that is the class that 'broke' working people like his own father: the poet as busker to the middle class, guiltily reprocessing his family histories for their delectation.

And this is what Hill is very conscious of in the most poignant poem in his sequence *Mercian Hymns* (1971). It's about his grandmother. Its title is 'Opus Anglicanum' (English work) and it opens with a reference to a letter of August 1877 in which the critic and social reformer John Ruskin describes being taken to see women in Worcestershire 'nailing' in a little cottage with 'a small forge, fed to constant brightness by the draught through the cottage, above whose roof its chimney rose: in front of it, on a little ledge, the glowing lengths of cut iron rod, to be dealt with at speed'. The families of these workers, Ruskin discovered, typically had an income, after rent and taxes, of '£55 a year, on which they had to feed and clothe themselves and their six children'. The nails made by these women were the very raw material of England's industrial power. When the nail was forged it 'fell aside, finished, on its proper heap; level-headed, wedge pointed, a thousand lives soon to depend daily on its driven grip of the iron way' (*Fors Clarigera*, 1877, August, xxix, p. 173).

Here is Hill's *Mercian Hymn XXV*, 'Opus Anglicanum'. The word 'darg', deliberately archaic, means a day's work; 'quick forge' is quoted from Shakespeare's *Henry V* where it celebrates the power of the 'working-house of thought' (Act V, Prologue, 23). You'll see that the young woman's life (the word 'bloom' is painfully placed in the poem) can be memorially spoken of, and her 'spent' and exploited history made witness to, but like the 'damson-bloom of dust' it can't be 'shaken by posthumous clamour', by crying after the dead: nothing material can be achieved for such lives in a poem like this, which can only speak in an act of brooding, and repeat itself in a self-contained circle.

XXV

Brooding on the eightieth letter of *Fors Clavigera*, I speak this in memory of my grandmother, whose childhood and prime womanhood were spent in the nailer's darg.

The nailshop stood back of the cottage, by the fold. It reeked stale mineral sweat. Sparks had furred its low roof. In dawn-light the troughed water floated a damson-bloom of dust –

not to be shaken by posthumous clamour. It is one thing to celebrate the 'quick forge', another to cradle a face hare-lipped by the searing wire.

Brooding on the eightieth letter of *Fors Clavigera*, I speak this in memory of my grandmother, whose childhood and prime womanhood were spent in the nailer's darg.

Geoffrey Hill's poetry has received considerable critical if not public atten-tion. His 1968 collection, *King Log*, first gave wide currency to 'September Song'. All but his most recent work is in his *Collected Poems* (Harmonds-worth, Penguin, 1985). His criticism, quoted above, is collected in his *The Lords of Limit* (New York, Oxford University Press, 1984). For many, he is and has been for a long time the most challenging and important poet writing in English. A distinguished volume of essays on Hill is edited by Peter Robinson (Milton Keynes, Open University Press, 1985). The essay by Gabriel Pearson contains some sharp remarks on 'September Song'. Christopher Ricks has been Hill's most high-profile champion. There are essays on Hill in Ricks's *The Force of Poetry* (Oxford, Clarendon Press, 1984). Tony Harrison is gener-ously represented in a *Selected Poems* (2nd edition, Harmondsworth, Pen-guin, 1987). The literature on the Holocaust is far too large a topic for this note but students who know Trevor Griffiths's play *Comedians* (London, Faber and Faber, 1976) will find material to connect interestingly with the discus-sion above. In terms of education and entitlement, a fascinating anthology of children's literature dealing with war and the Holocaust is *In Times of War*, edited by Carol Fox *et al.* (London, Pavilion Books, 2000).

23

BECKETT'S *NOT I*
Challenging the audience with a life, lost

Samuel Beckett's play *Not I* (1973) is presented in full in this chapter. Its challenge to audiences and to the actress for whom it was written, and its modernist rewriting of conventions, are discussed in connection with the play's presentation of an entire lifetime, lived in its social and geographical context, in a few minutes of theatre and audience time.

In November 1972, at the Forum Theatre of the Lincoln Centre in New York, and then in January 1973, at the Royal Court Theatre in London, audiences experienced for about thirteen minutes something for which even hardened theatre-goers and critics could hardly have been prepared. It was a searing experience. One member of the audience spoke of being bleached by it. One critic wrote of the play 'tearing into you like a grappling iron and dragging you after it, with or without your leave' (*Critical Heritage*, 1979, p. 330).

This is it. (After the title you'll see a 'Note': this describes the movement required by the on-stage 'Auditor' as specified in the stage-direction that follows. But remember that audiences would see neither the note nor the stage direction. Mouth says her lines very, very fast.)

Not I
Note

Movement: this consists in simple sideways raising of arms from sides and their falling back, in a gesture of helpless compassion. It lessens with each recurrence till scarcely perceptible at third. There is just enough pause to contain it as MOUTH recovers from vehement refusal to relinquish third person.

452

Stage in darkness but for MOUTH, *upstage audience right, about 8
feet above stage level, faintly lit from close-up and below, rest of face in
shadow. Invisible microphone.*

AUDITOR, *downstage audience left, tall standing figure, sex unde-
terminable, enveloped from head to foot in loose black djellaba, with
hood, fully faintly lit, standing on invisible podium about 4 feet high
shown by attitude alone to be facing diagonally across stage intent on*
MOUTH, *dead still throughout but for four brief movements where
indicated. See Note.*

As house lights down MOUTH'*s voice unintelligible behind curtain.
House lights out. Voice continues unintelligible behind curtain, 10
seconds. With rise of curtain ad-libbing from text as required leading
when curtain fully up and attention sufficient into:*

MOUTH: .... out ... into this world ... this world ... tiny
little thing ... before its time ... in a godfor— ... what? ..
girl? .. yes ... tiny little girl ... into this ... out into this
... before her time ... godforsaken hole called ... called ...
no matter ... parents unknown ... unheard of ... he having
vanished ... thin air ... no sooner buttoned up his breeches
... she similarly ... eight months later ... almost to the tick
... so no love ... spared that ... no love such as normally
vented on the ... speechless infant ... in the home ... no ...
nor indeed for that matter any of any kind ... no love of any
kind ... at any subsequent stage ... so typical affair ...
nothing of any note till coming up to sixty when— ... what?
.. seventy? .. good God! .. coming up to seventy ...
wandering in a field ... looking aimlessly for cowslips ... to
make a ball ... a few steps then stop ... stare into space ...
then on ... a few more ... stop and stare again ... so on ...
drifting around ... when suddenly ... gradually ... all went
out ... all that early April morning light ... and she found
herself in the— ... what? .. who?.. no! .. she! .. [*Pause and
movement 1.*].... found herself in the dark ... and if not
exactly ... insentient ... insentient ... for she could still
hear the buzzing ... so-called ... in the ears ... and a ray of
light came and went ... came and went ... such as the moon
might cast ... drifting ... in and out of cloud ... but so

dulled . . . feeling . . . feeling so dulled . . . she did not know
. . . what position she was in . . . imagine! . . what position
she was in! . . whether standing . . . or sitting . . . but the
brain— . . . what? . . kneeling? . . yes . . . whether standing
. . . or sitting . . . or kneeling . . . but the brain— . . .
what? . . lying? . . yes . . . whether standing . . . or sitting . . .
or kneeling . . . or lying . . . but the brain still . . . still . . . in a
way . . . for her first thought was . . . oh long after . . . sudden
flash . . . brought up as she had been to believe . . . with the
other waifs . . . in a merciful . . . [*Brief laugh.*] . . . God . . .
[*Good laugh.*] . . . first thought was . . . oh long after . . . sudden flash . . . she was being punished . . . for her sins . . . a
number of which then . . . further proof if proof were needed
. . . flashed through her mind . . . one after another . . . then
dismissed as foolish . . . oh long after . . . this thought dismissed . . . as she suddenly realized . . . gradually realized . . .
she was not suffering . . . imagine! . . not suffering! . . indeed
could not remember . . . off-hand . . . when she had suffered
less . . . unless of course she was . . . *meant* to be suffering . . .
ha! . . *thought* to be suffering . . . just as the odd time . . . in
her life . . . when clearly intended to be having pleasure . . .
she was in fact . . . having none . . . not the slightest . . . in
which case of course . . . that notion of punishment . . . for
some sin or other . . . or for the lot . . . or no particular reason
. . . for its own sake . . . thing she understood perfectly . . .
that notion of punishment . . . which had first occurred to her
. . . brought up as she had been to believe . . . with the other
waifs . . . in a merciful . . . [*Brief laugh.*] . . . God . . . [*Good
laugh.*] . . . first occurred to her . . . then dismissed . . . as
foolish . . . was perhaps not so foolish . . . after all . . . so on
. . . all that . . . vain reasonings . . . till another thought . . . oh
long after . . . sudden flash . . . very foolish really but— . . .
what? . . the buzzing? . . yes . . . all the time the buzzing . . .
so-called . . . in the ears . . . though of course actually . . . not
in the ears at all . . . in the skull . . dull roar in the skull . . .
and all the time this ray or beam . . . like moonbeam . . . but
probably not . . . certainly not . . . always the same spot . . .
now bright . . . now shrouded . . . but always the same spot

. . . as no moon could . . . no . . . no moon . . . just all part of
the same wish to . . . torment . . . though actually in point of
fact . . . not in the least . . . not a twinge . . . so far . . . ha! . .
so far . . . this other thought then . . . oh long after . . . sudden
flash . . . very foolish really but so like her . . . in a way . . .
that she might do well to . . . groan . . . on and off . . . writhe
she could not . . . as if in actual agony . . . but could not . . .
could not bring herself . . . some flaw in her make-up . . .
incapable of deceit . . . or the machine . . . more likely the
machine . . . so disconnected . . . never got the message . . . or
powerless to respond . . . like numbed . . . couldn't make the
sound . . . not any sound . . . no sound of any kind . . . no
screaming for help for example . . . should she feel so inclined
. . . scream . . . [*Screams.*] . . . then listen . . . [*Silence.*] . . .
scream again . . . [*Screams again.*] . . . then listen again . . .
[*Silence.*] . . . no . . . spared that . . . all silent as the grave . . .
no part— . . . what? . . the buzzing? . . yes . . . all silent but
for the buzzing . . . so-called . . . no part of her moving . . .
that she could feel . . . just the eyelids . . . presumably . . . on
and off . . . shut out the light . . . reflex they call it . . . no
feeling of any kind . . . but the lids . . . even best of times . . .
who feels them? . . opening . . . shutting . . . all that moisture
. . . but the brain still . . . still sufficiently . . . oh very much
so! . . at this stage . . . in control . . . under control . . . to
question even this . . . for on that April morning . . . so it
reasoned . . . that April morning . . . she fixing with her eye
. . . a distant bell . . . as she hastened towards it . . . fixing it
with her eye . . . lest it elude her . . . had not all gone out . . .
all that light . . . of itself . . . without any . . . any . . . on her
part . . . so on . . . so on it reasoned . . . vain questionings . . .
and all dead still . . . sweet silent as the grave . . . when suddenly . . . gradually . . . she realiz— . . . what? . . the buzzing? . . yes . . . all dead still but for the buzzing . . . when
suddenly she realized . . . words were— . . . what? . . who? . .
no! . . she! . . [*Pause and movement 2.*] . . . realized . . . words
were coming . . . imagine! . . words were coming . . . a voice
she did not recognize . . . at first . . . so long since it had
sounded . . . then finally had to admit . . . could be none other

. . . than her own . . . certain vowel sounds . . . she had never heard . . . elsewhere . . . so that people would stare . . . the rare occasions . . . once or twice a year . . . always winter some strange reason . . . stare at her uncomprehending . . . and now this stream . . . steady stream . . . she who had never . . . on the contrary . . . practically speechless . . . all her days . . . how she survived! . . even shopping . . . out shopping . . . busy shopping centre . . . supermart . . . just hand in the list . . . with the bag . . . old black shopping bag . . . then stand there waiting . . . any length of time . . . middle of the throng . . . motionless . . . staring into space . . . mouth half open as usual . . . till it was back in her hand . . . the bag back in her hand . . . then pay and go . . . not as much as good-bye . . . how she survived! . . and now this stream . . . not catching the half of it . . . not the quarter . . . no idea . . . what she was saying . . . imagine! . . no idea what she was saying! . . till she began trying to . . . delude herself . . . it was not hers at all . . . not her voice at all . . . and no doubt would have . . . vital she should . . . was on the point . . . after long efforts . . . when suddenly she felt . . . gradually she felt . . . her lips moving . . . imagine! . . her lips moving! . . as of course till then she had not . . . and not alone the lips . . . the cheeks . . . the jaws . . . the whole face . . . all those— . . . what? . . the tongue? . . yes . . . the tongue in the mouth . . . all those contortions without which . . . no speech possible . . . and yet in the ordinary way . . . not felt at all . . . so intent one is . . . on what one is saying . . . the whole being . . . hanging on its words . . . so that not only she had . . . had she . . . not only had she . . . to give up . . . admit hers alone . . . her voice alone . . . but this other awful thought . . . oh long after . . . sudden flash . . . even more awful if possible . . . that feeling was coming back . . . imagine! . . feeling coming back! . . starting at the top . . . then working down . . . the whole machine . . . but no . . . spared that . . . the mouth alone . . . so far . . . ha! . . so far . . . then thinking . . . oh long after . . . sudden flash . . . it can't go on . . . all this . . . all that . . . steady stream . . . straining to hear . . . make something of it . . . and her own thoughts . . . make something of them . . . all— . . . what! . . the

buzzing? . . yes . . . all the time the buzzing . . . so-called . . .
all that together . . . imagine! . . whole body like gone . . .
just the mouth . . . lips . . . cheeks . . . jaws . . . never— . . .
what? . . tongue? . . yes . . . lips . . . cheeks . . . jaws . . .
tongue . . . never still a second . . . mouth on fire . . . stream of
words . . . in her ear . . . practically in her ear . . . not catching
the half . . . not the quarter . . . no idea what she's saying . . .
imagine! . . no idea what she's saying! . . and can't stop . . . no
stopping it . . . she who but a moment before . . . but a
moment! . . could not make a sound . . . no sound of any kind
. . . now can't stop . . . imagine! . . can't stop the stream . . .
and the whole brain begging . . . something begging in the
brain . . . begging the mouth to stop . . . pause a moment . . .
if only for a moment . . . and no response . . . as if it hadn't
heard . . . or couldn't . . . couldn't pause a second . . . like
maddened . . . all that together . . . straining to hear . . . piece
it together . . . and the brain . . . raving away on its own . . .
trying to make sense of it . . . or make it stop . . . or in the past
. . . dragging up the past . . . flashes from all over . . . walks
mostly . . . walking all her days . . . day after day . . . a few
steps then stop . . . stare into space . . . then on . . . a few more
. . . stop and stare again . . . so on . . . drifting around . . . day
after day . . . or that time she cried . . . the one time she could
remember . . . since she was a baby . . . must have cried as a
baby . . . perhaps not . . . not essential to life . . . just the birth
cry to get her going . . . breathing . . . then no more till this
. . . old hag already . . . sitting staring at her hand . . . where
was it? . . Croker's Acres . . . one evening on the way home
. . . home! . . a little mound in Croker's Acres . . . dusk . . .
sitting staring at her hand . . . there in her lap . . . palm
upward . . . suddenly saw it wet . . . the palm . . . tears presumably . . . hers presumably . . . no one else for miles . . . no
sound . . . just the tears . . . sat and watched them dry . . . all
over in a second . . . or grabbing at straw . . . the brain . . .
flickering away on its own . . . quick grab and on . . . nothing
there . . . on to the next . . . bad as the voice . . . worse . . . as
little sense . . . all that together . . . can't— . . . what? . . the
buzzing? . . yes . . . all the time the buzzing . . . dull roar like

falls . . . and the beam . . . flickering on and off . . . starting to move around . . . like moonbeam but not . . . all part of the same . . . keep an eye on that too . . . corner of the eye . . . all that together . . . can't go on . . . God is love . . . she'll be purged . . . back in the field . . . morning sun . . . April . . . sink face down in the grass . . . nothing but the larks . . . so on . . . grabbing at the straw . . . straining to hear . . . the odd word . . . make some sense of it . . . whole body like gone . . . just the mouth . . . like maddened . . . and can't stop . . . no stopping it . . . something she— . . . something she had to— . . . what? . . who? . . no! . . she! . . [*Pause and movement 3.*] . . . something she had to— . . . what? . . the buzzing? . . yes . . . all the time the buzzing . . . dull roar . . . in the skull . . . and the beam . . . ferreting around . . . painless . . . so far . . . ha! . . so far . . . then thinking . . . oh long after . . . sudden flash . . . perhaps something she had to . . . had to . . . tell . . . could that be it? . . something she had to . . . tell . . . tiny little thing . . . before its time . . . godforsaken hole . . . no love . . . spared that . . . speechless all her days . . . practically speechless . . . how she survived! . . that time in court . . . what had she to say for herself . . . guilty or not guilty . . . stand up woman . . . speak up woman . . . stood there staring into space . . . mouth half open as usual . . . waiting to be led away . . . glad of the hand on her arm . . . now this . . . something she had to tell . . . could that be it? . . something that would tell . . . how it was . . . how she— . . . what? . . had been? . . yes . . . something that would tell how it had been . . . how she had lived . . . lived on and on . . . guilty or not . . . on and on . . . to be sixty . . . something she— . . . what? . . seventy? . . good God! . . on and on to be seventy . . . something she didn't know herself . . . wouldn't know if she heard . . . then forgiven . . . God is love . . . tender mercies . . . new every morning . . . back in the field . . . April morning . . . face in the grass . . . nothing but the larks . . . pick it up there . . . get on with it from there . . . another few— . . . what? . . not that? . . nothing to do with that? . . nothing she could tell? . . all right . . . nothing she could tell . . . try something else . . . think of something else . . . oh long after . . . sudden flash . . .

not that either . . . all right . . . something else again . . . so on
. . . hit on it in the end . . . think everything keep on long
enough . . . then forgiven . . . back in the— . . . what? . . not
that either? . . nothing to do with that either? . . nothing she
could think? . . all right . . . nothing she could tell . . . nothing she could think . . . nothing she— . . . what? . . who? . .
no! . . she! . . [*Pause and movement 4.*] . . . tiny little thing . . .
out before its time . . . godforsaken hole . . . no love . . . spared
that . . . speechless all her days . . . practically speechless . . .
even to herself . . . never out loud . . . but not completely . . .
sometimes sudden urge . . . once or twice a year . . . always
winter some strange reason . . . the long evenings . . . hours of
darkness . . . sudden urge to . . . tell . . . then rush out stop the
first she saw . . . nearest lavatory . . . start pouring it out . . .
steady stream . . . mad stuff . . . half the vowels wrong . . . no
one could follow . . . till she saw the stare she was getting . . .
then die of shame . . . crawl back in . . . once or twice a year
. . . always winter some strange reason . . . long hours of darkness . . . now this . . . this . . . quicker and quicker . . . the
words . . . the brain . . . flickering away like mad . . . quick
grab and on . . . nothing there . . . on somewhere else . . . try
somewhere else . . . all the time something begging . . . something in her begging . . . begging it all to stop . . .
unanswered . . . prayer unanswered . . . or unheard . . . too
faint . . . so on . . . keep on . . . trying . . . not knowing what
. . . what she was trying . . . what to try . . . whole body like
gone . . . just the mouth . . . like maddened . . . so on . . .
keep— . . . what? . . the buzzing? . . yes . . . all the time the
buzzing . . . dull roar like falls . . . in the skull . . . and the
beam . . . poking around . . . painless . . . so far . . . ha! . . so
far . . . all that . . . keep on . . . not knowing what . . . what
she was— . . . what? . . who? . . no! . . she! . . SHE! . . [*Pause.*]
. . . what she was trying . . . what to try . . . no matter . . .
keep on . . . [*Curtain starts down.*] . . . hit on it in the end
. . . then back . . . God is love . . . tender mercies . . . new
every morning . . . back in the field . . . April morning
. . . face in the grass . . . nothing but the larks . . . pick it
up—

*[Curtain fully down. House dark. Voice continues behind
curtain, unintelligible, 10 seconds, ceases as house lights up.]*

The critic for the *New Yorker* saw it as unprepared as the rest of the
audience. She described the 'stunning impact' of the pell-mell delivery
by Mouth of 'the pent-up words of a lifetime' and concluded that these
few minutes in the theatre were 'as densely packed' as any she'd
experienced anywhere. She added, in brackets: '(I have no idea what
the title means)' (*Critical Heritage*, 1979, pp. 328–9).

I think that must have been a typical response of first-time audiences without access to the text, that mixture of stunned admiration
and confusion. The question is inevitably raised: how many performances is it necessary for audiences to, as it were, undergo before
Mouth's true situation and the meaning of the title become clear? And
how does that rewrite the rule-book about going to the theatre, apart
from the related issue of how much or how little time audiences can
expect to spend with a play, having spent their money? When did you
last see a play that clearly demands you see it at least twice? Or one in
which audiences who have read the text beforehand not only know the
plot (plot?) but understand the title?

Students who, unprepared in any way, watch the video version (about
which more below) get very little apart from more or less stunned confusion first time round. A second viewing provides something amount-
ing to a biographical outline from Mouth's pell-mell delivery. Then to
see the text, particularly the note and the stage-direction, brings
illumination. A third viewing, after studying the text, affords a richer and
more totalising experience. But is that what Beckett wants? Isn't the
stunned confusion of the first unprepared viewing part of the challenge? As with *Bartleby* it's the viewer/reader whose responses are on
trial here. Do we turn away? Do we attend, try to understand, attend
again, try harder?

The critic for the London *New Statesman* (whose words I quoted at
the outset) wrote his review with knowledge of the text – which, incidentally, means that his review not only recommended the play but, as it
were, explained it, thus removing from potential audiences that first
stunned confusion. His justification is that *Not I* 'demands familiarity'
(*Critical Heritage*, 1979, p. 330). That must be right, in so far as the play
dramatises Mouth's desperate need to 'tell' what she has to tell and

the challenge to the audience to listen or turn away and refuse that familiarity, but it's not a comfortable or consoling familiarity that the play demands or offers, at least not at first.

You may not need, at this point, an outline of the life that is so desperately conveyed and in such fragmentary and flailing, jostling intensity – and it is a kind of disservice to summarise it, or anyone's life, in this way in any case, the kind of disservice that 'explaining' Bartleby presented. But here goes. Mouth was born and almost immediately orphaned, abandoned by both parents and brought up in a strictly religious institution. As an adult she wanders the countryside, avoiding people but occasionally impelled during winter to babble 'mad stuff' at strangers in public lavatories. We see glimpses of her lonely and helpless trips to a shop, of a mute appearance in court, of the one occasion she cried, in Croker's Acres. That's it, for some seventy years. Then something happened in a field. It grows dark, a ray of light shines on her, she hears a buzzing in the head, and her bodily senses are dulled. She thinks she's being punished then realises she isn't. Then her mouth begins to pour out a stream of words and feeling returns to her mouth, and only to her mouth. The stream of words may be something she has to tell, to tell 'how it was', or if not that 'something else' to be found 'somewhere else'. 'Raving away on its own' and 'dragging up the past' there's also 'something in her begging . . . begging it all to stop'.

And the title? Four times Mouth says 'what? . . who? . . no! . . she!' and this, according to the Note, is a 'vehement refusal to relinquish third person' – to refuse to admit that it's herself and not another that she is talking about – and that refusal is accompanied by the Auditor's movement, 'a gesture of helpless compassion' which lessens 'till scarcely perceptible'. The Auditor is the audience, though he/she is also a character as suggested below, and he is not only listening but, in effect, talking. *Not I* is a monologue but also a dialogue in which Mouth is answering a voice we don't hear, the voice putting questions to Mouth like 'but this is you you're talking about, isn't it?' So the theatre-audience, in another rewriting of conventions, is a character obliged to ask silent questions, to interrupt the torrent, and to no perceptible benefit.

The challenge of experiencing *Not I*, as suggested above, is the challenge to the audience to understand and to listen, to attend. To understand how this play works is then to understand that this is a human life, not a plot. Lives have non-events and events. The former far outweigh the latter and the latter, like the incident in the field, resist explanation. Whatever happened, it happened and we live with it or fail to. (Beckett had to hide his irritation with the American actress who kept pestering him with the question of what it was that had happened in the field.) And this is a human who needs help and who is refusing even to admit that the life is her own. To think or talk about oneself in the third person is a defence we all have recourse to, from childhood onwards. Not me, someone else. We use it in stress and we know what we're doing. Tom Waits's wonderfully comic-sad-drunken song 'The piano has been drinking' (not me) comes out of exactly the same defence mechanism as used by Mouth. But what if we lose all bearings and become adrift, a 'bit of wreck' like Bartleby or 'Wrecked, solitary, here – ' like Emily Dickinson ('I felt a Funeral')?

But the comparison should be closer to home and, for Beckett, it was. This is a very ordinary woman and there are thousands like her. We all know them, we avert our eyes and close our ears, we offer at best helpless compassion. These are the down and outs, the tramps, the bag-women. Benedict Nightingale, sitting in the theatre on that first night, found himself 'forcefully' picturing the image of a sad and deluded old woman whom he used to see as a child tramping the Kent countryside (*Critical Heritage*, 1979, p. 330). And Beckett knew that woman, women like that in Ireland 'stumbling down the lanes, in the ditches, beside the hedgerows. Ireland is full of them' (quoted in Knowlson, 1996, p. 590). And perhaps he heard it in Croker's Acres, a wide area of pasture-land where Sam Beckett used to wander as a child.

The subtitle of the third and most expressive of the Beckett biographies is 'The Last Modernist' (Cronin, 1996). It's a valid claim. And *Not I*, in its rewriting of the conventions of the theatrical experience itself, in its challenge and difficulty, in its concern with and deployment of the fragmentary and the self-divided, is a modernist classic. But Beckett's modernism is not the usual variety. Modernist writers, typically poets like Eliot and Pound, exhibit a lofty disregard for the everyday and ordinary people, and for social-political contexts, and their texts are positioned as existing in a kind of geographical everywhere or nowhere. Beckett criticism, from the start, appropriated his work too readily to high-modernism's concerns with existentialist or nihilist philosophy and its heady and private symbolism. Beckett frequently protested the simplicity of his work, famously ending his early novel *Watt* with 'no symbols where none intended'. And his own life, though famous now for reclusiveness, featured an endlessly generous series of kindnesses and charity to the less fortunate, with the same instinctive generosity as shown throughout his life by Dr Johnson with whom Beckett was always fascinated and about whose relationship with Mrs Thrale he started a playscript.

Beckett's modernism is grounded. It is intensely humane in its sympathies with lives led on the edge. *Not I* can be read, if it has to be, for instance (and as it has), as a demonstration of disconnected consciousness, with the Auditor as Mouth's Jungian shadow, but such readings rob it of its raw social-political power and its locality. *Not I* is an act of reclamation. It reclaims a life, an Irish life, a regrettably ordinary and routine life led by so many, and it asks us about our responses to such a life, by locking us in the theatre and forcing us to listen, to attend.

An Irish life. The Auditor is dressed in a 'loose black djellaba'. It is the case that one stimulus to composition was Beckett's sight of an attentively still mother awaiting her child in Tangiers (and of a painting he saw in Malta). But, again, the most telling context is the simple one. The Auditor was described by the *New Yorker*'s reviewer as 'in monk's garb' (*Critical Heritage*, 1979, p. 329) and by the *New Statesman*'s as 'cowled' (ibid. p. 333; a cowl is a monk's hood). The voice and the figure combined evoke, again, a very ordinary Irish context: the confessional. The confessor is putting those questions to Mouth to which she replies whenever the text says 'what?'. But the confessor/listener's compassion, in effect the compassion of the organised Catholic church, is 'helpless'. In later productions Beckett asked the Auditor to end by covering his ears (as in the Caravaggio painting in Malta) to block out the sound of Mouth's voice. Mouth finds the notion of a 'merciful god' irresistibly funny.

The role of Mouth was created for the brilliant Billie Whitelaw who, like Patrick Magee before her, Beckett responded to as a voice that he had always been hearing in his head. So Billie Whitelaw became, as it were, his route back to the woman in Ireland he 'actually heard'. Beckett was notoriously fastidious in rehearsal and Billie Whitelaw has given, as have others, vivid accounts of the technical problems and emotional traumas that were involved in the Royal Court production. Then there was a black-and-white BBC televised version in 1976. And for that, in an extraordinary stroke, Beckett got rid of the Auditor completely and agreed to have the camera focused in terrible close-up on Billie White-law's mouth. The effect is to make the television viewer his or her own Auditor in an even closer way than in the original. The problem of how we respond – the image on the screen is one that viewers instinctively flinch away from – is made even more immediate, and the notion that it is we who are asking those questions to which Mouth answers is made even more painfully explicit, now that there's no Auditor on stage to mediate for us.

One word of the text is pronounced very interestingly in Billie White-law's performance, and my guess is that this was on her initiative, with Beckett's approval. During those first gruelling rehearsals Whitelaw's own child was dangerously ill and this added to the terrible stresses of the play. The word 'baby' in the passage about Mouth crying – 'since she was a baby . . . must have cried as a baby . . . perhaps not' – is in Billie Whitelaw's performance pronounced 'babby'. I like to think that this pointed departure from BBC standard pronunciation was a tiny act of personal reclamation by a woman and a mother without whom the play would never have been written and whose voice Beckett heard in his head as he wrote it. Beckett later wrote the play *Footfalls* (1976) for Billie Whitelaw. The central character is called May. May was Beckett's mother's name.

Beckett's reputation, a misleading one, has been as a purveyor of fearsomely difficult, obscure and depressing plays. The mountain of reverential and heav-ily academic Beckett criticism has encouraged this view and the over-zealous policing of productions by the Beckett estate hasn't helped. The truth is that Beckett was principally a novelist for whom the writing of plays, at least in the first half of his career, was a light diversion. His novels and plays, many of the most important of which were first written in French and then translated by the author, are at least as comic as they are tragic. One of them, the early novel *Watt* (written in war-time and occupied France, where Beckett was a resistance-worker), is my first-equal funniest book ever written (equal with Vladimir Nabokov's *Pale Fire*). Hugh Kenner remains Beckett's most access-ible and stylish critic and his *The Stoic Comedians* (Berkeley, University of California, 1962) places his work in the context of comic writing from earlier periods, including Swift's. Kenner's *Reader's Guide* (London, Thames and

Hudson, 1973) is a good place to start. The two rival modern biographies are James Knowlson's *Damned to Fame: The Life of Samuel Beckett* (London, Bloomsbury, 1996) and Anthony Cronin's *Samuel Beckett: The Last Modernist* (London, HarperCollins, 1996): I agree with those who favour the latter, though it is less authoritative. Mel Gussow's *Conversations with (and about) Beckett* (London, Nick Hern Books, 1996) is very accessible. The reviews of *Not I* mentioned above are in the Beckett *Critical Heritage* volume (London, Routledge and Kegan Paul, 1979). Billie Whitelaw's memoirs, *Billie Whitelaw . . . Who He* (London, Hodder and Stoughton, 1995), contain her account of working with Beckett. An important book by Eoin O'Brien, *The Beckett Country* (Dublin, Black Cat Press, 1986), does the long-overdue job of locating Beckett's work in its Irish contexts. I very much hope you get the chance to see *Not I* in the theatre or in its televised form.

24

BISHOP'S AND
BERRYMAN'S POEMS
How to lose, and loss in this book

This last chapter stands a little further away from texts to survey a notion that can retrospectively be seen as dominant in this book, the notion of loss. The discussion moves to a consideration of a group of American poets in the second half of the twentieth century, and four poems are presented in full.

The title of a book published in America, and never in Britain, a collection of Geoffrey Hill's first three volumes of poetry, was *Somewhere is Such a Kingdom* (Boston, Houghton Mifflin, 1975), and it had an epigraph from Thomas Hobbes's *Leviathan* of 1651, which is probably when Marvell was writing his lyrics of garden and loss and just after Winstanley's commune was forcibly broken up. Here it is.

> Sometimes a man seeks what he hath lost; and from that place, and time, wherein he misses it, his mind runs back, from place to place, and time to time, to find where, and when he had it . . .

Perhaps he never had it. But that makes the search the more desperate and the sense of loss more agonising. It's because Heathcliff and Cathy never really possessed each other at all, that Heathcliff's terrible cry, in the novel's last stages, carries such a forceful charge. In effect it's the echoing vacancy at the heart of the Victorian novel, at a stroke disabling all those narratives of coming together and fulfilment.

> The most ordinary faces of men, and women – my own features mock me with a resemblance. The entire world is a dreadful

collection of memoranda that she did exist, and that I have lost her!

For Marvell the post-fall world is 'a rude heap together hurled'. Geoffrey Hill's poem 'Coplas' in his *Songbook of Sebastian Arrurruz* (1968) recognises and gives most brilliant force to the notion that not having possessed what is loved is the loss of sharpest intensity. Derisively, he quotes the so-called comforting wisdom of so-called common-sense.

> 'One cannot lose what one has not possessed.'
> So much for that abrasive gem.
> I can lose what I want. I want you.

Elsewhere in the *Songbook* 'you are outside, lost somewhere', only accessible in 'the dream where you are always to be found'. One of Hill's later poems, 'Damon's Lament for his Clorinda, Yorkshire 1654' from the collection *Tenebrae* (1978), explicitly invokes Marvell's Damon lyrics, but the date, 1654, as well as the lament, signals a loss because Marvell would have left Yorkshire and the Fairfax family by then. The Hill poem is set in a world where Damon and his scythe, as well as his Clorinda, have vanished.

> No sooner has the sun
> swung clear above earth's ridge than it is gone.
> We live like gleaners of its vestiges.

Loss affects, or infects, almost all the chapters in this book. *The Turn of the Screw* is like an enormously elaborate examination of the word itself. The story of Cathy and Heathcliff, for so many readers the purest expression of romantic one-ness, is a story that is constituted in loss, a series of wounding separations and losses to each other that structures their lives. But loss is the principal fact of our psychic lives. The state of consciousness itself is the recognition of loss: consciousness is the state of bereavement. Emily Dickinson (in 'A loss of something ever felt') has this.

> The first that I could recollect
> Bereft I was – of what I knew not.

The Narcissus story is the story of loss as love, love as loss, a story where layers of loss are folded within each other, or echo together. (A new translation of Ovid's Echo and Narcissus is in the Appendix that follows.) The Narcissus story was revisited by the psychoanalyst Jacques Lacan who identified a crucial moment in early childhood that he called the mirror-stage. The child looks in the mirror, perceives a human being with whom it merges and identifies, and thereby gains a new and narcissistic pleasure from that image of ideally whole completeness. This ideal is identified with what the child senses as the unbreakable wholeness connecting itself and the mother, a fantasy of completion in which, like Narcissus with his mirror-image but, unlike Narcissus in being satisfied, the child's every gesture is responded to by the mother.

The loss of that illusion structures all later desire and becomes a loss that has to be repeated in all our lives, as in all our narratives. Desire is driven by loss; narratives of desire are narratives of loss. The loss of Eden, paradise lost, the fall, is just the most forceful and culturally insistent of those narratives. All poems are acts of recovery from loss, reparations for loss. Every poet could say this of every poem.

> (I have made
> an elegy for myself it
> is true)

* * *

A group of American poets from the 1940s onwards saw themselves, perhaps like no other group since the early English Romantics, as in friendly competition with each other to write the great American poem or book of poetry. Prominent among these men, for they identified themselves as a group of men and expected their many girlfriends and wives (even the gifted writers among them) to support their enterprise, were Robert Lowell and John Berryman. But the group also included names less well-known today, like Randall Jarrell, Delmore Schwartz and Theodore Roethke. Their lives were messy, marked by spells of madness and institutionalisation, and they usually ended messily, often in suicide. The women coped as best as they could, keeping the men writing.

The most touching memorial to this group of poets is presented by the writer Eileen Simpson, who married Berryman in 1942, in her *Poets in their Youth*. One detail, about the effect on the women in the story, is very telling. Simpson tells of a writing fortnight she and Berryman spent with Lowell and his then wife Jean Stafford. Stafford was working on a novel but Lowell, working on his poems, would appear at her desk with a draft of a poem, and then another, and then another, expecting her to type each as he presented it, there and then. You might like to return to the sexual politics of the mid-sixteenth century as represented in Wyatt's 'They flee from me' in the first chapter at this point. 'I have seen them, gentle, tame and meek' . . .

It was John Berryman, as the group later dwindled with the deaths, who would memorialise the losses as they happened, as if gleaning the vestiges, while holding with increased desperation to the task for which he felt particularly marked out, appointed or self-appointed as their poet of loss. But loss had been Berryman's subject from the start. Virtually his first published poem, 'The Ball Poem', in his nicely entitled first volume *The Dispossessed* (1948), watches a boy losing his ball.

> People will take balls,
> Boys will be lost always, little boy,
> And no one buys a ball back.

And the end of the title poem in that volume, 'The Dispossessed', conveys a loss that is terminal, in a world where the sun is 'perishing', leaving everything 'done', nothing to be gleaned.

> The race
> is done. Drifts through, between the cold black trunks,
> the peachblow glory of the perishing sun
>
> in empty houses where old things take place.

The poems by Berryman in his extensive and autobiographical collection *The Dream Songs* (1964, 1968) ache with the loss of his fellow-writers as their deaths hit him. But the long elegy that is the *Songs* is, more or less openly, an elegy for himself as well as for the others, and the song that expresses that clearly is the very first. 'Henry' is Berryman's mouthpiece or persona or alter-ego in these songs (named, apparently, after Berryman's lugubrious dentist).

1

Huffy Henry hid   the day,
unappeasable Henry sulked.
I see his point, – a trying to put things over.
It was the thought that they thought
they could *do* it made Henry wicked & away.
But he should have come out and talked.

All the world like a woolen lover
once did seem on Henry's side.
Then came a departure.
Thereafter nothing fell out as it might or ought.
I don't see how Henry, pried
open for all the world to see, survived.

What he has now to say is a long
wonder the world can bear & be.
Once in a sycamore I was glad
all at the top, and I sang.
Hard on the land wears the strong sea
and empty grows every bed.

It's characteristically through his own self-involvement that Berryman comes at the loss of his contemporaries. Of Randall Jarrell, for instance, Berryman (in Song 90) sees that his own 'self-torturing' cannot 'restore one instant's good' to him.

The panic died and in the panic's dying
so did my old friend. I am headed west
also, also, somehow.

Delmore Schwartz's death was particularly messy and Berryman wrote a number of songs in response, as if unable to let go, or to let Delmore rest as he'd told himself he had to 'let Randall rest'. The last of the Schwartz songs (155) begins in typical self-torturing and a typical joke. Bellevue is a mental hospital.

> I can't get him out of my mind, out of my mind,
> Hé was out of his own mind for years,
> in police stations & Bellevue.

The comedy in Berryman's *Songs* is characteristically self-mocking, as in these two examples where Henry sees himself as doggy. This is from Song 14.

> [. . .] somehow a dog
> has taken itself & its tail considerably away
> into mountains or sea or sky, leaving
> behind: me, wag.

And this is from Song 54.

> I have been operating from *nothing*,
> like a dog after its tail
> more slowly, losing altitude.

The comedy gives the pervasive loss an air of jauntiness, as often in Emily Dickinson. The most frightening of the poems Berryman wrote about loss and his generation was published in his last volume *Delusions etc.* (1972), and the poem is among his last, before he took his own life. It's about himself. It's called 'He Resigns'. Here it is.

He Resigns

> Age, and the deaths, and the ghosts.
> Her having gone away
> in spirit from me. Hosts
> of regrets come & find me empty.
>
> I don't feel this will change.
> I don't want any thing

or person, familiar or strange.
I don't think I will sing

any more just now;
or ever. I must start
to sit with a blind brow
above an empty heart.

Or is that 'He Resigns'? It's the poem I've known since buying the
Faber collection *Delusions etc.* when it came out and while absorbing
the news of Berryman's death. But in preparing this chapter I happened to mislay my copy of *Delusions* and had to go in search of
another. The library in the college where I was working had instead a
volume called Berryman's *Collected Poems 1937–1971* (London, Faber
and Faber, 1989) and there, as 'He Resigns', was this. I skim-read it,
blinked, read it again. A misprint, surely. But no. (You may need to look
hard.)

He Resigns

Age, and the deaths, and the ghosts.
Her having gone away
in spirit from me. Hosts
of regrets come & find me empty.

I don't feel this will change.
I don't want any thing
or person, familiar or strange.
I don't think I will sing

any more just now;
ever. I must start
to sit with a blind brow
above an empty heart.

The handwritten deletion of that 'or' is, according to the *Collected
Poems* editor Charles Thornbury, very visibly marked on the typescript,
as well as more faintly on the photocopied printer's manuscript copy,

and it clearly represents Berryman's revision as the volume *Delusions* was being put together. (The version of the poem in *The Oxford Book of Short Poems* highhandedly repunctuates the poem, as it does its selection from Dickinson, disastrously changing that unnerving semicolon in the last verse to a comma.) The loss of that word 'or', especially after the semicolon, has the reader staring into the void on 'ever', suspended in as pure a state of loss as any poem could ever evoke.

The death of Berryman left just Robert Lowell from the original group. Lowell memorialised his loss in 'For John Berryman' in his *Day by Day* (1976), noting wryly that 'I used to want to live/to avoid your elegy' and 'you got there first'. The poem pays its respects in another way, when Lowell's line 'something so heavy lies on my heart' evokes Berryman's own bleakly terrible opening to an early Dream Song, 29.

> There sat down, once, a thing on Henry's heart
> só heavy, if he had a hundred years
> & more, & weeping, sleepless, in all them time
> Henry could not make good.

And that left another poet to write a poem 'in memoriam Robert Lowell' who died five years after Berryman and of natural causes, oddly enough, in 1977.

> ('Fun' – it always seemed to leave you at a loss . . .)

> You left North Haven, anchored in its rock,
> afloat in mystic blue . . . And now – you've left
> for good. You can't derange, or re-arrange,
> your poems again.

In a poem published three years earlier, this poet had memorialised a moment in 1918 of terrifying identity-loss from childhood.

> The sensation of falling off
> the round, turning world
> into cold, blue-black space [. . .]
> I scarcely dared to look
> to see what it was I was [. . .]

I knew that nothing stranger
had ever happened, that nothing
stranger could ever happen.

Those lines, from 'North Haven' (1979) and 'In the Waiting Room'
(1976), were by a poet not yet mentioned, on the edges of the group
we've been thinking about, to whom Robert Lowell dedicated his most
famous poem, 'Skunk Hour'. As the years have gone by, this poet's
works, though far fewer in number than those accumulated by Lowell
and Berryman, many of which became thin and lazy and diary-like in
manner, as if readers were bound to be compelled by everything these
rather narcissistic egos could scatter (derange or re-arrange) from their
typewriters, or as it were their wife's typewriter – this small body of
work now looks, for many readers, like the most highly crafted and
most poignantly indirect, and least narcissistic, poems written
anywhere in English in the second half of the twentieth century. (But,
conversely, this poet is not even mentioned in a recent guide to
twentieth-century American prose and poetry.)

It's just four published books, from 1946 to 1976 with some earlier
and later uncollected poems, and the voice and style are consistent
across the years. Here is 'Casabianca', from the collection *North &
South* (1946). It refers to an early nineteenth-century poem by Felicia
Hemans which opens with these familiar lines: 'The boy stood on the
burning deck/Whence all but he had fled;/The flame that lit the battle's
wreck/Shone round him o'er the dead.' This poem, also called 'Casabianca' (1829), a standard recital-task for later schoolchildren, com-
memorated an incident in the battle of the Nile (1798) when Nelson's
ships destroyed Napoleon's fleet, with enormous loss of life. Louis de
Casabianca assumed control when Napoleon's flagship went up in
flames, killing the commander of the fleet. Though wounded, he stayed
at his post while the ship burned. And his 10-year-old son refused to
leave him. Both were lost with the vessel.

Casabianca

Love's the boy stood on the burning deck
trying to recite 'The boy stood on

474

the burning deck.' Love's the son
  stood stammering elocution
  while the poor ship in flames went down.

Love's the obstinate boy, the ship,
even the swimming sailors, who
would like a schoolroom platform, too,
    or an excuse to stay
    on deck. And love's the burning boy.

The poet is Elizabeth Bishop. She died in 1979. The last published volume, *Geography III* (1976), contains just nine poems. One of them – to end on a personal note – I first heard read out on the radio and the effect was of having known it all my life.

Here, perhaps again, loss may return us to 'They flee from me' and the first chapter of this book. This last chapter, this book, if it does nothing else apart from sending you away to read and know the poems of Elizabeth Bishop, will have done enough.

One Art

The art of losing isn't hard to master;
so many things seem filled with the intent
to be lost that their loss is no disaster.

Lose something every day. Accept the fluster
of lost door keys, the hour badly spent.
The art of losing isn't hard to master.

Then practice losing farther, losing faster:
places, and names, and where it was you meant
to travel. None of these will bring disaster.

I lost my mother's watch. And look! my last, or
next-to-last, of three loved houses went.
The art of losing isn't hard to master.

I lost two cities, lovely ones. And, vaster,
some realms I owned, two rivers, a continent.
I miss them, but it wasn't a disaster.

— Even losing you (the joking voice, a gesture
I love) I shan't have lied. It's evident
the art of losing's not too hard to master
though it may look like (*Write* it!) like disaster.

The poet deliberately not mentioned above is Sylvia Plath. Not really part of the group discussed above, especially after coming to England, she none the less clearly wrote in ways that connect with the raw edginess and intimate intensities of Lowell and Berryman. She attended Lowell's master-classes in poetry. Berryman memorialised her suicide in a Dream Song. The sexual politics of the Plath story (or rather, the Sylvia Plath/Ted Hughes story), and what has become the Plath industry, is an enduring debate. *The Complete Poems of Elizabeth Bishop* (London, Chatto and Windus, 1991) is an affordable volume. A selection of Berryman's Dream Songs was included by the poet in his *Selected Poems* (London, Faber and Faber, 1972), and there's a usefully annotated selection of Robert Lowell (London, Faber and Faber, 1974). Eileen Simpson's excellent *Poets in their Youth* (New York, Random House, 1982) is commended above. To explore the notion of loss in our culture, readers could valuably start with Jonathan Dollimore's *Death, Desire and Loss in Western Culture* (London, Allen Lane, 1998), an important and challenging survey.

APPENDIX

OVID: ECHO AND NARCISSUS

A new translation of *Metamorphoses*, III, 339–510, by Ed Tattersall

Tiresias, famous throughout the towns of Boeotia, used to give fault-less answers to those who asked for his advice. Sky-blue Liriope made the first trial of his reliability and infallible voice. She was once enfolded in the meandering stream of the River Cephisus, who held her captive there and took her in his waters; from her swelling womb this nymph bore a child who even then was such as to incite love, and she called him Narcissus. The truth-revealing prophet was consulted about whether the child would ever see a long life and a ripe old age, and replied: 'So long as he does not know himself.' For a long time the prophet's utterance seemed meaningless, but its truth was shown by the outcome and event, the way Narcissus was to die and the unprecedented nature of his passion.

For Cephisus' son had reached sixteen and could be regarded as either a boy or a young man. Many youths, male and female, desired him, but with his slender form went such hardness and pride that not one of them, male or female, could touch him. A nymph endowed with a voice saw him driving nervous deer into the hunting nets. She was one who could not fail to answer anyone's words but could never be the first to speak – Echo, she who gives back sound.

Echo still had a body then, not just a voice; though garrulous she had no other use of her mouth than she has now – simply to repeat the last words from the many that she hears. Juno had brought this about because, on many occasions when she might have caught some nymph lying beneath her husband Jupiter on the mountain-side, Echo would cleverly detain the goddess in lengthy conversation until the nymph had escaped. When Juno realised this she said: 'You shall have

477

little power over this tongue, with which you tricked me, and the use of your voice shall be cut very short.' She carried out her threat. However, Echo does manage to make the end of whatever is said double and to repeat the words she has heard.

So when she saw Narcissus wandering through the trackless countryside she burned with longing and secretly followed his steps; the more she followed, the closer came the flame that burned her, just as when sulphur, smeared on the tops of torches, rapidly takes fire when another flame is brought near. Ah! How often she wanted to inflame him with soft words and approach him with gentle prayers! Her nature fought against her and did not allow her to begin, but it did allow her to hold herself ready, waiting for sounds to which she could send her own words in response.

The boy happened to be separated from his loyal band of friends and said: 'Is there anyone here?' – 'One here', Echo replied. He was amazed and looked all around. 'Come!' he called in a loud voice: she called him as he called. He looked round and as no one was coming called again: 'Why do you run from me?', and got back the same words as often as he said them. He persisted, beguiled by the image of the voice in counterpoint to his, and said: 'Here – let us come together!' and 'Come together!' she replied (and she would never more willingly reply to any sound); then she endorsed her words by coming out of the wood to throw her arms round his coveted neck. He ran off, saying: 'Keep your hands off! I should rather die than that you should have possession of me.' She replied no more than: 'Have possession of me.'

Now she hides rejected in the woods, covering her shamed face with leaves, and has lived in lonely caves from that moment on. Yet still her love holds fast, despite her repulse, and even grows along with her grief; sleepless sufferings thin her pitiable frame, emaciation contracts her skin, and all her body's moisture disappears into the air. Only a voice and bones survive, then only a voice – they say her bones were turned to stone. Then she hides in the woods and appears no more on the mountains, but the sound which lives in her is heard by all. Thus Narcissus had played with her feelings and those of other nymphs, and before that of several men. Then one of these despised lovers, lifting his hands to the skies, said: 'So may he love too, and not possess his love!', and Nemesis assented to his just prayers.

There was an unsullied pool, silver with shining water. No shepherds, no mountain-grazing she-goats or other herd had ever touched it; it was undisturbed by any bird or beast or the fall of a bough from a tree. Grass that the nearby water fed encircled it, and a forest which would allow the place no warming from the sun. Here the youth lay prone, worn out by eager hunting and the heat, drawn on by the beauty of the place and by its pool.

He desires to satisfy his thirst, but a different thirst has arisen; as he drinks he is captivated by the appearance of the shapeliness he can see, and falls for the promise of a body which in fact is a bodiless image. He marvels at his own self and hangs there motionless with his face fixed to the spot, like a statue formed from Parian marble; he lies on the ground and gazes at those twin stars, his eyes, at the hair befitting a Bacchus or Apollo, at the beardless cheeks and ivory neck, and the beauty of his face as its snowy radiance is coloured by a blush. He admires all those points for which he is admired. He recklessly desires himself and, self-approved, himself approves. He makes approaches and, so doing, is approached; he kindles the fire of love and likewise burns. Again and again he kisses the deceiving pool and dips his arms in the water to catch hold of the neck he can see – yet he cannot take himself in his own arms. He does not know what he sees, but whatever it is he burns with desire for it, and the very error that deceives him spurs his eyes to stare.

Fool, why vainly chase after fleeting images? What you seek exists nowhere, what you love you will lose the moment you turn away. What you see is the shadow of a reflected shape: it has nothing of itself, but comes with you and remains with you; it would leave with you too – if you had the power to go.

No thought of food or sleep can drag him away, but sprawling on the shaded grass he watches the deceiving shape with an insatiable eye, and it is through his own eyes that he perishes. Raising himself up a little and holding out his arms to the surrounding forests, he calls out: 'Has anyone, you forests, ever loved more cruelly? You should know, for you have offered happy concealment to many lovers. Or do you remember anyone in all the many epochs of your long life who has pined away like me? He pleases me and I can see him, but what I see and what pleases me I cannot find: some great error grips me in my love. And – to increase my pain – it is not a vast sea which parts us or a road or mountains or the locked gates of a city wall: we are held apart by just a tiny bit of water! He himself must long to be embraced, for whenever I stretch to kiss the shining water, he struggles towards me with his face upturned. You would think he could be touched: only the smallest obstacle prevents our loving. Wherever you are, come out here! Why do you deceive me, unequalled youth? Where do you go when I move towards you? Surely I have neither the looks nor the age which you would wish to avoid, and I too have been loved by the nymphs. With your friendly face you lead me to hope for something, and whenever I stretch out my arms to you you stretch yours back; you smile at me when I smile; I have often noticed your tears when I cry; you send back signals by your nod, and – I believe from the movement of your lovely mouth – you respond to me with words which never reach my ears.

I myself am he: I know it, my image does not deceive me. I burn with love for myself; I cause the flames which I must endure. What am I to do? Should I accept advances or make them? And what advances would I make? What I long for is within myself: my own wealth has made me poor. If only I could separate myself from my own body! I wish for something unheard of in a lover – the absence of what I love. Now pain has destroyed my strength and I have little time left to live. I am being extinguished in the prime of life, but death is no sorrow to me as by dying I shall lay down my sorrows. I could wish for my beloved to live longer but now, our two hearts joined together, we shall share the same last breath as we die.'

So he spoke and, almost out of his mind, returned to gaze at the same face and ruffled the water with his tears; as the pool moved the reflected shape became obscured. When he saw it going away he yelled out: 'Where are you escaping to? Stay and don't desert me, cruel one – I am your lover! Let me at least see what I cannot touch; let me feed this pathetic mania!' As he grieved he undid the upper edge of his tunic and beat his nude breast with hands as white as marble. His beaten breast took on a rosy colour, like apples which blush in part, in part remaining pale, or like clusters of unripe grapes when they assume a purple tint.

Seeing this in the water, which had now regained its smooth surface, he could not bear it any longer, but, just as yellow wax melts in a little heat, or the morning frost as the sun grows warm, so he, wasted by love, dissolved and was slowly consumed by the hidden fire; and now he had neither his former colouring (white and red blended together) nor strength and vigour nor the qualities which so recently had pleased the onlooker; nor did that body remain which Echo had once loved. Yet when she saw him she grieved despite her angry memories, and whenever the poor boy said: 'Alas!' she repeated with echoing voice: 'Alas!'; and when he beat his own arms, she gave back the sound of beating.

These were his last words as he looked into the familiar water: 'Ah, dear boy, loved so vainly!', and the place spoke back just those words; when he said: 'Farewell!', 'Farewell!' said Echo too. He drooped his tired head on the green grass. Death closed his eyes even as they were admiring their master's beauty; then he was received into the halls of the underworld and saw himself in the waters of the Styx. His Naiad sisters lamented and placed cuttings of hair on their brother's tomb. The Dryads also wailed, and as they did so Echo returned the sound.

And now they were preparing the pyre, the torches for brandishing and the bier. His body however was nowhere – in its place they found a yellow flower, its centre enclosed in white petals.

Translator's note:
Latin's strict system of inflections (different word endings for different functions of the same word within a larger group of words) paradoxically allows the author greater freedom in the arrangement of the words. Latin poets routinely exploit such possibilities, and Ovid in this passage has graphically reflected his subject matter by making words and groups of words echo and mirror each other, for example by immediate repetition, or by juxtaposing a verb in the active with the same verb in the passive, or by continual play with personal pronouns, especially reflexives. Thus Narcissus acts and is acted upon by his reflection, and is simultaneously both subject and object, self and other. An English prose translation can only reflect these verbal devices very approximately – as it were through ruffled water.